WARRIOR NATION

For Morris —
Thank you. I
hope you enjoy,

A.

WARRIOR NATION

A History of the Red Lake Ojibwe

ANTON TREUER

MINNESOTA
HISTORICAL
SOCIETY PRESS

Boundaries depicted in the maps used in this book do not represent the legal position of the Red Lake Band of Chippewa Indians nor limit any future claims or disputes relating to boundaries.

www.mnhspress.org

The Minnesota Historical Society Press is a member of the Association of American University Presses.

Manufactured in the United States of America

10 9 8 7 6 5 4 3 2

♾ The paper used in this publication meets the minimum requirements of the American National Standard for Information Sciences—Permanence for Printed Library Materials, ANSI Z39.48-1984.

International Standard Book Number
ISBN: 978-0-87351-963-2 (paper)
ISBN: 978-0-87351-968-7 (e-book)

Library of Congress Cataloging-in-Publication Data
Treuer, Anton.
    Warrior nation : a history of the Red Lake Ojibwe / Anton Treuer.
       pages cm
    Includes bibliographical references and index.
    ISBN 978-0-87351-963-2 (pbk. : alk. paper) — ISBN 978-0-87351-968-7 (ebook)
    1. Red Lake Band of Chippewa Indians, Minnesota—History. 2. Red Lake Band
    of Chippewa Indians, Minnesota—Politics and government. 3. Red Lake Band of
    Chippewa Indians, Minnesota—Biography. 4. Ojibwa Indians—Government relations.
    5. Red Lake Indian Reservation (Minn.)—History. 6. Red Lake Indian Reservation
    (Minn.)—Biography. I. Title. II. Title: History of the Red Lake Ojibwe.
    E99.C6T76 2015
    977.004'97333—dc23

                                                                                            2015028414

This and other Minnesota Historical Society Press books are available from popular e-book vendors.

Warrior Nation was designed and set in type by Judy Gilats. The text face is Cardea and the display faces are Railroad Gothic and Benton Sans.

For Thomas J. Stillday and Anna C. Gibbs, who bridged the knowledge of Leonard Hawk, Dan Raincloud, Nodin Wind, and the ancient ones before them to the present generation and dedicated their lives to ensuring the future vitality and legacy of Red Lake ceremonial life for the benefit of Ojibwe people everywhere.

◆

For my son, Elias Treuer—the blood of chiefs—with high hopes that you can study the amazing accomplishments of the great political and spiritual leaders of our people and use those lessons to help make the world a better place.

◆

And for Justin Beaulieu, Samuel Strong, Vincent Staples-Graves, Marguerite Secola, Marcus Tyler, Harvey Roy III, Elizabeth Strong, Rose Barrett, Bryanna Grimes, Don Kingbird, Donovan Sather, Delana Smith, Nate Taylor, Stacey Thunder, Wes May, Roger "Spanky" White, Liz White, Tito Ybarra, and all the other young citizens of Red Lake who have already devoted so much of their energy to the betterment of the Red Lake people. The political patrimony, culture, and language of this incredible native nation are already in your hands. I believe in it. And I believe in you.

Contents

Author's Note

WARRIOR NATION IS A POLITICAL HISTORY OF Red Lake. It is organized in seven main chapters, each a biography of an important Red Lake leader at a different point in time. Red Lake had many important historical figures, and telling Red Lake's history through these leaders is not intended to diminish any others. Each biographical feature should be seen not as the most important person of his or her time, but as a window into the evolving political culture of the Red Lake nation. This work tries to include the contributions of women at Red Lake even though it is a political history and, until recently, Red Lake's political leaders were primarily men. This effort is addressed in the narrative directly and through the chapter on Anna Gibbs. The research process, available historical resources, and the direct participation of Red Lake's tribal council in this project also shaped the work. A more thorough discussion of these issues prefaces the bibliography.

WARRIOR NATION

Battle River

OJIBWE RUNNERS SPRINTED THROUGH THE village near Ponemah Point on the north shore of Lower Red Lake with the call to arms. Dakota warriors were on the east shore of the lake several miles away, and they were prepared to kill or drive out all of the Ojibwe in the region. They had already killed one Ojibwe trapper and wounded another. Ojibwe warriors grabbed their war clubs, spears, and bows. It was about 1760, and a couple of men even had muskets, obtained in trade with the French at Lake Superior. The Ojibwe sallied forth by the hundreds, gathering strength from scattered wigwams and settlements along the north shore of the lake as they sped toward their enemy, most by canoe and others on foot, eager to defend their homes and families. They approached the mouth of a small river, known at the time simply as Zaagiing (the outlet), and found hundreds of Dakota massing on the banks of the river, ready to fight.[1]

The Ojibwe had just established a village at the narrows between Upper and Lower Red Lakes over the preceding year. The area would later be called Ponemah Point (Obaashiing), and a village and population center five miles to the east would be known as both Cross Lake (Aazhooding) and Ponemah. The Ponemah Ojibwe were part of a large front of Ojibwe that had attacked the Dakota with many hundreds of warriors and had driven them from their homes. The late Fannie Johns (Ogimaakwe, or Queen) from Red Lake said that when the Ojibwe first settled there Ponemah was the only Ojibwe settlement at Red Lake and the Dakota still lived in villages along the south shore. They could see the distant smoke from one another's fires every day. The Dakota sent numerous scouts to Ponemah to evaluate their enemy's strength and determine the best time and place to attack. Johns said there were three Ojibwe medicine men in Ponemah who performed a ceremony with hand drums, fire, and medicine to obscure the village and create an illusion of overpowering numbers to deter Dakota attacks. She said the effect was so profound that hundreds of Dakota abandoned the idea of driving the Ojibwe out of Ponemah and voluntarily packed up their families to move west where hunting was easier and their families would be free from the danger of continued warfare. When the Dakota who stayed finally rallied their warriors to drive the Ojibwe out, their numbers were already greatly reduced from the voluntary relocation of many Dakota families.[2]

The Ojibwe occupation of Ponemah came as part of a much larger territorial advance where the Ojibwe displaced the Dakota from their villages in many places at Leech Lake, Lake Winnibigoshish, and the area surrounding Upper and Lower Red Lake. In Ponemah, the Ojibwe immediately built wigwams and palisades, bringing their children and elders there to live, with full knowledge that the Dakota would come back to challenge the Ojibwe claim to the land. Today some people marvel at the bravery and audacity of the territorial claim of the Ojibwe and their apparent reckless willingness to risk the lives of their entire families to make Red Lake their home. This was due in part to the fact that the Ojibwe warriors were also full-time providers, and there was no way to leave dependents behind in cases of war or they would surely starve. But the Ojibwe were also warriors. They had fought their way west for generations—long before European contact. From their original homeland on the Atlantic Coast, the Ojibwe had forayed west through the eastern and central Great Lakes for more than fifteen hundred years. The population density on the East Coast was very high, and food shortages caused by occasional droughts sometimes created intense conflict between the numerous indigenous groups there over the land. As the Ojibwe defended themselves from the Iroquois Confederacy and other tribes in the east, prophets appeared among them with a series of visions and a powerful message to move west to "the land where food grows on water." This clear reference to wild rice is a big part of what brought the Ojibwe through the Great Lakes to Red Lake.[3]

The movement of the people was driven by deeply held spiritual belief, a practical understanding of land and food resources, and conflict in the east. Their path to Red Lake was two thousand miles long, traversed by birchbark canoe, and occurred over fifteen hundred years. New villages were established along the way, new friendships with other tribes were forged, and sometimes new enemies were made of those who occupied the land before them. The migration itself played a significant role in the Ojibwe's emergence as a distinct people, different from their cousins the Ottawa and Potawatomi. At one time those tribes, like all tribes in the Algonquian language family, were the same people. But the geographic separation of the groups and different historical experiences led their cultures and even their languages to diverge.[4]

The Ojibwe split into two groups at Sault Ste. Marie, Michigan. One went north of Lake Superior, the other south. As the two groups converged again west of the big lake, dialect differences in their shared language were already cemented. Red Lake was dominated by people who took the north route. Mille Lacs and later White Earth were dominated by those who went south. Leech Lake was settled by both groups. The journey was fraught with danger and conflict. Those who survived—the ones who made it to Red Lake—had honed exceptional skills as hunters, trappers, fishermen, rice harvesters, canoe travelers, and warriors.[5]

Today the Ojibwe and Dakota are fast friends. In the 1860s, the Dakota gave the Ojibwe a series of ceremonial drums as peace offerings to cement friendship and goodwill between the tribes. Those drums remain a vibrant and vital part of the modern Ojibwe ceremonial experience today. People from both tribes regularly attend each other's powwows, ceremonies, and social and political functions. The Mdewakanton Dakota from Shakopee, Minnesota, in particular have been very generous with the Ojibwe, especially those at Red Lake— funding casino expansions, a skate park, and a new Boys and Girls Club. Most Ojibwe people now feel that it was folly to make war on their brothers in arms because the Ojibwe and Dakota share much common history, common struggle against political, economic, and social injustice, and even common bloodlines.

The Ojibwe did not come to colonize the Dakota—tribal territorial conflict was nothing akin to American Manifest Destiny. But with hindsight, we know that the Ojibwe dispossessed the Dakota—a cold, calculated, violent wrong. The Dakota committed the same wrong on the Gros Ventre, Arikara, Hidatsa, and Cheyenne who likely occupied Red Lake before them, even though many details of exactly how and when that happened have been swallowed by the clear, icy waters of the lake itself. But in the minds of the people at the time it must have seemed entirely different. The Dakota saw the Ojibwe as invaders. But the Ojibwe saw the Dakota the same way. They too were defending small children, villages, and lifeways.[6]

As the Ojibwe warriors descended on the Dakota host, they were filled with a sense of purpose. Their spiritual prophets had told them to move here. They had been fulfilling that prophecy through generations of arduous travel and conflict. As they neared the completion of that quest, they must have seen their actions as justified: they were where they were supposed to be and doing what they were supposed to do, as their ancestors had done for many generations.

Like an angry bear who knew the woods belonged to her, fearing for her cubs, the Ojibwe rushed the battlefield. Most tribal battles were over in a matter of minutes, with minimal casualties and a hasty retreat by the outmatched party. But this battle raged on all day. The Dakota were determined to reclaim their rightful home. The Ojibwe were determined to protect theirs. Arrows, spears, and occasional musket fire rained down on the Dakota at first, but most of the violence was hand-to-hand, with war clubs. Casualties were staggering on both sides. The Dakota gave no ground and offered no retreat. The Ojibwe gave no quarter. As more and more Ojibwe descended on the scene, they enveloped the Dakota and overwhelmed them. Some of the Dakota escaped and fled to the Sandy River outlet in wooden dugout canoes. The Ponemah warriors pursued them around the lake in faster birchbark canoes and overtook them at the outlet. No Dakota surrendered and none were spared.

As the Ojibwe regrouped at Battle River and examined the battlefield, they must have been more shocked and horrified than exultant at their victory. Many Ojibwe were wounded. All the survivors were completely exhausted. Hundreds of Ojibwe and Dakota lay dead, their tribal identities now indiscernible. Their blood ran together so thickly that the entire river was filled with their life fluids. The water turned scarlet and streamed forth into the lake in a giant bright red plume.

Nothing would be the same again. Although the Dakota came back to Red Lake in small war parties for many more years, they could never again muster the force necessary to retake Red Lake. The sovereignty and territorial claim of the Ojibwe to the lake and the land were secured from then on. Even the names of places were forever altered. The river outlet was no longer called Zaagiing (the outlet), but Gaa-danapananiding (the place of slaughter). It was the permanent resting place for many of the bravest Dakota and Ojibwe warriors of the time. In English, the river would be called Battle River. Standing on its bloody banks, the Red Lake warriors watched the entire lake change color as the red water streamed forth, and the meaning of the Ojibwe name for the lake itself changed. The lake had always been called Miskwaagamiiwi-zaaga'igan by the Ojibwe, meaning "the lake with the red body of water," in reference to the tannins from the tamarack trees that colored many of the tributaries in the watershed red, in stark contrast to the crystal-clear body of lake water. The name described the flow of the red creeks into the lake. But after the battle, as the blood of two nations coursed into the lake, the description took on a new and deeper meaning, defined by this seminal historical event. In English, it is known simply as Red Lake.[7]

Over the next two hundred years the Red Lake Ojibwe continued to demonstrate exceptional leadership and resilience—avoiding allotment of their lands and state government intrusions into their sovereignty, establishing a modern representative tribal government forty years before any other tribe in the United States while preserving the respected positions of their traditional chiefs, developing a reservation economy that supported traditional fish harvesting and lifeways, and maintaining the highest tribal language fluency rate in the Great Lakes region and the Northern Plains. The lake and the people who live there are imbued with an amazing history—deeper than anyone might imagine.

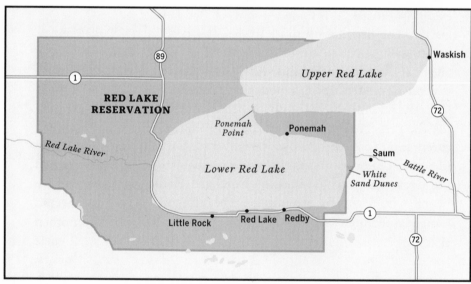

Red Lake reservation and traditional territory

1

White Thunderbird and the Seven Clans

> They built a high embankment of earth, for defence, around their lodges, and took every means in their power to escape the notice of the Ojibways—even discarding the use of the gun on account of its loud report, and using the primitive bow and arrows.
>
> WILLIAM WARREN, *on the secret Dakota village at what would become Thief River Falls*

White Thunderbird

The Ojibwe (Chippewa) at Red Lake grew in numbers and solidified their control over the land after the Battle River fight, keeping a constant eye on the horizon. By 1770, the Dakota could no longer challenge Ojibwe ownership of Red Lake, but they could still make them pay for taking the land. One day a group of warriors encountered a small Dakota war party somewhere in the vicinity of Mahnomen Creek by the northeast shore of Lower Red Lake. They used eagle bone whistles, war whoops, and runners to call for reinforcements, and chased the Dakota on land and by canoe. After driving them off, the Ojibwe were returning to their daily activities when one of the warriors discovered a young Dakota boy crouched down in the brush where the Dakota war party had originally been hiding. The boy was too small to successfully run away from grown men, and now he was without family or community. In tribal warfare, anyone could be an honorable target—elders or children, women or men. Ponemah warriors were seasoned and tough, but not heartless. They saw an innocent brown face and, taking pity on the young boy, one of the warriors took him as a captive, but made him his son.[1]

The adoption of child war captives was not unique to Red Lake. In 1824, William H. Keating observed that throughout Ojibwe country, "The children are generally spared and incorporated into families, where they frequently meet with tolerably good treatment." But this time the impact was greater than anyone could have foreseen.[2]

The boy was given an Ojibwe name—White Thunderbird (Waabi-bines). He was raised as an Ojibwe and lived the rest of his years in the Red Lake village of Ponemah, taking an Ojibwe wife and having children. Today his descendants make up one of the largest family groups at Red Lake—including the Greenleaf, Hawk, Oakgrove, and Whitefeather families—and among them are some of Red Lake's most prominent leaders, including hereditary chiefs, spiritual leaders, and elected tribal chairmen. The adoption of this Dakota boy, this simple act of kindness, both enabled and symbolized a powerful change in the cultural and political configuration of the Ojibwe people at Red Lake.

The Ojibwe families at Red Lake grew stronger every year after the Battle River fight. The primary villages at Warroad, Ponemah, Redby, and Red Lake swelled with new children. New people migrated to Red Lake as well. Among them was Sweet Leaf (Wiishkoobag), veteran of an Ojibwe–Dakota battle at Crow Wing in 1768 and chief at Leech Lake for several years afterward. He quickly rose to prominence at Red Lake. Sweet Leaf's acceptance as a leader at Red Lake, like White Thunderbird's, showed Red Lake's readily evolving and adaptable political culture.

Wild rice, game, berries, and fish were abundant throughout the region. Red Lake warriors ranged freely for a hundred miles in all directions, pressing their territorial claims, protecting their people, hunting, trapping, and fishing. Small villages and family enclaves were established at present-day Warren, Minnesota, then at Pembina, North Dakota, and eventually along the Red River of the North. By 1800, some groups had established new villages at Roseau River, Manitoba, and soon after that at Turtle Mountain, North Dakota. Even today those Ojibwe communities claim Red Lake as their motherland.[3]

In the late 1700s and early 1800s, more Ojibwe and even a few Ottawa and Cree families came from all over the Great Lakes to settle and live at Red Lake. The newcomers brought some new ideas and even some different ways of expressing them. The fabric of social life and political function at Red Lake was evolving, even while the seasons and cycle of the traditional harvest economy remained steadfast. Some kinds of change were obvious, such as the creation of a new Ojibwe political nexus for the people at Red Lake. Other kinds of change, such as language and culture variation, are harder to identify. What made the Red Lake Ojibwe different from the Leech Lake Ojibwe and other communities in the same language group was more than physical location. Language, culture, customs, natural-resource harvest practices, political traditions, and relations with other tribes morphed into something entirely new. This metamorphosis was an ongoing process long before nonnative people came to the region or made an effort to change native people. The Red Lake Ojibwe were an ancient people, but they were something new at the same time. The contrast between cultural continuity and change was a defining feature in the emergence of the Red Lake Ojibwe as a distinct group, and it remains so today.[4]

The Battle River fight cemented Ojibwe control of Red Lake in 1760. But the things that made the Red Lake Ojibwe such a distinct and dynamic people had been developing for fifteen hundred years before their occupation of northwestern Minnesota. The structure of chieftainship, the clan system, the unique positions of spiritual leaders, the role of women in society, and the relationships between the Ojibwe and the Dakota, the French, the British, and eventually the Americans all served to separate and distinguish the people of Red Lake from other Ojibwe communities and tribes. Those distinctions are what strengthened the people at Red Lake and enabled them to build a small collection of warriors and their families into one of the most powerful tribal nations in North America.

The Seven Clans

In 1989, Johnson Loud was among hundreds who attended the one hundredth anniversary commemoration of the 1889 Nelson Act, an act of the U.S. Congress and subsequent negotiation with Red Lake tribal chiefs that ceded vast tracts of Red Lake land and converted the remaining unceded Red Lake lands into a reservation. Loud was more than a Red Lake band member; he was a student of his tribe's history and leadership and a gifted artist. He had been commissioned to develop a new symbol for the Red Lake Nation, one that resonated with its rich history, tradition, and continued sovereignty. That symbol was officially adopted by the Red Lake government as its flag and seal in 1989.[5]

When Loud developed the Red Lake tribal flag, he studied clan representation on the reservation. Although he did not include every clan at Red Lake on the flag, he did include the clans of all hereditary chiefs and the largest and most common ones represented among the tribal population. Seven original Red Lake clans were put on the flag: bear (makwa), turtle (mikinaak), bullhead (owaazisii), otter (nigig), eagle (migizi), marten (waabizheshi), and kingfisher (ogiishkimanisii).

Formally acknowledging these seven clans as primary symbols on the Red Lake Nation flag said a great deal about the culture, government, and history of Red Lake. Although some of the research is contradictory, scholars who have studied Ojibwe clans all agree on one thing: the traditional Ojibwe leadership clans were loon (maang) and crane (ajijaak). Chieftainship was passed down hereditarily through the father's side, and these two clans dominated all of the civil chieftainships in Ojibwe country. Red Lake had more than a dozen hereditary chiefs in 1989. Their lineage could be traced all the way back to the Ojibwe settlement of Red Lake. But not one of them was from the loon or crane clans.[6]

The people of Red Lake are quintessentially Ojibwe, as reflected in their language, culture, and customs. Red Lake has one of the most intact chieftainship traditions of all Ojibwe communities anywhere. Many tribes do not know or keep records of important genealogical information, and almost none use that information to determine leadership responsibilities or for other political purposes (other than tribal enrollment). But at Red Lake, genealogy is the primary determining factor in civil chieftainship even today. And though Red Lake also has adopted a democratic process for electing tribal representatives and the tribal chair, the chiefs are determined by heredity and participate in all political functions of the tribal council today as hereditary civil chiefs.

The lack of traditional Ojibwe leadership clans among the Red Lake chieftainship reflects a dynamic that was introduced in the late 1700s. To understand it, we return again to the Dakota boy adopted and raised as an Ojibwe—White Thunderbird.

When White Thunderbird was captured and adopted he was old enough to know who he was. He was Dakota, and the Dakota had a complicated kin system that established relationships and obligations throughout one's extended family. The Dakota also had a clan system like their Siouan cousins the Ho-Chunk (Winnebago) and most tribes in North America. Since the 1900s, the Dakota clan system has become defunct—a thread pulled from their cultural tapestry that is no longer recoverable. Their kin system remains intact, as do many other critical features of Dakota culture, but clan is no more.

All of this becomes very important in understanding Red Lake chiefs, clans, and governance today. When White Thunderbird was adopted, the adopting family had a choice: they could formally adopt White Thunderbird into the clan of the family patriarch, or they could adopt him without formally changing his clan. They chose the latter. As a result, even though White Thunderbird was adopted as an Ojibwe he retained his Dakota clan, becoming the first Ojibwe person at Red Lake from the kingfisher clan. Even today his clan is emblazoned on the Red Lake Nation flag and on Red Lake Nation automobile license plates, and his clan is one of the most widely represented at Red Lake. In addition, as people from Red Lake established new villages at Turtle Mountain, North Dakota, and Roseau River, Manitoba, members of the kingfisher clan were among the settlers of the new Ojibwe communities there. Today the kingfisher clan is common at Red Lake, Roseau River, and Turtle Mountain, rare almost everywhere else, and virtually unheard of in the eastern reaches of Ojibwe country.[7]

White Thunderbird introduced the kingfisher clan to Red Lake. But his story was not completely anomalous. The wolf clan was also introduced to the Ojibwe through Dakota paternity. More common among the St. Croix, Mille Lacs, and White Earth bands, the wolf clan is also a large and important clan in Ojibwe culture. The Dakota exerted a profound influence and sparked many transformations in Ojibwe culture. The spiritual and political impacts reverberate to this day.[8]

Clans are vital to Ojibwe identity today, and in the 1700s they were even more important. The nature of clans underwent significant changes, but many clan taboos and protocols were established early on and remain unchanged. Clan was central to Ojibwe spirituality. Clan protocol structured marriage and village life. Marriage between people of the same clan was one of the strongest taboos in Ojibwe culture and people could be killed for violating it.[9]

Clans were a strictly patrilineal birthright and established a spiritual connection for the clan member with an animal, bird, or water creature. Even when Ojibwe married non-Indians, the patrilineal structure of the clan system was not altered. Instead, as a birthright (not a ceremonial adoption), children with a nonnative father were automatically adopted into an existing clan. The eagle clan was the adopting clan at Red Lake. As Red Lake grew with new migrants from other parts of Ojibwe country and new additions like White Thunderbird, the number of clans there grew to more than twenty. While some Ojibwe communities struggled with cultural retention in the face of missionary activity, clans stayed strong at Red Lake regardless of the people's changing faith traditions.[10]

Red Lake was settled by warriors, and warrior clans dominate the membership of Red Lake even today, especially marten and bear. Because the Red Lake warrior clans found themselves occupying new territory without significant representation from the traditional chief clans, political duties had to be assumed by members of other clans.[11]

In 1850, Ojibwe missionary George Copway wrote: "The rulers of the Ojibways were inheritors of the power they held. However, when new country was conquered, or new dominions annexed, the first rulers were elected to their offices. Afterwards, the descendants of these elected chiefs ruled the nation, or tribe, and thus power became hereditary." Explorers Henry Schoolcraft, James Duane Doty, and Charles Christopher Trowbridge concur. In 1820, Trowbridge wrote:

The Chieftainship descends from father to son, and the women are always excluded, so that the line becomes extinct on the death of the last male of the old line. When this happens to be the case (but I believe it seldom happens), the vacancy is filled by election of the man most valiant, brave and powerful, or the most celebrated for wisdom and eloquence; and he inherits the title of chief together with all the honors of the last in power. This practice is never deviated from except by some daring fellow, who usurping the authority holds the tribe in awe by his ferocity or the influence of numerous relatives devoted to his interest. Such a one however is soon disposed of by his enemies.[12]

The first chiefs at Red Lake were elected, but the succession of chieftainship lines afterward remained for the most part hereditary, passed on from father to son, much as it had been for centuries. The initial election of chiefs at Red Lake meant that hereditary leadership rights were dispersed among various warrior clans, primarily bear, marten, and kingfisher. Ironically, Dakota bloodlines and clans were well represented among the Ojibwe warriors and chiefs at Red Lake— including those who continued to fight and dispossess the Dakota.[13]

The clans represented when chiefs were originally elected at Red Lake retained their leadership positions even when new waves of Ojibwe people from other clans settled there. The overwhelming majority of Red Lake Ojibwe today are of the bear, eagle, marten, bullhead, kingfisher, and turtle clans. Other clans include sturgeon (name) and caribou (adik). Not all are represented on the tribal flag. Marriage with people from other tribal communities accounts for most of the expanding clan representation at Red Lake today.[14]

At Red Lake many different people led in war, ceremony, and politics. Red Lakers were warriors. There were no formal military leaders. Nobody ever told someone else to fight or told others to follow. When tough, successful warriors went off to war, less-experienced warriors went with them. When Red Lake was attacked, everyone fought back. In some Ojibwe communities, such as Mille Lacs, there were designated head warriors or war chiefs, but not at Red Lake. At Red Lake, people were inspired not by position, but by action.[15]

Religious leadership at Red Lake was similar to military leadership in many ways. Nobody was obligated to lead and nobody had to follow. People went to successful healers and stayed away from those who did not have the gift. They went to ceremonies with people they trusted and could not be bothered with anyone else. Spiritual leaders did teach what they knew to the people closest to them, and there were some ceremonial leadership dynasties at Red Lake, especially in Ponemah. But spiritual leaders, like military ones, had to prove their worth.

Political leadership was a hereditary birthright. But here too, leaders had to earn their position. If a hereditary chief tried to control anyone or tell people what to do, he was shunned, or people would move a little farther down the lakeshore, or to a different village. If a chief upset or offended a large family, they would move to a new area, start a new village, and elect a new chief. This happened many times at Red Lake, and the base of hereditary chiefs grew and diversified (by family and clan) as the tribe expanded throughout northwestern Minnesota.

White Thunderbird was born a Dakota, raised Ojibwe, and rose to a position of respect in Ponemah, eventually becoming one of the first elected chiefs at Miquam Bay (Mikwami-wiikwedong, or Ice Bay), southeast of Ponemah. Cultural change at Red Lake made possible his rise in status. Cultural continuity enabled him to pass not just the kingfisher clan, but also his leadership position, on to his son.

The White Sand Dunes

They call it the White Sand Dunes (Chi-waasadaawangideg). It is the most exposed and windward part of Red Lake. Prevailing northwest winds whip at the trees and pound surf against the shore. In the winter, snowdrifts sometimes reach twenty feet in height because all the snow on the lake is piled up on the southeast shore, burying the road. In the spring, ice heaves topple trees and push the earth into large, sandy ridges. The dunes closest to the water, devoid of plants and covered in translucent sand, glow white as they reflect sunlight and are visible from twelve miles across the lake.[16]

When the Dakota lived at Red Lake, they buried their dead at the White Sand Dunes in large earthen mounds, still discernible among the natural ridges farthest from the shore, now topped with maple and ash trees. The Ojibwe never adopted mound burials at Red Lake, preferring instead to inter their dead wherever they lived. In the winter, they buried their dead in spirit homes above the earth, and even built scaffolds to house them. In all other seasons they were buried in shallow graves in front of the family wigwams, and later houses. At Ponemah, that remains the custom today, although scaffolds have been abandoned now in favor of ground burials, even in winter.[17]

The White Sand Dunes is a sacred place. Bald eagles nest in the trees along the shore and feed in large numbers on smaller fish forced into the shallows by wave action. The dunes are exposed to the wind and water, and bird, water, and animal life of all kinds abounds. So do powerful spirits. People do water ceremonies here in the spring and fall, make offerings, pray, and come searching for answers. There are platforms in the trees all along the lakeshore where young men and women come to fast, giving up food and water for up to four days to seek visions—spiritual awakenings to help them heal, teach, and lead. Some come away with medicine, Indian names to give to others, authority to run sweat-lodge ceremonies, or new songs.

Political, military, social, and religious leaders at Red Lake have always been guided by spiritual practice. From the Battle River fight to the present, meetings of peace and war, endeavors of hunting and harvest, and all of Red Lake's political councils have always begun with a pipe ceremony. Tribal chairmen at Red Lake customarily introduce themselves with their clans and the native names obtained from dreams or visions while fasting. In 1827, Thomas L. McKenney wrote, "[They] live, and die, confirmed in the belief that they are acting the part which the dream, or some other impression, pointed out to them as indispensable." At Red Lake, that tradition has never died.[18]

Red Lakers often say that they fiercely embrace one of the most libertarian cultures in the world. If someone has a vision while fasting, he or she could use that vision to give people their Indian names. If someone dreamed about a hand drum with a blue circle and cedar sticks tied inside of it, the person would make that drum. If someone dreamed about songs for a ceremony, he or she would bring those songs to that ceremony. If a Dakota boy was adopted into the Ojibwe community and his clan was kingfisher, everyone accepted it. The people were free and empowered. Red Lake was spiritually vibrant. New ceremonies and new ways of doing old ceremonies were born and reborn at the White Sand Dunes many times. That freedom was the heart of Red Lake's libertarianism—broad-minded, open, and growing. This dynamic explains why one family did its first animal-kill feast (*oshkinitaagewin*) one way, while two hundred yards away another family did it just a little bit differently. Both families were right. There was no rulebook, bible, or institution to shape such decisions. Creating formal social and ceremonial positions was avoided. People were guided by spiritual processes more than by ancient rules.[19]

The spiritual freedom enjoyed at Red Lake had its frustrations. If someone dreamed about doing a ceremony a certain way, nobody was obligated to attend. In fact, although people were not apt to judge their neighbors for their unique ways of doing things, they were also unlikely to abandon their own. And they would never tolerate someone else trying to impose a cultural idea or practice on others. Time and again, Red Lakers struggled to lead when presenting new and revolutionary ideas—whether around spirituality, war, or politics. The idea or the vision wasn't rejected, but people could rarely tolerate its being implemented.

When Red Lakers were expanding their domain, it was easy to accommodate divergent social, political, and cultural ideas. People just packed up and moved to a new part of the expanding territory where there was nobody to question the legitimacy of the ideas or their leaders. But when the treaty period began, land loss froze the freedom to expand. Culture did not change overnight, but the physical space had helped create the cultural space, and both were increasingly confined. Now when people had different ways of doing things, they had to tolerate and even accommodate one another.

Compounding the tension this cultural dynamic created was the fact that Red Lake, being on the western frontier of Ojibwe country, was dominated by Ojibwe people from farther east who had the greatest motivation to move. That motivation often emerged from this same cultural process farther east—people with new ideas moved west to get the space they needed to carry out new visions. This is part of what made Red Lake so vibrant and innovative, so full of new ideas and new visions, yet at the same time so resistant to picking up other people's visions. Red Lake was also dominated by warriors—anyone who told them what to do was in for a fight.

The cultural process was not gender-specific. Women and men both innovated, fasted, dreamed, and led. Clans and chieftainship at Red Lake were patrilineal, but society was matrilocal. Women owned the family dwelling and had great authority in marriage and divorce, even more so than in eastern parts of Ojibwe country. In ceremonies, both men and women played important leadership roles. Women and men often sat on opposite sides of ceremonial lodges to symbolically reinforce the understanding that men and women had equal voice in rituals.[20]

Women at Red Lake controlled the most important endeavor of the people there: they ran the economy. Groundbreaking scholarship by Brenda Child has illuminated and deepened our understanding of the role of women in Ojibwe economies, especially at Red Lake. Women dominated the economic activity of Ojibwe communities by producing most of the food, clothes, and lodges, and tanning most of the furs for trade. They also did most of the wild rice harvesting, gathering of berries, drying and storing of meat, and maple sugar harvesting, although there was no gender taboo for anyone who participated, and whole families engaged in all such activities.[21]

The gendered division of labor at Red Lake meant that families functioned best with both men and women, which put economic pressure on the marriage structure. There were fewer men at Red Lake because many died in warfare, arduous travel, and fishing on dangerously thin ice or rough water. As a result, Red Lake, like many Ojibwe communities, embraced polygamy through the 1800s. Polygamy evolved out of need, but persisted after the need began to dissipate. Men sometimes had more than one wife, but women could not have more than one husband. As mortality rates declined for men at Red Lake, women rejected the practice of polygamy. Their power to do so shows that polygamy was more about economic family structure than about sexual power. Assimilation pressure from missionaries and government officials surely played a role in influencing Ojibwe perceptions of family, but polygamy was abandoned in Ponemah (where nobody converted to Christianity) at the same time that it was abandoned in Redby, Red Lake, and Little Rock (where most people converted).[22]

When Red Lake was attacked, both men and women defended themselves. Men usually pursued war away from home, but not exclusively. Chiefs were usually men, but women often exerted leadership influence. Over time, women at Red Lake grew their authority in many realms. Fannie Johns and Susan Hallett each in turn became village matriarchs and history keepers. Anna Gibbs broke through gender barriers and became the most widely respected spiritual leader in Ponemah.[23]

Because Red Lake was so fiercely libertarian, because people had their own deep sense of personal spiritual empowerment and agency, because the people were so resistant to being told what to do, leading was a challenge. People loved their freedom so much that they required consensus to engage in joint political action, rather than anyone having to suffer the imposition of someone else's will. Red Lake was so spiritually vibrant and innovative that there was great diversity in local customs. Consensus was expected but hard to achieve. But on rare and special occasions, when someone had a truly compelling spiritual vision, it motivated broad and sometimes permanent change. The people who brought such visions forward had great influence, and their leadership prevailed across generations.

King Bird (Ogimaa-bines), who was a spiritual leader in the Battle River area near the White Sand Dunes, was given the gift of song. His vision was so powerful that he reshaped Ojibwe music across the region and his descendants (the large Kingbird family of Red Lake) remain one of the most musically gifted families in the region today. They inherit his spiritual gift, and they embrace it, sitting boys at the drum or on their fathers' laps to learn Ojibwe music from the age of four. Many of Red Lake's most prominent political and spiritual leaders built their influence through this same spiritual process, in this same spiritual place—Anna Gibbs, Thomas Stillday Jr., Dan Raincloud, Nodin Wind, and many more.

From the arrival of the first Ojibwe in Red Lake around 1760 to the present, the key to leadership in social, political, and military matters has always been influence, and influence had to be earned. Leadership was not limited to men and it did not happen in great halls of power, through legislation, or by leading armies into battle. It happened at the White Sand Dunes.

Red Lake Warrior Politics

There was something in the water at Red Lake, a genuine spiritual force that bonded people to that place and empowered them with a fearless sense of potential. Because seemingly nothing could stop them and nobody outside or inside their communities could tell anybody else what to do, people were inherently resistant to following. In this unique cultural environment, people were forced to build and sharpen certain skills: toughness, resilience, adaptation, and collaboration. The land and people shaped chiefs of remarkable ability to innovate and adapt to new political environments without allowing their own to be assimilated. Those leaders reshaped Red Lake's political culture over and over—connected and identifiable to their ancestors, but new and forward thinking at the same time.

During the first hundred years of Ojibwe settlement at Red Lake, the Ojibwe became one of the most numerous tribes in North America and built hundreds of primary villages from Quebec to Montana and from Illinois to northern Manitoba. The Ojibwe people did not function as one nation politically in spite of sharing many key aspects of language and culture. Within the Red Lake region there were networks of shared political and military communication, but each village was independent. There was no head chief, king, or other top official; rather, there were numerous chiefs from many distinct villages. Even neighboring places like Ponemah had different chiefs than nearby Battle River, Miquam Bay, and Ponemah Point. Nobody was chief of them all.

Ojibwe leadership dynamics were changing before the Ojibwe came to Red Lake, but its settlement was the catalyst for even more profound cultural changes in leadership. Because clan designation did not restrict chieftainship at Red Lake and new villages were being established not just along the lakeshore but throughout northwestern Minnesota, new leaders and new lines of chieftainship were out of necessity being established throughout the late 1700s and early 1800s.

As had been the custom throughout Ojibwe country, if there was a major political disagreement, one group often moved down the river or along the lakeshore and established a new village—but changes accelerated in Red Lake. New villages and chiefs emerged at Warroad, Blackduck, Warren, Red Lake River, Clearwater River, Sandy River, the north shore of Upper Red Lake, and throughout the region. For generations, anyone who exerted too much control got left behind in Michigan, Wisconsin, or eastern Ontario, and the same thing happened at Red Lake as well, as people left again to establish new villages at Turtle Mountain, Roseau River, and elsewhere.

Red Lake was home to warriors who believed in personal agency and self-directed power. To the people there, that was a sign of strength, and it spoke to the power of the people rather than the power of chiefs. At Red Lake, chiefs did not speak for all the people, and village chiefs never spoke for people outside of their respective villages. But French, British, and American officials always expected them to do so. That made for awkward diplomacy between Red Lake leaders and white folk. It also strained intratribal relations and politics. This caused trouble enough during the fur trade era, but when American officials wanted Red Lake chiefs to permit land cessions, it became painful.

Even though each village was independent, American officials grouped all Indians throughout the Red Lake region together and considered them a single band. This was a Euro-American construct, not an indigenous one. Calling the Ojibwe living in villages on the shores of Upper Red Lake, Lower Red Lake, the Red Lake River, the Thief River, and Lake of the Woods "the Red Lake Band" did not make them a unified political group. The idea of collective political or cultural identity emerged later, and even today is contested by many Red Lake Ojibwe.[24]

The chiefs of the Red Lake Band of Chippewa (as the Americans called them) never made decisions about politics, economics, or warfare as a united group before the American government tried to convince them to sell their lands at the Old Crossing Treaty in 1863. From then on, although many people at Red Lake took issue with anyone speaking on behalf of people who did not live in a particular chief's village, the representative nature of Red Lake's tribal politics increased.

Decision making often took a long time at Red Lake because the political culture made chiefs humble and reluctant to speak on someone else's behalf. The process was grassroots, cooperative, and consensus-oriented. Political council began with a smoking of the pipe, prayers for guidance, and invoking the creator, the spirits in the wind, the water, mother earth, the clans, and local spirits like those at the White Sand Dunes. The very word for council, *zagaswe'idiwin*, literally means "a smoking." When leaders could not arrive at consensus, nobody could overpower a smaller faction or force them to adhere to the will of the majority. Instead, smaller factions and leaders who could not align with the majority simply left the council.[25]

Chiefs did not have the power to command or control, but they did have the power to abstain from decisions or walk away from council, an act that usually negated the power of the council to speak for the entire community. When a faction or village chief refused to participate in council or broke away from an ongoing council, the council's authority was diminished and able only to speak for the villages still represented. This posed a major problem at every land cession. In 1863, Redby chief He Who Is Spoken To (Medwe-ganoonind) and all of the Ponemah chiefs refused to sign off on the land cession. He Who Is Spoken To walked away from the treaty signing; Ponemah boycotted the council altogether. In 1889, several chiefs, including all of the Ponemah chiefs, refused to sign the agreement for the land cession. That the government took their land anyway was seen as a fundamental betrayal. U.S. officials called it a binding agreement between nations.

The British and Americans tried to manipulate Red Lake leadership culture to their advantage. Through the gifting of medals and flags, they repeatedly declared that cooperative Indians were chiefs. The people of Red Lake were completely unimpressed by assertions of position from anyone of any race. According to George Copway, "Fear of the nation's censure acted as a mighty band, binding all in one social, honourable compact. They would not as brutes be whipped into duty. They would as men be persuaded to the right." Nothing could trump Red Lake reliance on consensus politics, hereditary chieftainship rights, and earned influence.[26]

Red Lake chiefs who did want to shape the will of a council had two primary ways to do it—showing and telling. Showing meant action—demonstrations of raw spiritual power, bold ideas in motion, or actions of service and self-sacrifice. Telling meant engaged listening first, respectful speaking second. An established reputation and advanced years usually helped. Establishing influence in council required deep relationships and oratorical skill—patient and pointed at the same time. Paul LeJeune wrote of the Ojibwe, "All the authority of their chief is in his tongue's end, for he is powerful in so far as he is eloquent."[27]

The culture at Red Lake was highly resistant to political gamesmanship. Wealth accumulation was a foreign concept, and chiefs often had fewer possessions than their people. In 1838, Anna Jameson noted, "the chief is seldom either so well lodged or so well dressed as the others." Johann Kohl wrote:

As long as a man has anything, according to the moral law of the Indians, he must share it with those who want; and no one can attain any degree of respect among them who does not do so most liberally. They are almost communists and hence there are no rich men among them. . . . Frequently, when a chief receives very handsome goods, either in exchange for his peltry, or as a recognition of his high position, he will throw them all in a heap, call his followers, and divide all among them. If he grow[s] very zealous he will pull off his shirt and give it away, and say, "So you see, I have now nothing more to give; I am poorer than any one of you, and I commend myself to your charity."[28]

A chief was expected to be generous with food, trade goods, and eventually treaty payments. This kept chiefs humble and service-minded. But during the treaty period, American diplomats undermined this value. Red Lake chiefs became financial arbiters, with the very powerful position of not just negotiating the land deals, but also handing out the cash. Some were even granted private land grants. How chiefs were treated was starting to change. Who was chief mattered more than ever before.[29]

The Way of the Red Lake Warrior

There was a reason for everything Red Lakers did. The people were devoted to family, collaborative, deeply spiritual, hardworking, and extremely respectful. Red Lake warriors did not look for or live by violence, but they could be fiercely protective of the people and place they loved. War was a means to an end, not a lifeway. But it did have its reasons, and even some rules.

Ojibwe warriors came to Red Lake for territory, for spiritual quest fulfillment, for strategic advantage in protecting their families, and for greater ease of access to food. They stayed in Red Lake for the same reasons. Missionary Samuel Pond summed up the territorial incentives for Ojibwe–Dakota conflict:

If they were to live at all, they must have a country to live in; and if they were to live by hunting, they must have a very large country, from which all others were excluded. Such a country they had, not because their enemies were willing they should occupy it, but because they were able and willing to defend it by force of arms. If they had not resisted the encroachments of their enemies, they would soon have been deprived of the means of subsistence and must have perished. If they would have game to kill, they must kill men too.[30]

The Red Lake Ojibwe often waged war for practical reasons such as food and safety. But there were cultural beliefs about war that kept Red Lake in conflict even when there were no practical reasons to fight. Red Lakers believed that the body was a temporary house for a person's soul. They were not humans looking for a spiritual experience; they were spirits having a temporary human experience. They did not have souls; they were souls, and they had bodies for a little while. When someone died, his or her body went back to the earth, but the soul lived forever and traveled to the spirit world. When someone was killed, the killing had the potential to offend the departing soul and inhibit his or her departure to the place of never-ending happiness. Something had to be done about that.

When someone was murdered or killed in war, there were ceremonial options to remove the potential offense to his or her soul and enable a peaceful departure to the spirit world. One way was through initiation into the medicine dance, the primary religious society of the Ojibwe. Another common alternative was through a peaceful reconciliation between the killer and the family of the victim. This custom was variously called "covering the dead," "paying the body," or "wiping off the blood." The murderer, or representatives of that person's family or community, offered gifts and food, as Frederic Baraga observed: "Sometimes the relatives of the killed are appeased by the relatives of the murderer, by great presents." William W. Warren called it "to heal the matter *Indian fashion,* paying in goods for the lives lost." This usually resolved intratribal Ojibwe-Ojibwe violence but was hard to make happen in intertribal Dakota-Ojibwe violence.[31]

When peaceful options for removing offense to a departing soul were not available, the bereaved family could remove it themselves by seeking revenge. One early Ojibwe missionary observed: "their departed relatives will not rest in peace unless some human beings are sacrificed to them." Around 1800, when Red Lakers settled Pembina, one of the early chiefs there, Lynx Head (Bizhiwoshtigwaan), said: "We bear with us . . . those that were our friends and children, but we cannot lay them down, except [when] we come into the camp of our enemies." Thus even when it was not critical to Red Lake territorial defense, Red Lake warriors often went to war for this cultural reason. Successful warriors returning from battle performed ceremonies to remove the offenses on the souls of their own dead relatives. Different families had different ways to perform this kind of ceremony. One of the most common was through the scalp dance.[32]

Red Lakers did scalp. The scalp was brought home and used as a tool to remove the offense on the souls of family members killed by enemies. Henry Schoolcraft observed an Ojibwe scalp dance on July 10, 1832, conducted at the graves of family members killed in war. Scalping was considered honorable because it was not done for the purpose of disrespectful mutilation but for respectful ceremony for beloved relatives. Through prayer and dance, the offended spirit for whom vengeance was taken could be sent on to the spirit world. The scalp was believed to house the spirit of the slain person. Victorious warriors customarily blackened their faces after battle as a symbol of mourning for those they had slain. Often, they put tobacco down at the camp of their overrun enemies as an offering to the spirits whom they may have offended in exacting their revenge.[33]

Because this custom was shared across the region, it was also considered an honor to be scalped. One Ojibwe warrior said, "we consider it an honour to have the scalps of our countrymen exhibited in the villages of our enemies, in testimony of our valour." Joseph Nicollet said, "They consider it an honor to be scalped. Not to be scalped is a sign of contempt." At Warroad, the local chief, Sword (Ashaweshk), led a defensive party against a Dakota raid and was knocked unconscious and half of his scalp was removed. He survived and considered the wound an exceptional honor.[34]

For the first hundred years of Ojibwe settlement at Red Lake, Ojibwe-Dakota war persisted. Territorial pressure eased after a few decades, but the cultural drivers for conflict endured. At the same time that conflict continued, peaceful interconnections between the Ojibwe and Dakota also deepened. White Thunderbird's adoption at Ponemah was not anomalous. Many Dakota were adopted into Ojibwe communities and vice versa. There were also many intertribal marriages between the Ojibwe and Dakota. Dakota chiefs Wabasha and Red Wing had Ojibwe heritage. Ojibwe chiefs Big Foot, White

Fisher, and Flat Mouth had Dakota ancestors. From the beginning of Ojibwe settlement in northwestern Minnesota to the present, most Red Lake Ojibwe have had Dakota blood running through their veins. Even during periods of conflict, Red Lake Ojibwe traveled far onto the plains to hunt buffalo, often in the peaceful company of Dakota under temporary truces. The Ojibwe called such truces *biindigodaad-iwin* ("to enter one another's lodges"). Ojibwe and Dakota hunters literally entered one another's lodges, slept in them together, smoked the same pipes, and formed friendships and sometimes marriages. When they returned to Red Lake, territorial or cultural imperatives might have them at war with one another again at any time.[35]

The land changes quickly west of Red Lake, and the nature of warfare changed just as fast. Rivers and creeks flow through northwestern Minnesota, coursing west and north to and then through the Red River Valley. In 1800, Alexander Henry reported that the Ojibwe traveled throughout their newly acquired territory by canoe and had few horses compared to Plains tribes. The Dakota had had easy access to horses for nearly one hundred years already. Their transition to plains life was greatly aided by their close relationships with the western Lakota. Horses provided a great advantage in warfare when the Red Lakers stepped out of the shelter of the forests. In 1798, one Red Lake chief said: "While they keep to the Plains with their Horses we are not a match for them; for we being foot men, they could get windward of us, and set fire to the grass. When we marched for the woods, they would be there before us, dismount and under cover fire on us. Until we have horses like them, we must keep to the Woods and leave the Plains to them."[36]

In those early days, everything else worked to the benefit of the Ojibwe in war. Red Lake was upstream from Dakota villages. When traveling in their own territory, Red Lakers could cover the distance to enemies quickly by canoe. When retreating, their birchbark canoes were faster and more buoyant than Dakota dugouts.

The lure of better hunting increased their territorial ambitions, and realizing those ambitions required horses. From 1800 to 1820, the Red Lake Ojibwe began to build horse herds for travel, hunting, and war. Red Lakers started to rely heavily on big-game hunting too, especially woodland caribou, moose, elk, deer, and buffalo. That took them everywhere in the Red River Valley and even farther out onto the plains. By the time of the Nelson Act in 1889, most families had at least one horse, and many families had many horses. In Ponemah, a wild horse herd grew from stray and runaway mustangs. The Ponemah feral herd persisted through the 1970s, within the memory of many reservation residents today. The acquisition of horses made Red Lake unique among Minnesota's Ojibwe communities in the early 1800s, encouraging cultural evolution in hunting and war and setting up Red Lake as the staging ground for Ojibwe settlement of Roseau River, Pembina, Turtle Mountain, and numerous Ojibwe communities in Manitoba.[37]

Another advantage Red Lake had over the Dakota was geographical. Red Lake was continually being reinforced by Ojibwe migrants from eastern Ojibwe communities. The Ojibwe had greater ease of access to guns in trade and more furs to trade for whatever they needed. All Ojibwe enemies were on one front, whereas the Dakota had enemies in almost every direction. The Ojibwe also had a lot more friends than the Dakota. They had powerful European trade alliances and strong military allies in the Cree and Assiniboine. They even forged an alliance with the Mandan. The Dakota were often overwhelmed—they could not fight everyone all at once.

In 1800, Ojibwe from Red Lake went to one of the Mandan villages to parlay with the Mandan, Cree, and Assiniboine. While they sat in council, the Dakota attacked. The Mandan fought them alone until their chief called out to the attackers, "Depart from our village, or we will let upon you our friends, the Ojibbeways, who have been sitting here all day, and are now fresh and unwearied." The attackers replied, "This is a vain boast made with a design to conceal your weakness. You have no Ojibbeways in your house, and if you had hundreds, we neither fear nor regard them. The Ojibbeways are women, and if your village were full of them, we would, for that reason, sooner come among you." The Ojibwe and their allies sallied forth from behind the fortified walls of the Mandan village in a spirited attack and forced the Dakota into a rapid retreat.[38]

Red Lakers had practical and cultural reasons for fighting, but leading a war party was not an easy thing. If a Red Laker wanted to put a war expedition together, he was rarely stopped, but war leaders also could not command people to follow them. Such actions were entirely voluntary on the part of both participants and leaders. There

Wild horses at Red Lake, 1941

were times when Ojibwe people did participate en masse in military events—driving the Dakota out of Red Lake, for example, or when attacked. But usually offensive military events were small and lacked any real command-and-control directive. Red Lakers were not soldiers—shaped and molded into uniform fighting machines. They were warriors—unique, independent, highly skilled, and spiritually empowered and motivated. For Red Lakers, the way of the warrior was not a culture of conflict, even though conflict was part of the culture. It was a path to safety, protection, a higher standard of living, and spiritual responsibility. It was about building their communities, not destroying someone else's.

Red Lake Warriors at War

As soon as the Ojibwe settled Red Lake, they became a juggernaut of military power in the region. Red Lake was protected by Ojibwe communities to the north, south, and east. In turn, it became the linchpin that buffered and protected those places from Dakota attacks. With the birchbark canoe and the gun, Red Lakers were masters of the water; having horses in significant numbers enabled them to push westward after 1800.

Red Lakers were accomplished fishermen, rice harvesters, hunters, and warriors. They had clear advantages in their conflict with the Dakota—better technology, a more easily defended homeland, greater numbers, and more allies. They intentionally pushed the Dakota westward, but even if someone at Red Lake wanted to stop it, there was no way to control the dynamic at play. More and more Ojibwe people were coming to Red Lake. More and more Red Lakers were spinning off in small family groups and lesser villages throughout northwestern Minnesota. Buffalo, elk, and woodland caribou hunting was excellent. Fish were plentiful. Wild rice was abundant. And it was at least as safe as anywhere else in Ojibwe country. The Red Lake people who spread throughout the region were simply trying to live; they did not intend to have any particular cultural impact beyond their own flourishing. But from 1790 to 1863, Red Lakers gave birth to the Plains Ojibwe and settled Pembina, Turtle Mountain, and many communities in Manitoba. They also contributed greatly to the rise of the Métis.

Red Lake was on the move immediately after the Battle River fight in 1760, and by the late 1700s was sending war parties directly to Sisseton to attack the Dakota. The Dakota sent war parties to Red Lake throughout the early missionary period in the 1850s, but the Dakota had no choice but to relocate most of their people off of the Red River war road to Sisseton and Lake Traverse. When Father George Anthony Belcourt came to Pembina in 1831, he said, "The Crees and Assiniboins regard themselves as equally masters of these lands with the Chippewas, having acquired them jointly with the latter." The Cree and Assiniboine established new villages in Manitoba while the Red Lake Ojibwe established Roseau River, Manitoba, and Pembina, North Dakota. In 1790, Pembina was populated almost entirely with Ojibwe people from Red Lake and Lake of the Woods. By 1795, it was impervious to Dakota attack. Alexander Henry, who established a trading post at Pembina in 1798, said that the people at Pembina still considered themselves Red Lake Ojibwe, even though the village grew rapidly to more than two thousand, with many Ojibwe and even Ottawa from farther east moving there.[39]

The Spanish and British sparred over trading rights on the plains in the late 1700s when Red Lakers were settling Pembina. The Spanish had trading posts on the Missouri River; the British had posts at Winnipeg. Tribes from the entire region traveled overland and by canoe to connect with both. In 1796, the Spanish complained that the Red Lake and Pembina Ojibwe were in the British interest and hostile to their traders along the Missouri River. In 1797, the North West Company established a trading post at Pembina. In 1798, the Hudson's Bay Company followed suit.[40]

By 1800, the Red Lake Ojibwe were able not just to fortify and build the village at Pembina but to range far onto the plains, hunting buffalo and fighting the Dakota. The Red River Valley was now Ojibwe territory. The Dakota at Lake Traverse were hard-pressed by the Red Lakers. At the same time, Leech Lake Ojibwe established a new village at Otter Tail Lake, Minnesota, which is close to the mouth of the Otter Tail River near Wahpeton, North Dakota. Some reports claimed that Red Lake Ojibwe traveled as far as the Rocky Mountains, and they frequently began to camp at Turtle Mountain, North Dakota. In 1806, Alexander Henry reported a large settlement of Ojibwe and Cree at Turtle Mountain.[41]

Ojibwe territorial pressure kept mounting. In 1803, Dakota chiefs Red Thunder and Standing Buffalo moved from Sisseton to Lake Traverse to consolidate the Dakota population for better defense because of repeated Ojibwe attacks. The Ojibwe now sought control of Spirit Lake (Devils Lake), North Dakota, a populous Dakota village. In 1805, large numbers of Red Lake and Pembina Ojibwe, Ottawa, and Cree made joint hunting camps around Spirit Lake. That year there were at least three significant battles between the Ojibwe and Dakota around the lake. Pembina Ojibwe chiefs Little Clam (Esens) and Little Chief (Ogimaans) were killed in separate attacks.[42]

The Dakota tried to push back. In 1821, they killed two whites and several Ojibwe traders in Red Lake territory. In 1823, Dakota scouts ran into Count Giacomo Beltrami's expedition on the Red Lake River, which was guided by Red Lake Ojibwe. The Ojibwe guides deserted the expedition immediately and fled back to Red Lake. William H. Keating came to the Red River Valley in 1824 and reported that the Red Lake Ojibwe had well-established distinctions between residents of various villages, calling the Ojibwe at the Red River outlet *zaagiiwininiwag* ("people of the outlet") and those in villages on the shore of Red Lake *miskwaagamiiwi-zaaga'iganininiwag* ("people of Red Lake"). Major Stephen Long embarked on five major exploring and surveying expeditions in the region, affirming the observations of Keating and Beltrami about sustained Dakota counterattacks against Red Lake. Long reported that Black Man (Makadewinini) and Great Hare (Chi-waabooz) were chiefs at Red Lake at this time.[43]

Red Lake's greatest influence in bringing the Ojibwe to the plains lay in the settlement of Pembina, Roseau, and Turtle Mountain. Once those villages were established, their population grew rapidly. Throughout the region, small, independent villages were popping up as the Ojibwe population moved west and increasingly occupied territory. The independence of each of these communities was soon unquestioned. Red Lake was not controlling new settlements as part of a common polity, but rather was supporting their settlement and independence. From Turtle Mountain and Pembina, the Ojibwe expanded throughout the Northern Plains. In 1824–25, the Ojibwe established a village on the prairie between Turtle Mountain and Bismarck on Buffalo Lodge Lake (Bizhiki Endaad) by present-day Towner, North Dakota, hunting buffalo and planting corn. It was the object of ferocious Dakota attacks. From 1829 to 1832, Kenneth McKenzie and George Catlin observed numerous Ojibwe warriors on the plains as far west as the Yellowstone River.[44]

Red Lake's expansion onto the plains was not entirely violent; long periods of genuinely cooperative peace punctuated the territorial advance of the Ojibwe. In 1836–37, the Red Lake, Pembina, and Otter Tail Lake Ojibwe were peacefully hunting together with the Wah'petonwan Dakota. William Aitkin withdrew the American Fur Company trading post at Otter Tail Lake because the Ojibwe preferred to trade at the Dakota post at Lake Traverse. Red Lake Ojibwe frequently journeyed far onto the plains, sometimes independently, sometimes in the company of their relatives from Pembina, Leech Lake, or Otter Tail Lake. In 1836, it was reported that Red Lakers made annual hunting trips to the Sheyenne River, on the edge of the Ojibwe–Dakota territorial boundary.[45]

Although the Ojibwe gained substantial territory fighting the

Dakota, it cost lives and daily stress. Red Lake chief Great Wind (Chi-noodin) claimed to have taken more than fifty Dakota scalps in various battles west of the Red River and in Manitoba. Dakota warriors were equally celebrated, and the cost for both sides was tremendous. In the late 1840s, the Ojibwe built huge breastworks of earth, logs, and stone around their satellite villages in the vicinity of Turtle Mountain to better protect themselves from enemy attack. In 1847, the Ojibwe from Otter Tail and Leech Lakes ceded land for a tiny payment of guns, blankets, and traps, with no financial remuneration, in order to have the Ho-Chunk (Winnebago) and Menominee relocated to Long Prairie, Minnesota, as a buffer from Dakota attacks.[46]

We do not know how long White Thunderbird lived, but his impact rippled through time. He brought the Dakota kingfisher clan to the Ojibwe and his descendants were among the Red Lake warriors who pushed west. Even today the kingfisher is one of the most widely represented clans among the Plains Ojibwe. As the kingfishers spread, so too did the spiritual, military, social, and political culture of Red Lake.

Red Lake and Making the Métis

When Red Lakers settled Pembina in the late 1700s it was strictly an Ojibwe community, an offshoot of the population at Red Lake. That changed over the next fifty years. Cree, Assiniboine, and Ottawa Indians settled there along with the Ojibwe, as did many French and British trappers and traders. The French government left Canada after signing the Treaty of Paris in 1763 at the conclusion of the French and Indian War. Their fur traders, many of whom had intermarried with Indians or had Indian blood themselves, were left behind. At Pembina, Indians from these four tribes and two European nations mingled, mixed, and married for generations. Ojibwe and French were the largest groups there, and out of their sustained fraternization a new culture and people was born: the Métis. They had their own language, Michif, largely consisting of Ojibwe verbs and French nouns. Eventually, they evolved their own way of doing things and their own political and military ambitions.

The Métis did not see themselves as French, British, Ojibwe, or Cree. Like the Red Lakers who established Pembina, they highly valued their freedom from European military and political control. Like

Red Lakers, they also felt free from one another—nobody could tell
them what to do or how to live. But through the 1800s, they increasingly felt distinct from Red Lake. Many of them were Catholic, a
belief brought by the French Catholic settlers at Pembina. That was
reinforced with the arrival of Catholic missionaries: Fathers Severe
Joseph Nicolas Dumoulin and Joseph Norbert Provencher in 1818,
Father George Anthony Belcourt in 1831, and Father Joseph Goiffon
in 1856. The Métis had operated as traders before coming to Pembina
and continued that economic lifestyle afterward, eventually domi-
nating the Red River trade by canoe and overland by oxcart. The Red
Lakers who settled at Pembina had no objections to so many Europeans coming to their community to live. They were trading partners
for Red Lake trappers and buffalo hunters. They were military allies
in fending off Dakota attacks. And they were often friends and family
as well. By the time it was evident that the Métis were distinct from
the Ojibwe and a force in their own right, there was both no need to
interrupt Métis ascension and no way to do it.[47]

After a few generations, the Métis at Pembina were thoroughly
racially mixed, often referred to as *bois brûlés* (burnt wood) because
of their dark complexions. Some of the Métis population called
themselves *gens libres,* or free men, because they were the descendants of liberated French indentured servants. In 1811, the Earl of
Selkirk brought many Scottish peasants to Pembina. Like the French
coureurs de bois (traders) there, they too absorbed into the Métis population. Joseph Renville, Simon McGillivray, Lyman Warren, and
other traders among the Ojibwe married native women. Their children were mixed bloods, but not Métis. Métis did not mean mixed
blood—it was more than that. The Métis had a hybrid culture and
a distinct language of their own. Many were mixed bloods, but that
was not a requirement to be part of the new culture at Pembina.[48]

The Métis played contending trading companies off of one
another with great skill. The Hudson's Bay Company and the North
West Company had a bitter economic rivalry that sometimes got
bloody and often engulfed the Métis community. In 1823, Major
Stephen Long established an American presence at Pembina. Soon
the American Fur Company was competing with the British. The
Métis were growing economically, politically, militarily, and in
sheer numbers.[49]

Like the Red Lakers, the Métis acquired horses and hunted buffalo. For decades, Métis friendship and alliance with their relatives at Red Lake kept Pembina safe from overwhelming Dakota attack. By 1830, the Ojibwe and Métis dominated the Red River Valley. Alfred Brunson estimated the population in the valley to be 25,000 people, most being Métis and Ojibwe. The Dakota, who still fought the Ojibwe and Métis, feared being overwhelmed and wrote two letters in 1844 to Métis leader Cuthbert Grant in an attempt to establish peace. Over the next two decades, the Métis increasingly handled their own defense independently and spread across Manitoba. Turtle Mountain, which, like Pembina, began as an Ojibwe community around 1805, was by 1845 populated with large numbers of Métis, Cree, and Ojibwe.[50]

In many ways, Red Lake helped give birth to the Métis. Then the Métis grew in power, influence, and numbers, imprinting heavily on the Ojibwe community at Turtle Mountain, and forming many independent Métis communities in Canada. They eventually tried to gain independence there, fighting the British during the Louis Riel Rebellion in 1869 along the Red River and then during the North-West Rebellion in 1885. After their military defeats, some Métis maintained independent cultural enclaves in Canada. Some took refuge and absorbed into white communities in the United States and Canada. And some sought refuge in Ojibwe and other tribal communities, especially at Turtle Mountain, White Earth, and Red Lake. Father Thomas Borgerding, who served as Catholic priest at Red Lake for many years, estimated that twenty-five hundred Ojibwe, Métis, and French were buried at St. Mary's Catholic Cemetery in Red Lake by the time of the Nelson Act in 1889.[51]

The Red Lake Warrior Economy

White Thunderbird's era at Red Lake saw significant cultural and political change, and during that same period the tribal economy was also transformed. Like all Ojibwe, Red Lakers were harvesters. Failure to consistently produce food by traditional harvest methods meant starvation and death. They lived in a place that was cold, harsh, and forbidding, but also lush and full of resources.

The nature of the harvest at Red Lake changed over the first few generations of Ojibwe settlement. West of Red Lake was the Red River Valley—home to the most densely concentrated elk and buffalo herds in the world, with numerous smaller lakes and rivers that were less impressive than Red Lake for fishing but excellent habitat for moose and woodland caribou, which were numerous there. Red Lakers followed the path of least resistance. They hunted the big game west of Red Lake and throughout the Red River Valley. Once Red Lakers had horses, they ranged farther and farther onto the plains and came to depend more and more on the chase. They retained all their other resources and skills, but their diet and culture were transformed.[52]

Red Lakers were trappers too. As the fur trade grew and Europeans got closer to Red Lake and easier to trade with directly, the importance of trapping increased, which led Red Lakers to diversify their economy. Everyone at Red Lake had to know about harvesting of all kinds. But increasingly, some of the Red Lake people became specialists at trapping while others specialized in buffalo hunting. In 1794-95, the North West Company reported 211 otter pelts and 1,500 beaver harvested at Red Lake and brought to Grand Portage for sale. In 1806, the company established a post at Red Lake.[53]

In 1796, North West Company trader Jean Baptiste Cadotte Jr. (later Anglicized as John Baptiste Cadotte) spent the winter at Sandy Lake, Minnesota, and traveled extensively around Red Lake. Man of the Rapids (Bawatigoowinini), one of Cadotte's Ojibwe guides, stayed in Red Lake, got married, and raised a family. When William Warren interviewed him nearly sixty years later, he was the sole surviving member of the expedition. Warren claimed that Red Lake chief Feathers in Different Directions (Wewanjigwan) regarded the arrival of the Cadotte expedition in 1796 as a date when Red Lake was safely and undisputedly in Ojibwe hands.[54]

The North West Company, Hudson's Bay Company, and even Spanish traders on the Missouri River were vying for the Red Lake fur business. In 1823, the United States began to assert more influence in the region with a series of exploratory and political missions. In 1847, the American Fur Company built a post on the south shore of Red Lake. That building was still standing in 1888 when Thomas Borgerding and John G. Morrison charted the area.[55]

The fur trade led to an evolution in the culture at Red Lake. Collaboration and collective harvest had dominated Ojibwe practices there for generations. Now, while those values were still important, they were infused with new ideas about specialized skill, individual ownership of and profit from the harvest, and intratribal trade and commerce. Red Lakers began to supply Leech Lakers with buffalo meat and fish. Red Lake and Leech Lake Ojibwe cut an overland trail from Pike Bay to Lake Andrusia, past the southern tip of Turtle River Lake, across high ground north of Lake Julia, to Mud Lake, and then to the Red Lake villages. Commerce grew. The American Fur Company saw the potential of the intratribal and intertribal trade and built a post on Little Turtle Lake. It was charted by Ralph H. Dickinson in 1897. Many Leech Lake families were soon traveling the trail not just to trade, but to join in hunting the Red River Valley. That deepened relationships between Leech Lake and Red Lake families. In 1849, Jonathan E. Fletcher, Winnebago Indian agent, reported that a Dakota war party attacked the Leech Lakers at Lake Winnibigoshish. Red Lake warriors rallied and ran over the new overland trail to reinforce the Ojibwe at Leech Lake and drove the Dakota war party out.[56]

As Red Lakers embraced new kinds of hunting, travel, and trade, they also experimented with farming. Northwestern Minnesota is ecologically diverse. The Red River Valley has some of the best farmland in the world. But north of Red Lake is primarily swamp and nearly impossible to cultivate. Along the immediate western shoreline of Red Lake is a microclimate, with nitrate-rich topsoil well suited to farming cereal grains. When the Ojibwe arrived in Red Lake, they had knowledge of traditional tribal crops such as corn, tobacco, and squash—crops that were not widely farmed at first but that grew in importance over time.

In 1837, Ojibwe people in central Minnesota ceded land to the U.S. government for the first time, and white settlers came close to Red Lake territory to stay. That process only grew, and gradually exerted pressure on Red Lakers to become more sedentary. Missionaries came to Red Lake at the same time, and Red Lakers were happy to add to their ancient knowledge of farming with European foods, especially cereal grains.

The initial success of farming at Red Lake was widely documented by government officials and missionaries. In the winter of 1842-43, fifty families from Leech Lake and other Ojibwe communities

wintered at Red Lake and were fed from the surplus grain and vege-
table harvests. Alfred Brunson, agent at La Pointe, bought a hundred
dollars' worth of the Red Lake corn surplus for agency use in Wisconsin. In 1850, the Office of Indian Affairs reported, "The Red Lake and
Pembina bands derive their subsistence chiefly from agriculture. To
this mode of life they have been led by the persuasions of their excellent missionaries . . . according to the estimates of their traders, they
will this year produce not less than two thousand bushels of corn. In
the winter season they move their camps west of Red River to hunt
the buffalo which still abound in that region." The commissioner of
Indian affairs reported the following year:

> The prospect of success at Red Lake is more encouraging than at either
> of the other stations (Cass Lake and Winnipeg Lake). The band at that
> place will raise the present season an abundant supply of corn and pota-
> toes. They are becoming more industrious and marking more rapid
> improvement than any other band in the territory. They are beginning
> to feel in some measure, the importance of educating their children. . . .
> The soil at Red Lake is the best I have seen in the territory and produces
> abundantly almost all kinds of grain and vegetables; and the lake also
> abounds in excellent fish.[57]

In 1853, Indian agent D. B. Herriman reported that Indian farmers
at Red Lake were producing wheat with a yield of forty-five bushels
per acre. In 1869 seven thousand bushels of grain were harvested at
Red Lake. Because farming was so successful in the microclimate on
Red Lake's western shore and in the Red River Valley, many government officials assumed it would be the same elsewhere in Red Lake
territory; that was a miscalculation for which Red Lakers and many
white settlers ultimately paid a heavy price. But where farming was
good, it was great, and even today some Red Lake families still operate farms commercially on the west end of the reservation.[58]

Red Lake chiefs at this time included Feathers in Different Directions and Crooked Arm (Gaawashkweniked). Feathers in Different
Directions, Crooked Arm, and other chiefs at Red Lake often parlayed with the U.S. government through councils. In 1856, the chiefs
forbade the government from cutting any more timber on Red Lake
land unless the government first built a council house and a house for
each family in each community. It was a powerful statement, even

though they did not get full concessions. The request showed that Red Lake leaders were thinking of their people first and were pro-actively engaging the U.S. government rather than passively waiting for white men to act. There was no doubt that whites coveted Red Lake land, and the chiefs could feel the pressure building. As early as 1851, Governor Alexander Ramsey tried to initiate a land cession at Red Lake, but he was unsuccessful.[59]

Red Lake warriors traveled where they wanted. They hunted where they wanted. They suffered few restrictions, except those that were self-imposed. The people respected their chiefs, but chiefs did not rule—they represented. The chiefs were primarily spokesmen, and if they deviated from the will of the people, they simply stood alone. The Americans looked at the chiefs differently than the people of Red Lake did, and when the government finally came after the land, it tested not just the Red Lake harvest, hunting, fur, and farm economy, but the very structure of Red Lake's political culture. Big changes were at hand.

The Secret City

From the Battle River fight in 1760 to the Old Crossing Treaty in 1863, the influence of the Red Lake Ojibwe continued to grow in the region. It must have seemed like nobody could challenge Red Lake's rise. Imagine the surprise of the Red Lake warriors to learn that de-spite everything they had accomplished, there was a secret Dakota village in the heart of their territory.

In the late 1820s, a group of Cree and Assiniboine made a tem-porary peace with the Dakota, during which someone disclosed the existence of a large Dakota village at the outlet of the Thief River into the Red Lake River. The Cree told the Red Lake Ojibwe, and the Ojibwe dispatched scouts to see if any of this was true.

Red Lake scouts confirmed that there was indeed a secret Dakota village. The Dakota had built a massive earthen palisade around their village. It was impossible to see their lodges from any distance with-out breaching the dirt embankment, which not only concealed the village but also protected it from enemy attack. The Dakota hunted only with bows and arrows to avoid any discernible noise. They kept fires small and as smokeless as possible to avoid detection. There were

Ojibwe villages around that location in every direction for at least one hundred miles. We can only imagine the full scope of lifestyle concessions the Dakota must have made and the constant state of fear they must have lived in. They too must have loved the land and the life it supported to have taken such an incredible risk in staying.

Amazingly, the Dakota had successfully avoided detection at the secret village since the Ojibwe occupied Red Lake in 1760, more than sixty years. There were ten lodges in the village, roughly a hundred people. The Red Lakers called the place Gimoojaki-ziibi (Secret River), because the Dakota had for so long maintained a secret community there even while the Ojibwe were literally living and hunting all around them. Traders mispronounced it as Gimoodaki-ziibi (Thief River), and the translation stuck in English.

The secret village galvanized Red Lake to unite in a way rarely seen. Nobody commanded them, but they all answered the call for war. Moose Dung (Moozoo-moo), who was born around 1800, was already a distinguished warrior, and one of the leaders of the attack. Sun Shining Through (Mizhakiyaasige) was a young and ambitious warrior who had just arrived in Red Lake from Michigan. Together, Moose Dung, Sun Shining Through, and many other warriors whose names are no longer remembered planned a devastating attack. The Red Lake war party was huge, consisting of hundreds of warriors. They surrounded the village and stormed over the earthen palisades, completely annihilating the village—every man, woman, elder, and child.[60]

Red Lakers won the battle, but they suffered many casualties. The Dakota had been preparing for this attack for generations. They were ready. Fortifications were strong, and the Dakota knew they were fighting for their lives. Sun Shining Through was wounded so severely that he had to be dragged on a travois all the way back to Red Lake, although he lived many more years.[61]

Crushing the Dakota at Thief River was but one chapter in a long saga of complicated conflict. The battle at Thief River elevated Sun Shining Through to prominence as a Red Lake warrior. He led a subsequent attack at Shakopee, in southern Minnesota, in which two of his brothers were killed. He then led a major retributory offensive and came back to Red Lake with thirty Dakota scalps. By the time he became an elder he had represented Red Lake for so long and led so many successful war parties that people began to call him by a new

English nickname, "Business." He was a monolingual Ojibwe speaker, but he loved this one English word. In 1889, scribes at the Nelson Act councils thought it had to be an Ojibwe word and wrote it down with two different spellings as Pus-se-naus and Pah-se-nos. The interpreters could not figure out the word's true meaning or origin, so they asked him, and he simply said, "Slapping the Flies," his metaphor for killing Dakotas.[62]

Moose Dung stayed at what would become Thief River Falls and built a village. By 1863, forty-two Ojibwe families had moved there and he was widely acclaimed as their chief. The Thief River fight marked the beginning of something else: the many disparate villages in the Red Lake region had done something together. Their village autonomy was unaltered, but the idea and the source for an ideological shift from village to nation was emerging. The people of the Red Lake region had separate villages, but they shared land, resources, and military ambitions. Political cohesion was far from certain, but it was possible.

White Thunderbird's descendants now served as village chiefs at Ponemah and were members of Ojibwe and Métis communities across millions of acres of territory in the woodlands and the plains, in both the United States and Canada. White Thunderbird was both a symbol of and spark for cultural change. Red Lake's politics, economics, and culture were altered by the presence of White Thunderbird and others like him, making them distinct from those of other Ojibwe communities, and stronger than ever before. The warrior nation was on the rise.

Moose Dung, before 1877

2

Moose Dung and the Old Crossing Treaty

"My heart is bleeding when I hear you talk. I am sorry, for the reason that the Great Father thinks so lightly of our land. . . . I do not want this at all. . . . I tell you frankly that I do not accept it, and shall go home instantly."

HE WHO IS SPOKEN TO

The View at Old Crossing, Minnesota

The topography of the land changes between the tall stands of virgin pine forest on the south shore of Red Lake and the hardwoods on the west end, to the shallow and meandering Thief River, quickly giving way to wide-open space in the midst of the tallgrass prairie. In 1863, the Red River Valley was dominated by the tallgrass prairie, which covered the entire western third of Minnesota and extended north into Manitoba and south as far as Missouri. It was covered in lush grass, fertile, verdant growth that dwarfed everything on the Great Plains. The Red River Valley sustained the densest herds of buffalo and elk in the world. The shallow lakes dotting the landscape formed a central corridor for the duck and goose migrations of North America. Moose and woodland caribou abounded. It was paradise to the Red Lake Ojibwe.[1]

Although the villages on the shores of Red Lake were the largest, there were numerous smaller villages throughout the region as well whose people hunted, traveled, and harvested in the Red River Valley.

43

Moose Dung and forty-two families lived at the Thief River outlet. Fannie Johns and other tribal elders remembered well growing up in the heart of the Red River Valley near present-day Warren, Minnesota, in Pembina, North Dakota, and all over the Minnesota prairie.

The cool, damp autumn wind whipped at the weathered faces of the Red Lake chiefs. In 1863, Moose Dung was a venerable elder with many grandchildren, tough and seasoned in both war and politics. His eldest son, Red Robed (Meskokonayed), was with him. He was thirty-one, and emerging as a capable successor chief at Thief River. There was little natural shelter from the elements along the high banks at the Old Crossing of the Red Lake River (present-day Huot) in northwestern Minnesota. A large entourage of white land speculators, government officials, translators, and Indian agents faced the Red Lake chiefs. The wind blew through their beards and woolen overcoats without discrimination. They cared little for the buffalo, elk, and big bluestem grass. They looked at the land differently from the Red Lake leadership, and they envisioned a different future for the land, but they saw paradise too. They must have imagined the land as it looks in the spring today—deep, dark, fertile soil for miles and miles in all directions, as far as the eye can see.

It was hard for any of them to fully know just how rich the land really was, but they could imagine it, and even the wildest of those dreams came true. The Red Lake lands in the Red River Valley today are among the easiest to irrigate, plant, and fertilize. The topsoil is twice as thick and three times as nitrate laden as most other American farmland. Two transcontinental railroads and two branches of the interstate highway system bisect the valley to transport harvests to market. While the Red Lake chiefs saw the natural splendor of the land and the bird, fish, and animal resources that sustained their people, the white leaders they had to interact with in 1863 saw the largest swath of Grade A agricultural land in the world.

Moose Dung's Strategy of Resistance and Dakota Lessons

In 1863, Moose Dung could still see the earth embankments of the now-empty secret Dakota village every day from his wigwam at what would become Thief River Falls. There were more than four hundred

Ojibwe in the village there, and he had been their chief most of his adult life. He was not just a chief; he was also a warrior. He had not lived a long life by being foolish. War had taught him not just to be brave, but to be wise. He had avoided at least as many battles as he fought. Looking at the remnants of the secret village, he must have been constantly reminded that it was wise to start a fight only when the outcome of the battle was already decided in one's favor.

Moose Dung could see that the Dakota were outmatched by the U.S. government. In 1819, the U.S. Army built Fort Snelling at one of the most sacred Dakota places—Bdote, at the confluence of the Minnesota and Mississippi Rivers. It now served as the staging ground for systematic dispossession of the Dakota through negotiation, coercion, and military action. In 1849, Minnesota became an official territory, and in 1858, a state. The environmental and human landscape of Minnesota was completely transformed in half a lifetime.

The Dakota fought. The U.S.-Dakota War in 1862 transformed the region and the nation. Between four hundred and eight hundred white civilians were killed, and more than two thousand Dakota, in battles, concentration camps, and retributory military campaigns. The remaining Dakota fled for their lives or were held as prisoners of war. Thirty-eight Dakota were hanged in Mankato that year, in the largest mass execution in the nation's history. Alexander Ramsey said, "The Sioux Indians of Minnesota must be exterminated or driven forever beyond the borders of the state." He fulfilled that promise, and then set his eyes on Ojibwe land at Red Lake.[2]

In 1862, when the U.S.-Dakota War broke out, Dakota chief Little Crow sent a beaded belt and pipe to the Red Lake chiefs to invite them to join him in alliance against the Americans. Moose Dung, He Who Is Spoken To, and other Red Lake chiefs refused. Eventually, the Red Lake chiefs turned the items over to U.S. military officials. Years later, Major Edwin Clark deposited them in a pioneer museum at the Godfrey House.

Mississippi Ojibwe chief Hole in the Day (Bagone-giizhig) threatened to join the Dakota and sent runners to Red Lake with a call for aid. The Red Lake chiefs refused Hole in the Day as well, even while Ojibwe chiefs at Leech and Otter Tail Lakes took white prisoners, burned down the Indian agencies and missions, and marched to Crow Wing, the site of Fort Ripley. Hole in the Day's invitations were an elaborate manipulation, timed perfectly with commissioner of Indian affairs William P. Dole's visit to Minnesota and the outbreak of the U.S.-Dakota War to get their attention on the chief's grievances. Hole in the Day very nearly embroiled the Ojibwe in the conflict, but Red Lake's refusal helped prevent further escalation.[3]

Some of the Pembina Ojibwe pillaged steamboats on the Red River in 1862, although nobody was killed. Red Lake chief Little Rock (Asiniiwab) was present during the 1862 depredations, leading some American officials to believe that the Red Lake Ojibwe participated directly. It was a significant source of contention during the early phase of the 1863 treaty talks, although it appears from the treaty records that this was more of a threat and manipulation strategy for the American treaty commissioners than a serious concern.[4]

Red Lake's refusal to participate in the U.S.-Dakota War of 1862 avoided conflict but it did little to ease white avarice, land hunger, or fear. White fear convinced the U.S. government to be diplomatic with Moose Dung so as not to risk war with the Ojibwe, but it also strengthened the government's resolve to get Indians pushed to the margins in Minnesota. That added to the pressure on Red Lake land.[5]

The Minnesota Dakota imploded. Thousands were killed, chased westward, imprisoned, or forcibly evicted. The U.S. Army marched right across the plains, igniting wars with the western Lakota and other plains tribes. This strengthened the Ojibwe military position against the Dakota, but it was so closely followed by American convergence on Red Lake that it proved not to be a relief from tension, but rather a shift to a new nexus of stresses.

Ojibwe-Dakota relations changed after 1862. Conflict between the two tribes came to a close. Both tribes had concerns far greater than tribal skirmishes. Some Minnesota Dakota took refuge in Canada, cementing friendship with resident Dakota relatives and former Ojibwe enemies in a large regional peace conference. There were lingering resentments, but the Ojibwe-Dakota peace was real, and many of the new Dakota arrivals stayed permanently. Some returned to Minnesota years later.[6]

Shortly after the U.S.-Dakota War, the Dakota presented the Ojibwe with a series of ceremonial drums to cement peace between their nations. According to the drum legend, it was now against the will of the Great Spirit for the Ojibwe and the Dakota to kill each

other. Ojibwe men who were given positions on the drums were seasoned veterans who had killed Dakotas. Those who had been in charge
of the war now had to be in charge of the peace—a critical teaching of
the drums. Drum members then passed their positions down hereditarily. Ceremonial drums made and preserved peace between the
Ojibwe and the Dakota. They also reaffirmed the importance of ceremonial leaders, heredity, and warriors in Ojibwe culture.[7]

Ceremonial drum culture also gave birth to the modern powwow.
In 1990, Red Lake spiritual leader Adam Lussier wrote down and
shared the drum legend with his protégés on the powwow circuit,
explaining that the reason men drum while singing at powwows and
women sing without drumming was out of respect for the Dakota
woman, Tail Feather Woman (Wanaanikwe), whose vision in the
1860s inspired the ceremonial drum, which in turn spawned modern Ojibwe powwow singing. In Tail Feather Woman's vision, only
men touched the drum, but women sat behind and danced around
the men, singing with them.[8]

Moose Dung was at the height of his power through the U.S.-Dakota
War and subsequent Ojibwe-Dakota peace. He must have seen the
futility of a protracted struggle with
the Americans and determined to
bargain for the best possible outcome in impossible times. There
was no way to win. Red Lakers could
fight, lose, and sign treaties at the
point of a gun or they could ratio-
nally predict such an outcome and
bargain under duress. Either way,
Moose Dung had to preserve what
he could of the Red Lake homeland
under unbearable pressure.

Alexander Ramsey successfully
engineered the destruction of the
Minnesota Dakota in 1862. In 1863,
he traveled north to present-day

Governor Alexander Ramsey, about 1863

Huot, Minnesota, leading a military detachment and treaty delegation to the Old Crossing of the Red Lake River. Moose Dung was waiting for him. Ramsey and the chief each had a strategy as they squared off for the first time. They both had a lot to learn.

Hundred-Year Floods: Bracing for the Red Lake River Surge

Moose Dung's long life in the Red River Valley taught him many things. The Red Lake River flooded often in the spring, as winter snows melted under April rains and rushed out of Red Lake and many smaller rivers and creeks, swelling the Red Lake River and the Red River of the North. The lowland flood plains were dangerous in the spring because dramatic warm-ups or heavy precipitation sometimes brought on the floods with little warning. Moose Dung knew what to do. He brought his people to the sugar bush for the harvest every spring and stayed until the water had its way.

The land was incredibly adaptable, like a massive multimillion-acre sponge, pooling and absorbing the water, then sending it downstream. The moisture fluctuations added nutrients to the soil, recharged the wetlands, and maintained the Red River Valley paradise the chief loved so much. Every hundred years or so, the spring floods were truly torrential, awe-inspiring, destructive and rejuvenating at the same time—causing massive erosion and cutting new channels in the Red Lake River. Those floods were the kind that altered tribal lifestyles—relocating villages and reordering life.

The arrival of whites in the Red River Valley was like the coming of predictable spring floods. White folk were traders or travelers, explorers or diplomats. Moose Dung watched them come, and sometimes they asked him for things like trade goods or supplies or Indian guides from his village. He obliged them when it was convenient and refused them when it wasn't. Like the river in May, they eventually receded and village life returned to normal. But Moose Dung could see the progression of white settlement in the wake of U.S.-Ojibwe treaties across central Minnesota. By 1863, he knew that something bigger was brewing. It was like watching the snow pile up in an unusually hard winter. Inevitably, it would melt, and when it did it had the potential to generate one of those hundred-year floods that forced villages to move and reordered life as people knew it.

Moose Dung must have watched with trepidation as the U.S. government began to come after Ojibwe land in central Minnesota. He had responsibilities to his village and little power or desire to deal with things beyond that. The exceptional level of freedom and libertarian idealism at Red Lake was a great blessing in many ways, but when new enemies invaded the Red River Valley and war clubs were insufficient to deal with the threat, the cultural barrier to unification of tribal leadership diffused power and made it harder to muster a vigorous response. The best that Moose Dung could do was to intently watch what transpired elsewhere in Ojibwe country so as to be better prepared when the government came after him.

While the U.S. government was busy killing and driving off the Dakota, it was also concocting plans to relocate the Ojibwe and come after Moose Dung's home in the Red River Valley. Eager to put distance between Indians and the whites in Minnesota who were ravenous for tribal land but unwilling to go to war against the Ojibwe to achieve that, the government used a series of piecemeal land cessions and removal propositions to accomplish its goals. In a letter to President Abraham Lincoln, Mississippi Ojibwe chief Hole in the Day complained that the U.S. government was trying to relocate the Ojibwe "as far as possible from the white people."[9]

In 1863, there was a convergence of interests at Red Lake that put special pressure on Moose Dung and other tribal leaders. In addition to the white fear of Indians that had exploded in 1862, growing railroad and logging industries were fueling American economic growth. Ojibwe territory in northwestern Minnesota contained not only a massive piece of Grade A agricultural land, but also some of the finest stands of white pine in the region, and speculators believed that the iron-ore deposits in the Arrowhead region of northeastern Minnesota might extend across the state. The economic interests of railroad, mining, and timber tycoons, along with those of the white settlers, brought unprecedented pressure to bear on the Ojibwe to cede their homelands in northwestern Minnesota.

Economic incentives were paramount in the call for Red Lake land cessions, but missionaries helped drive the effort as well. Protestant,

Catholic, and Episcopal missionaries wanted to see the people of
Red Lake concentrated in larger villages on smaller tracts of land to
make their missionary work easier. Henry B. Whipple, John Johnson, George Copway, George C. Tanner, Thomas L. Grace, Joseph
A. Gilfillan, and other missionaries had sought for years to pressure
the U.S. government to seek land cessions from the Ojibwe, concentrate them on smaller tracts of land and villages, and force them to
become Christian yeoman farmers. It was part of their agenda for
cultural change and conversion of the Ojibwe.[10]

In 1825, the Lake Superior and Mississippi Ojibwe signed their
first U.S. government treaty at Prairie du Chien, Wisconsin. Moose
Dung stayed away. It was ostensibly a peace and friendship treaty to
draw lines between Ojibwe and Dakota lands all the way from the
Wisconsin woodlands to the Red River Valley and into the Great
Plains. For the Americans, it set the stage for subsequent land cessions. For Moose Dung, it meant nothing. Red Lakers were busy
changing those territory lines with their war clubs. Little Buck
(Ayaabens) and Descender (Niisideshish) both signed the treaty in
1825 and later moved to Red Lake, but no established chiefs at Red
Lake had anything to do with the agreement at Prairie du Chien.[11]

In 1837, the Lake Superior and Mississippi Ojibwe signed their
first major land cession treaty in Minnesota, which ceded lands on
the Mississippi River, south of Mille Lacs Lake, and along the St.
Croix River to the U.S. government. At Red Lake, daily life continued
as before, but white settlers began to pour into the ceded lands to the
south, and pressure for further land sales mounted. Traders William
A. Aitkin and Lyman M. Warren were each paid more than $25,000
out of the money owed to the Ojibwe for the sale of their land. Both
represented the American Fur Company, which conducted lots of
trade with the Mississippi and Lake Superior Ojibwe, although their
claims were probably inflated. Besides representing the American
Fur Company, Lyman Warren also served as interpreter for the Lac
du Flambeau and Lac Courte Oreilles delegations at the treaty negotiations. More than fifty other traders also laid claim to Ojibwe annuities. To Moose Dung, watching from a distance, it must have been
obvious that none of the white men engaged in the treaty process
were on the side of the Indians.[12]

One large section of land at a time, the Ojibwe bands in Minnesota ceded most their homelands, retaining eleven different reservations, and being swallowed by the surge of white settlement that followed. Eventually, many of the new reservations were ceded as well, including those at Pokegama Lake, Rabbit Lake, and Gull Lake. The government worked on relocation plans for the Minnesota Ojibwe—to Isle Royale, Leech Lake, and White Earth. In 1850, the government tried to concentrate the Wisconsin and Michigan Ojibwe at Sandy Lake, Minnesota. The government mismanaged communication and food rations, and hundreds of Ojibwe died from food poisoning, dysentery, or exposure as they fled the disaster. Red Lake was remote enough to avoid these catastrophes and the people there held on, but there was no doubt that the swell was rolling their way.[13]

From the Red River Valley to Ponemah Point, Moose Dung and other Red Lake leaders were worried. They had not ceded any land or compromised their position in any way, but life was changing. The buffalo population was declining, not from tribal harvest (which had been sustainable for thousands of years), but from the spread of white settlement outside of Red Lake's sovereign domain. White settlers killed buffalo for sport and for food, but also to remove them from the landscape to enable agricultural development. Buffalo hides were sold on the market for factory machine belts. Eventually, professional hunters completed the extermination of the buffalo in the Red River Valley, funded by bounties on buffalo established by the military and the federal government to cripple the food supply of the Plains Indians and starve them into submission. Red Lakers had not laid a hand on a white man, but still they had less food to eat.[14]

When Red Lakers traveled the road to Leech Lake or by canoe to Nett Lake and Lake Vermilion, which they did often (especially to harvest wild rice), they encountered white people on lands ceded by other bands, reducing their access to harvest food and hunt game. The fur trade was less profitable because of volatile and declining European demand for furs and decreased access to trapping territory south of Red Lake. For the first time in their history, the people of Red Lake had restricted food resources and faced a declining standard of living.

Moose Dung and other Red Lake region chiefs still held undisputed control of more than 20 million acres of land. There was a leadership crisis in some Ojibwe communities as cooperative and uncooperative chiefs played off one another and vied for position and influence with the Americans. That pattern did not emerge at Red Lake, and it never would. But that didn't prevent Alexander Ramsey from making his way to the Old Crossing. The government had tried several times to treat with the Red Lake chiefs for a land cession, but nobody was willing to entertain such a discussion. In 1862, Ramsey had already set in motion plans to get the land from Moose Dung. He met with Commissioner of Indian Affairs Dole and John G. Nicolay, President Lincoln's influential private secretary. Dole and Nicolay assembled a caravan with two hundred cattle and thirty wagons to treat with the Red Lakers, but the U.S.-Dakota War broke out as they reached Fort Abercrombie and army officers at the post commandeered all of the supplies, inadvertently delaying the Old Crossing negotiations for nearly two years. By 1863, Ramsey was once again ready for Red Lake, with a freshly stoked hatred of Indians.[15]

Moose Dung had seen many kinds of hardship. He had seen good weather and bad. He had watched from a distance all of the humiliations, manipulations, and outright lies visited upon the other Ojibwe bands in Minnesota. He had already accomplished much for his people and prepared in every way he could. But even though the snow was piled high and a hundred-year flood seemed imminent, there was no way he could predict or control the path of this river when it raged.

The High Banks at Old Crossing

The villages along Red Lake's south shore were empty in September 1863. It was the Wild Ricing Moon, and most of the women and children were gathering the fall harvest in the smaller lakes and rivers. Moose Dung stood on the shore of the Red Lake River with more than five hundred Red Lake chiefs and warriors. Some brought their families. Ashley C. Morrill was with them. Morrill was a smart, intense, and seasoned Indian agent, handpicked by Ramsey to serve as one of the treaty commissioners. Morrill explained to the chiefs prior to their arrival at Old Crossing that Ramsey wanted them to cede all of their lands in the Red River Valley. Moose Dung knew that the treaty might forever alter the Red Lake way of life, but the concept of land ownership and sale was new and not well understood.

The chiefs had a lot questions, and Morrill insisted that they wait for Ramsey to get any answers.

Although Morrill was quick to tell the chiefs about the money, supplies, and annuities the government planned to distribute, that was not why the Red Lakers were there. They all felt a strong obligation to look out for their future generations. There was a lot at stake in Red Lake's first treaty with the U.S. government, and Morrill and Ramsey were not to be trusted.[16]

Moose Dung chose the Old Crossing on the Red Lake River, now Huot, Minnesota, for the treaty negotiations. It was an auspicious place. The barren, windswept hilltops disguise a natural bowl along the riverbank full of black ash, oak, elm, and cottonwood. It provides good shelter from the elements in September and early October, as the changing leaves are still falling from the trees. Old Crossing is a natural river ford as well, and in 1863 it was heavily traveled by Indians and fur traders.

The treaty council was supposed to take place in the summer and be concluded before the autumn ricing time. Morrill traveled first to Red Lake and then to Moose Dung's village on the Thief River, arriving with most of the Red Lake delegates. The Pembina chiefs were notified of the treaty council but not accompanied by government officials. Ramsey was delayed in St. Paul waiting for the shipment of supplies and treaty goods, which didn't even arrive until August. The Civil War plagued Ramsey's logistics at every turn. The U.S. Army was still embroiled in a brutal, vengeful roundup of Dakota people all over southern Minnesota. That was just the beginning of tensions and problems.

Ramsey wanted to treat with the Pembina Ojibwe and the Red Lake Ojibwe at the same time. This was complicated by the fact that the Red River Métis were already breaking away from any allegiance to the mainstream U.S. or Canadian governments and from tribal communities. In 1869-70, this break would become the basis for a major independence movement and war in Canada under the leadership of Louis Riel. In 1863, it meant that the Pembina Ojibwe (who were inextricably tied to the Métis movement) and the Red Lake Ojibwe did not want to sign the same documents, negotiate in each other's presence, or share any resources. Ramsey had not even arrived and already the warriors were restless. When treaty talks commenced, the

Red Lake Ojibwe brought 579 Indians and 24 so-called half-breeds to the council and the Pembina Ojibwe brought 352 Indians and 663 half-breeds. The distinctions between Indians and half-breeds are not often made today, except on tribal enrollment forms, but in 1863, those distinctions made a tremendous difference for annuities, allotments, politics, and the power to negotiate treaties.

Ramsey had a short-term and a long-term plan for the Red Lake Ojibwe. He wrote about the negotiations that "It was, in their view, a matter of much less consequence what they surrendered, than what they obtained in exchange for the surrender." In other words, Ramsey felt confident that he could get the Indians to sign if the annuities and the spoils from the signing itself were sufficient to excite the tribal leadership.[17]

Ramsey correctly concluded that the soil across the entire proposed land cession was "of extraordinary fertility and finely adapted to the production of small grains." Of the unceded lands around Red Lake, he said, "The tract reserved for their future occupancy, while abounding in game, fish, fields of rice, and other resources adapted to the primitive wants of the Indian, is, from the nature of the surface, which may be generally described as a series of impassable swales, entirely valueless to a civilized people."[18]

Ramsey was definitely thinking ahead: "This plan contemplates the extension of settlement, of mail, telegraph, and eventually steamboat and railroad communications throughout the whole belt of fertile valleys which span the west half of the continent, from the Red river." Unbeknownst to the Red Lake chiefs, Ramsey also advocated for relocation of the Indian agency from Red Lake to Leech Lake so that the Red Lake Indians could be "taught to look upon it as their future home." In other words, even before the treaty was negotiated, Ramsey did not intend that its protections of Red Lake land in perpetuity would stand. He wanted to concentrate and relocate the entire tribal population of Red Lake at Leech Lake. He knew that to make relocation possible without bloodshed, they had to be whittled away one land cession at a time.[19]

Ramsey finally made it to Old Crossing in late September. Morrill was sitting between the Red Lake and Pembina delegations pulling at his beard. Mississippi Ojibwe chief Hole in the Day the Younger arrived uninvited, further testing the patience of Moose Dung and

Red Lake chief Little Rock. Personalities were as frosty as the weather when the first council began.

The Interloper: Hole in the Day at Old Crossing

Mississippi Ojibwe chief Hole in the Day disrupted and very nearly broke up the treaty proceedings at the first assembly. On June 7, 1863, Hole in the Day wrote a letter to President Abraham Lincoln, requesting permission to represent the U.S. government at Old Crossing in their effort to obtain a land cession from the Red Lake and Pembina Ojibwe. His request was denied, but he went to the treaty council anyway, this time ostensibly to represent native interests. Moose Dung and Little Rock stopped him and he was denied admission again. But as the first council assembled, Hole in the Day again tried to insert himself in the parlay for his own purposes.[20]

Ramsey was thrilled to have Hole in the Day there. He wrote, "No circumstance of my interview with the Indians had a happier effect in assuaging their discontent than the address made by Hole-in-the-Day, of Gull Lake, to their chiefs, and which was marked by a breadth and elevation of views which are rare among his race. He advised them to submit cheerfully to the provisions of the treaty, since their Great Father willed it." Surely, no other statement could have made Ramsey happier, but the Red Lake chiefs had an entirely different view of Hole in the Day's presence. The treaty council secretary wrote: "The presence of Hole-in-the-Day and several other chiefs from Leech Lake, who were not parties to the proposed treaty, gave great umbrage to the Red Lake chiefs. They were especially distrustful and jealous of Hole-in-the-Day, whom they suspected of coming there with a view to influence the proceedings in some way for his own benefit. They carried this feeling to such an extent that they refused to speak to or recognize him in any way, and set spies on his track."[21]

When the first council began on September 23, 1863, Red Lake chief Little Rock brought the issue to a head. He addressed Ramsey directly: "My friend, I am very sorry to say that there is something squeezing me very hard, and filling me with great grief since I have been here. My friend, I am very sorry to say that what fills me with grief is something which you have along with you. We never would have expected it. I thought we had a friendly feeling between us, and that we could lay our views openly before you; but it is now impossible to speak freely before you. My friend, if you will help me to remove out of the way the thing that is filling us with grief, I shall be grateful." Little Rock then gestured to Hole in the Day, singling him out as the source of contention.

Hole in the Day made a spirited defense of his reasons for attending the council, but in the end it was to no avail. The Red Lake and Pembina chiefs negotiated their own treaty. Hole in the Day was accustomed to being at the center of treaty negotiations, but he traveled to Old Crossing with little support, and the Red Lake chiefs were numerous, assembled with their war clubs, chief bonnets, and otter-skin turbans, displaying feathers earned in battle. He had to back down or risk a physical confrontation. Hole in the Day's motives were obvious—he sought financial payment for his band and himself, to impress American officials for future leverage, and to continue to expand his authority in white and Indian circles as he had done successfully for his entire chieftainship, rising from village chief to regional political power. But he met his match with Moose Dung and Little Rock and retreated from the council.

Feathers and Quills

The first councils showcased a clash of cultures. The treaty commission secretary wrote of the Red Lake delegation: "The Red Lakers are among the purest representatives extant on the continent of the Indian race in its original characteristics—a fact which they owe to their geographical isolation from the influences which have corrupted the blood and modified the manners of other Indian communities; and another reason is, that the occasion was one of extraordinary importance to the Indians concerned, constituting a supreme crisis in their history, and especially fitted, from the nature of the topics involved, to call out all their mental resources, and all their political and ethical ideas."[22]

Ramsey came with a mind to get signatures for the land sale, not to negotiate on terms. He frequently threatened to hold the people of Red Lake responsible for the steamboat attacks on the Red River on August 25, 1862, and during the first few councils, Little Rock adamantly insisted that nobody from Red Lake had killed a white man

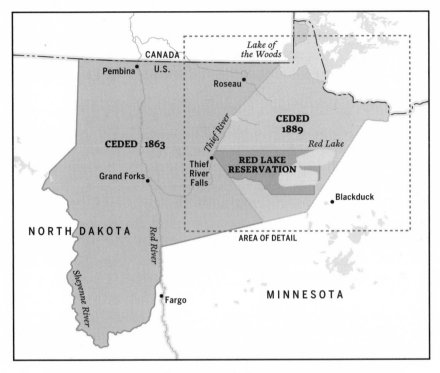

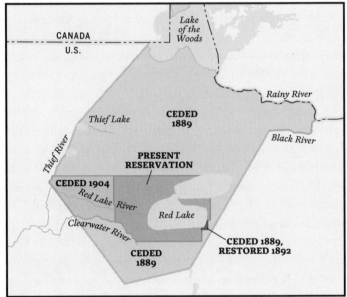

Red Lake land cessions, as interpreted and surveyed by the U.S. government

or caused any trouble in 1862. At one point, Little Rock exclaimed, "I am afraid your war-club is raised behind me, ready to fall upon me." Ultimately, Ramsey agreed not to hold Red Lake accountable, and this paved the way for acceptance of the treaty even more than the haggling over terms of the land sale.[23]

Ramsey's initial offer was to purchase the entire 11 million acres—most of the Red River Valley and a large chunk of the North Dakota Plains—for $20,000 per year for twenty years. He also offered terms to each of the chiefs for their personal interest: an annual stipend of $150, paid out of land-sale annuities, plus a onetime payment of $500 to each for the construction of a modern house. The government also agreed to improve the road the Indians had already cut from Red Lake to Leech Lake. In addition, Ramsey offered to provide home-steads of 160 acres each for half-breeds and mixed bloods.

Moose Dung insisted on staying at Thief River, and Ramsey agreed to provide 640 acres for a reservation for the forty-two families there and another 640-acre reservation for Pembina chief Red Bear at Pembina. The total payment from the U.S. government was to be $510,000. As early as 1861, traders had claimed that $150,000 was owed them by the Red Lake Indians for trade goods and wanted the treaty to resolve their debt. Their claims were both real and fabri-cated, and no external agency ever audited the traders' books; Tru-man A. Warren, who served as an interpreter, was also the traders' representative at Old Crossing. Most of their claims were validated and paid out of the annuities.[24]

Moose Dung and other Red Lake leaders probably did not fully comprehend the extent and impact of the 11 million–acre land sale. Key phrases such as "privilege of," "pleasure of the President," "relinquish and convey," and "right, title and interest" did not trans-late well in Ojibwe. Moose Dung and the other chiefs operated with the understanding that their relationship with the land was gov-erned by use for residence and hunting. Title meant little to them. The commissioners were not specifically asking to restrict Ojibwe use (that came later). They seemed willing to make accommodations for the village residents at Thief River to stay where they were, and over 3 million acres of land around Upper and Lower Red Lakes was not even being considered for this land cession, which focused exclusively on the 11 million–acre Red River Valley. The Red Lakers thought their homeland and ability to harvest was protected and focused more on getting paid. The full impact of the land cession on Red Lake's use of the Red River Valley was not understood by the Indians until after the valley flooded with white settlers and Ojibwe access was cut off.[25]

None of the subsequent council time was used to reduce the size of the land sale. Such a request was never made. Instead, the focus was on maximizing compensation. Little Rock did most of the speaking for Red Lake in the first several councils:

> We should be very sorry for you to set a value upon the land for us and make us an offer as you did yesterday, before you heard our offer. . . . The Master of Life gave us the river and the water thereof to drink, and the woods and the roads we depend on for subsistence, and you are mistaken if you think we derive no benefits from them. The Master of Life gave it to us for an inheritance, and gave us the animals for food and clothing. . . . My dependence is on that prairie. The Master of Life has placed upon these prairies animals from which I live. Their meat is my food, and their skins are my clothing. It seems now that the white man is passing backward and forward, and wresting these prairies from our hands, and taking this food from my mouth. . . . We want you distinctly to understand that the proposition you made us yesterday (twenty thousand dollars for the right of way) we do not accept; we do not think of it at all.

Little Rock also insisted several times on the retention of use rights to the land sold: "If they sold the land they could still occupy and hunt over it as heretofore . . . the privilege, for many years at least, of hunting over these lands as before. They would thus lose nothing they now have, while they would gain much they have not." Again, later in the proceedings, he repeated: "Though they cede the land to the government, they will continue for many years to have the privilege of hunting over it as heretofore . . . then permit them to use it as heretofore, to hunt for game in the woods and prairies, and to fish in the streams."[26]

The Red Lake chiefs insisted that they be compensated for the land all the way to Devils Lake. Little Rock said: "This land used to belong to the Sioux, and so did the [Red] lake. While the Sioux were in quiet possession of that country my ancestors had not laid down the tomahawk. We drove them, as it were, towards the Rocky mountains; and

when we had driven them off, then we claimed the land as our own.
. . . Whenever our people go to hunt for the Sioux they do not find
them on the Sheyenne, but have to go clear beyond. The bones of the
Chippewas are scattered all along the Sheyenne river, and that is the
reason we consider it belongs to us."[27]

The chiefs also discovered ways to manipulate the commission for
provisions. Little Rock would sit and tap his pipe, saying, "There is
a mistake, but the place where it is is in the bottom of my pipe." The
council would then have to break for tobacco to be provided. Some
of this was ritual, but it was also a tug-of-war over power dynamics.[28]

One night the camp was alarmed at the news that Dakota war parties were in the area. Little Rock, He Who Is Spoken To, and Sun
Shining Through rallied the Red Lake warriors and sent out scouts,
but there was no attack. The council resumed the next day.

The commission had been in council for eight days straight, with
Little Rock doing most of the speaking for Red Lake, when the most
influential chiefs rose to speak. This was the Red Lake way. The voices
that had the greatest weight came last. The oldest and most powerful was Moose Dung. Second was He Who Is Spoken To, of Redby,
who was younger but represented the largest group of Indians on the
south shore of Red Lake. They used Little Rock as a spokesman and
proxy, and Little Rock worked all the small things out of the way—
like Hole in the Day and tobacco provisions. What was said in the
formal councils was only a fraction of the political discourse that was
going on in the Red Lake camp. The substance of the conversations
behind the scenes is not known, but there was an obvious rift in the
tribal leadership.

He Who Is Spoken To had lost his father earlier in 1863, and had
just assumed the mantle of leadership. He had promised his father
as he lay dying to never surrender Red Lake to the whites. He Who
Is Spoken To was fifty-six years old, new to his position, but wise to
the manipulations of treaty commissioners. At six feet four inches in
height he towered over the treaty commissioners. He had both gravi-
tas and influence when he spoke on September 30, 1863: "My heart
is bleeding when I hear you talk. I am sorry, for the reason that the
Great Father [President Lincoln] thinks so lightly of our land . . . I do
not want this at all . . . I tell you frankly that I do not accept it, and
shall go home instantly." The chief rose from his seat, shook hands

with Ramsey, and without saying a word, walked out of the treaty proceedings, never to return.[29]

Sun Shining Through, the highly respected warrior who helped lead the Ojibwe attack on the secret village at Thief River in the late 1820s, also left. He was not active in the negotiations, but he was roughly the same age as He Who Is Spoken To, and also carried a lot of respect. Moose Dung and Sun Shining Through had fought together against the Dakota. Moose Dung must have been affected by the lack of faith Sun Shining Through and He Who Is Spoken To had in Ramsey and the proposed agreement.[30]

Moose Dung now faced a tough choice. The other Red Lake chiefs stayed at the Old Crossing. They saw Ramsey's wagons loaded with goods, but more than anything, they saw Moose Dung not capitulating and not leaving. It must have occurred to the chief that leaving would have set Ramsey back because all the other chiefs were likely to follow his lead. But there was a chance that they would break ranks with him. There was also a very real possibility that Ramsey would get his way without Moose Dung's consent or come back with more troops and force the issue. The chief had to think about the future.

Moose Dung insisted that alcohol not be allowed on any Red Lake lands. Article 7 was added to the treaty, "prohibiting the introduction and sale of spirituous liquors in the Indian country." Moose Dung was pleased with that much, saying, "Father, you have hit my heart in the right spot, in speaking of the liquor as you did. That is what I don't want in my land, because it is a source of trouble and poverty."[31]

Moose Dung had been developing a strategy for this moment. The late 1820s, the destruction of the secret Dakota village at Thief River, where Moose Dung now kept his wigwam, showed the importance of winning battles. The chief knew to buy time when outmatched and assert himself when it produced results. If he walked away, he might lose influence both with his people and with Ramsey. If he signed, they would lose the land.

Ramsey and Morrill were steeped in a culture of individualism and materialism. They wanted the land and its resources. Moose Dung came from a culture that valued collective benefit and generosity. He wanted to protect the Red Lake way of life. Ramsey valued resources whereas Moose Dung valued relationships. As a matter of core operating values, a strategy for survival, and very likely not fully comprehending how the land cession would impact Red Lake access to and use of the territory, Moose Dung must have thought he was both protecting his people and getting them a significant payment from the government. He moved to accommodate—feathers on his head and quill in his hand.

Signing with Moose Dung and his son Red Robed were seven other Red Lake chiefs: Little Rock, Crooked Arm (Gaawashkweniked), Big Indian (Gichi-anishinaabe), Four Skies (Niiyo-giizhig), Dropping Wind (Mezhakeyaash), Leading Feather (Niigaanigwaneb), and Berry Hunter (Miindawewing). The Pembina chiefs did less speaking at the council than the Red Lake delegation. Six of them signed the treaty: Red Bear (Misko-makwa), Little Shell (Esens), Summer Wolverine (Niibini-gwiingwa'aage), Night Sky (Dibiki-giizhig), Joseph Gornon, and Joseph Montreuil. Paul H. Beaulieu, Peter Roy, and Truman A. Warren did all of the interpreting.

The Old Crossing Treaty was signed on October 3, 1863. Annuities were dispersed the following day. He Who Is Spoken To returned to receive his share of the annuities and then departed. He did not go back to Redby. Instead, he traveled south to White Earth, searching for Henry B. Whipple, Episcopal missionary and his close friend. Whipple was a complicated public figure. By 1886, he was representing the government in a coercive effort to gain major land cessions from Red Lake. He strongly advocated for allotment, relocation, land cession, and conversion. But he also felt that such changes needed tribal consent and that great nations needed to be honest when getting land from Indians. In 1863, the government was not entirely honest with the Red Lake leadership. He Who Is Spoken To succeeded in getting Whipple fired up about the government's mistreatment of the Red Lake leadership. Whipple wrote:

> We treat as an independent nation a people whom we will not permit to exercise one single element of that sovereign power which is necessary to a nation's existence. The treaty is usually conceived and executed in fraud. The ostensible parties to the treaty are the government of the United States and the Indians; the *real* parties are the Indian agents, traders, and politicians. The avowed purpose of the treaty is for a Christian nation to acquire certain lands at a fair price, and make provision that the purchase-money shall be wisely expended, so as to secure the civilization of the Indians. The real design is to pay certain worthless

Bishop Henry B. Whipple, about 1860

debts of the Indian traders, to satisfy such claims, good or bad, against the Indians, as have been or may be made, and to create places where political favorites may receive their reward for political service. . . . Those chiefs who cannot be bribed or deceived by false interpretations have in some instances been deposed, and more pliable tools appointed in their place.[32]

The Red Lake delegates were pleased to receive their annuities in 1863, but none of them felt good about the treaty itself. As the gravity of the land loss became clear and white men such as Henry B. Whipple explained to them what it meant, the chiefs were deeply worried. On March 15, 1864, Whipple wrote that the Old Crossing Treaty was "from beginning to end a fraud and must sooner or later bring another Indian war." More than 120 years later, the *Red River Daily* agreed: "When this treaty was negotiated, the Chippewa Indian leaders were conned into turning over 11 million acres of prime real estate in Northwestern Minnesota and Northeastern North Dakota for about half a million dollars. As far as real-estate deals go, the ceding of the Red River Valley ranks up there with the Manhattan deal, the Louisiana Purchase, and the Alaska deal. It has been characterized as one of the most dishonest and fraudulent deals ever made."[33]

The Red Lake Beaulieus

Paul H. Beaulieu, one of the Old Crossing translators, was a descendant of French Catholic loyalists during the Huguenot rebellions in France (1621-29), which earned the family royal standing by decree of the king. François Hudon de Beaulieu was the first in his line to come to North America, establishing residence in Canada. Five generations later, Bazile Hudon de Beaulieu (1785-1838) became a trader with the North West Company at La Pointe, Wisconsin. He was the first in the Beaulieu line to become an American and the first to marry an Ojibwe woman—Margaret Racine (Ogimaa-giizhigookwe, or Queen of the Sky), the daughter of prominent Lac du Flambeau Ojibwe chief White Raven (Waabi-gaagaagi). Each generation of the Beaulieu family married into Ojibwe families after that, and the large Beaulieu, Fairbanks, and Van Wert families at White Earth and Red Lake all descend from them.

Paul H. Beaulieu (1820-97) was a mixed blood, but he did not operate strictly in Indian interests. He was fluent in French, English, and Ojibwe, but sometimes struggled with translating the Red Lake dialect and the subtle metaphors employed by some of the Red Lake chiefs, and this exacerbated communication difficulties at the treaty councils. Paul H. Beaulieu's siblings, cousins, and children were some of the most powerful figures in the government service at White Earth and Red Lake.[34]

Beaulieu allegiances shifted over time as more of the subsequent generations married into big native families. Paul H. Beaulieu's son, Clement Abraham Hudon de Beaulieu (1844-1930), married Mary Gurneau and Margaret Jourdain at the same time and kept a house for each wife directly across the road from each other at Red Lake. This marked a departure from Catholic doctrine with regard to marriage for the Beaulieus, and a tighter embrace of ancient Ojibwe tradition. Clement A. H. Beaulieu had seven children with Mary and another eight children with Margaret, including one named Paul. Paul H. Beaulieu's grandson, Paul H. Beaulieu (1889–1955), went on to advise the 1909 Red Lake chiefs delegation, coauthor the tribe's first constitution in 1918, and mentor his son-in-law, Roger Jourdain, the tribe's first elected chairman. He was a tribal patriot, not a government agent.

From Old Crossing to Washington

The ink dried slowly in the cool autumn air at Old Crossing. He Who Is Spoken To walked to White Earth, looking for allies to help him adjust treaty terms, and had some success. Henry B. Whipple had a lot of influence in Minnesota and Washington, and agreed to travel with the Red Lake chiefs to the nation's capital in an attempt to redress matters. Moose Dung was still considered the primary Red Lake political patriarch. He helped convince other Red Lake chiefs to join the delegation. Red Bear was the ranking representative from Pembina.

Moose Dung, He Who Is Spoken To, Red Bear, and the other delegates spent two weeks meeting and greeting dozens of white politicians and Office of Indian Affairs employees. Whipple helped them get audiences, translated, and advocated for them. The effort was exceptionally difficult. Some politicians resisted treaty ratification because they wanted more concessions from the chiefs, not a redress of their grievances. They agreed to clarify language in the treaty so that all lands west to Devils Lake were included in the cession. Moose Dung and He Who Is Spoken To managed to get some of the stipulated trader claims and chief bonuses removed or reduced. They also successfully added language to appropriate funds from the ceded land sales for a sawmill. The buffalo were declining and the Red Lake chiefs wanted to grow a new economy to provide for the people. Timber harvest was part of their plan. A small payment was added for damages.

Senators were used to buying leverage in pork-barrel politics with one another and they insisted on the same strategy with the chiefs, even when Red Lake delegates objected. They designated "head chiefs," even though there was no such position, and they wrote in provisions for the head chiefs to receive five thousand dollars as personal stipends and made special land grants to mixed bloods.

Whipple was distraught over the shenanigans, and wrote that advocating for better terms for Red Lake was "one of the severest personal conflicts." He later wrote to Joel Bassett of his disdain for "this
abominable Indian system." On April 12, 1864, the treaty changes
were finalized and pushed through the Senate.[35]

Hither Comes the Flood

The flood of white settlement began right away in the spring of 1864.
Title transferred from the Red Lake Indians to the U.S. government
for the entire land cession. Moose Dung's tiny 640-acre parcel was
soon an island. First came timber speculators and harvesters. Then
the government began granting private parcels to white settlers.
First hundreds, then thousands came to the region. The white arrivals were busy clear-cutting the forested areas to the east and clearing
and plowing the Red River Valley's tallgrass prairie into farms. They
killed off much of the big game and the predators. They tried to bend
the land to their purposes; it was inconceivable to them that the land
might have a legitimate purpose of its own. Settlers and lumbermen
came after Moose Dung too, asking him to sell his private 640-acre
parcel, sell the timber on the parcel, or lease it. He refused. His people were still living there, still in their ancestral village. The people
had not changed, but the human landscape around them was transforming rapidly.[36]

In 1867, other Ojibwe groups in Minnesota signed another treaty
with the U.S. government, which established the White Earth reservation. The White Earth treaty reduced the size of the Leech Lake
reservation and pressured the Ojibwe residents at Pokegama, Rabbit
Lake, Mille Lacs, and Sandy Lake to move to White Earth. White
Earth was designated as a relocation destination for Ojibwe from all
over the region. Although Red Lake avoided immediate pressure to
move, the creation of White Earth opened even more land across
Minnesota to white settlement and catalyzed the explosion of white
settlement in the Red River Valley.

Some of the Ojibwe families retreated from the white timber and
agricultural feeding frenzy. Most of the ones who left went to the big
water at Red Lake. That was all unceded Red Lake land. Fishing was
good. Their cousins were welcoming. In 1890, the large Lussier fam-

ily moved from the land the tribe ceded in North Dakota to Red Lake. Some moved north to Canada or west to Turtle Mountain. The people from smaller Ojibwe villages in northwestern Minnesota had no choice but to move. White folk owned the native homes, wigwams, land parcels, villages, and hunting lands. They could not stay in their own wigwams without real fear of violence. The U.S. Army played no role in this dispossession, but the effect was the same. The tallgrass prairie of the Red River Valley was no longer an Indian place; it wasn't even a prairie anymore. It was America's breadbasket.[37]

Moose Dung held on at his Thief River village with his family. It was a heartbreaking time. He died in 1872. The people now had to look to his son, Red Robed, and to the chiefs on Red Lake's south shore, such as He Who Is Spoken To, for guidance and protection. It was hard to feel optimistic while the floodwaters raged so ferociously, but there was still a lot of fight in the Red Lake warriors. Hard times tested human mettle, and what was breaking could be reforged into something stronger than ever. For that, the warriors needed every tool—the war club, the pipe, the feather, and the quill.

He Who Is Spoken To, 1891

3

He Who Is Spoken To and the Nelson Act

"[He Who Is Spoken To was] six feet and four inches in height, straight as an arrow, with flashing eyes, frank, open countenance, and as dignified in bearing as one of a kingly race."

HENRY WHIPPLE

The Promise

He Who Is Spoken To (Medwe-ganoonind) gave the signal and Little Frenchman (Wemitigoozhiins) beckoned to Henry M. Rice to stand before the chiefs. It was July 6, 1889, and the tiny government school building at Red Lake was packed. Red Lake's chiefs and warriors were standing shoulder to shoulder, a sea of otter-skin turbans and feathers (each earned in battle). Hundreds more Ojibwe were standing outside, peering in through the windows and the open door. The wind whipped across the field in front of the building, ruffling the braids and feathers of those who could not get inside.[1]

Rice rose to his feet and raised his hands four times as a sign of his solemn promise to the spirits in the wind, the rising sun, and all creation that the Red Lake Ojibwe would keep in perpetuity all of Upper Red Lake and Lower Red Lake—as long as grasses grow and rivers flow. In Ojibwe culture, four is a sacred number, symbolizing the four directions, four layers of earth, and four layers of sky. Frank English and Bad Day (Maji-giizhig) were among the hundreds who watched Rice make the promise, and their depositions about the

69

event are one of the primary sources of information about it. Neither English nor Bad Day provides an analysis of the symbolism of Rice's quadruple pledge, but this was a common Red Lake protocol. The first of Rice's four hands-raised promises was a promise to the east. The second was to the south as he repeated the pledge, again raising his hands, palms outstretched, assuring the spirits and the people in attendance that he and the government would never violate their oath. His third pledge was to the west as he again held up his hands, offered his words, and promised the lakes to the Ojibwe for all time. His last vow was to the north, as he raised his hands a fourth time, guaranteeing the Red Lake Ojibwe's sovereign domain over their sacred lakes. He Who Is Spoken To then nodded again to Little Frenchman, who called forth Bishop Martin Marty. Marty followed the same protocol and repeated Rice's promise.[2]

Henry Rice was one of the most influential white men in Minnesota in 1889. He had negotiated many treaties and contracts with Indian nations. On behalf of the U.S. government he had promised them many things. But his promise to the Red Lake Ojibwe was unprecedented.

The chiefs lined up behind He Who Is Spoken To. Most were advanced in years, weathered from decades of life on the shores of Red Lake. They were providers—fishermen, hunters, trappers, rice harvesters. They were statesmen too, although they did not usually see themselves that way. They had helped build the villages that were home to their people. Most had represented those communities at the Old Crossing land-cession treaty in 1863. They helped shape the evolving identity of their people as it shifted from a village focus to a more collective one. And they embodied the libertarian ideals and tenacious identification with the lakes that defined Red Lakers as different from their cousins in other Ojibwe communities. They were tough people, but uncompromisingly loyal and honest.

They would sign nothing unless it protected the exclusive tribal ownership of both Upper and Lower Red Lake and all the land for at least a mile from the lakeshore. Rice assured them of the president's good intentions. For an agreement between tribal leaders, that might have been enough, but He Who Is Spoken To and the other chiefs at Red Lake had been learning the hard way about America's broken promises after the 1863 Old Crossing Treaty. They insisted that Rice prove it—in the Indian custom and the way of the white man. They wanted an authentic statement and solemn vow to the spirits of the land that they would retain all of Upper and Lower Red Lake, and they also wanted it in writing.

If Rice had any trepidation, he did not let it show. He stood steadfast for all to see and made the promise that the Red Lake Ojibwe would keep all of Upper Red Lake and all of Lower Red Lake. He did so in the Indian custom, and that promise has never been forgotten at Red Lake. That promise was alluded to in the 1889 Nelson Act council proceedings and incorporated on the map approved by He Who Is Spoken To. It was affirmed in communications by the Office of Indian Affairs, and further attested to in thirteen independent affidavits taken in 1930 by Indian and white participants in the 1889 negotiations between the Red Lake leadership and the Rice commission.[3]

Today, a third of Upper Red Lake is excluded from the reservation boundaries at Red Lake (as those boundaries are currently viewed and treated by the U.S. government). There are white homes and resorts along the shore at Waskish, on Upper Red Lake. Rice's words float in the wind there still, but the people of Red Lake are the only ones who continue to hear them. They bear no ill against the white residents there, but they know that the land rightfully belongs to them. There has never been a legal or political action to alter Rice's promise, and there has never been an effort by the U.S. government to rectify the breaking of their word and the taking of Upper Red Lake. To contemporary Red Lake residents it remains one of the most painful wrongs in a long history of injuries and injustices in their relationship with the United States.

Critical new sources of information on this event are contained in the Red Lake Archives and inform this work. They include depositions taken in 1930 from thirteen people who participated in the 1889 treaty councils—tribal members and the white Catholic priest, Thomas Borgerding. They also include important and reliable oral histories and a wide range of legal and political correspondence and documentation about land issues stemming from the 1889 Nelson Act. Few people have seen the documents in the Red Lake Archives and many white people have long-vested emotional and financial interests in Upper Red Lake now. This is a chapter of history that not many people know and some might wish to dispute. At the time of this writing, it remains unresolved and there is a lot at stake for everyone.[4]

While the Floodwaters Raged: Red Lake and Manifest Destiny, 1863–1889

He Who Is Spoken To watched white settlers flood into the Red River Valley by the thousands. It was like a hundred-year flood on the Red Lake River, rushing over sandy soil—no dam would stop the water from reaching its destination. The best response was a careful series of redirections, diversions, and protections to shape the flow, mitigate the damage, and protect the most fundamental parts of the homeland.

The Ojibwe scattered throughout the areas ceded by the Old Crossing Treaty had to abandon their homes, trapping areas, wild rice beds, and hunting lands. Some squatted or sneaked back to hunt elk and moose. A few even sought refuge with friendly white settlers and stayed. Moose Dung's village at Thief River was slowly eroding away as more and more of his people moved to Red Lake, Redby, Ponemah, Warroad, Roseau, and Turtle Mountain. Within a decade, the land rushes and tide of white settlement engulfed the territory. Soon it became unsafe to rely on the goodwill of white settlers, who were eager to take advantage of their private land grants and make the Red River Valley their home. To the east and south, towns sprang up almost overnight. There was a deluge of speculation in land, mining, railroad, and timber.

The economy at Red Lake was changing quickly. Before the Old Crossing Treaty, the people of Red Lake regularly hunted buffalo throughout the Red River Valley west of Red Lake and far out onto the plains in North Dakota. But within just a few short years white settlers and bounty hunters had decimated the buffalo herds. By 1869, even the Pembina Ojibwe were destitute because of the implosion of the buffalo population. The flood of white settlers into northwestern Minnesota compounded the land loss from the Old Crossing Treaty: the Red Lake people had less land on which to hunt, rice, and trap, and there was a significant decline in animal populations. Dr. C. P. Allen, who was stationed at the Red Lake Agency in 1873, wrote: "While they possess in common with any minority people, some defects of character, my heart goes out in sympathy to them in their abjectly distressed condition." The strain of the treaty period was evident and growing.[5]

The people of Red Lake still held more than 3 million acres of land. That land was not a reservation. It had never been ceded to the U.S. government. The eastern half of that unceded land base comprised the largest stand of virgin pine forest in the region. Mining interests wanted to prospect for iron ore, inspired by the massive deposits already located east of Red Lake. Settlers, amazed by the agricultural productivity of the Red River Valley, wanted to see if the rest of Red Lake's land was just as rich. Henry Whipple, Thomas Grace, Thomas Wilkinson, John Johnson, George Copway, and other missionaries wanted to concentrate the Red Lake and other Ojibwe in order to more easily convert them. White settlers were terrified of Indians after the U.S.-Dakota War in 1862, and anything that pushed brown people off the landscape was usually viewed in a positive light. The people of Red Lake held on, prepared for the pressure that was sure to follow, and considered the best strategies for survival—what could be compromised, and what could never be lost.

The Red Lake Ojibwe lived in several communities on more than 3 million acres of unceded land after the Old Crossing Treaty in 1863. They watched in horror as the tide of white settlement engulfed Ojibwe communities to their east and south. By the time of the Old Crossing Treaty, a wave of land cessions and relocation efforts had disrupted many Ojibwe communities in Minnesota. Efforts were made to relocate all Minnesota Ojibwe to Sandy Lake (1850), Isle Royale (1862), Leech Lake (1863), and White Earth (1867). Red Lake was to be next.[6]

Traders received vast sums of money from Ojibwe land payments, sometimes more than the Indians themselves. Traders like Truman Warren and missionaries like John Johnson received private land grants from Ojibwe treaties. Nobody seemed interested in treating the Ojibwe fairly. To white folk, Indians were simply obstacles to be overcome.[7]

The Ojibwe population was boiling with discontent. The 1855 treaty ceded most of the land owned by the Pillager, Lake Superior, and Mississippi Ojibwe, establishing reservations for those bands on portions of their homelands. Within twelve years, even some of the new reservations, including those at Gull Lake, Rabbit Lake, and Lake Pokegama, were ceded, forcing the relocation of their people first to Leech Lake and then to White Earth. In 1863, the Rabbit Lake Ojibwe killed Crossing Sky (Aazhawaa-giizhig) and two other chiefs for negotiating the treaty that ceded their reservation. Leech Lakers, furious with chief Flat Mouth (Eshkibagikoonzh) for agreeing to further land cessions, killed the horse he used to travel to the train station for his trip to Washington. Even after ceding most of his band's homeland, Mississippi Ojibwe chief Hole in the Day said, "It is for us to say wether [sic] we shall move or not." But as the land filled with whites, it became more and more difficult to enforce such a position.[8]

Pressure was mounting at Red Lake. The Office of Indian Affairs opened a subagency at Leech Lake in 1866, and from then until 1900, Red Lake was usually administered from Onigum at Leech Lake, and sometimes from White Earth. In 1879, Leech Lake, Red Lake, and White Earth were temporarily consolidated. There were periods afterward when Red Lake was administered independently, but it was a battle for the Red Lake chiefs to establish and maintain direct contact with the U.S. government when they wanted it. As late as the 1960s, the location of the Indian Affairs office was still a major issue of dispute.[9]

He Who Is Spoken To was not content to wait for the government to come after Red Lake. In 1866, he was part of a Red Lake delegation to Washington that sought to redress critical issues remaining from the Old Crossing negotiations regarding late or missing treaty payments and inaccurate land surveys. He Who Is Spoken To was not satisfied with the results of his trip to Washington, and he continued to assert Red Lake interests with government officials, traders, and missionaries. It was frustrating and scary, but not futile.[10]

New surveys of the Old Crossing land cession were conducted in 1873 and 1879, but they did not draw the boundary line as understood by the chiefs at Old Crossing. Although Indians often did not fully understand the legal language of treaties and surveys in the 1800s, the surveys were fraught with errors and fraud and Red Lakers were paying the price. White settlers and businessmen were prospering at Ojibwe expense, and it would not take much to spark a war. He Who Is Spoken To frequently conversed with Henry Whipple about Red Lake's position. Whipple supported a relocation policy, but he was sincere friends with He Who Is Spoken To. Whipple wrote to the commissioner of Indian affairs in 1866: "Unless the government desires to destroy its influence with the entire body of Chippewas, they are bound to recognize to the fullest extent all its pledges to the Indians."[11]

Red Lake was growing as more Ojibwe people from Michigan, Wisconsin, Minnesota, North Dakota, and Manitoba moved there, seeking sanctuary from the exploding white population around them. Joseph Nedeau Sr. (1797–1888) moved to Red Lake from Winnipeg in 1860. His son, Joseph Nedeau Jr. (1829–1921), built the large Nedeau family at Red Lake. There were many others as well.[12]

Ojibwe chiefs at Red Lake, Leech Lake, and White Earth worked to dampen the influence of new arrivals to Ojibwe country. The Canadian Métis sought independence in Canada during the Red River Rebellion of 1869–70. Their population was severely disrupted, and many Métis sought refuge in Ojibwe communities in Minnesota and North Dakota. The Métis and other mixed-blood traders usually had financial, religious, and social interests that were quite different from the resident Ojibwe population. It did not take long for Ojibwe leaders to realize that the interests of the Métis and mixed-blood traders were often not in sync with those of the Ojibwe. Hole in the Day formalized that position in the White Earth removal treaty in 1867: "no part of the annuities provided for in this or any former treaty with the Chippewas of the Mississippi bands shall be paid to any half-breed or mixed-blood, except those who actually live with their people upon one of the reservations belonging to the Chippewa Indians."[13]

The errors and fraud in the surveys made after the Old Crossing Treaty and the Pillager, Lake Superior, and Mississippi Ojibwe treaties in 1863 and 1864 had serious consequences. Whites were occupying land that Indians understood to belong to them. A tiny parcel of land along the overland trail between Red Lake and Leech Lake was excluded from the Leech Lake reservation by survey error: the small hamlet of Spaulding in Beltrami County, located by Peterson Lake, north of Bemidji. White settlers and businessmen took advantage of this and set up several saloons in the parcels excluded from the reservation by survey error at Long Lake and Campbell Lake for a time, profiteering from Indian misery and undermining an intentional prohibition of alcohol established by Moose Dung and He Who Is Spoken To in the Old Crossing Treaty.

In 1871, a power struggle between the House and the Senate in Washington, DC, terminated the power of the United States to make treaties with native nations. From this point on the government had to resort to congressional acts and executive orders to formally change Indian land tenure. It seems strange that the United States would allow a technicality to stop them from making treaties when more than 3 million acres of land around Upper and Lower Red Lakes in Minnesota remained unceded. But there were many ways to get land from Indians, and the government found them.

The end of treaty making had a significant impact on Red Lake's ability to keep so much of its land. Although credit deservedly goes to the tribal leaders who navigated this difficult time, Red Lake's geographic isolation and the fact that it was one of the last tribes in the United States to hold unceded lands offered them some protection as the government moved to further erode the Red Lake land base.[14]

As land opened for white settlement and logging all around Red Lake, the government began to build dams to help private timber businesses float their logs to mills and markets. Dams on Leech Lake, Lake Winnibigoshish, Pine River, Rum River, and Pokegama Falls flooded Ojibwe villages and cemeteries and drowned much of the area's wild rice and lowbush cranberry. The Ojibwe were not properly consulted or compensated. He Who Is Spoken To and other Ojibwe leaders complained loudly, and government commissions were established in 1881 and 1883 that documented the damage and even promised reparations. Reports from Henry H. Sibley, William R. Marshall, and Joseph A. Gilfillan were formally submitted to Congress in 1884 and 1885, but they were ignored in each successive congressional session.[15]

The government also took steps to attack tribal sovereignty. The Major Crimes Act was passed in 1885 and gave U.S. federal courts unilateral jurisdiction in cases of murder, manslaughter, rape, assault, arson, burglary, and larceny. This severely undermined the power previously retained by tribes to administer justice on their own behalf. From then on, chiefs would no longer be the arbiters of justice for their own people in any but minor offenses. None of that was immediately understood by He Who Is Spoken To or his fellow chiefs at Red Lake. But it became clear the following year when a Red Laker accidentally killed another and was arrested for murder, brought to St. Paul, and arraigned in federal court. The chiefs were stripped of their power to see justice done the Red Lake way, and the man accused of a crime had to navigate a foreign court system more than two hundred miles from home.[16]

Pressure on Red Lake was coming to a head. Lucius Q. C. Lamar, secretary of the interior, wrote: "They found the Red Lake band in possession of and occupying a large tract of well-timbered and otherwise valuable land, estimated to contain about 3,200,000 acres, of which they were making no practical use." In 1885, Henry Whipple wrote to every U.S. senator and congressman, President Grover Cleveland, and select members of his administration to push for stronger efforts to concentrate the Ojibwe at White Earth and Red Lake: "The Leech Lake, Cass Lake, Winnibagoshish, Oak Point, Sandy Lake and Mille Lac Indians cannot be protected where they are at or led to civilization." Whipple hoped to select a small group of cooperative chiefs to bring to Washington and secure the relocation of their bands: "Great care must be taken to secure only those chiefs . . . whose influence is on the side of civilization." Whipple's friendship with He Who Is Spoken To and unabashed criticism of policy makers who did not honor Indian treaties did not stop him from picking chiefs representative of his mission rather than the views of their people to advance his goals.[17]

He Who Is Spoken To must have felt betrayed by Whipple. The chief converted to Christianity, encouraged his people to do the same, and strongly advocated for peace, tolerance, and temperance while he continued to fight for Red Lake's land and political interests. Whipple deepened his personal relationship with the chief at the same time that he was a primary advocate for Red Lake land cession and Ojibwe removal.

In 1886, Whipple's advocacy paid off as he successfully helped influence legislative action to forward his religious mission and relocation of the Minnesota Ojibwe population. Red Lake land issues were bundled with relocation for the other Minnesota Ojibwe. A new congressional commission was proposed to address relief for and civilization of the Ojibwe in Minnesota. The politics got complicated in Washington as the legislative approval for the commission was buried in congressional committees, but it was attached to the appropriation bill and ratified on May 15 of that year. It was named the Northwest Indian Commission.

Knute Nelson, who was elected to the U.S. House of Representatives from the newly established Fifth Minnesota District in 1883, engineered the primary legislative push for Whipple's plan. Nelson and Whipple were testing the waters for a major land cession from Red Lake, to pave the way for allotment, relocation, timber harvesting, and assimilation programs. Instead of protecting He Who Is Spoken To or the people of Red Lake, Whipple had emboldened the forces arrayed against them.

He Who Is Spoken To was seasoned now. He was eighty-two years old. He had dealt with missionaries and American politicians for decades. He objected to and never signed the Old Crossing Treaty, but he was there for all the councils and politics in 1863. He liked Whipple, but he also knew that the bishop would not have his best interests at heart in 1886. The chiefs at Red Lake were looking to him for leadership now, so He Who Is Spoken To rose to his full and considerable height and went out to meet the Northwest Indian Commission.

On Knute Nelson's recommendation, President Cleveland appointed Whipple, Charles F. Larrabee, and John V. Wright as commissioners and instructed them to get permission for a land cession from Red Lake and consolidate the rest of the Minnesota Ojibwe there or at White Earth. He Who Is Spoken To knew that he now had to be as smart as he was strong.

He Who Is Spoken To and the Chipmunk

He Who Is Spoken To called Congressman Knute Nelson the Chipmunk (Agongos, translated as ground squirrel in the council logs). In Ojibwe culture, the chipmunk is notoriously annoying; according to Ojibwe legend, the animal earned the stripes on his back in a karma-inspired owl attack. Nelson was a Norwegian immigrant, so calling him *agongos* served both to label him as an outsider (it was the Ojibwe term for Norwegians) and to draw attention to the annoyance his manners, presence, and politics caused He Who Is Spoken To throughout the proceedings for the Northwest Indian Commission— and afterward.[18]

He Who Is Spoken To opened the first council with Henry Whipple and the Northwest Indian Commission in Red Lake on August 17, 1886. Simultaneously, Congressman Nelson was working with Senator Henry L. Dawes in Washington, DC, to create legislation that would enable and legitimize white control of Indian land within reservation boundaries. They succeeded in passing a major change in national Indian law that set up the policy of allotment and laid the groundwork for one of the most trying times in Red Lake history. Congress passed the General Allotment Act, often called the Dawes Act (after its primary sponsor, Henry L. Dawes), on February 8, 1887, although most of the legislative work was done in 1886 while the Northwest Indian Commission was in Red Lake and other Ojibwe communities.[19]

Farming, timber, mining, and railroad interests wanted access to the Indian land within reservation borders. Missionaries wanted Indians to convert to Christianity and feared that the reservation system, by grouping Indians together, encouraged unity among native people and allowed them to retain too much of their culture. The Dawes Act allowed the government to break up the communal ownership of tribal land, establish private ownership of land parcels on reservations, and open "surplus" reservation land not allotted to Indians for white settlement. It was an "enabling" act, meaning that it set up the policy that then had to be implemented on a case-by-case basis.

He Who Is Spoken To must have felt sick to his stomach as his friend Henry Whipple worked with fellow commissioners Charles Larrabee and John Wright in 1886 to convince all of the Minnesota Ojibwe to move to White Earth, accept allotments, and pave the way for further white settlement. Because the U.S. government could no longer make treaties with Indians, the report of the Northwest Indian Commission was to serve as the basis for further congressional action to advance these stated goals.[20]

He Who Is Spoken To showered Whipple with complaints. The White Earth reservation was created in 1867 and included part of Red Lake's unceded land; Red Lake was never consulted or compensated. The government took the northeastern four townships off of the White Earth reservation by executive order and opened them for logging and settlement. The land was within the unceded Red Lake

Red Robed, 1899

land base and now was full of white loggers and settlers; again, Red Lake was not consulted or compensated. The 1873 and 1879 surveys intended to correct previous border errors from the Old Crossing Treaty of 1863 were themselves incorrect. He Who Is Spoken To pushed Red Robed, the son of Moose Dung, to operate as spokesman on the Old Crossing survey errors. In a telling exchange between Red Robed and Commissioner Larrabee, the issue was laid on the table.

On August 19, 1886, Red Robed stood before the committee and spoke: "We have written a great many times, but we have never received a satisfactory answer. We do not know any of our chiefs who have ceded this land; we cannot find the name of a single chief who has ever ceded this land or signed his name to a paper."[21]

Larrabee had to concede misunderstanding and error on the part of the government: "We can see the possibility of a misunderstanding having been made at the time. . . . But it is not in our power to rectify that mistake at the present time. We are very sorry that the error was made."

Red Robed was adamant: "We do not accept your proposition. . . . I do not want anyone outside to set a value upon my land. This property belongs to us, the Red Lake Indians. That is the conclusion we have arrived at, and that is the conclusion we have all arrived at."

The Red Lakers were unhappy, and rightfully so. Annuity payments were past due. Dams were flooding wild rice and lowbush cranberry crops east of Red Lake. Red Lake chiefs would never consent to relocate. White people were cutting timber on tribal land without permission and offering no compensation.

He Who Is Spoken To explained the progression of timber speculation and growing white intrusion at Red Lake. In 1868, the first sawmill at Red Lake was opened at Mill Creek. At its inception, the sawmill served no immediate benefit to the people of Red Lake. Most of the cutting was done by white lumbermen and most of the value-added work went to the U.S. government or nonnative companies. The mill was just a tool used by white timber interests to accelerate their operations because booming logs onto the lake was the most efficient way to move them to mill or float them to Crookston and get them to market.[22]

White timber cutting at Red Lake was growing far faster than the permission to do it. In 1871, the commissioner of Indian affairs began to regularly report on timber resources at Red Lake, estimating 50 to 75 million board feet of harvestable timber. That estimate proved conservative in the long run, but it was high enough to spur political action to get at Red Lake's vast timber resources. In 1872, the commissioner of Indian affairs outlined specific plans and recommendations for timber harvesting by white citizens and businesses at Red Lake. In 1874, a road was built connecting Red Lake to White Earth. Logging was accelerating throughout the region. The Red Lake mill sawed 300,000 board feet in 1874 and 375,000 in 1875. In 1877, white speculators were successfully taking greater control of logging operations at Red Lake. A storm destroyed the boom at Red Lake, and the reconstruction in 1877 disrupted operations. The Red Lake mill milled only 177,000 board feet that year—floated down Mud Creek, boomed and towed on the lake, and processed by the mill. Meanwhile white-owned operations in Crookston and other mill sites were processing vast quantities of timber harvested throughout the region. In 1885, it was reported that "Timber cutting and logging operations are carried on from both sides of the International line, and the vast extent of the timber zone renders it utterly impossible to protect the timber from wholesale theft."[23]

In 1885, Omar H. Case was commissioned to survey a proposed route for a railroad from Brainerd to Red Lake Falls to get at the Red Lake timber. The land, easements, and right-of-way on the proposed route were to be owned by Brainerd and Northwestern Railway Company. The same year, House Resolution 4384 was introduced to appraise and sell timber on the unceded land at Red Lake.[24]

He Who Is Spoken To was furious about the cutting, and also because very little of the maneuvering for access to Red Lake timber had the consent of the chiefs. Because government regulations permitted Indians to cut "dead and down" timber, white timber speculators were starting numerous forest fires and then hiring Indians to cut the torched timber. By the time He Who Is Spoken To brought the issue before Whipple at the council meeting, sanctioned Red Lake timber operations had brought more than 850,000 board feet to mill. Unsanctioned white cutting at Red Lake and dead and down cutting in arson areas brought multiple times that amount of timber to white mills in the region. The chiefs complained about arson fires on tribal land, but the government simply responded with an official approval of the already established dead and down timber policy. Fires set by whites plagued Red Lake for decades afterward.[25]

When Whipple read the government's proposed terms to the assembled chiefs at the Northwest Indian Commission council, He Who Is Spoken To was exasperated. The government wanted to relocate Ojibwe from elsewhere in Minnesota to Red Lake. The chief was composed but clear: "We wish to live alone on our premises; we do not wish any other Indians to come here." The chiefs were, however, willing to cede 2 million acres of land if the government could meet their other terms about retaining the lakes and avoiding allotment, but they likely never fully imagined what would come next. Commissioner of Indian Affairs John D. C. Atkins could barely contain his zeal in his letter to the president: "The portion ceded embraces a vast timber zone, said to be of incalculable value." One report estimated the initial cut value to be more than $3 million. That was in the end a fraction of the proceeds from Red Lake timber.[26]

At the Northwest Indian Commission council, He Who Was Spoken To was clear on the Red Lake position—the chiefs would not agree to allotment. Whipple still kept articles 4-7 of the agreement unaltered, and they all pertained to allotting the reservation at a later date, firmly establishing that as the expectation for future action.[27]

Whipple was at times greatly influenced by He Who Is Spoken To and saw the chief as a force for the civilization of the Red Lake people. But Whipple had no respect for tribal culture or worldview. The bishop said, "There must be some reason of this great difference between the white and the red man. . . . The white man has learned to use this world for the purposes for which the Great Spirit made it; it was not made for a few deer to run over."[28]

The agreement proposed by the Northwest Indian Commission was designed primarily to enable the timber boom. It included a stipulation on lake access that was particularly maddening to the Red Lake chiefs: "Free and unobstructed navigation of Red Lake is granted." Tensions were high for the first six days of councils. He Who Was Spoken To was frustrated that his position on allotment was not sufficient to remove all articles from the agreement that pertained to the subject. Increasingly, his frustration spread from the commissioners and the government's position to the interpreters for failure to deliver his position in a clear and convincing way. On August 20,

He Who Is Spoken To, aged and venerable, normally composed and soft-spoken, tore into the translators: "My friends, I consider you my friends. There are only the Sioux that harm us: just such Sioux as you are." The chief extended his index finger and pointed directly at the translators—Fred Smith, John Beaulieu, and Paul H. Beaulieu—as being the "Sioux" because they were causing so much harm. In Ojibwe culture, pointing is customarily done with the lips rather than a finger, which is a direct challenge and usually considered especially rude, but at that point the chief probably did not care.[29]

As the council meetings with the Northwest Indian Commission progressed, He Who Is Spoken To regained his composure and grew more assertive. His diplomacy paid off as Whipple wrote the first line of the agreement between Red Lake and the U.S. government: "It should be premised that the Red Lake Reservation has never been ceded to the United States." He Who Is Spoken To succeeded in getting the government to stipulate that land-sale proceeds would be used to build schools, purchase farm equipment, and construct a house for each Red Lake head of household. Essentially, the agreement required Red Lakers to sell their land to pay for their own assimilation. It was a lot to ask, but He Who Is Spoken To clearly saw the need for Red Lake to economically evolve without giving up the lakes.[30]

The deciding moment for the Northwest Indian Commission at Red Lake came with a bold, proactive move by He Who Is Spoken To. He called a recess after six days of meetings, and returned to council on August 23, declaring: "I am prepared at the present time to show you the amount of land that we wish to retain as a reservation hereafter." He then produced a map with carefully drawn lines for a new reservation at Red Lake that encompassed all of Upper and Lower Red Lakes and land for at least a mile around the lakeshore. He appealed to the commissioners to help sort out financial terms that were fair for the cession, but his primary concern was to keep all of both lakes.[31]

Whipple and Larrabee were not expecting this and scrambled to make an appropriate response. Ultimately, Whipple read a legal description of the boundary line: "Beginning at a point 1 mile due north of the most northerly point of Red Lake; thence due east to a point due north of a point 1 mile due east of the most easterly point of Red Lake." This roughly corresponded to what He Who Is Spoken To had drawn on the map and certainly included all of Upper and

Lower Red Lake. The chiefs already had trouble with the translating team and probably did not follow all of the legal description, but they knew their territory and were in unanimous agreement with the chief's map, which covered the most important issue of the day. They had saved Upper and Lower Red Lake for Red Lake's exclusive use and ownership. The chiefs lined up behind He Who Is Spoken To and signed the amended agreement with the Northwest Indian Commission, starting with Leading Feather (Niigaanigwaneb), Red Robed, Little Frenchman, and Praying Day (Anami'e-giizhig).[32]

To the Red Lake leadership, it appeared that they had fought a tough diplomatic battle and emerged scathed, but with the lakes intact. Under the circumstances, that was the best they could have hoped for. Whipple, Larrabee, and Wright got most of what they wanted, but not everything Knute Nelson had expected.

Commissioner of Indian Affairs Atkins wrote of the Northwest Indian Commission's Red Lake agreement: "With the Red Lake agreement I am not so well satisfied. . . . Indians have in this reservation only the aboriginal right of occupancy, the ultimate title being in the United States, which has never established the reservation by treaty, law, or executive order." Nevertheless, Lucius Q. C. Lamar, secretary of the interior, approved the commission findings and the Red Lake agreement over Atkins's objection.[33]

The work of the Northwest Indian Commission, including the Red Lake agreement, still needed congressional approval. As leader of the commission, Whipple had pushed the Indians as far as he could, and his relationships with many Ojibwe leaders, including He Who Is Spoken To, were forever tarnished. Red Lake had kept the lakes in spite of Whipple, not because of him. The agreed-upon land cession would be hard for Red Lake to live with. But Whipple was still advocating for Ojibwe relocation, conversion, and land cessions. Whipple tried to preserve what was left of his respect in the Ojibwe world, including bringing issues and potential solutions to the newly established Indian Court of Claims, which was designed to expedite solutions to the now numerous Indian land-claims cases in federal court. Many tribes had been defrauded in the treaty process and sued the government. The Indian Court of Claims was created to address tribal legal grievances and clear disputed titles that might impede the speed of white land acquisition in Indian country. Red Lake did not get much relief from the Indian Court of Claims or Whipple's other advocacy, but the complaints were so voluminous and serious that Congress knew it would have to do something.

Nobody in Washington was prepared to act in the best interests of the Red Lake Ojibwe. Their voting constituents were white landowners; and their financial supporters were white timber speculators and railroad tycoons. So the politicians went to work, undoing most of He Who Is Spoken To's hard-won concessions and any remaining faith the Red Lake chiefs had in the U.S. government. Knute Nelson, the Chipmunk, led the effort. Knute Nelson had a plan to make both the commissioner of Indian affairs and all of his own land-hungry and timber-hungry constituents happy. He gathered his allies and shifted his focus from the Indians to white politicians, with devastating effect.[34]

The Nelson Act: Chipmunk in the House

Knute Nelson scurried all over Minnesota and Washington, DC, meeting with timber barons, railroad owners, politicians, and constituents. Congress did even more favor-trading and pork-barrel political maneuvering in those days, so the congressman had a lot of interests to line up before bringing legislation to the floor of the House. The Northwest Indian Commission had been authorized by Congress on May 15, 1886. The councils at Red Lake were held August 17–23, 1886. The commission submitted its report to Congress on March 1, 1887. On January 4, 1888, Nelson finally had his support in place and introduced a bill for "the relief and civilization of the Red Lake Chippewa."[35]

Nelson's bill included a major land cession at Red Lake as agreed, but also included allotment and relocation of the Red Lake Ojibwe. Instead of an immediate vote on the floor, Nelson's bill was sent to committee so that seasoned political veterans of the Indian land business could leverage his work to accelerate their own plans for Ojibwe land and timber. Nelson anticipated this move, and had already won assignment to the Committee on Indian Affairs. The committees spent hours deliberating on Nelson's bill, primarily figuring out how to dissect Red Lake's land, separating agricultural land from timber sections, ensuring adequate supplies of timber products for rapidly growing settlements on the Red River, and selecting the best methods for timber exploitation and farmland conversion for white settlers. Agricultural land was valued at one dollar per acre; timberland was valued at three dollars per acre, an increased valuation by congressional amendment. Twice before, Congress had taken up Red Lake land issues (1884 and 1886)—both before and contemporaneously with the work of the Northwest Indian Commission—but those efforts stalled each time because plans were not fast enough or forceful enough or provided too many protections for Indians.[36]

Nobody in Congress advocated for Red Lake's interests—fair financial terms and keeping all of Upper Red Lake and Lower Red Lake in tribal hands. Whipple did get traction with a few legislators about honoring the stipulated agreement and not dispossessing the Red Lakers so fast that it might inhibit their adoption of Christianity and farming practices. One congressman objected to the sealed auction process proposed in the legislation: "The methods provided by these agreements for the disposal of the lands to be acquired from the Indians are novel, vicious, and dangerous in the extreme."[37]

Some members of the committee felt strongly that the Red Lake chiefs should give consent for the land acquisition and that too much had changed from the agreement originally brought to Congress by the Northwest Indian Commission. Knute Nelson knew that getting consent at Red Lake would be extremely difficult, especially because He Who Is Spoken To had already drawn up his own map for the reservation and refused to consent to allotment. So Nelson developed a novel and unscrupulous idea for obtaining Red Lake's consent and inserted it into the legislation. The legislation was broadened to impose allotment on all Ojibwe reservations in Minnesota and require all Ojibwe to take their allotments at White Earth or Red Lake. This would advance relocation efforts and gather even greater political support for the legislation. The Nelson Act stipulated that a new commission would be created to travel to each reservation and obtain signatures from two-thirds of the male residents at each one. Except at Red Lake. The requirement for Red Lake's consent was different from all the other Ojibwe bands. While everyone else needed two-thirds of adult males to sign the agreement for it to be binding, Red Lake was deemed to be in consent if two-thirds of the male Ojibwe in Minnesota signed off on the Nelson Act, even if the accepting signatories were residents of different reservations. If Red Lake voted against the act, the land cession and allotment could still be imposed if other Ojibwe elsewhere in Minnesota agreed to it.[38]

On March 1, 1888, an amended bill was sent to the floor of the House. Instead of proposing any specific action for Red Lake, the amended version called for "the relief and civilization of the Minnesota Chippewa." Nelson's trick to obtain consent for the legislation at Red Lake survived committee work and floor debates. Alabama congressman James E. Cobb proposed one major amendment on the floor. While the legislation stipulated that the Minnesota Ojibwe had to take their allotments at Red Lake or White Earth, Cobb's amendment allowed for tribal members to choose whether to stay on their home reservations or move. Nelson was not pleased, but he had already pushed every issue beyond normal ethical standards to get the bill passed, so he said simply, "I have no objection." By the time the bill was put to a vote, Nelson had lined up so many votes from the power brokers engaged in the timber, railroad, and land speculation that it was adopted without a roll call and with no significant dissension. It passed 131 to 33.[39]

In the Senate, Henry Dawes inserted himself into the proceedings. Dawes was from Massachusetts but was a primary architect of the General Allotment Act that governed the Ojibwe in Minnesota. He wanted to make sure that every effort was made to streamline the allotment process and accelerate land acquisition. Red Lake could set a precedent for allotment issues elsewhere in the country. He wanted to make sure there were no obstacles to his efforts to open Indian land for white settlement. Dawes rewrote Nelson's land-cession bill for Red Lake, turning it into a much larger land-cession, relocation, and allotment act governing all of the Ojibwe in Minnesota. The Nelson Act was revised to implement the allotment provisions of the Dawes Act, implement the recommendations of the Northwest Indian Commission for a land cession from Red Lake, cede all Minnesota Ojibwe reservations except Red Lake and White Earth, and remove all Minnesota Ojibwe to those two locations. The bill emerged with committee support and won Senate approval on January 14, 1889. In spite of Dawes's heavy hand, it is still commonly called the Nelson Act.

Tribal consent was still required, and it would prove difficult to obtain. The U.S. Chippewa Commission was created to get the necessary tribal signatures to implement the Nelson Act and carry out the land transfers. The act called for a land cession of 2,905,000 acres at Red Lake, but offered no maps or legal descriptions. That would have to be decided in council with He Who Is Spoken To at Red Lake. Henry M. Rice, seasoned treaty negotiator and Minnesota politician, was appointed chairman of the U.S. Chippewa Commission and charged with conducting the cession negotiations and reservation censuses and obtaining consent from the Indians.[40]

Most Minnesotans celebrated Knute Nelson for his contributions to the state. He was elected governor and served from 1893 to 1895. He then won continual reelection as senator from 1895 to 1923. But at Red Lake, the kindest thing people could think of to call him was the Chipmunk.

Henry M. Rice and the U.S. Chippewa Commission

On July 4, 1889, He Who Is Spoken To stood before all the chiefs and many warriors at Red Lake. His hair was long and gray, with a slight wave and no braids. His normally gentle countenance was covered in a stern growl as, unflinching in the summer sun, he stared down Henry Rice, who stood an entire head shorter than the chief. "We don't feel pleased to see a man like Mr. Nelson antagonize any of our interests," said the chief.[41]

Knute Nelson's work with the Northwest Indian Commission was still fresh in the minds of the Red Lake chiefs. Through Whipple and the Northwest Indian Commission, Nelson made many promises. They were all retracted now; the Chipmunk had delivered on none of them.

Nelson, Whipple, Larrabee, and Wright, who had carried out the work of the Northwest Indian Commission, stayed far away from Red Lake when the new U.S. Chippewa Commission arrived. They were all invited to join the U.S. Chippewa Commission by President Benjamin Harrison, but they knew better. Their names and reputations would do more harm than good in any effort to get tribal consent for the provisions of the Nelson Act. Many white folk in many places saw them as people who had befriended the Indians, but to the people of Red Lake, they were the ones who betrayed them.

President Harrison appointed Bishop Martin Marty and Joseph B. Whiting to work with Henry Rice on the commission. They began on June 11, 1889. Rice knew that obtaining tribal consent for the Nelson Act would be extremely difficult. He immediately consulted with Bishop Henry Whipple and Archbishop John Ireland to gather the support of Minnesota's major missionary organizations and seek their direct involvement in the negotiations. Respect for Whipple among Minnesota's tribal communities was real but waning fast after passage of the Nelson Act. His influence had the potential to make the work of the commission a lot more palatable in Indian country—or a lot more difficult. Whipple appointed E. Steele Peake to represent Episcopalian interests with the commission. Ireland appointed Father Aloysius Hermanutz to represent the Catholics. President Harrison informed the U.S. Senate that their work would be difficult because the government still owed so much money to the Indians and had a poor track record of delivering goods, honoring promises, and providing protections for the tribes and tribal members. He wrote that the Ojibwe had "an indisposition to treat with the Government for further concessions while its obligations incurred under former agreements are unkept."[42]

Joseph B. Whiting was not as annoying as Knute Nelson, but he also irritated the chiefs. Rice could tell that Whiting was more hindrance than help, so he asked him to talk less and used him to work on the provisions and food arrangements. For that, the chiefs called Whiting The Hunter (Giiyosewinini).

The Nelson Act was a bold piece of legislation. By calling for the transfer of 2,905,000 acres of Red Lake land to the U.S. government, the relocation of numerous tribal villages, and the allotment of Indian land across Minnesota, including Red Lake, its terms risked outright war between the Ojibwe and the U.S. government. But the government still needed Ojibwe signatures to make it happen. President Harrison directed the commission to get the signatures for the Nelson Act from every Ojibwe community in Minnesota. The commissioners did not have the authority to alter the act itself, and that put a serious limitation on their ability to get concessions and negotiate terms.

He Who Is Spoken To and most of the Red Lake chiefs present in 1889 were also part of the Old Crossing Treaty, and they felt betrayed by the government. Compensation was smaller than promised because the traders took so much from the annuity payments. Many payments were delayed. The survey work was late and the Red Lake chiefs considered it inaccurate. Leading Feather made this statement to the U.S. Chippewa Commission:

> We consider that the Government did not keep its agreement, according to our understanding. There is lots of money yet due the Red Lake Indians which they should have in their hands.. I was selected to and did show the line to the surveyors. The Indians define the line of the cession, starting from the mouth of the Thief River, thence to Rice River; right then straight to Little Birch Lake. The Government surveys do not comply with that line; somebody has cut it off. . . . It is a fact that that land we considered belonged to the Red Lake Indians.[43]

Snow Goose (Wewe) summed up the sentiment of the Red Lake chiefs: "There are many things which come inside the line of the reservation which can be compared to the works of the devil, and I am unable to estimate the amount of the damage done by these things. You see how tall I am. If I should be able to stand in the midst of the money, of the value of the damages, what had been stolen from us, it would go over my head."[44]

The only substantive ally Rice had at Red Lake was Bishop Martin Marty. Marty was based out of Sioux Falls, but he held quite a bit of sway with the Red Lake Catholics. Father Thomas Borgerding, who observed all of the council meetings, summarized the background politics and noted a crucial success of the chiefs:

> Some of the Catholic Indians here held a council and kind of agreed that it was not right to hold out against the bill because of Bishop Marty who was encouraging them to accept it. They succeeded in getting the others to agree, so it ended in a compromise offered the Red Lake Indians by the Commissioners; the Red Lake Indians might take a diminished reservation and would not have to take allotments, and that this diminished reservation need not be pooled with the other Indians of Minnesota. Of course, the Commissioners had no right to promise on the basis of a compromise and for many years there was considerable trouble about this diminished condition because the compromise was never ratified in Washington.[45]

Red Lake Councils

The Chippewa Commission knew that its toughest work would be at Red Lake. Red Lake had no reservation. Moose Dung's son Red Robed had a 640-acre plot at Thief River, technically considered a private land grant. Red Lakers were masters of 3,260,000 acres of unceded Indian land that stretched from Beltrami County to the Canadian border. They had never endured relocation, removal, allotment, or the scourge of legalized alcohol—and they were not interested in any of those things. If Red Lake was to be a relocation destination for other Ojibwe people, their consent to the Nelson Act was a critical first step. The Chippewa Commission arrived on June 29, 1889, and stayed in nonstop council meetings until July 8, 1889.

As had happened at the Old Crossing treaty negotiations in 1863, there were serious translation issues in 1889. Paul H. Beaulieu and Mary C. English served as interpreters. Their Ojibwe skills were as good as anyone's in the government service, but some dialect differences, metaphors, and key concepts did not translate well. In 1863, the councils focused on a treaty negotiation; in 1889, the councils were intended to obtain consent for an act of Congress. The difference was probably not well understood by tribal leaders, and it hampered their ability to bargain for better terms. It is likely that they did not fully comprehend the terms under negotiation—everyone knew it, but the commissioners did not care.[46]

Rice wrote: "We found them intelligent, dignified, and courteous, but for several days indisposed to give a favorable hearing." They opposed almost every term in the Nelson Act and had very little trust that the government would accurately incorporate or adhere to their demands. Praying Day complained bitterly about white encroachment: "I can see my property going to waste; they are stealing from me on every side; I never received a cent for it."[47]

The chiefs insisted that all land was to be held in common for the benefit of all the people at Red Lake. There was no way they would consent to allotment. They extended that understanding to the water as well, articulated as "the right to use in common all the water-ways."[48]

The chiefs refused to open up the reservation to alcohol sale or use. He Who Treads the Earth from the South (Zhaawanookamigishkang) said, "no liquor shall ever come on this reservation. It would be

Praying Day, 1896

the ruin of all these persons that you see here should that misfortune come to them."[49]

The chiefs also consistently insisted that the people of Red Lake remain in possession of all of Upper and Lower Red Lakes, and all the land for at least one mile from the lake shore in all directions, "to a point due north of a point 1 mile east from the easterly end of the lower Red Lake." The tribal delegates relied heavily on the maps used during negotiations. Rice assured them, "We do not ask you to sign the paper until we have your full and free consent to the reservation that will be marked out to you." The chiefs insisted on all of Upper and Lower Red Lakes being part of the retained reservation; no part of either lake could be excluded from their exclusive control, within the reservation boundaries. He Who Is Spoken To told the commissioners: "This property under discussion called Red Lake is my property. These persons whom you see before you are my children. They own this place the same as I own it. My friends, I ask that we reserve the whole of the lake as ours and our grand-children hereafter."[50]

Father Thomas Borgerding, who was present for all negotiations, was deposed and gave statements in 1921, 1926, 1930, and again in 1948. "One thing that the Indians insisted upon was that they keep this lake as their own," he said. "They said it was their warehouse and that it would provide for them when they were hungry." Borgerding told the Court of Claims:

> There was especially one thing they seemed to be very anxious, they repeated it different times, they wanted to keep their lake intact so that they would have that as their warehouse, as they expressed themselves or at-tas-soh-we-cumig, as they called that. That is a word they used frequently. It means a storehouse or warehouse and that is the word they used for their government warehouses where they kept the provisions, you know. They had a warehouse up there at that time and that was the word they used. That is the word they used for that lake and they wanted to keep that for their warehouse. They said whenever they were hungry they went to the warehouse and got their food and so they wanted to keep that. They were very insistent on that one point. That was repeatedly mentioned. I do not know whether it is mentioned in the reports of the councils as strongly as they mentioned it in their speeches. It seemed to me when I read their reports of the councils later on I did not notice that they insisted upon that so strongly, that it was not as strongly reported as they had done in their speeches.[51]

The chiefs closely scrutinized the map, ensuring that both Upper and Lower Red Lakes and all the land for at least a mile around them was included in the reservation. The entire tribal delegation, commissioners, interpreters, and witnesses viewed the delineations on the map. When it was done, He Who Is Spoken To said, "We wish to guaranty to our posterity some security; that is why we demand the reservation we have outlined on that paper."[52]

It is astonishing to read the attitudes of the commissioners today: they truly believed that the people of Red Lake did not need the land, did not benefit from it, and did not properly use it. Rice told the assembled chiefs that the whites "want to get their lands so as to make use of them, as they are now lying useless." He continued: "You are here surrounded by your lands, which are rich and full of good things, but you can not make use of them. You are just like the man would be on the shore of that lake: the lake is full of good fish, but he has no hook and no net, and has nothing to take the fish out with, so he starves for want of something to eat. So the Great Council invites you now to dispose of those lands which you do not need."[53]

Rice's line of reasoning only served to alienate the chiefs. Leading Cloud (Niigaanakwad) opened the third council meeting on July 3, 1889, and stated: "I stand before you as the spokesman of the band, and to show you that my assertion is correct, I proclaim it by a rising vote." More than two-thirds of the Indians rose to their feet in support of Leading Cloud. He then continued: "Your mission here is a failure. We never wish hereafter to sign any instrument. . . . We never signed an instrument in which we did not have a voice. . . . We shall return to our respective homes." Leading Cloud never did sign a consent for the act. Stands Forever (Gebegaabaw) reminded the Red Lake delegates, "We do not believe it is in our best interest to comply with their request." Nothing had changed for the Red Lakers by the fifth council. Snow Goose told the commissioners flatly, "I don't want to accept your propositions, I love my reservation very much; I don't want to sell it."[54]

The Red Lake chiefs also insisted that they be provided with the infrastructure to alter their lifeways. If they had to surrender hunting land, they demanded a sawmill, cattle, materials for fencing and farming, and houses for their tribal members. They knew that the concessions proposed were significant and had the potential to completely alter their lifeways, so they insisted on all the necessary support for the inevitable adjustment to farming, ranching, and logging industries.

The Red Lake Ojibwe had more land than any other Ojibwe band and the most to lose. Tribal leaders insisted that their payments not be prorated with those of other bands. Praying Day said, "Whatever belongs to the Red Lake Indians, we do not want consolidated with the money of any other band." The chiefs were also steadfast that no part of the land-sale proceeds go to traders for debt settlement. They knew all too well how traders fleeced their annuities.[55]

He Who Is Spoken To had limited power to change the terms of the Nelson Act. It was an act of Congress that had already passed both houses and become law. The U.S. Chippewa Commission had authority to obtain consent from Red Lakers, but not to change the legislation. The chief pushed for concessions where he could get them and did make some progress despite the difficult circumstances.

Dead and Down Timber

The arson by white timber speculators and timber exploitation came up repeatedly during the U.S. Chippewa Commission councils. Usually the timber companies employed some Indians in order to comply with federal regulations, but sometimes they didn't even bother with that. The Indians had no protection for their homes or resources. Leading Cloud laid the issue out before Henry Rice: "It is not the Indians who set fires to the pines that are burning, it is the whites. There are so many of them going about the country unknown to us. It is not to be laid to the Indians, and our Great Father ought not to allow any of his white children to come on the reservation here and set fire to the pines. If an Indian had been guilty of going to a white man's country and causing so much ruin and havoc the Indian would have been punished."[56]

He Who Is Spoken To added: "In passing Mrs. Warren's place, there was a fire raging to the west of the road. The woman told me that there was not an Indian in the country; that the fire had been set by settlers. We never set fire to our pine." Little Frenchman said, "We are surrounded by whites; they keep thieving from us and setting fires. We are not to blame for the destruction of any property on the reservation."[57]

Sensing their desperation about the timber exploitation, the commissioners tried to use it as a land-selling argument—Red Lake should sell the land and get some money for it before the whites stole all the timber. Joseph B. Whiting said, "Unless something is done for you now, five years hence this vast body of timber will be destroyed." Martin Marty added, "The rest of the land which is now being used up, stolen from you, or burnt off will be taken hold of by the Great Father for his children. He will sell your pine." None of that motivated He Who Is Spoken To to change his position. The issue remained unresolved in the council with the U.S. Chippewa Commission and went on to plague Red Lake for decades to come.[58]

Allotment

The Nelson Act, as originally proposed, required all of the Indians in Minnesota to relocate to White Earth or Red Lake. But as the bill was being debated in Congress, it became clear that such a monumental change might trigger physical violence over the land, so James E. Cobb amended the bill to allow the Ojibwe to take allotments in either the designated relocation areas or their home reservations.[59]

The Red Lake chiefs were united in opposition to allotment. They did not want Indians from other reservations moving to Red Lake to take allotments, and they did not want to break up the communal ownership of land. He Who Is Spoken To spoke for the entire delegation: "I said that I was opposed to having allotments made to us; I do not look with favor on the allotment plan. . . . I will never consent to the allotment plan. I wish to lay out a reservation here, where we can remain with our bands forever. I mean to stand fast to my decision." The chief never retreated from this position throughout the negotiations. He later stated: "We wish that any land we possess should be not only for our own benefit, but for our posterity, our grandchildren hereafter. . . . We think that we should own in common everything that pertains to us; with those that are suffering in poverty, just the same as we are."[60]

The Nelson Act enabled allotment at Red Lake and every other Ojibwe reservation in Minnesota, and the law was not altered through the council deliberations. However, He Who Is Spoken To was so adamant in opposition to allotment that the issue was a clear deal killer for the commissioners. They agreed to postpone the issue and not to proceed with allotment at Red Lake within the boundaries of the new reservation. Some allotments would be made in the ceded lands at Warroad and other places outside of the main reservation. The postponement of allotment was a major victory for the Red Lake leaders because it altered the course the government had planned for them and kept the reservation land base intact. For many decades after the Nelson Act, the government kept trying to allot Red Lake. Every Red Lake chief and tribal leader had to fight the same battle over and over again, from He Who Is Spoken To through the Peter Graves era until Roger Jourdain became chairman at Red Lake in 1959.

Saving the Lake

He Who Is Spoken To knew from years of experience that white men often had trouble hearing their own words in the strong northwest wind at Red Lake; and the wind seemed to howl every time Rice started to talk. The chief had backed the government away from immediately allotting Red Lake. He successfully reinforced the prohibition of alcohol on the reservation. He hammered the commission about timber fraud, Old Crossing survey lines, and late annuities. He must have felt like he was getting nowhere with the commissioners at times, but he did accomplish many things. He saved Red Lake from the same fate as the other Ojibwe reservations in Minnesota, most of which lost over 90 percent of the land inside their reservation borders. This was Red Lake's biggest issue that had to be addressed, so the chief devised a plan to keep the sacred lakes in Red Lake hands.

He Who Is Spoken To knew how important it was to have initiative. When Henry Whipple brought the Northwest Indian Commission to Red Lake in 1886 to ask for the lakes, the chief's use of pre-drawn maps and proactive diplomacy caught the bishop off guard. Red Lake kept the lakes that time. He needed something even stronger now.

He Who Is Spoken To could sense that Rice was in a difficult position during the negotiations, although there was no way for him to know the depth of the commissioner's entanglements. Rice had many political and economic allies who wanted railroad and timber business opened at Red Lake, including the use of Upper Red Lake to boom logs from rail to water. Prominent among them were Cushman K. Davis and Charles R. Davis. Cushman K. Davis was U.S. senator from Minnesota in 1887-90. Charles R. Davis was a Minnesota state congressman in 1889-90, state senator in 1891-95, and a U.S. congressman from 1903 to 1925. The Davis business plans required lake access, so Rice was under considerable personal and political pressure. Above all though, Rice was tasked to get Red Lake consent for an act of Congress that had already passed through the legislature. He was pretending to negotiate when he did not have authority to completely reconfigure the legislation. He Who Is Spoken To and the other Red Lake chiefs were recalcitrant and unwilling to make excessive concessions, so Rice had to compromise more than he wanted and worried that President Harrison would see his concessions as a failure of duty.

The venerable chief pulled Rice aside and offered a compelling compromise. So far nobody at Red Lake seemed likely to sign off on the Nelson Act. When He Who Is Spoken To said that Rice would get his signatures if Red Lake got the lakes, the commissioner listened intently. He Who Is Spoken To explained that the prohibition of alcohol, avoiding allotment, and maintaining Red Lake's independence from the other Ojibwe bands were critical, but that they now had acceptable agreement on those issues. What the chiefs needed most of all was an infallible assurance that they would keep every inch of Upper Red Lake and Lower Red Lake and at least a mile in every direction around it for eternity. If the commission offered anything less, nobody would sign. Rice agreed.[61]

The chief told Rice he would have to guarantee his words the Red Lake way when the council met that day inside the government school. There was a flurry of activity in Red Lake, as chiefs, warriors, and tribal residents filled the school building and crowded around outside the structure, peering in the windows. Although the level of trust must have been very low, anticipation was clearly high. When everyone was assembled, He Who Is Spoken To nodded to Little Frenchman, who beckoned Rice, and the commissioner stood facing east with his palms outstretched and promised that the people of Red Lake would keep all of both lakes for all time. He turned to the south, the west, and the north, repeating the pledge each time. The people saw. The spirits in the earth, the sky, and the water all saw and heard.

Rice made his promise the Red Lake way, and now He Who Is Spoken To wanted to see it made again in the way of the white man. A large map of the region was laid out on a table in front of the entire council assembly. The chief marked out a boundary for the new reservation with both lakes inside the boundary lines and told the commissioners that this was the final offer.

Rice might have thought he was playing nice with the promise ceremony before the council, but treaty records would have to go to Washington. He must have felt like he was boxed into a corner. There is a telling passage in the published treaty log, where the map is laid before them and Rice is pleading with He Who Is Spoken To, saying: "We have heard your proposition, and we think we can perhaps change the lines so as to give you all you want, and very much more than you will have use for—you, your children, grand-children, and great-grand-children—and still please the Great Father much better than by following accurately the line you suggest. You have made some mistakes in your lines; we think we can change them so it will be much better for you." Rice's backpedaling about the reservation lines was not lost on the Red Lake leadership. He Who Is Spoken To, Red Robed, and the other chiefs staunchly refused any alteration of the lines already drawn on the map. He Who Treads the Earth from the South leaned over the map on the table and looked Rice in the eyes, saying, "I want to know if you will leave a copy of the arrangement here."[62]

The treaty log says that as soon as Rice finished this parlay, "The Commissioners then consulted with each other and with the Indians individually about the lines of the proposed reservation." Having no success at convincing anyone to change his mind, Rice left the map unaltered, with the reservation lines including all of both lakes. He said simply, "The most important question has now been settled. The only doubt we have is as to whether the Government of the United States will approve of our yielding so much, but we will do the best we can." Immediately after that comment, He Who Is Spoken To grabbed a quill and signed the document abruptly before any alterations could be made. Most of the other chiefs followed suit.[63]

Consent for the Nelson Act

There was a feeling of relief at Red Lake. They had saved the lakes, delayed allotment for a later fight, kept alcohol illegal, and raised critical issues around logging, surveys, and treaty payments. The band was selling land, but it was protecting what it considered most important.

The people at Red Lake were going to receive annuities too, and they welcomed this support at such a stressful time. In 1889, the destruction of the buffalo herds in the Red River Valley and the explosion of white settlement all around the borders of Red Lake's unceded land base forced them to live on a fraction of their former land with only a fraction of their former food production. Spring planting and summer crops were not looking good, and many failed that fall.

He Who Is Spoken To had just fought an impressive diplomatic battle in the councils. He was the warrior protecting the people, representing eighty-three families on the south shore of Lower Red Lake. When he signed, many were ready to follow suit. They all saw the ceremony at the school and many saw the maps inside the school too. Leading Feather, who was seventy-one years old, signed after He Who Is Spoken To. Red Robed, now age fifty-seven, representing forty-two families at Thief River, signed next. Praying Day, Sits Alone (Ne'etoowab), and Noon Day (Naawakwe-giizhig) followed suit.

The Nelson Act stipulated a vote from all adult men in each Ojibwe community. Following their chiefs, many warriors from Red Lake also signed their consent for the act. Not everyone was convinced that Rice's ceremonial promise, the map, and the final council deliberations would be sufficient to keep the government off the lakes. There was a growing collective political culture at Red Lake, but libertarian warriors always did what they felt was right.

Most of the chiefs from Ponemah boycotted the councils, or came as observers only, and they all refused to sign consent for the Nelson Act. Changing Feathers (Aanjigwaneb) was one of the few Ponemah chiefs to engage in the councils. He wanted to make sure that his objection to the act was noted in the record. He was fifty years old and younger than several other Ponemah chiefs who refused to even paddle across the lake to attend. Little Wind (Noodinoons) of Ponemah, later known as Nodin Wind, also observed but refused to sign. Ponemah leaders had now refused to agree to both the Old Crossing and Nelson Act land cessions.

Chiefs from the south shore of Red Lake refused to consent as well. Leading Cloud's rejection was notable because during the council he stood to address the commissioners with a "rising vote" and two-thirds of the council attendees stood with him to acknowledge his authority as spokesman. Dawn Flight (Waabanikweyaash) also refused to sign over concerns that his relatives at Lake of the Woods

would be ostracized. Rice painted a different picture in his correspondence: "At Red Lake the assent of all the Indians to the agreement was
obtained except a few called 'pagans,' residing on the northern shore
of the lake."[64]

And then there was the complicated matter of the signatures. The
Nelson Act required each reservation to obtain signatures from two-
thirds of the male residents of that reservation. Red Lake was deemed
to be in consent if two-thirds of the male Ojibwe in Minnesota signed
off on the Nelson Act, even if the accepting signatories were residents
of different reservations. The official U.S. government census conducted at Red Lake in preparation for the Nelson Act showed 1,168
tribal members, of which 303 were adult men. The 247 signatures
acquired at Red Lake met the government's two-thirds requirement,
though barely.[65]

The documented consent at Red Lake for the Nelson Act is
deceptive and incomplete—a fabrication by omission. Most of the
Ponemah Indians boycotted the negotiations. Most were excluded
from the census and not counted as proper "no" votes.

In fact, included in the official transcript of the Nelson Act is a
reference to He Who Is Spoken To as representing eighty-three
families on the south shore of Red Lake and Red Robed (sometimes
called Moose Dung the Younger) as representing forty-two families
from Thief River. If there were only ten people per family (and likely
the number was higher because people had many children in those
days and often had grandparents living in their homes), the number
would be closer to 1,250. A census taken at Red Lake in 1892, three
years after the Nelson Act, tallied 1,259 tribal members. And the 1889
and 1892 census figures do not include most people from Ponemah,
Warroad, or outlying communities in the ceded lands. Warroad and
the outlying communities were geographically too far away to be in
the realm of awareness for government officials who did most of the
census work. Ponemah residents avoided government officials as a
normal practice, and made special efforts to avoid anyone associated
with the 1863 and 1889 land cessions. The village of Ponemah today
is half the size of Red Lake village. The relative size difference was
likely to have been comparable then. As early as 1845, Francis Pierz
reported as many as 1,400 people on the south shore of Lower Red
Lake alone. The likely population at Red Lake in 1889 was probably

more than 2,000, of whom 500 or more were adult men. The 247 consenting men at Red Lake in 1889 constituted less than half of the adult male population. Some of the consenting Indians on the list appear to have consented more than once as well, such as Stands Forever, who signed on lines ten and seventeen.[66]

The fact that Red Lake's own tribal population did not meet the two-thirds threshold required in the legislation did not automatically invalidate the act at Red Lake. However, because there was a substantial error in the census information for the Nelson Act at Red Lake, it is reasonable to assume that there was a similar error (intentional or inadvertent) on other reservations. It is quite possible that the documented tribal support for the Nelson Act was actually insufficient to properly authenticate the land cession at Red Lake. That casts a cloud over the validity of the entire 3.2 million-acre Red Lake land cession in 1889—and everything else in the Nelson Act.

Taking the Lake

Today, the village of Waskish on the eastern shore of Upper Red Lake consists entirely of white homes and resorts. It is the only developed part of the lakeshore. With all we know of the U.S. Chippewa Commission, the Nelson Act, the maps, and the signing process, this should not be possible. The chiefs and citizens of Red Lake never ceded the lake. It was taken.

Paul H. Beaulieu (1820-97), who served as government interpreter at Red Lake's major land cessions in 1863 and 1889, kept his papers, notes, and letters, and gave them to his grandson, Paul H. Beaulieu (1889-1955). Paul H. Beaulieu the younger (Mashkikiwenzii, or Old Medicine Man) married Mary McIvers (Waawaasekwe, or Shimmering Woman), a member of the Citizen band of Potawatomi from Shawnee, Oklahoma. They raised their children and set their deepest roots at Red Lake. The Beaulieu family identity was shifting from mixed-blood fur traders and government agents to Red Lake tribal citizens and leaders. They were a Red Lake Ojibwe family now. Paul H. Beaulieu, the grandson, went on to become adviser to the Red Lake chief delegation in 1909 and coauthor with Peter Graves of the constitution for the General Council of the Red Lake Band of Chippewa Indians in 1918. He was in constant contact with the Red

Lake chiefs who had signed the Nelson Act. He was the inheritor of many Beaulieu family documents and letters, including his grandfather's treaty council notes from Red Lake in 1863 and 1889. Beaulieu had a deep understanding of the entire U.S. Chippewa Commission process.[67]

Beaulieu said that as soon as the U.S. Chippewa Commission obtained signatures from He Who Is Spoken To and other Red Lake chiefs and warriors, Henry M. Rice walked out of Red Lake, took out the map with He Who Is Spoken To's demarcations, and changed them, cutting off a section of Upper Red Lake on purpose to make room for timber booming operations on Upper Red Lake and the railroad proposed by his cronies Cushman K. Davis and Charles R. Davis.

Cushman K. Davis left a voluminous paper trail of advocacy for the Duluth and Winnipeg Railway Company. In 1890, shortly after Rice submitted the U.S. Chippewa Commission report to Congress, commissioner of Indian affairs Thomas J. Morgan wrote to secretary of the interior John W. Noble: "This Office has received informally by reference from Senator C. K. Davis, a copy of the articles of incorporation of the Duluth and Winnipeg Railway Company, together with the charter of said Company from the state of Minnesota, and also two maps (in duplicate) of the definite location of a portion of the line of railway it proposes to construct through the Indian lands . . . within the Red Lake Reservation." The maps enclosed with that letter show the northeastern section of the lake *inside the diminished reservation* but the proposed railroad cutting across Red Lake land on the reservation.[68]

According to Paul H. Beaulieu, Henry Rice illegally altered the U.S. Chippewa Commission map that was agreed upon and included with the signature pages for the Nelson Act. Rice grabbed all copies of the map and signature pages, leaving no duplicates at Red Lake when he departed.

Paul H. Beaulieu's daughter, Margaret Beaulieu, married Roger Jourdain, who went on to become Red Lake's first elected tribal chairman. Beaulieu spent countless hours grooming Jourdain as a political and scholarly protégé. Jourdain had a photographic memory. Beaulieu's documents burned up when Roger Jourdain's house was destroyed in an arson fire in 1979, but Jourdain carefully dictated his exceptional recall of their contents to Don Allery as part of a major biographical history project in the 1980s. Jourdain's recollection of Paul H. Beaulieu's knowledge of the Chippewa Commission cannot be ignored.

Beaulieu told Jourdain repeatedly that the parties to the Nelson Act agreed upon a one-mile buffer around Upper and Lower Red Lakes but that Rice doctored the map after the signing. If so, that alteration of the map was illegal—never agreed to by the chiefs or people of Red Lake. And it is a theft that to this day has seen no just compensation or remedy. Rice concluded the councils with other Ojibwe bands, completed his report, signed it on December 26, 1889, and sent it to the Office of Indian Affairs, which reviewed and commented on the report and submitted it to Congress.[69]

The family of Henry Rice eventually archived his correspondence and personal papers at the Minnesota Historical Society. Official federal documents ended up at the National Archives, mainly the branch in Washington, DC, but some in Chicago and many in Kansas City as well. Missing from those documents are accurate copies of the maps and sections of the official U.S. Chippewa Commission council transcripts. The work of the U.S. Chippewa Commission was hardly transparent to begin with, but the omission of critical records is telling. There is no way to prove that formal government records were altered, but there can be no doubt that many of them are missing. The Rice papers also do not have detailed correspondence or notes on this chapter of Rice's life, although his other major political services are copiously documented in his papers.

In 1989, Dan Needham Sr., the grandson of Sun Shining Through ("Slapping the Flies" in the Nelson Act documents), recorded an account of the taking of the lake that corroborates that of Paul H. Beaulieu and Roger Jourdain:

> They [the chiefs] wanted the reservation to be a square block of land from Thief River to a mile north of Waskish and a mile east, then straight down. They made a map showing what they wanted. But they only made one map. I don't know why they didn't make two maps.
>
> Commissioner Rice, he took that map. He took it down to St. Paul. And he wasn't feeling very good about the way the Indians treated him. He couldn't allot them, he couldn't move them. He was so mad at the Indians, he said, "Damn it, I'm going to get a piece of that lakeshore." So,

when he got down there, he moved the lines over. He changed those lines on the east side of the lake. Drew them further in and took part of that lake. He drew the north lake the way it is now. And he also took a piece away from Blackduck bridge. They had a line running across there, they had a half mile of that shoreline on the map. And he changed that. Chairman Rice changed it. He stole our land from us. He stole it outright.[70]

Thomas Borgerding was the Catholic priest at Red Lake in 1889, and was present at the negotiations with the U.S. Chippewa Commission. He was deposed as part of the discovery process in a major related Ojibwe land-claims case in 1930. He was a close personal friend and professional colleague of Bishop Martin Marty. His deposition is a powerful affirmation of the understanding that the people of Red Lake have of the theft of the lake:

[The Ojibwe] wanted to keep their lands and be free there and especially the lake. That was repeatedly mentioned and when I read the proceedings later on of the council as they were published by the government I do not remember to have noticed where such stress was laid upon their insisting on the keeping of the lake as their property. There was an old map . . . the Rand-McNally. . . . So they designated the lines as close as they could. They drew them. The Indians made them and the Commissioners agreed on those lines. . . . They were to have those lands indefinitely. Not simply that they were to be held for a short time. . . . There was especially one thing they seemed to be very anxious, they repeated it different times, they wanted to keep their lake intact so that they would have that as their warehouse, as they expressed themselves or at-tas-soh-we-cum-ig, as they called that. That is a word that they used frequently. It means a storehouse or warehouse. . . . It was not as strongly reported as they had done in their speeches. . . . [The map] included the Upper Lake. . . . I know the Indians were very anxious to keep both lakes. All during the deliberations and also in the private conferences they talked about keeping those lakes.

The impression I got was that they were exceeding their powers and on the strength of that one evening after the council was over . . . I went privately to see Mr. Rice and I asked him how he could promise such things to the Indians because evidently no authority was given to him in the Act to promise such things to the Indians. . . . [H]e was evidently embarrassed when I said that to him, embarrassed for an immediate answer. . . . They did not want allotments, very plainly and repeatedly, and that was never taken back.[71]

Bad Day was deposed on August 21, 1930. He testified about his personal observations of the councils with Henry Rice: "The reservation land was defined by the Indians, which way it was to run, and it included both lakes. There wasn't any of the lakes that was to be outside of the reservation. . . . The Chiefs defined the lines. . . . The reservation line was to include all of the lakes. . . . He [Rice] was made to raise his hand to swear and then he said that this land that was reserved was to belong to the Red Lake Indians alone and that their children will have the benefit of it." Joseph C. Roy also testified about the Nelson Act councils. According to Roy, the chiefs said, "We will sign it, that is, if we get this reservation." Rice replied, "Yes, you will get it."[72]

In spite of Rice's probable alteration of the map after the signing, the correspondence about the Nelson Act and treaty documents still made it clear that Red Lake retained all of both lakes. On February 26, 1896, M. R. Baldwin, who chaired the U.S. Chippewa Commission within the Office of Indian Affairs, was as surprised as the Red Lake chiefs that anyone thought to cut off the eastern portion of Upper Red Lake from the reservation. He wrote to Hoke Smith, secretary of the interior, that the claim of the Red Lake Ojibwe to "occupancy of this country is beyond question or doubt. It would seem therefore, that they are right in their demands and entitled to the valuable agricultural and timber lands (some 200,000 acres) now claimed to belong to the Public Domain and occupied by settlers and lumbermen." Although Smith's reference to "this country" might sound ambiguous by itself, within the context of his letters it is obvious that he was speaking specifically to Red Lake ownership of Upper Red Lake, which was not only the primary parcel contested by the Red Lake leadership at the time, but also the section being specifically discussed in his letter.[73]

After the U.S. Chippewa Commission got signatures at Red Lake, the reservation boundaries had to be surveyed and marked. Here too the government made errors in abundance and even committed outright fraud. The verbal agreement with the Chippewa Commission was to establish a reservation of 700,000 acres, but when the surveys were completed, the reservation was only 663,452 acres. John F. Norrish, Minnesota surveyor general, wrote to George A. Burbank, surveyor, in 1891, "I have today consulted with Mr. Rice who made the agreement with the Indians and he states that according to Rand McNally Map which was the basis of their negotiations the Northwest corner of the Lake Is shown to be much farther North." Of course, Rice's response also has to be measured in light of the possibility that he deliberately altered the reservation line on the map and did not want to get caught in a lie or named as an agent of fraud or deception.[74]

Norrish was informed by his field staff that "irregularities are found on line between ranges 43 and 44, through townships 154, 155, and 156. These excessive and defective measurements should have been noted . . . to show that the north boundary of the diminished R.L.I. Reservation is *not* a township line. . . . The errors above noted must be corrected as soon as practicable and should be extended to the eastward."[75]

A resurvey in 1901 uncovered gross negligence and fraud in the survey work. The General Land Office informed the surveyor general, "this shows that the deputy *moved the corner of an accepted survey,* but failed to cover up the fraud by destroying evidence of location of the corner, and by mistake sent in his field notes of the old survey of this Red Lake Indian Reservation. . . . The conclusion must be that the deputy fraudulently moved the reservation boundary corners to suit his convenience. In view of these evidences of gross fraud and incompetency you will notify the deputy that he may have thirty days in which to show cause."[76]

The deputy ignored the directive of the General Land Office. The pace of white settlement was so torrential and the frenzy of the timber boom at Red Lake so profound that nobody stopped it. The commissioners had misrepresented the government's intentions to the Red Lake leadership, altered an agreed-upon map, and reinforced the theft with fraudulent surveys. But no politician wanted to humiliate Henry Rice, revisit the work of the U.S. Chippewa Commission, or investigate, slow, or stop white settlement and timber exploitation. All the financial backers of the railroad, timber, and agricultural industries were directly benefiting from the taking of the lake, as were numerous white settlers. Minnesota Indians were not citizens or constituents of American politicians.

The only recourse for He Who Is Spoken To and the other Red Lake chiefs was to negotiate with the Office of Indian Affairs, which had oversight of the U.S. Chippewa Commission that defrauded them in the first place. The first battle over the taking of the lake had been lost and it was bitterly unfair. But seasoned warriors such as He Who Is Spoken To knew that the battle for the lake had really just begun.

Enter the Pine Barons

Taking the lake was an intentional act designed to enable, accelerate, and legitimize the exploitation of Red Lake timber. The timber business was the biggest and fastest-growing commercial enterprise in the country at the time. Even before Red Lake ceded land as part of the Nelson Act agreement in 1889, the timber business was building and booming legally and illegally all over Red Lake. The Nelson Act uncorked an explosion of harvesting, settlement, millwork, and contracting. At Red Lake, the people and the place were permanently altered.

White homesteading in the freshly ceded lands had to wait for months of survey work, so the government began to open access to Red Lake's timber in other ways as soon as the Ojibwe councils were complete. On October 16, 1889, the president of the United States loosened the authorization for the cutting of dead and down timber at Red Lake. If there was a fire, the tall timber was considered dead and therefore harvestable, even if the trees were still alive. That touched off a flurry of burning and cutting. Every timber company vying for the resource started burning Red Lake's forestland. This practice began long before the Nelson Act was signed, but it accelerated rapidly after the president's executive order. The people of Red Lake received no restitution and had no remedy.

Through exploitation of dead and down timber laws the white harvest of tribal forests grew exponentially: 11 million board feet cut in 1889-90, 15 million in 1890-91, 18 million in 1891-92. All of that cutting was done through dead and down timber laws on acreage torched by nonnative people to enable their harvest. Soon, Congress began to pass laws that allowed cutting timber without going through the time-consuming arson process. Most of that happened through riders to appropriation bills and various congressional acts. Soon whites were cutting 75 million feet per year on Minnesota reservations, especially Red Lake. There was wanton fraud on many levels. Some reservation timber contracts required hiring Indians, but Office of Indian Affairs special agent James Jenkins reported that only 15 percent of the work was being done by Indians.[77]

At Red Lake, pine on ceded lands was valued at $25 to $50 million. The actual worth was even higher, but that was more than enough to encourage all kinds of disregard for tribal people, property, and sovereign rights. Timber companies often hired criminals to work the logging camps, both because there was a serious labor shortage and because it helped advance their economic interests to employ people willing to coerce or force tribal people out of the way if they resisted company work.[78]

The secretary of the interior was responsible for timber surveys. In 1891, John W. Noble authorized the first timber survey at Red Lake, legitimizing harvests already made and calculating the value of timber for future cutting. In 1893, the new secretary of the interior, Hoke Smith, dismissed Noble's report and established a new timber commission. Twenty-seven people worked on the survey and many federal and state politicians—William Bull, Silas Lamoreux, Darwin S. Hall, and Andrew Douglas especially—did what they could to get their people involved in the process. The entire timber survey and investigation devolved into political squabbling and then defunding issues for the timber surveys. The cutting continued unabated.[79]

Red Lake saw a flurry of white business operations. In 1894, Jim and Pat Meehan ran a log-booming business from the Blackduck and Battle Rivers, floating logs to the Red Lake River outlet and then to the Thief River Falls mill (which they owned). The lake teemed with huge steam barges operated by white men, including the *Mudhen, Martin Lally, Jim Meehan, Jim Anderson, Michael Kelly,* and later the *Margarite,* the *Chippewa,* the *Beltrami,* the *Viking,* and the *J. P. Kinney.* In 1899, a railroad was completed up to the high banks for dumping logs into Lower Red Lake to be floated down to Crookston. The largest of the colossal barges shuffled up to a million feet of logs across Lower Red Lake.[80]

In 1896, new legislation delineated procedures for timber sales by advertised auction and sealed private bid. Timber companies pushed more auction venues and smaller minimum parcel sizes to make oversight more difficult because of the sheer volume of transactions.

Even though millions of acres were being cut, they were often bid for in tiny forty-acre parcels.

The people of Red Lake, however, were not profiting from the cutting of their pine. Thomas J. Morgan wrote, "Although surrounded by pine forests, they have not boards enough to make coffins for the dead. Their houses are in dilapidated condition, and for the want of material cannot be repaired." Although the Indians owned the land, whites controlled the timber resources, and they did not share the profits. Exploitation was so shameless and rampant that some politicians began to push back against the powerful timber lobby. In 1897, the government disallowed commercial cutting on dead and down timber, forcing the dead and down harvest to be allotted through small contracts with native laborers. The effect of the law was to encourage white timber speculators to set fires and then establish contracts with the Indians to cut the timber.[81]

By 1897, the Nelson Act land surveys and homesteading had allowed so much white land ownership and timber contracting that the need for dead and down timber laws to exploit the resource went into decline. Dead and down cutting did continue after the legal change in 1897, largely because it was the most expedient way to access the timber within the main reservation. So did the arson fires. In 1898, 4.5 million board feet of dead and down timber were cut at Red Lake on contracts executed before the legal change. Other forms of timber harvest continued to escalate during the same time period.[82]

The railroad was extended to Fosston in 1892, bringing government freight in while logs went out. The roads between Fosston and Red Lake were busy with white traffic to and from the reservation. In 1898, the Minneapolis, Red Lake, and Manitoba Railroad was built from Nebish to Red Lake, a distance of nine miles. It was extended to Bemidji in 1905. The sole purpose for the construction of this railroad was the movement of timber. Nearly 55,000 tons of logs were freighted over the rail line for the Thomas B. Walker and Shevlin-Carpenter lumber companies in the first year. John and Lester Van House also ran logs, supplies, and people by horse on a line from Red Lake to Solway. The timber network impacted all aspects of life at Red Lake.[83]

Attending the auctions and profiting considerably from Red Lake timber were many of Minnesota's famous timber tycoons and well-known local fortune seekers. They often colluded at auctions to keep prices low. Much of the Red Lake timber was auctioned in Crookston, where the Weyerhaeuser, Shevlin, Wright, Davis, and Meehan family patriarchs took turns as the sole bidders for vast tracts of land, one parcel at a time, until hundreds of thousands of acres of timber had been disposed of as cheaply as possible. John G. Morrison Jr., a businessman and Office of Indian Affairs official at Red Lake, recalled: "They decided to divide it up. C. A. Smith would take this area; Weyerhaeuser would take this area; Crookston this one; Grand Forks this one; and Meehan Brothers of the Thief River Falls Lumber Company this one. After this deal, when any tract of land was offered it was bid on only by the firm having it in its agreed area." Many cuts were auctioned or privately bid at half the price recorded for dead and down timber prior to the Nelson Act. Entire townships were bid without contest.[84]

The appointment of David R. Francis and then Cornelius N. Bliss as secretary of the interior (in 1896 and 1897) unleashed a torrent of evidence about the timber fraud, most of which is included in each year's Commissioner of Indian Affairs Report. Senator Cushman K. Davis and Representative Loren Fletcher were in frequent communication with Thomas H. Shevlin, a local timber speculator, and Silas Lamoreux, commissioner of the General Land Office (1893–97), about timber bids, appraisal teams, and other land and timber speculation issues. The collusion of interests is impossible to ignore. To be certain, Davis, Shevlin, and Fletcher shared financial interests that benefited from the political actions of Davis and Fletcher and the oversight (or lack of it) from various commissioners of Indian affairs and the General Land Office. The Nicholas-Chisholm and Wild Rice lumber companies colluded with one another to fix bid prices for timber for a period of several years with the full knowledge of each commissioner of Indian affairs.

The dead and down timber exploitation and arson fires were so widespread at Red Lake that the government had no choice but to launch a formal investigation. On March 1, 1899, the Indian Appropriation Act ordered an investigation into timber fraud at Red Lake. Secretary of the interior Ethan A. Hitchcock put a temporary moratorium on cutting at Red Lake starting on March 30, 1899. That put considerable pressure on the investigators to finish their work quickly so everyone could get back to logging.[85]

A second investigation into collusion and fraud was authorized in 1902, but had no more success than the first one because the Office of Indian Affairs did not have the stomach to investigate itself or the General Land Office, and after acquiring affidavits from several timber speculators stating that they had not committed fraud, everyone was acquitted and the investigation was formally abandoned. The investigation brought no remedy to the people of Red Lake. Timber cutting continued at the same pace.

While the rate of white timber harvesting at Red Lake grew and grew, so did the pace of white settlement and political development in the northland. The official white population of Red Lake County went from zero in 1889 to 12,195 by 1900. Beltrami County, which comprises a significant portion of the Red Lake reservation, was established in 1897. Minnesota's white population went from 6,000 in 1850 to 172,000 in 1860, to 1.3 million in 1890, and to 1.8 million in 1900. White settlement and political expansion kept oxygenating the fire of economic activity around Red Lake timber.[86]

It took decades to focus any attention on arson fires. In 1912, the government finally appropriated funds for fire prevention. Three lookout towers were built at Red Lake. Nathan J. Head, a Red Lake enrollee who worked sporadically for the Indian agency, became Red Lake's first forest ranger and continued in that position for another five years. His work did slow the rate of arson at Red Lake.[87]

Minnesota politicians and businessmen were still trying to find ways to get at Red Lake timber in the World War I era. A major congressional report stated that Red Lake still had "the finest stand of white pine that has ever grown on God's footstool." Knute Nelson was still leading the effort. His success at opening up Red Lake lands for white settlement and logging won him financial backing for his political career and lots of love from the white folk flooding into Red Lake's ceded lands to set up farms. Nelson had completed his terms as U.S. representative and governor of Minnesota, and he had been U.S. senator since 1895.[88]

On January 7, 1915, Senator Nelson introduced legislation to convert a large piece of the Red Lake reservation into a national forest so it could be managed by the federal government instead of by tribal leaders. This would allow it to be systematically cut, as had been done at Leech Lake. The bill stalled out in the first session, but slipped through in the next as an attachment to the Indian Appropriation Act, creating the Red Lake Indian Forest. The only objection to the legislation was from an Illinois legislator who pointed out that the cession was without tribal consent and in direct opposition to every stated position of the tribal chiefs in the congressional record. His objection had little effect.[89]

Creating the Red Lake Indian Forest altered power dynamics because it allowed the transfer of titles and execution of timber contracts at the discretion of the secretary of the interior. The creation of a national forest does not protect the timber from being cut. Only national parks do that, and only fairly recently in their history. The creation of national forests simply puts those forests under management of the U.S. Forest Service, through auspices of the Department of the Interior. More than 107,000 acres of Red Lake land were transferred to the Red Lake Indian Forest by 1916. That enabled the government to manage the cutting of timber on those lands without interference from Red Lake's chiefs. There can be no mistake about the intention of the legislation, which read: "Said forest shall be administered by the Secretary of the Interior in accordance with the principles of scientific forestry, with a view to the production of successive timber crops thereon, and he is hereby authorized to sell and manufacture . . . pine and oak." The chiefs would not administer the resource or the proceeds. The creation of the forest was about sustained harvest, not environmental protection. By 1952, more than 207 million board feet of timber were cut from the Red Lake Indian Forest.[90]

A host of lumbermen, foresters, government officials, and non-native businessmen again came to survey Red Lake's timberland. In 1917, a liberal contract was awarded to the International Lumber Company, classifying 80 percent of the timber as dead and down—a gross misrepresentation that enabled the company to pad its take, with the support of the secretary of the interior. That year, the company clear-cut 105,042,800 board feet under the new contract on the south shore of Lower Red Lake. The timber was hauled by sleigh to the Minnesota, Red Lake, and Manitoba rail line and sent to Bemidji, and then on to International Falls via the Northern Pacific. After the cutting, the profiteering of middlemen, and the settlement of accounts, a fraction of the proceeds were deposited to the Red Lake trust account. No consent was given by Red Lake's leadership or its citizens. The law was justified as a means to better the condition of Red Lake Indians, but its effect was to enrich the lumbermen.[91]

He Who Is Spoken To knew that there was no way to keep the timber predators away from Red Lake's forests, so he worked with the other chiefs to make sure that the people of Red Lake profited from the logging and millwork as much as possible. The Red Lake tribal mill was not properly maintained after 1880, and after 1889 most of the work was subcontracted to nonnative mills. In 1899, Captain William A. Mercer, acting agent for Leech Lake Agency, which had oversight of Red Lake, recommended the construction of a new mill at Red Lake. After years of lobbying, the Red Lake mill at Shell Lake was abandoned and a much larger facility was constructed at Red Lake in 1907. It was able to mill more than 1 million board feet every year.[92]

The entire logging business was a great frustration to the chiefs. When they allowed cutting on the reservation, about two-thirds of the timber sale proceeds were routinely directed to cover the costs of cutting, milling, and administration of operations, much of it going off the reservation to nonnative contractors and loggers. Only about a third ended up being deposited into accounts for the benefit of the Red Lake people. This rate did improve some in the early 1900s because the frenzy of timber speculation started to slow across the region, as evidenced by the very detailed reports to the commissioner of Indian affairs.[93]

Compounding their frustration with the system and its formulas was the growing network of white business interests that operated with a belief that the chiefs and their people were obstacles to white economic expansion rather than human beings with legitimate vested interests in the land and its resources. Every time the chiefs turned their heads, someone had found a new way to undermine their authority or get at their land's resources. In 1904, a major windstorm leveled acres of trees around Ponemah. The Office of Indian Affairs sent word to local contractors, most of them nonnative, to help with the cleanup. They carried off and milled 23 million board feet of timber. In 1905, another blowdown resulted in 18 million board feet of special cutting. There were some Indians who worked the cuts, and some of the millwork was done at Red Lake, but none of the operation was conducted with the advice or consent of the chiefs, and most of the money was funneled off of the reservation.[94]

The timber harvest at Red Lake was huge, and it was all enabled by the Nelson Act. Prior to the Nelson Act, the cut and mill rate for Red Lake was never above 1 million board feet. From 1889 to 1906, Red Lake reported an average annual cut of 16 million board feet. A group of forestry students from the University of Minnesota came to Red Lake in 1909 and conducted a timber survey; they estimated there was an additional 125 million board feet of readily harvestable timber on the reservation. The pressure on Red Lake's land and timber would continue for many decades.[95]

By 1900, the timber industry in Minnesota employed 20,000 loggers. Minneapolis became the world's largest lumber market, and three of the four largest mills in the United States were in Minnesota. The population explosion in Minnesota was driven in large part by the timber industry. With incredible fortitude and resilience, He Who Is Spoken To and the chiefs at Red Lake did what they could to redirect and shape the pressure on their people, land, and resources.[96]

The Western Townships

He Who Is Spoken To passed away in 1898 at the age of ninety-one. He was an excellent peacetime leader who was forced to lead in a time of diplomatic conflict. In that effort, he had wisdom, insight, and stamina beyond his years. Without his advocacy and influence, Red Lake likely would have suffered a far more devastating loss of land through allotment. A baptized Episcopalian, he was buried at the cemetery behind the Church of St. Antipas in Redby. Henry Whipple purchased his marble headstone, whether from a sense of duty, love, or guilt is hard to know. The headstone, shaped as an oak cross, bore the inscription, "In memory of Madwaganonint, Head Chief of the Red Lake Indians, always faithful and true. He has gone to his reward."[97]

Perpetual Wind (Gabe-noodin), He Who Is Spoken To's son, and Moose Dung's son Red Robed now had to shoulder the chief's burden. The pressure on Red Lake's land was as intense as it had been at any time in He Who Is Spoken To's life. The people lost a lot of land,

Perpetual Wind, 1900

but they gained a great deal of knowledge from him about how to fight this ancient battle against new adversaries, and now with new leaders.

The Red Lake survey fraud was so pervasive that it still plagues contemporary survey work across Minnesota, even many miles away from the reservation and ceded lands. After 1889, surveyors working off of erroneous corner section markers from Red Lake misaligned and cut off townships and private land parcels, leaving two contradictory survey posts in different parts of the same sections all over northern Minnesota.

The Nelson Act surveys cut off not only a huge section of Upper Red Lake, but a large section of Lower Red Lake as well. The timber there was promptly logged off. Loggers and Indians, operating with completely different understandings of boundaries, were in a state of perpetual tension. The Office of Indian Affairs advised President Harrison to defuse the situation and avoid a violent incident. (They may also have worried that a court case could validate Red Lake's claim to all of both lakes.) Henry Rice also recommended that all of

Lower Red Lake be kept in the reservation. His statement led the commissioner of Indian affairs to request a retrocession for "justice and necessity." On November 21, 1892, Harrison issued an executive order to restore acreage wrongly cut off from the reservation around Lower Red Lake. The restoration was a gross under-correction that served to avoid immediate conflict but did not affirm the boundary as it was understood by the chiefs at Red Lake. The under-correction was an issue in Red Lake's subsequent forestry court case and the still-unresolved land issues stemming from the Nelson Act.[98]

Efforts to enable private white access to Red Lake lands continued for decades after the Nelson Act. On April 17, 1900, legislators pushed through special legislation to approve a new railroad, telephone, and telegraph easement across five townships of tribal land at the mouth of the Baudette River along the Rainy River. There was no effort to consult with tribal leaders or obtain their consent. In 1901, the congressional appropriation bill included an amendment that allowed the sale of reservation lands without treaties, presidential orders, or congressional commissions, but simply via independent negotiations. The legislative change was an elaborate circumvention of the protections for Red Lake lands in the Nelson Act.[99]

In 1902, rapid white settlement led to political changes, including the creation of new counties and the subdivision of counties into new townships. Two full townships and three fractional ones were created in Clearwater County inside the boundaries of the Red Lake reservation. This was a simple organizational act that did not involve land loss (although those who engineered it hoped and planned for the future allotment of the reservation), but it was all accomplished unbeknownst to the Red Lake leadership. This might seem like a trivial municipal division, but it was the beginning of a long process of dividing Red Lake lands into gerrymandered minority districts within the county system. Red Lakers were not U.S. citizens and did not even have the right to vote yet, but they were being politically pieced out decades before such developments. The goal at that time was to ease the acquisition of their land, but it later helped to ensure their political marginalization and disempowerment.[100]

While private and municipal interests moved to strengthen their political and economic positions, the U.S. government again came after Red Lake land. The impetus this time was from private white citizens, and it was enabled by the 1901 appropriation bill's provision allowing independent sales of Red Lake land. On January 30, 1902, Frank H. Kratka, mayor of Thief River Falls, traveled to Washington, DC. There were roughly two thousand whites living at Thief River Falls at that time, and the white population had eclipsed the tribal population at Moose Dung's old village site.

Red Robed, Moose Dung's son, tried to preserve his father's legacy and protect Ojibwe interests. He sometimes introduced himself as Moose Dung the Younger. The logging and agricultural businesses allayed against Red Robed were formidable. The Ojibwe land there was not held in common by all tribal members with the rest of Red Lake's land. It was a private parcel owned by Moose Dung, and then Red Robed after Moose Dung died. Starting in 1891, Red Robed leased and later sold off chunks of the Thief River homeland one small piece at a time, using the proceeds to purchase food and help the Ojibwe at Thief River Falls survive.[101]

Patrick and James Meehan leased a section of Moose Dung's land grant from Red Robed in 1891 and set up a sawmill. In 1894, the same section was also leased to Ray W. Jones, creating a major conflict between Jones and the Meehans. Red Robed did not understand all of the legal language and the white settlers were moving so fast that they often did not bother speaking to one another or examining all of the contracts being put in front of Red Robed to sign. Jones and the Meehans both wanted to work sawmills on Red Robed's land. Their contest eventually went all the way to the U.S. Supreme Court, which decided on October 30, 1899, that the Meehans had the superior claim because the land was private land, not tribal land, and afforded no special status or legal protection. Red Robed testified in the case, saying: "I did not have anything to do with making a lease of a part of a section of land to Ray W. Jones of Minneapolis, Mr. Kellog [sic] used his own words, and read it to me, he asked me if I wanted to lease my land to build a sawmill on, for twenty years he told me he would give me $200.00 a year, I just listened to him and never said a word back. I did not consent to that proposition."[102]

The Ojibwe were increasingly desperate for food, whites were hungry for their land, and Moose Dung's land grant at Thief River became taxable. Red Robed was hard-pressed to hold on to his father's land grant. In 1895, he began to sell portions of it. By the time

Mayor Kratka set out to get the last of the land at Thief River Falls and extend white settlement deeper into Red Lake's unceded reservation lands, most of Moose Dung's section had already been sold.

When Kratka went to Washington, most of the Ojibwe residents at Thief River Falls had been moved to Red Lake, Little Rock, Redby, Ponemah, or Warroad. Some stayed at Thief River, and a few others married into or sought refuge with white families in the original Old Crossing region.

Kratka got an appointment with Ethan A. Hitchcock, secretary of the interior. He wanted the government to obtain a formal land cession of Red Robed's remaining acreage and an additional eleven townships of Red Lake agricultural land on the western section of the reservation. Kratka succeeded in getting Hitchcock to appoint a special inspector to negotiate for the land cession. There was little resistance from bureaucrats, politicians, or white citizens. The mayor had letters from every Minnesota congressman and U.S. senators Moses E. Clapp and Knute Nelson in support of his proposal. Clapp won a special election in 1900 to replace Cushman K. Davis, who died in office. Davis was a major proponent of railroad and timber businesses, and Clapp was just as eager and well supported by those same lobbies.[103]

The only contest to the proposed legislation came from the state of Minnesota, which brought suit not to protect Red Lake or its land rights, but to claim that the state's survey work showed that the state, and not the federal government, held jurisdiction and land ownership around Thief River. The case was dismissed. Thanks to the 1901 appropriations bill, Congress did not need to authorize a commission or make any effort to treat for Red Lake land; this action was entirely orchestrated by the Office of Indian Affairs (OIA) at the request of Kratka. On February 10, 1902, the OIA sent James McLaughlin to negotiate the land cession with the Red Lake leadership. McLaughlin was a career employee of the OIA and was already notorious for having ordered the arrest of Sitting Bull in which the Lakota chief was murdered. McLaughlin arrived on March 4, 1902, and opened council with the Red Lake chiefs at the Red Lake Agency building.[104]

Peter Graves served as interpreter, along with Joseph C. Roy and C. W. Morrison. Graves was a young and well-educated mixed blood. He worked for the government in 1902, but he was also looking out for Red Lake interests. His unique role as an insider with both the

Ojibwe community and the government enabled him to influence the tribal diplomatic position and the means of delivering it. Graves helped the chiefs prepare a list of requests in the form of a formal petition. This shift from verbal to written communication marked an intentional communication strategy for the chiefs that would eventually propel them to orchestrate even greater internal tribal political transformation.

The chiefs were hopeful that the council would provide a meaningful opportunity to redress numerous grievances. They presented McLaughlin with a litany of government wrongs—survey fraud and error, illegal timber harvesting on tribal land, land classifications (timber and agricultural land were priced differently), mismanagement of tribal trust funds, whites fishing on Red Lake, and especially the theft of part of Upper Red Lake. Tribal leaders were also worried that the government wanted to allot the rest of Red Lake. White Earth now owned only seven percent of its own reservation. Red Lakers did not want a similar fate.[105]

Perpetual Wind and Red Robed did most of the talking for Red Lake. Red Robed complained bitterly about the Chipmunk (Senator Knute Nelson). Red Robed had met with Nelson in Washington to address land issues at Red Lake in 1899, but according to Red Robed, "He would not give me an answer. He simply walked out of the office without his hat. I am looking for an answer." The chiefs pressed McLaughlin for remedies and protections. They refused any overture for allotment. McLaughlin responded, "I am not here to force allotments upon you people, although I know it would be for your own good." Stands Forever was blunt with McLaughlin: "The reservation that will be left after we cede the western portion, we want it to be an Indian reservation for all time to come, and that we shall never be required to take allotments within the boundary thereof."[106]

McLaughlin offered little rectification. He stipulated a price of $1.25 per acre for reservation land and offered to double the size of allotments. He asked the Red Lakers to cede 256,152 acres for $1 million with 25 percent paid immediately and the rest in installments for fifteen years. The chiefs were wary of government officials from long experience. The presence of more than one hundred warriors at the councils reminded everyone that the entire tribe was paying close attention.

The chiefs were evolving their diplomatic style. They developed a thirteen-point petition that they wanted addressed in any new agreement. It is probably the clearest articulation of the Red Lake position in any of their agreements with the U.S. government. Their critical points included holding the diminished reservation in common, no cutting of timber on the reservation without tribal consent, no allotments, no railroad inside the reservation, no construction of dams, tribal power to control enrollment, tribal power to control residency, tribal control of their trust funds, and all financial issues to be brought before the Court of Claims for redress.

Two other stipulations spoke directly to the evolving identity of the Red Lake people. Their eleventh petition item stated: "After all the pine timber on the ceded lands of our reservation under the act of 1889 has been cut, making the waterways for the removal of the timber no longer necessary, the waterways for commercial purposes within our reservation to be closed." Red Lake wanted to reassert tribal control over its land and water.[107]

The twelfth item in the petition was important too: "this reservation, heretofore known as Red Lake and Pembina Band of Chippewa to be changed so as to be hereafter known as the Red Lake Chippewa, as all Pembina of this reservation have become Red Lake Indians by intermarriage or long residence." Both residence and marriage helped acculturate and assimilate the Pembina Ojibwe into Red Lake families and identities. Now the chiefs who represented Ojibwe from Thief River, Pembina, Red Lake, Little Rock, and Warroad all intended to live in the same place and wanted to be known simply as Red Lakers.[108]

For the families still living at Thief River Falls and in the eleven townships being considered for cession, this was a difficult time, and McLaughlin played a hard hand. They asked what would happen if they stayed at Thief River, and McLaughlin told them that allotments could be made, and their treaty payments would be offset and reduced. Most Red Lakers voiced distrust of any reduction in benefits or sale proceeds; moreover, they were certain that the government would not protect them. Thief River Falls was swarming with white settlers who had little respect for Indians or their homes.

He Who Treads the Earth from the South told McLaughlin: "I have a grave out at my place. I did not want the white man to disregard the grave. I came up here from there some time ago, and a Norwegian set my house on fire and burned it up. The only thing I have there now is the little garden that I had when I had my house. I don't want to stay over there. I want to come here." He Who Treads the Earth from the South loved his land at Thief River Falls, but he hated the perpetual state of fear, the lack of protection for his family and his property, and the avarice of white settlers.[109]

Arrangements were made to move the 129 Ojibwe still living at Thief River to Red Lake, including exhuming the remains of family members for reinternment on the diminished reservation. Private land grants were promised to two families that wanted to stay off the reservation in their ancestral village at Warroad. John KaKay-Geesick (Gaagige-giizhig, or Everlasting Sky), his brother Sturgeon Leaf (Namebag), and Little Raven (Gaagaagiins) were each to receive one-hundred-acre plots.[110]

The chiefs were pleased that most of their terms were heard and agreed upon. They signed the agreement on March 17, 1902. Perpetual Wind (age sixty-seven) and Red Robed (age seventy) signed first, followed by Striped Day (Beshi-giizhig), Sits Alone, Praying Day, Changing Feathers, and Stands Forever. Peter Graves and Joseph Roy, who worked for the government as interpreters, also signed as Red Lake Indians. A total of 220 Red Lake men signed the agreement.[111]

James McLaughlin took the agreement and signature roll and submitted everything to Ethan A. Hitchcock, who then directed William A. Jones, commissioner of Indian affairs, to draft a bill for the legislature. On March 28, 1902, only eleven days after the conclusion of the council at Red Lake, Congress was considering a bill for the cession of Red Lake's western townships.

Senator Moses E. Clapp consolidated the council log, correspondence, and agreement, added them to the congressional record, and argued for the bill. It passed in the Senate on April 18, 1902, and then in the House of Representatives on May 8, 1902. It bogged down in committee afterward as various politicians wrangled over appropriating money for the agreed-upon land purchase. Some favored no appropriation, instead proposing to sell the land to homesteaders and pay Red Lake out of the proceeds. In 1903, this procedure was passed without amendment or objection—but it required tribal consent.

McLaughlin again traveled to Red Lake to tell the tribal leaders that the deal they had negotiated with the government had been changed. They would not receive money for the land ceded up front as agreed. They would have to wait until it was sold off to whites one small parcel at a time, and the process would likely take decades to complete. Red Robed and other chiefs were furious. If McLaughlin spoke for the "great father," how could the agreement he made be rejected by the "great father"? The new agreement also called for Red Lake to give the state of Minnesota twenty-two sections of land for schools, an additional land cession without agreement or satisfactory compensation. The chiefs, who considered that the terms had already been negotiated and agreed to in good faith, refused to consent to a different arrangement.[112]

Senator Moses E. Clapp and Representative Halvor Steenerson were not going to let Red Lake keep its land just because the chiefs had a problem with the government's changing the agreement. Clapp pushed through another bill to extinguish Red Lake title to the eleven townships and it won easy passage in the Senate. On February 5, 1904, Representative Steenerson came out of his congressional committee with a substitute bill that no longer required tribal consent. It provided for the land cession previously agreed to but stripped out all of the other hard-won terms the chiefs had negotiated. Article 4 even stipulated the continued right to allotment for Red Lake Indians, meaning that the chiefs would have to keep fighting that battle even after having clearly refused allotments in 1889 and again in 1902. On February 20, 1904, commissioner of Indian affairs William A. Jones wrote an editorial in defense of the legislation, arguing that the consent of Indians at Red Lake should not be required for the sale of their land.[113]

The terms Red Lake agreed to in 1902 were never honored; now they had to contend with the ones imposed in 1904 even after formally rejecting them. No payments were forthcoming, and they had to keep fighting pressure to allot their unceded land. The Ojibwe people living at Moose Dung's old village site now had to move to Red Lake. Rudolph Berg, a young Norwegian settler fluent in Ojibwe, translated for Red Robed's people as they identified graves for exhumation at Thief River Falls and reburial at Red Lake. Joseph Duchamp was paid $14.50 per body for the dig work. All remains were loaded on a shallow river barge, the *Dan Patch,* and brought up to Red Lake.

Nobody knows exactly what happened to the bodies, but they were not all properly buried on the reservation as agreed. Francis Blake (Waabi-giniw, or White Eagle) wrote about the event in his book *We Have the Right to Exist* (which he published with his Ojibwe name spelled Wub-e-ke-niew). He believed that the bodies were dumped at Frogs' Bridge for convenience because the barge could not navigate the shallow upper reaches of the Red Lake River. Today, Red Lakers call the Frogs' Bridge area Silent City.[114]

The auctions began at Thief River Falls on June 20, 1904, and continued there, at Crookston, and other locations until the ceded land was sold off. As soon as white settlers moved in, they started pushing the Indians out. In 1908, Knut Austin wrote that Red Lakers "annoy the settlers by hunting and killing all kinds of game in and out of season: that they shoot moose, ducks, and trap mink . . . they gather the berries, such as cranberries." Enforcement of private property rights for white settlers came swift and hard. Many Red Lakers were arrested and charged with trespass or violation of state game laws.[115]

One of the primary reasons the Red Lakers refused to consent to the amended agreement was the difficulty they predicted in being paid. Those fears proved well founded. The Red Lake trust fund netted $1,265,000 in land-sale proceeds from the land cession, spread over a sustained period of time. It was a long struggle for the tribe to get access to its money while it was held in trust by the federal government. All the while, the Red Lake people struggled as they adapted to life with less land to harvest on and increasing poverty.

Eventually, local residents at Thief River tried to acknowledge the taking of the land and commemorate Moose Dung and Red Robed. In 1976, a plaque and statue of Moose Dung were erected at Thief River Falls in an event attended by local white citizens and Red Lake tribal officials.[116]

Ongoing Land Pressure after the Nelson Act

The reservation at Red Lake got smaller after 1904. The Red Lake Ojibwe now retained 636,964 acres of their nearly 20 million–acre land base. The chiefs held on, and successfully avoided allotment on the main reservation. The government kept trying, but the chiefs' resilience on that issue was one of the most significant victories for Red

Lake in the entire treaty period. Nevertheless, businesses, churches, schools, and government officials did find other ways to get at Red Lake land within the diminished reservation.

The process of white land acquisition inside the reservation was ongoing for several years prior to the 1904 land cession, and accelerated afterward. On June 25, 1897, Thomas H. Shevlin, president of the St. Hilaire Lumber Company, obtained permission from the Office of Indian Affairs to build a temporary logging railroad across the reservation. St. Hilaire then contracted with the Halvorson-Richards Company to log the reservation—without contract, letter of permission, or legislative approval. It employed more than a hundred workmen from Chicago at the township of Nebish that summer. The railway was completed to the Red Lake landing by December 1898. John Lind served as governor of Minnesota from 1899 to 1901. While in office, Lind worked his political connections to advance railroad interests; afterward, the railroad returned the favors.[117]

In June 1904, John Lind (former governor of Minnesota), C. A. Smith (timber tycoon), and Andreas Ueland (Lind's former law partner and now a judge) assumed embedded controlling financial interests in the Minneapolis, Red Lake, and Manitoba Railroad Company and used their power to create the Red Lake Transportation Company. They set the hub for the railroad in Bemidji and completed the north spur all the way to Redby by 1906. The spur had 33.5 miles of track with a long trestle directly into Red Lake and included construction of a modern depot. Their plans did not stop there. An entire half section of land at the village of Redby was platted specifically for the white-owned railroad company's private ownership.[118]

The business parties pushing for the Redby land grants for the railroad did a lot of work with politicians to get the railroad expansion approved and obtain the land cession from Red Lake. They succeeded in getting legislative approval for the cession on April 8, 1904, followed by endorsement of the Indian agent on April 26, 1904. But the Office of Indian Affairs denied their land patent in June over political squabbles, so they had to start all over. A new piece of legislation on February 8, 1905, successfully sailed through and got the white railroad company a 320-acre private land cession and right-of-way through Red Lake lands.[119]

This arrangement gave C. A. Smith a huge advantage in cost margins for transporting timber and getting first access and best net price for clear-cutting Red Lake. The Crookston Lumber Company, which operated in Red Lake's ceded land in the Red River Valley, continued to compete, but it protested loudly. The Great Northern Railway developed a spur line at Wilton all the way to Island Lake in 1905, but Smith's direct line to Red Lake was catching most of the direct business. In 1910, Alfred L. Molander, another major timber contractor and subsidiary of C. A. Smith, took over administration of the Redby rail line. In response, the Crookston Lumber Company surveyed for its own railroad, the Wilton and Northern. It took over the spur line from Wilton to Island Lake on the old Great Northern route. Railroad was faster and more efficient, lost less timber, and was a more expeditious way to get lumber to market than transporting logs on lakes and rivers. So much money was being made off of timber at Red Lake that it was worth it for private logging companies to build private railroads at their own expense.

In 1912, the Red Lake line still won most of the timber traffic and the Crookston Lumber Company reconciled with the competition. There was money enough to bury the bad feelings between them— still at the expense of the Red Lake people and the environment. In 1916, 50 million board feet of timber were cut at Red Lake in contract by John Moberg and shipped through the Red Lake line to Bemidji and then to Cass Lake for milling. Even smaller mill and boom operations were overwhelmed with business. Turtle Lake, north of Bemidji, got so full of logs that the entire lake was covered from shore to shore. It took months to process and ship all the timber.

Once the timber was harvested, the logging companies began to sell their acreage, starting in the late 1800s but very actively in the 1910s. Intermediaries such as the Solway Land Company routinely sold land to white settlers for two to five dollars per acre. J. J. Opsahl was an early real-estate mogul in the northland, moving white settlers into new tracts and facilitating property transfers. Soon the diminished Red Lake reservation was an island surrounded by a sea of white settlement. In 1920, a congressional report said that Red Lake was different from all other Ojibwe reservations in Minnesota because it had avoided allotment, there was no white settlement on the diminished reservation, and few Indians were farming. Avoiding allotment on the reservation was a testament to Red Lake resilience, but also served as a call to action for the already busy land, timber, and missionary efforts directed at Red Lake.[120]

From the Nelson Act to World War I, politicians like Halvor Steenerson focused not only on getting Red Lake's land and timber resources but on simultaneously transforming the entire ecosystem and natural environment at Red Lake. It started on May 15, 1896, when lands ceded in the Nelson Act were opened for white settlement. Settlers flocked to Bemidji, Thief River Falls, Crookston, Roseau, Warroad, Blackduck, Red Lake Falls, and the other border towns around Red Lake from all over the United States and several European countries. A 1896 homestead circular read: "To qualify as a homesteader, the person needs to be head of a family or over 21 years of age, and a citizen of the U.S. or at least have filed a Declaration of Intent to become a citizen." There were so many white squatters and sooners that the *Crookston Times* ran an article with the headline, "NOW GIT! That Is What Uncle Sam Says to Red Lake Sooners." A tidal wave of white settlement enveloped Red Lake. White settlers anticipated finding the same rich land white farmers had obtained in the Old Crossing land rushes, but the 1889 ceded lands were largely wetlands and swamps that were not well suited for agricultural development. The Crookston Land Office handled the first several bundles of sales of ceded Red Lake timber and farmland. Soon struggling white settlers were calling for dramatic public action to make the swamps tillable farmland.[121]

Halvor Steenerson was happy to champion their cause. Red Lake insistence in the 1902 petition that no dams be built at Red Lake was completely ignored. In 1904, Steenerson introduced legislation to build a dam at Red Lake and spend more than $1 million to drain the swamps north of Red Lake for farming. He even proposed a massive ditching and dam development to drop the lake level by eight feet.[122]

In 1904, he addressed Congress: "I have a bill pending before the Committee on Food Control to get permission to build a dam at the outlet of the Red Lake and to drain those lands. If we get a proper outlet for those lands, the lands . . . will be most valuable. They are the richest lands in the world. . . . We have organized a drainage district which will spend over a million dollars."[123]

Many settlers hoped Steenerson and other politicians would enable them to farm and increase the value of their newly acquired parcels.

They petitioned for both ditches and homesteads and got them. By 1909, ditching efforts were under way throughout Red Lake's ceded lands, digging hundreds of miles of ditches to drain the great bogs. All of Thief Lake was drained. White land prospectors were brought by boat across Red Lake up the Tamarac and Red Lake Rivers to scout sites. Today, that would be a violation of sovereignty, but it was common practice then. Soon Beltrami County held more than $3 million in ditch bond debt to pay for all the effort. Many white farms were lost in tax forfeiture.[124]

In 1918, A. D. Johnson became Beltrami County auditor and reported: "When I took office as auditor in 1918 quite a bit of land north of Red Lake had become tax-delinquent, and the future of that country did not look good. Ditches were still being constructed because there were still many advocates and enthusiasts. Before the ditching ceased Beltrami County had about 1400 miles of ditch . . . of no value to anyone." In fact, they were trying to drain a swamp more than three times the size of the state of Rhode Island. The task was environmentally impossible and financially grotesque. Up to 1917, not a single request for ditching work was refused or delayed. Across the ceded lands, 1,507 miles of ditches were dug, with more than $3 million in bonds and another $3 million in liens, with an annual tax forfeiture rate of 15 percent by 1918. By 1927, only ten years later, 77 percent of the white homesteads in the ceded lands failed and went into tax forfeiture. By 1931, the foreclosure rate was 90 percent. In 1933, Red Lake leaders were still fighting to stop drainage efforts, including a massive dam and drainage project on the Red Lake outlet.

Although people on and off the reservation today think of Red Lake as a "closed reservation," from 1889 to 1918 Red Lake was swarming with nonnative activity. Steamboats operated all over the lake, and hundreds of white loggers, mill workers, steamboat operators, farmers, and service personnel lived, worked, and did business at Red Lake. There were many stores in Red Lake for groceries, farming implements, and supplies. Red Lake village was a supply hub and travel stop for numerous white settlers heading to the Old Crossing settlement area, the Red River Valley, and the ceded lands, as well as transient workers in the timber business on the newly ceded lands. By the early 1890s, several hotels operated in the village of Red Lake and did a lively business, including ones owned by Joseph C. Roy,

William R. Spears, John George Morrison Sr., and Selam Fairbanks.
Most of the hotel owners also operated stores in Red Lake. Dan Needham Sr. recalled:

> I think it was 1904 when I first went to Bemidji. You could still see
> stumps in the streets, you know. It wasn't all cleared yet.
>
> Red Lake used to be the main town for this area. People going through
> in all directions, settlers, they'd stop in Red Lake for their supplies. That
> used to be their main stopping place.
>
> Red Lake was a bigger town than it is now. A little livelier. We had
> three hotels in town. Five grocery stores and one clothing store, a barber
> shop.
>
> The hotels were always filled with traveling salesmen. They'd supply
> the stores. And all the settlers around the country would go to Red Lake
> to buy their stuff.

Red Lake even got a movie theater in 1918.[125]

Red Lake was a frequent tourist destination for white settlers and
area visitors. The Red Lake and Manitoba Railway Company, which
operated the line to Redby, arranged frequent pleasure trips to Red
Lake. In the early 1900s they ran every Sunday, usually attended by
as many as two hundred people. Attendees got a round-trip rail fare
and a day on Lower Red Lake in one of the two-story steam barges,
including tours of the Redby town site, Sandy River outlet, and the
west end.[126]

White occupancy, business, and tourist use of Lower Red Lake
and tribal lands across the reservation slowed a little bit when Peter
Graves helped develop the General Council of the Red Lake Band of
Chippewa Indians in 1918, which enabled the Ojibwe to assert more
self-governance. But the land and water at Red Lake was not really
controlled by Indians until after the 1934 Indian Reorganization Act,
and by some measures not until after Red Lake established a new
constitution in 1958. That does not diminish the status of the tribe in
any way; it makes their success at reclaiming their space afterward
all the more impressive.

The Red Lake Ojibwe endured many injustices in their land deal-
ings with the U.S. government. They ceded 11 million acres in 1863
through the Old Crossing Treaty. They lost another 3.2 million acres
in 1889 through the Nelson Act. They lost an additional 256,152 acres

through the 1902-04 Thief River Falls land cession. Survey fraud and error cost Red Lake another 52,477 acres. An additional 32,000 acres around Baudette were excluded from a repatriation land transfer and held in legal contest for years. Red Lake surrendered, lost, or was robbed of a grand total of 14,540,142 acres of land.

In 1913, the House Committee Report on Indian Affairs examined tribal land issues at White Earth and Red Lake, and concluded: "Considering [the Indians'] unsophisticated character, the operations of great and greedy lumber concerns and anxious speculators in farming lands, the march of settlement, and the great influence such interest could wield with the Government . . . it is but natural that results such as we found were likely to follow sooner or later. In this instance it was sooner."[127]

Red Lake won some battles too. The reservation and reclaimed ceded lands total 825,654 acres today (roughly 441 square miles). Of that land, 636,964 acres is the diminished reservation, of which 407,668 is land, and the rest water. An additional 156,698 acres of ceded lands have been restored to the tribe north of Red Lake proper. Considering all of the relentless pressure on Red Lake's land and natural resources, it is stunning to see not what they have lost, but what they have retained.[128]

Allotment was enabled by the Nelson Act and the 1904 land-cession bill. In 1930, Thomas Borgerding, Catholic priest at Red Lake, testified before the Court of Claims: "I thought it would be a good thing, but I have changed my opinion since and after nearly forty years I have looked upon the allotments as one of the worst things that ever happened to the Indians." The chiefs had to fight repeated attempts to allot the main reservation from 1889 to 1934. Ironically, outside of the main diminished reservation, Red Lakers had a very different fight trying to get allotments and private land parcels so they could stay in their homes while their lands filled with white settlers. For Red Lake allottees who had spent years petitioning for parcels to enable them to live in their ancestral villages at Roseau, at Warroad, and in the Northwest Angle, the struggle continued. In 1895, John KaKayGeesick, who had just assumed the position of chief at Warroad in place of his father Sword, protested the Nelson Act land cession that had laid the legal basis for taking the land he lived on— and to which he was not party. After taking the land without consent of the local residents at Warroad, the government refused to make any accommodation for them for many years. In 1895, Daniel M. Browning, commissioner of Indian affairs, wrote to secretary of the interior Hoke Smith: "They are American born and are known as men who have never ceded any of their rights under any treaty, and have never asked for or received aid in any manner from the United States in the way of annuities; that they were born upon and have always resided upon the lands which they now ask the United States to confirm to them in lieu of any allotments which the government might assign to them upon the Red Lake reservation."[129]

The allotments were finally made at Warroad and the Northwest Angle after the 1904 cession of the eleven western townships. John KaKayGeesick had 102 acres of land allotted at the outlet of the Roseau River near Warroad. Little Raven had a hundred-acre allotment in the Northwest Angle. KaKayGeesick's brother, Sturgeon Leaf, had a ninety-acre allotment at Warroad. Their tribal enrollment at Red Lake was questioned, and again they had to spend years advocating for their political and legal inclusion as part of the Red Lake reservation. It is an ongoing battle for many of them.

The Ojibwe stayed in their ancestral villages at Roseau and Warroad even while white towns grew up right next to them. The Roseau village was at the present-day hamlet of Ross. The Warroad village was on the beach of Lake of the Woods. Over time, many of the Ojibwe residents moved to Red Lake, but several large families stayed. Today, most of their descendants are members of the Gibbs, Jones, Holenday, Godin, Angus, Accobee, Thunder, KaKayGeesick, Boucha, Sandy, Lightning, Gibbons, Pawasson, Cobenais, and Crow families.

Other families applied for allotments so they could stay elsewhere in the ceded lands north of Red Lake and in the Thief River region. Among them was a woman named Queen of the Water (Onabi-ogimaayobiikwe). She was summarily denied an allotment because the government wanted the Indians out of Thief River Falls and her village was represented by Moose Dung and Red Robed in 1863, 1889, and 1902. In the eyes of the government, her chiefs had already sold the land at Thief River Falls (whereas the Warroad families had never sold their land interests). She was forced to evacuate her residence and move to Red Lake.

Bark lodges at Le Claire, Lake of the Woods, June 19, 1900

The Source

The traumatic effects of the individual tragedies and collective loss experienced at Red Lake over the theft of the land and the lake cannot be minimized. It still burns in the minds and hearts of tribal members today. But in spite of all the taking, coercion, and manipulation, Red Lake endured. In fact, it has fared better than most tribes. Through dedicated leadership in impossible times, it avoided allotment, maintained its traditional leadership structure, and held on to its language and lifeways, always with an eye to building something stronger and better.

The diplomatic wrangling over the Nelson Act and subsequent efforts to get at Red Lake land forced a new response from tribal leaders during a difficult time. He Who Is Spoken To led that response, and he did something remarkable at Red Lake. He pulled the people together in unprecedented political and cultural cohesion. At Old Crossing in 1863, tribal leaders came from many different villages in the Red Lake region. They had many shared interests and values, and that shaped an emergent collective political identity. In the end, He Who Is Spoken To refused to sign the treaty while Moose Dung acquiesced. The people did not speak with one voice. But when Henry Rice came to Red Lake in 1889, He Who Is Spoken To did get the chiefs to speak with one voice. Politically and culturally, this evolution was truly formative.

Through it all, there were human beings who led the effort to protect the people and place at Red Lake. In this extraordinary libertarian social and political culture, they rose up and rallied others behind them to fight off foreign ideas, intrusions into their sovereignty, and attacks on their lifeways. It took warriors to lead warriors, and there were many who distinguished themselves—Red Robed, Perpetual Wind, He Who Treads the Earth from the South, and most especially He Who Is Spoken To. They ensured that the people of Red Lake would not be mere victims and would be more than survivors—that they would endure, evolve, grow, and rise again, like a phoenix from the center of the lake.

The village of Redby is usually referred to as Madaabiimog (The Landing) because it is the best canoe and boat landing on Lower Red Lake. For generations it has been the customary base for fishermen and is home to the Red Lake Fisheries, the tribe's contemporary commercial fish operation. He Who Is Spoken To lived here, and the location of his wigwam was just several hundred yards from the landing. It was both his home and his political center.

For generations, Red Lakers have called the area where Chief He Who Is Spoken To lived Ondatamaaning (The Source), a reference to his indelible influence at Red Lake. The name remains as a special recognition of He Who Is Spoken To's enduring reputation and legacy. Before He Who Is Spoken To, Red Lake was a gathering of scattered villages, each with its own leaders. After He Who Is Spoken To, those villages coalesced into something greater. Redby was not just the local source of chiefly power under He Who Is Spoken To. It was the source of the new Red Lake nation.[130]

Nodin Wind, 1970s

4

Nodin Wind
and the War on Culture

"We understand that this government gives its subjects the freedom of worshipping as he chooses and
we cannot understand why we are deprived of this
privilege."

Nodin Wind

Little Wind

They called him many things: grand medicine, healer, spiritual
leader, chief, Ponemah pagan, Red Lake patriot, Wind. To the people of Ponemah he was simply Noodinoons (Little Wind) and no
other word could encompass what he meant to them. He always introduced himself as Noodinoons to government officials, including
President William Howard Taft (whom he met in 1909). Officials
wrote his name down as Nodin (with a short "o" and without the
diminutive *-oons*). When pressed for his last name by government officials, he simply gave them a rough English translation—Wind. That
was the form his name took on government correspondence, letters
addressed to him by the Office of Indian Affairs, and even his tribal
enrollment at Red Lake. Because Noodinoons means Little Wind, he
sometimes added Junior to the end of his name, even though he was
not a junior in its English understanding and use. Nodin Wind Jr. is a
name still widely remembered across the Red Lake reservation today
and throughout Ojibwe country.[1]

137

In Ojibwe tribal communities Wind is best remembered for his spiritual service to the people. He ran the medicine dance in Ponemah. He was one of the first spiritual leaders in Ojibwe country to regularly travel and help people in communities other than his own. This is common practice for Ojibwe spiritual leaders today, but in the late 1800s and early 1900s, local spiritual leaders served their communities and there was both no need to look elsewhere and a fear of offending local elders if one did. But Wind was an exceptional healer and speaker, called upon to perform life ceremonies and officiate at funerals for hereditary chiefs and tribal citizens in Mille Lacs and elsewhere in Minnesota and Wisconsin.[2]

Nodin Wind lived a long life, from 1874 to 1981. His children Reuben, Maude, and Dorothy were born in wigwams, and he continued to live in a wigwam until well after World War I. He never attended school and never learned to read or write in English, but through translators he wrote some of the most compelling letters and political statements by any leader from Red Lake. His longevity, service, and status afforded him deep respect throughout Indian country and in the nonnative world. Among other accolades, he was named grand marshal for the Fourth of July parade in Bemidji in 1976. At the age of 102, he had lived through more than half of the American nation's two-hundred-year history.[3]

What people at Red Lake might not know or fully appreciate is the indelible mark Wind made on the tribe's political evolution. He was from Ponemah, and Ponemah is a very special place. Even today the people there claim to have a 100 percent traditional Ojibwe religious belief and funeral practice. No church or missionary movement succeeded there in spite of numerous efforts.

Anna C. Gibbs, who today has inherited Wind's position as Ponemah's primary spiritual leader, says that the missionaries failed "because it was simply not meant to be." But Gibbs has no doubt that it was Nodin Wind and the rest of the stalwarts at Ponemah who most consistently exhibited Red Lake's warrior spirit. Their efforts are what kept the traditions alive in spite of repeated missionary efforts to eradicate their customs. It was warriors from Ponemah who defeated the Dakota at Battle River to secure the lakes for the Ojibwe; and it was warriors from Ponemah who chased away the missionaries. The community had greater control of the school, blocked numerous assimilation efforts, and even drove off army recruiters at gunpoint. Today they bury their dead in their front yards as they have for generations—for longer than the United States has been a country. The people of Ponemah are also often extremely distrustful of outside influences and the outsiders who bring them.[4]

Ponemah chiefs boycotted the Old Crossing Treaty negotiations in 1863. Most Ponemah chiefs stayed away from the Nelson Act councils in 1889 and the Thief River land-cession councils in 1902 and 1903. The people of Ponemah usually did not trust the government, and for good reason. They often saw themselves as separate from the white world rather than inextricably linked to it. And before Nodin Wind assumed political leadership in Ponemah, they usually saw themselves as separate from the native nation growing out of the villages on the south shore of Red Lake. Nodin Wind was a healer, a bridge builder, and a relentless warrior. He led Ponemah's successful resistance to the war on Ojibwe culture, and at the same time he united Ponemah with the other villages on the reservation as part of a common tribal nation.

The Battle for Souls: Missionary Movements at Red Lake

People from Christian faith communities today often look at missionaries as self-sacrificing humanitarians, hardworking, dedicated idealists who gave up everything to help distressed populations around the world. The missionaries usually saw themselves in exactly the same way. But human beings do not see the world as it is, but as they are. To the people of Red Lake, the arrival of missionaries presented a complicated mix of cultural attack, language erosion, political intervention, new ideas and technology, and economic opportunity. Further complicating matters, the missionaries may have believed deeply in their work but often did not get along with one another. In fact, various Catholic, Episcopalian, and other Protestant factions openly argued, fought, and undermined one another's efforts. The feud over converts at Red Lake between Henry B. Whipple (Episcopalian) and Ignaz Tomazin (Catholic) was especially long and often mean-spirited. No wonder, then, that the people of Red Lake had such varied responses to the missionaries. Some individuals and even entire communities embraced them, while some resisted every attempt at conversion.[5]

In addition to the struggles between traditional Ojibwe people and missionaries and between the various denominations themselves, there were often clashes with politicians, some of whom supported the missionaries and others who countermanded or even forbade some of their work. At the outset of early missionary activity at Red Lake, such a conflict immediately shaped the landscape of mission efforts for years to come. Alexander Ramsey, the governor of Minnesota Territory from 1849 to 1853, was at odds with missionaries over Indian education policy. The missionaries wanted to educate Minnesota Indians, teach them English, convert them, and convince them to abandon their ancient ways and beliefs. They saw such efforts as progress and truly believed that through conversion, assimilation, and education Indians could be afforded greater economic opportunity. Ramsey was not opposed to the conversion of Indians. On the contrary, he saw their conversion and religious assimilation as a path to their pacification. But he did not believe that Indians should be provided equal economic opportunities. He did not believe Indians were capable or worthy of a place in American society. The missionaries supported academic education. Ramsey opposed academics for Indians and wanted only education that would train them for manual labor.[6]

In 1852, when the people of Red Lake still controlled more than 20 million acres of unceded land and only the first few waves of missionaries had visited them, Ramsey ordered all Minnesota Indian mission schools closed. If they wouldn't educate the Indians his way, they would not educate them at all. Indian agent D. B. Herriman supported Ramsey: "Let books be a secondary consideration except to those who are too young to handle tools." Ramsey left the territorial governorship in 1853, but he returned after statehood as the second governor of Minnesota, from 1860 to 1863. He was then continually reelected as U.S. senator from 1863 to 1875. For more than twenty years, he was in a powerful position to influence Indian policy in Minnesota. When it came to educating Indians, Ramsey did not always get his way, but he slowed and stymied academic educational efforts for Indians at their very genesis. The missionaries eventually found ways to work around Ramsey. That's when their efforts and the conflicts began in earnest.[7]

There is a diversity of faith traditions at Red Lake today, but the denominational breakdown of the communities shows striking disparities. All current differences are directly connected to missionary successes and failures in the 1800s. Today, although Ponemah remains a traditional Ojibwe religious community, in the villages of Little Rock and Red Lake, around 90 percent of the people are Catholic and five percent are Episcopalian. In Redby, about 15 percent of the population are Episcopalian and roughly 80 percent are Catholic. There are members of various Protestant denominations on the south shore of Red Lake as well and a small but growing number of people who hang on to or have reconnected with their ancient traditional Ojibwe religion. The Catholics, Episcopalians, and other Protestants on the south shore of Red Lake are quick to point out that religion and customs are not the same thing. They still take great pride in their native identity, hunting practices, music, and dance.[8]

The story of Catholicism in Ojibwe country is complicated. There are more than 250,000 Ojibwe people in the United States and Canada today. Although in many areas the tribal population predominately follows traditional Ojibwe religious beliefs, where Ojibwe people are Christian, they are most often Catholic. The French had a long, sustained relationship with the Ojibwe from 1600 to 1763. They intentionally sent only men into Ojibwe country and as a matter of policy directed them to marry and make babies with Ojibwe women. Thousands of mixed French–Ojibwe children were produced by this policy. After the French and Indian War (1754–63), the French government severed ties with the Ojibwe, but it left all French people behind (French-speaking Quebecois in Canada, French-speaking Creoles in Louisiana, and Métis and French-speaking mixed bloods everywhere else). From 1763 to 1812, the British hired the largely mixed French–Ojibwe population as traders, and once the Americans came to Ojibwe country and pushed out the British, they hired the very same people.

The French were Catholic. In 1627, they passed an ordinance allowing Indians who converted to Catholicism to be citizens of the realm. They insisted that the offspring of their marriages with

Ojibwe women be baptized Catholic. They often sent their boys to France for Catholic education. They arranged marriages for their girls to advance their trade and political goals. The role of patriarchy and sexism in the evolving French trade empire among the Ojibwe is well documented in Sylvia Van Kirk's book *Many Tender Ties: Women in Fur-Trade Society*.[9]

When the fur trade imploded in the middle of the 1800s, some of the mixed French-Ojibwe Catholics left and eventually assimilated into mainstream nonnative communities. Some French-Ojibwe Catholics forged an entirely new identity as Métis, spoke a hybrid French-Ojibwe language called Michif, and vied for political independence in Canada during the Louis Riel Rebellion in 1869-70. Many more mixed French-Ojibwe Catholics stayed in native communities such as Red Lake.[10]

Such was the case for Paul H. Beaulieu (1889-1955)—a descendant of French royalty and Red Lake Ojibwe warriors. The French Beaulieus had been Catholics for fifteen hundred years; and most of the Beaulieus with Ojibwe blood had been Catholic for generations before coming to Red Lake. Paul H. Beaulieu was an ardent Catholic and a Red Lake tribal patriot. Even today, the population of Red Lake is dominated by French surnames like Jourdain, Beaulieu, Lussier, Gurneau, Bellanger, Nedeau, Bedeau, DeFoe, and DesJarlait. The Catholics had a head start long before missionaries ever made it to Red Lake.

As the French empire collapsed and its Catholic subjects and progeny adapted to their new reality in divergent ways, the Catholic church was not content to leave the fate of their religion to chance. It made sustained efforts to support Catholics throughout Ojibwe country and to convert those who were not members of the faith. That brought lots of Catholic missionaries to Red Lake.[11]

Red Lake was an Ojibwe stronghold in the 1800s. In spite of the long French-Ojibwe connection and the presence of some Catholics at Red Lake, the missionary movement took decades to get established, first swirling around the edges of Red Lake's territory and then slowly establishing a foothold on the south shore.

Because Red Lake was politically and militarily impregnable in the early 1800s, Catholic missionaries had greater success at first developing connections with Catholic Métis in Manitoba and the Red

River trade routes and using that as a base of operations to expand into more traditional Ojibwe communities. Counterintuitive though it may appear, that brought the Catholics to Red Lake from west to east. Fathers Severe Joseph Nicolas Dumoulin and Joseph Norbert Provencher made it to Pembina in 1818. They built the St. Boniface Catholic mission at Pembina, which is located at the present-day intersection of Minnesota, North Dakota, and Manitoba, on the banks of the Red River. They mainly focused on white and Métis traders and settlers, but Pembina was a crossroads for Red Lakers who came there regularly to hunt buffalo. In 1831, Father George Anthony Belcourt came to Pembina. By 1848, he was busy trying to muster political and financial support for the mission, writing to Henry H. Sibley and others. Father Joseph Goiffon arrived in 1856 and further strengthened the efforts at Pembina. Belcourt and Goiffon reinforced the effort in Pembina and frequently corresponded about the "wild" Indians from Red Lake who came through Pembina, often to attack the Dakota at Sisseton and to hunt buffalo. Eventually, they convinced the church to try a mission directly at Red Lake.[12]

Far to the east of Red Lake, Father Frederic Baraga influenced the eventual mission at Red Lake as well. In 1835, Baraga was stationed at La Pointe (Madeline Island in northern Wisconsin). In 1836, he met with Father Francis Pierz at Fond du Lac. The Catholics had a steady feud going with Reverend Benjamin Taylor Kavanaugh and other Methodist missionaries over territory and converts. They strategized about a move to Red Lake. Pierz was greatly influenced by Baraga, who had a Catholic conversion plan for all of Ojibwe territory. Pierz and Baraga conducted most of their correspondence and conversations in German, another shared affinity between them. Once the church began thinking about Red Lake in response to the Pembina missionary advocacy, it was Pierz who engineered the first attempt.[13]

In 1852, Pierz was transferred to Crow Wing in central Minnesota. He had his hands full competing with Episcopal missionaries, navigating Ramsey's ban on academic education of Indians, and dealing with Ojibwe leaders during the height of treaty politics, land-cession treaties, and tribal community upheaval. In 1858, Pierz and Father Lawrence Lautischar left Crow Wing, arriving in the village of Red Lake on August 15. They had great initial success. Pierz had a deep knowledge of homeopathic remedies for common illnesses, which he shared with anyone who wanted them. His openness and the effect of his tinctures and herbs provided a perfect segue to spiritual influence. The population at Red Lake relied heavily on traditional Ojibwe medicine. Pierz's work with healing had as much effect as anything else he did to win people's trust. In a few short months Pierz and Lautischar built a church and mission and developed plans for a school. They called it St. Mary's. There were still some Catholics at Red Lake from the old French connections. Pierz and Lautischar won many early converts and the mission was off to a promising start.

Pierz took a trip that fall to check on other Catholic efforts in the state and Lautischar was left in charge. He was thirty-eight years old, young and ambitious. He desperately wanted to prove his worth to the mission and to Pierz. At great risk, he traveled to Ponemah in December. There were no roads to Ponemah at that time. Access was possible only by boat in the summer or across the ice in the winter. He made it to Ponemah but had little success and got a cool reception from the local residents, who were steadfast in their adherence to traditional Ojibwe religion. As he left for the return walk to Red Lake village, the northwestern winds whipped across the lake, driving through his robes and sapping his strength. Eventually, a rescue party found his lifeless body. Pierz was devastated. He wrote to Baraga:

> Father Lautischar . . . made his way alone, fasting and praying, over twelve miles of difficult traveling to the other side of Red Lake to visit a sick heathen. Deceived by the mildness of the morning's weather, too lightly clad, he intended to make the journey to and back in one day, praying uninterruptedly and putting forth every physical effort. He would take neither a companion, nor a dog, nor more clothing and food. On his return journey, the wind, which had been from the south, changed, and, during the night, a stormy wind swept over the lake with piercing cold. The servant of God succumbed to this. Many traces of his having knelt on the snow which covered the ice on Red Lake on the journey out and back evidenced.[14]

After Lautischar died, the mission at Red Lake was temporarily abandoned. Pierz was overextended and had nobody to staff it. He came to Red Lake sporadically from 1858 to 1867. His efforts did maintain a base of converts in the three villages on the south shore of Red Lake—Little Rock, Red Lake, and Redby.[15]

In 1862, during the U.S.-Dakota War, the Red Lake chiefs refused Hole in the Day's request to go to war with the whites. They were never afraid of a fight, but there had to be a compelling reason for them to make such a bold move. Pierz believed that the influence of the Catholic Ojibwe at Red Lake did much to dissuade Red Lake participation in the violence.[16]

In 1863, desperate for more clergy, Pierz traveled to Europe to recruit, and he brought back with him Joseph F. Buh and Ignaz Tomazin. Pierz sent Buh to White Earth, but put him in charge of the Red Lake mission, which Buh administered and where he had extended stays from 1867 to 1875. Tomazin took over that responsibility in 1875 and eventually moved to Red Lake to staff the mission himself from 1879 to 1883. That marked the permanent establishment of nonnative Catholic clergy at Red Lake. Aloysius Hermanutz assumed leadership of the Catholic mission from 1883 to 1888, and he brought visitors from the church who would leverage an even bigger expansion of Catholicism on the reservation.

In 1887, Katharine, Louise, and Elizabeth Drexel, all biological sisters and nuns from Philadelphia, visited Red Lake. They were astounded at the poverty they saw, and immediately recommended the posting of permanent missionaries and nuns to Red Lake. The church responded and St. Mary's Mission was established.[17]

In 1888, Thomas Borgerding and Father Simon Lampe arrived at Red Lake with two monks and the first two nuns. They acquired the old American Fur Company store building and opened a Catholic mission school there. The first student was the daughter of Rising Sky (Ombi-giizhig). In 1889, the Red Lake chiefs approved a land grant to the Catholic church. St. Mary's Mission now began the construction of a new mission, school, and church campus, most of which still stands today. The first building went up in 1889, and many more were added over subsequent years. A boarding school opened in 1889 in the old American Fur Company building and then moved into a larger log building later that year. By 1900, it had more than eighty students. The school soon became a contract school, funded, albeit erratically at times, by the federal government until 1940. In spite of a policy of separation of church and state, the federal government often funded religious schools, especially in Indian communities. When the government stopped subsidizing the school, the General

Council of the Red Lake Band of Chippewa Indians financially supported the Catholic school. The main church was constructed in 1893 and remodeled in 1956. Two buildings burned in 1904 and 1905 but were rebuilt in 1916.

Father Borgerding spent the next fifty years at Red Lake. He died on November 28, 1956, at age ninety-five, the oldest priest in the United States at the time. He recruited many different priests to serve on the reservation during his tenure there: Felix Nelles (1898–1900), Julius Locnikar (1906–07), Florian Locnikar (1915–41), Egbert Goeb (1940–55), Leo Hoppe (1941–47), Benno Watrin (1947–52), Omer Maus (1952–54), Columban Kremer (1952–56), Albin Fruth (1955), and Cassian Osendorf (1956). Roger Jourdain was impressed with Father Florian Locnikar, who smoked cigars and played tennis with the school kids, taking on two kids at a time.[18]

The Catholics didn't try to convert anyone in Ponemah between 1858 and 1941. Physical access was difficult, and, more important, the residents were never interested. In 1941, Florian Locnikar, unable to get permission from local residents for a land grant to build a church there, tried holding mass at the private residences of Tom Cain Sr. and Rod Henry. Cain and Henry were polite hosts, but not Catholics. The effect was the same. Again, they had no success gaining converts in Ponemah.[19]

Although Catholics dominate the Christian experience at Red Lake, they by no means monopolize it. Catholics have been converting Ojibwe people for four hundred years, and they had the influence of the French colonial regime on their side. The other denominations that came to Red Lake have been at it for around 150 years. They too had an impact.

After the Catholics, the Episcopal missionaries had the most influence at Red Lake. The first Episcopalians arrived in 1861: Henry B. Whipple and E. Steele Peake. It took another fifteen years for them to open the first Episcopal mission. In 1876, Joseph Alexander Gilfillan brought an Episcopal delegation from White Earth, including Reverends Samuel Madison, Fred W. Smith, Joseph Charette, and George Johnson. In Red Lake village, they converted an old log house to church use and started the mission in 1877. Madison and Smith officiated. Madison died that year and Smith left the following year. They were replaced by Reverend Mark Hart in 1879. In 1880, they

St. John-in-the-Wilderness Episcopal Church, about 1895

built a new church out of rough-hewn logs and named it St. John-in-the-Wilderness. Today it is the oldest standing building on the reservation. Reverends Charles T. Wright, Frederick Willis, Heman F. Parshall, and Thomas Phillips successively kept St. John-in-the-Wilderness going. In 1896, the Episcopal church in Red Lake housed one of America's twelve Sybil Carter Indian Mission and Lace Industry Association charters, employing ten local Red Lake women.[20]

In 1877, thrilled with their success at establishing the Episcopal mission in Red Lake, Frederick Smith, George Smith, and Joseph A. Gilfillan came to Ponemah to establish a new mission among the "pagans." Like Catholic missionaries before him, Gilfillan heard about Ponemah on the other side of the lake and the absence of any Christian influence there and decided to try his luck at converting the residents. The missionaries were so thoroughly and consistently rejected by the local population in Ponemah that they abandoned the thought of successfully converting anyone, boarded their boats, and started out across the lake to Red Lake. As the group departed, they were caught in a wicked storm and windblown for more than twelve miles, eventually landing in Redby. Seeking shelter in the bur oaks on the shoreline, they wondered if the experience was a sign from God.[21]

They reached out to the local chief at Redby—none other than He Who Is Spoken To, the venerable seventy-one-year-old stalwart who had refused to give his consent for the 1863 Old Crossing Treaty— and requested permission to build the Church of St. Antipas and an Episcopal mission. The village of Redby, which had the best landing on the lake and would eventually be home to the sawmill, the timber boom docks, and the commercial fishery, also became the center of the Episcopal effort at Red Lake.

The chief agreed to convert—a major coup for the Episcopalians. He Who Is Spoken To accepted baptism and confirmation. Whipple came to Red Lake to perform the chief's baptismal rite. The chief was more than a convert. He told Whipple, "I want your religion for my people." Whipple had two young clergymen, Frederick Smith and Samuel Nabicum, work with the chief to get more conversions.[22]

Whipple came back to Redby to perform a new round of confirmations. Eleven young men from Redby lined up to participate in the ceremony. Whipple wrote of the event: "When I called the candidates forward Madwaganonint came first and stood at one end of the chancel rail. I was surprised for the moment, thinking the dear man had not understood that confirmation was not to be repeated. But as the candidates came forward, the chief counted them on his fingers, and when all had come he bowed to me and reverently took his seat. As their chief, he considered it his duty to see that the young men fulfilled their promises. He more truly represented the patriarchal chieftain and counselor than any Indian I have known."[23]

Afterward, the chief frequently walked through the village with a bell, summoning the people to mass. The chief's efforts to help Whipple gain converts earned him the bishop's lifetime friendship.

Whipple consecrated the cemetery in Redby. He Who Is Spoken To was deeply appreciative. Whipple also advocated justice for the Red Lake Ojibwe in their treatment by the government, again earning great respect from the chief. It made Whipple's role as government agent for the Northwest Indian Commission, negotiating for land cessions from Red Lake in 1886, all the more painful. The chief had to stand up to his friend and religious mentor to fight for the people and their land.

St. Antipas Episcopal Church and congregation, about 1900

The log church built in Redby burned down in 1910 and was replaced with the help of a private donation from Whipple's wife. It is still used today. The clergy in Redby included over the years Reverends Julius Brown, H. O. Danielson, William Hanks, Clifford Walin, Clyde Benner, Albert Wilson, and Thomas Phillips. By the 1920s, the Episcopal effort focused on Redby more than on Red Lake. In 1957, there were around a hundred Episcopal converts in Red Lake village and another 250 in Redby.[24]

Methodists, Presbyterians, and Lutherans also tried to set up missions in Red Lake. Most struggled to gain converts. Those open to Christianity were already saturated with missionaries, and the Ponemah residents just weren't interested. But the missionaries were persistent.

Frederick Ayer, a thirty-nine-year-old teacher and missionary, was the primary impetus for the first formal mission at Red Lake. After the Wisconsin Ojibwe ceded most of northern Wisconsin to the U.S. government in 1842, Leech Lake and Red Lake became the largest Ojibwe communities in the United States without a mission and with relative safety from Dakota attack. This was a major concern for missionaries because in 1841 the Dakota attacked the Ojibwe village at Pokegama Lake (between Lake Lena and Mille Lacs). Casualties were high and the Ojibwe survivors abandoned the village for more than a year. Presbyterian missionaries were present during the attack and found the killing of their converts, their own safety concerns, and the expense and practicality of running a mission with no Indians very distressing. Ayer partnered with Sherman Hall, Edmund F. Ely, and William T. Boutwell to create the Western Evangelical Missionary Society for the purpose of establishing missions at Leech Lake and Red Lake and then extending their work westward from there. William E. Bigglestone called Ayer "a conquistador after souls."[25]

At Red Lake village, near the mouth of Pike Creek, Ayer established the first Presbyterian mission on Red Lake and kept at it from 1842 to 1857. He put David Brainerd Spencer in charge. Alonzo Barnard and Sela G. Wright arrived on August 14, 1843. Wright kept excellent records and made the earliest grammatical sketch of the Ojibwe-language dialects at Red Lake, all archived now as the Sela G. Wright Papers at Oberlin College. In the fall of 1843, Reverend Sherman Hall opened a mission school in Red Lake. There is no way to know the substance of the many conversations between the missionaries and Red Lake leaders in the early years of the missionary effort. It does seem clear that some of the chiefs had a great deal of skepticism about the promises being made. One of Red Lake's chiefs told Ayer, Spencer, and Hall that if after four years' time everything they promised came true, he would protect them. The chief's parting words were: "Gaa-ikidoyaan, ningii-ikid." It translates as "I meant what I said." They recorded it as his name.[26]

The Presbyterian Board of Foreign Missions administered the school from 1843 to 1845. In 1845, the Congregationalist American Missionary Association took charge of the school and mission in a special agreement with the Presbyterian Board of Foreign Missions. In 1847, Barnard and Spencer moved to Leech Lake to establish a new mission on the high ground between Buck Lake and Cass Lake (the site of present-day Camp Chippewa), also operating Minnesota's first printing press. In 1848, the Western Evangelical Missionary Society, which was the organization used to start the mission, was absorbed by the American Missionary Association.[27]

On May 31, 1851, John P. Bardwell reported for the American Missionary Association to Luke Lea, the commissioner of Indian affairs: "At Red Lake a school has been taught 9 months, the number of scholars registered is 21; average attendance is 9. Many of the children enter the school almost, and some entirely, in a state of nudity, and we are obliged to furnish them clothing." In 1852, Bardwell said that the school at Red Lake was showing progress. In 1853, one of the Indian agents, D. B. Herriman, reported that most Red Lakers were dressing like whites.[28]

In 1852, Bardwell made plans for a mission to Ponemah as well: "A new station has been commenced on the north side of Red Lake, at a place called by the Indians, Uebashingie, a strait or place the wind blows through. Our missionaries are now erecting buildings at that place, but will not be able to commence a school before another season."[29]

The initial success of the Presbyterians and Congregationalists in launching Red Lake's first mission school came to an abrupt halt when Ramsey forbade academic education of Indians in 1852. The school limped along for a few more years, but most of the staff relocated by 1855, and the school was abandoned. The Congregationalists had administrative oversight of the school until 1857, but operations had already stopped for a couple of years by the time that officially ended. The missionaries at Red Lake struggled with the arduous travel to and from the mission. Some of them got cholera. Alonzo Barnard's wife died from illness. David Spencer's wife died from a stray Dakota bullet in a raid. Internal support for the mission waned at the same time that external pressure was brought to bear on the school. The Western Evangelical Society and the American Missionary Association spent more than $50,000 on mission and school operations by the time they closed. They had converted twenty people at Red Lake in sixteen years.[30]

It was fifteen years later, in 1871, when the American Missionary Association returned to Red Lake. Sela G. Wright reestablished the school with a focus on manual labor training in order to appease political opponents. In 1875, Reverend Francis Spees was stationed at Red Lake. In spite of the renewed effort, the Protestants never got as many converts as the Catholics and Episcopalians. Hoping to grow their church in "untilled soil," they once again set their sights on Ponemah.[31]

Ponemah was not just the most isolated of the villages around Red Lake; it was the most traditional. The medicine dance thrived there. As the missionaries descended on Red Lake and Redby in the 1800s, several of the traditional families from those communities migrated to Ponemah so they could be in their own faith community without constant pressure from missionaries and neighbors to convert. The people of Ponemah were inherently resistant to religious assimilation.[32]

In 1928, Alrich Olson and Ernest Pearson traveled to Ponemah to establish what they hoped would be the first successful mission there. Mission activity had little success, other than getting local kids to play basketball. In 1954, Reverend Samuel A. Fast obtained permission from the General Council of the Red Lake Band of Chippewa Indians and funds from the Northern Gospel Mission to move a government school building to Ponemah and renovate it as the Wah-Bun Bible Chapel.[33]

Wah-Bun stood for more than fifty years—long enough for Erwin F. Mittelholtz to get a picture and call it Ponemah's first permanent Christian church. The tribal council repeatedly approved a lease to the Northern Gospel Mission to maintain the facility. On Christmas Eve the church provided food and gifts for children, and locals attended once in a while. Eugene and Alfreda Stillday were married there in 1956. Neither converted to Christianity, but the facility served their needs. In the end, the mission never accomplished its mission—nobody from Ponemah converted to Christianity. In 1982, an arsonist burned the church to the ground. Up in flames was how all the missionary efforts ended at Ponemah. Nobody has tried to sway the population toward Christianity since.[34]

Ponemah Pagans

Since 1874, Nodin Wind had watched many of the missionaries come to Ponemah and leave. But he was more than a passive observer of history. As an emerging leader, he played a central role in Ponemah's resistance to the war on culture. The people of Ponemah, derisively referred to as pagans by the Office of Indian Affairs, missionaries, and sometimes their cousins on the south shore of Lower Red Lake, were steadfast in resisting every political, educational, religious, and cultural intrusion.

After boycotting land-cession negotiations in 1863, 1889, 1902, and 1903, the Ponemah Ojibwe continued to fight the construction of schools and missions with astounding consistency and vigor. And through it all, Ponemah showed its greatest strength in voicing not what its people were against, but what they were for. In the face of incredible adversity, they kept the language and the culture alive.

The pressure exerted on the people of Ponemah to convert, move, or assimilate was tremendous. For Nodin Wind and many other Ponemah residents, it simply strengthened their resolve. In 1879, Father Ignaz Tomazin broke up a ceremonial dance at Little Rock. According to Father Thomas Borgerding, "The Indians were beating a big drum. Impulsively he drew his knife and cut the drumhead so they could no longer use it." While many Red Lakers retreated from ceremonial life in response to persecution, Ponemah residents moved their drum ceremonies to secluded locations and kept them going. When a white photographer named Roland Reed came to Ponemah in 1907, King Bird chased him off and told him to "get out at once and not come back." When U.S. army recruiters came to Ponemah during World War I, John Greenleaf's mother barricaded her son in their house and stuck a shotgun through the boards on the window. The recruiters turned around and left.[35]

Chasing off army recruiters was easy enough, but the war on culture was just taking shape at Ponemah in the early 1900s. In 1916, Walter F. Dickens, the agency superintendent, wrote to two of the Ponemah chiefs—Lone Feather (Nezhikegwaneb) and Pelican Sky (Azhede-giizhig):

> My friends, it has been reported to me that you have been taking a very active part in the dances recently held on the "point" and that it was necessary for Mr. Breckner and Mr. Stanard to direct you not to dance anymore, also that you made excuses to the effect that the government had reference to the Squaw Dances and not to the medicine dances when they requested that you discontinue your foolish abuse and over indulgence in dancing last winter. In this connection your attention is called to the law regarding the practice of Indian Medicine Men on the reservation, and a further violation of this law will be properly punished by me. . . . It is unlawful for you to continue in these medicine dances and I trust that you will assist me in suppressing these dances and follow the laws as outlined for your direction by

the Honorable Commissioner of Indian Affairs and the government at Washington.[36]

Nodin Wind, Ponemah's well-respected spiritual leader and an emerging political force, rallied to the defense of Ponemah culture. He answered Dickens with a petition signed by eighty Ponemah residents:

> We Indians living in the vicinity of Ponemah, on the Red Lake Reservation, Minnesota, protest against the ruling of the Indian Department at Washington, D.C., prohibiting the ancient Indian ceremony, known to the white man as the "Grand Medicine Dance." We base our protest on the following grounds.
>
> The so called Grand Medicine Dance is not a dance in any sense of the term. It is simply a gathering of Men, Women, and children for the purpose of giving praise to the Great Spirit, thanking him for the manifold blessings bestowed upon the tribe and praying for continued health, happiness and long life.
>
> The beating of the drum is simply an accompaniment to the songs of praise, uttered by the congregation. As in every church of the white man, piano or organ is found for the purpose.
>
> There is no medicine present at this ceremony and nothing that is supposed to be medicine: it is strictly a religious ceremony and nothing else.
>
> To illustrate, let us say that an Indian has been sick for some time and eventually recovers: the members of his family and friends will give the so called Grand Medicine Dance as a token of respect and thanks to the Great Spirit, in other words, to God, for his recovery. On the other hand, should he die, the same ceremony will be performed, changed of course to deep regrets, instead of rejoicing.
>
> Among the whites the minister is called to administer salvation to the sick or dying and after death the minister is again called for the same purpose.
>
> We understand that this government gives its subjects the freedom of worshipping as he chooses and we cannot understand why we are deprived of this privilege.[37]

This exchange was part of a long and painful story. In 1883, the U.S. commissioner of Indian affairs created a "Code of Indian Offenses" and used it to persecute tribal religious practice. Until 1933, the Office of Indian Affairs used circulars to direct Indian agents to

Dance at Red Lake, about 1915

suppress tribal ceremonies. Circular 1665 instructed Indian agents to ban and break up tribal dances, religious ceremonies, and give-aways, even after Indians became U.S. citizens in 1924. On February 24, 1923, Charles H. Burke, commissioner of Indian affairs, issued an order prohibiting powwows at Red Lake. The order was disseminated directly to tribal members with a message that read, "You do yourselves and your families great injustice when at dances you give away money or other property, perhaps clothing, a cow, a horse or a team and a wagon." The First Amendment to the U.S. Constitution was insufficient to provide for the religious freedom of Indians the way it did for Americans of other races.[38]

At Ponemah, suppression of the medicine dance was especially onerous. The Office of Indian Affairs even required permits for Ponemah Indians to visit other reservations, fearing that their "pagan ways" would influence other Ojibwe people. In 1917, Minnesota governor Joseph A. A. Burnquist defended government suppression of the medicine dance at Ponemah, saying simply that it was, "the only thing to do." The commissioner of Indian affairs wrote of the Ponemah medicine dance in 1917, "The old and harmful practices of the Indians, which are clearly detrimental to their progress and welfare, cannot be tolerated even under the guise of religious ceremony." Ponemah resident Peter Martin was incarcerated that year for participating in the medicine dance and his treaty payments were withheld by the Office of Indian Affairs.[39]

In 1926, Ponemah resident Still Day (Obizaani-giizhig) testified to the U.S. Senate Committee on Indian Affairs: "I have been told that they are going to stop my religion, so I will have no religion at all. The religion has been given to me. That is the reason I have a religion, because it has been given to me. God has given me this religion. . . . He was going to stop my religion; that is, the grand medicine. I never ask anybody or try to induce anybody to join the grand medicine lodge."[40]

The pressure on the medicine dance at Ponemah eased somewhat in 1934 when commissioner of Indian affairs John Collier retracted Circular 1665. Traditional Ojibwe on the reservation still chafed under the yoke of unfair treatment. It wasn't until 1978 that the American Indian Religious Freedom Act formally extended protection from religious persecution to Indians.[41]

Nodin Wind and the people of Ponemah hung on through many hard years. The medicine dance used to draw crowds of non-lodge members as observers. After the war on culture, they performed the medicine dance in secret. The access roads to ceremony locations were not marked, and they remain that way even today. The ceremony was truncated as well, so that it was over by the time someone might arrive to shut it down. That too is an entrenched part of the custom in Ponemah today.[42]

In Ponemah, traditional wake services last two nights and the funeral services begin in the morning of the day of the funeral because the feast and ceremony are time consuming and elaborate. After the government began to persecute traditional ceremonies, formal obituaries and funeral announcements in Ponemah always carried the same format. The wake was secretly conducted on the first night with no public announcement. No religion was mentioned, but simply,

"Services in the Indian Custom." And the start time listed in every Ponemah obituary and funeral notice was 2 PM on the day of the funeral. That was the time when the main ceremony was over and all that was left was interment of the body. That too was an intentional decision made by culture keepers to protect their ways from outside interference by keeping ceremonial doings secret. Most of the Ponemah funerals in the 1990s still formally listed a start time after their conclusion, although since then more of the notices are providing accurate start times and open invites to wake and funeral services. Active suppression of tribal religion by the government and missionary interference with traditional religious practices only served to heighten Ponemah's cultural isolation.

Medicine Men and Doctors

Every aspect of pre-reservation life at Red Lake was conducive to excellent health. The traditional diet included fish, moose, elk, caribou, deer, and small game—boiled, not fried. Abundant berries, tubers, and mushrooms provided nutrition. Wild rice, which was less prolific on Red Lake proper, abounded in the smaller lakes and rivers throughout the region, and proved a critical staple. People were always active, as a necessary means of survival, so they were physically fit. Reading through treaty logs, signature pages, and scattered archival references, it is stunning to note the number of Red Lake citizens described as very old—not just Nodin Wind, who died at 106, but the entire body of tribal citizens who enjoyed a life that was by many measures much longer and healthier than what most Red Lakers experience today.[43]

Diet and lifestyle explain much of what has changed. When the people of Red Lake ceded land, they ceded access to critical healthy food resources. The gap between what was available and what was needed was filled any way possible. People continued to harvest traditional foods, just less of them. As partial payment for the land sold, the government sent not just cash, but food annuities—flour and lard. So people figured out how to make fry bread and started to fry their fish and wild game. People became much more sedentary as well, because they were restricted and discouraged from travel on land that no longer belonged to them.

Besides diet and lifestyle changes, the health of people at Red Lake was also compromised by the introduction of diseases previously not experienced and unknown. Smallpox and then tuberculosis ravaged the population. Red Lake's isolation from continual exposure to the European germ pool ended with the beginning of the missionary period. The tribal population had little natural immunity to many foreign diseases, which hit the people very hard. As the pace of white settlement around Red Lake increased, so did the frequency of new outbreaks. Ancient knowledge of medicines and healing was well suited for what the Ojibwe had experienced prior to contact, but they struggled at least as much as Europeans did in trying to cure smallpox. Government officials had no faith in indigenous remedies and would never just leave Red Lake alone. The people had to forge a new way forward.[44]

The Office of Indian Affairs started staffing doctors at the Indian agency in 1865, which is when Dr. V. P. Kennedy was assigned to Red Lake. He was followed by many others: C. P. Allen (1873-79), H. W. Brent (1881), J. R. Hollowbrush (1885), Wallace E. Belt (1889), George S. Lescher (1889), G. S. Davidson (1896-1900), Julius Silverstein (1900), and a Dr. Schneider (1901). The doctors tended to the sick, but they had limited tools to deal with smallpox. There is no cure for smallpox. Vaccinations had been developed as early as the late 1700s, but little effort was made to inoculate Red Lakers before 1900. The global push to eradicate the disease by vaccination didn't begin until 1967. It was not until the early 1970s that Red Lake, like the rest of the country, didn't have to worry about the disease, which was eradicated by 1980.[45]

The arrival of Western medical help at Red Lake was limited to one field doctor who was sporadically available while tending to a widely scattered tribal population. There was no emergency triage or ambulance service. At the same time that service was emerging and very limited, the practice of Western medicine served to further undermine the status of traditional Ojibwe healers and erode tribal culture and ceremony.

All the while, the people really suffered. In 1901, a smallpox epidemic broke out in Ponemah. Students were quarantined at the school and were eventually vaccinated. Care was never consistent. In 1905, the government boarding schools at Red Lake and Ponemah had to open hospitals to treat students with tuberculosis and other illnesses. Disease spread quickly in the schools' tight quarters.[46]

In 1912, E. B. Merritt, who was contracted to do fieldwork at Red Lake for the Office of Indian Affairs, wrote a scathing report of medical conditions at the schools and sent it to William H. Bishop, superintendent for Red Lake Indian School, as well as to several prominent lawmakers. Merritt's letter noted that only three boys and three girls were vaccinated at the Ponemah school. He also reported: "The bathing facilities in the Cross Lake [Ponemah] School consist of one bath tub, used by both boys and girls at different hours. The matron states that she bathes two pupils in a tub at once. She also states that on occasions of low water as many as eight pupils have been bathed in the same water." Water shortages were common because the school had a shallow well and high demand. Poor hygiene caused trachoma and other eye problems. Merritt reported: "infections of the eye resulting in ulcerations and leaving corneal scars appear to be more serious . . . 10.9% of the entire enrollment here have permanent defective vision fully developed as the result of eye infection."[47]

In 1914, Red Lake was one of the first reservations in the United States to open an Indian hospital. This created emergency-room service capability for the south shore of Red Lake. There was still no ambulance service and the facility was small and understaffed in comparison to the need.[48]

The influenza epidemic in 1918, which killed 675,000 Americans, hit Red Lake hard. Red Lake children in residential boarding schools suffered disproportionately. Children who died at far-off boarding schools in Haskell, Kansas, and Carlisle, Pennsylvania, were buried in the schools' cemeteries. For the people of Red Lake, losing children to disease was horrible, but not to get their bodies back for burial was unbearable. And for traditional families, not having any authority to decide the religious choices over the funerals was even worse. Although influenza was especially terrible in 1918, tuberculosis probably claimed more lives than influenza and smallpox in subsequent years. Again, the crowded conditions in boarding schools exacerbated the spread of the disease.[49]

In 1955, the Indian hospital was remodeled and the following year converted to administration by the U.S. Public Health Service, as it remains today. The hospital had a field physician for several more years before moving to on-site outpatient service only.

Missionary and health practices at Red Lake significantly changed the cultural landscape. More and more Red Lakers were going to church than to the lodge. More and more were going to the hospital than to traditional healers. In the early 1900s, Dr. Thomas Rodwell reported, "The Indians under my professional charge have now almost entirely given up their grand medicine ideas and are availing themselves of the professional services and remedies of Agency physician." But the war on culture had just begun.[50]

Education for Assimilation

"Schools are less expensive than war. It costs less to educate an Indian than it does to shoot him." Reverend Lyman Abbott, the Congregationalist missionary who uttered these words, was one of many voices advocating for the education of native children. He, and others like him, were not simply evil men trying to hurt Indians. They thought their ideas were in the best interests of the Indian people. As their Indian education practices enveloped Red Lake, many Red Lakers must have felt that with friends like these, they didn't need enemies.[51]

After the Red Lake Presbyterian mission school closed, some of the church personnel picked up work at the government schools as they were slowly established over the next twenty years. In fact, most government day schools and boarding schools for Indians actually required church attendance and infused Christian teaching (usually Protestant) into the curriculum and protocol of the schools.[52]

The Red Lake people had mixed feelings about education. Nodin Wind and most of the Ponemah population remained exceptionally distrustful of educators because they were self-proclaimed assimilators. Wind would never embrace a war on his own culture. But in Red Lake village, the growing Catholic population saw more opportunity than betrayal in embracing education.

Some openly advocated for the government to build them a school. Captain Hassler reported in 1869, "They are a sober, industrious, and well-behaved tribe. . . . They have made earnest and repeated requests for a school." In 1870, Lieutenant George Atcheson wrote, "Of late years the educational interests of these people have been entirely neglected. No provision is made by the government for this purpose, and no religious association has assumed the burden of sustaining schools or missions at this point." Ramsey's plan to limit Indian education to preparation for manual labor seemed to be working.[53]

Atcheson's report got traction with President Ulysses S. Grant in 1870. Grant successfully rearranged assignments and responsibilities in the Office of Indian Affairs. Military officers would no longer be the reporting and administrative agents to the tribes. All such managerial responsibilities shifted to Indian agents administered by the Office of Indian Affairs. In addition, Grant encouraged missionary activities and church-sponsored schools in Indian country. He was trying in part to depoliticize treaty work and administration, but also to save money in a tough budget environment by getting more work and infrastructure development out of religious groups and the private sector. Catholic, Episcopal, and Congregationalist mission work at Red Lake immediately accelerated.

In 1873, the U.S. government appropriated funds for a government school in Red Lake. Funding was too limited to make the school residential right away, so a tiny green day school was built. In 1877, the government expanded the facility to a boarding school with capacity for fifty students. Such schools usually operated on the contract model, with federal funding support to pay private, religious, or public entities to run the schools. In 1879, there was a big change at Red Lake. Under the auspices of the U.S. government's new Indian boarding-school policy and funding model, the school would now be administered directly by the Office of Indian Affairs, which no longer provided funding to a third party, but ran the school itself. The facility was soon overloaded to fifty-eight, although average attendance was fifty-two. Operations expanded further in 1885, when the government attached and opened a day school with capacity for twenty students. Monthly attendance averaged sixty-eight, with a high one month of 123. The campus was expanded in 1896.[54]

That same year, Robert M. Allen reported that many Red Lake families sent their children to the government and mission schools voluntarily. Enrollment at the government boarding school was fifty-four students, and seventy more at St. Mary's. In spite of the growing support that many Red Lakers were showing for the school, the commissioner of Indian affairs implemented a new attendance policy at Red Lake. Attendance was now compulsory and parents who failed to comply would be fined or imprisoned. This policy was part of a nationwide effort to use education as a means to eradicate tribal culture.[55]

Inside the schools, nothing was being taught and no method of teaching was being used that did anything to strengthen the identity of native children. The schools were run in English with physical punishment for anyone caught speaking Ojibwe. The schools were residential, cutting children off from their homes and families, even on weekends, no matter how close they might be to the school. The students received little nurturing, more discipline, and a steady barrage of attacks on tribal beliefs and customs. Most of the teachers and administrators were white, although there were some notable exceptions. Francis Blake described his experience at St. Mary's in Red Lake:

> There was a trough, with a pipe with holes drilled in it, for the water. We washed in cold water. . . .
>
> At six-thirty, we were lined up and marched to Mass, which was celebrated in Latin. . . .
>
> The Nuns and the Prefect carried a clipboard with all our names on it, and during the day they kept track of all of our infractions of school rules, including saying a single word of *Ahnishinahbœó'jibway*. We had to be in bed by ten o'clock at night. The lights were turned off, and then in a few minutes, they were turned on again. The Prefect would go down the rows of beds in the dormitory. We never knew at whose bed he was going to stop. He would turn down the blanket, and take his strap to us as we lay in our beds, and beat us. . . . Other discipline included "running the gauntlet," in which the child to be punished had to go between two lines of children, and the children in the lines had to kick and hit the child who was running. If the Prefect thought that the child had not been hit enough, they would make them run through again, or single out those of us who had not hit and kicked, and make us beat on them. The discipline at the U.S. Government and Mission Schools also included chloroforming children. The smell of chloroform and ether still haunt me.[56]

The use of education to wage war on tribal culture at Red Lake deepened over time. In 1899, the Indian Appropriation Act included a set-aside of $35,000 for construction of a new school plant at Red

Lake plus $20,000 for three smaller schools in Minnesota at Bena, Cass Lake, and Ponemah. Construction began immediately in Red Lake, but not in Ponemah. Dan Needham Sr. reflected on the school construction effort in Ponemah: "The government wanted to start a school over there in Ponemah in the early 1900's. The Indians didn't want no school yet. They'd say, 'Go on and tell them we'll meet them Baanimaa.' 'Baanimaa' means 'after a while.' But you know, they're bound to change the words. These delegates wanted to convince the Indians to have a school, so they'd say, 'Well, let's go to Ponemah.' They thought that was the name of the town. That's where it got its name."[57]

Many Ponemah residents today have stories and jokes about the origin of the town's name. Often, they revolve around the corruption of the Ojibwe word *baanimaa* and resistance to schools, missionaries, treaties, and marriage proposals to outsiders. Although that's not likely the true linguistic origin of the word, there can be no doubt that for the people there assimilation would have to come *baanimaa,* always. In Ojibwe, Ponemah Point is called Obaashiing, but the village itself is called Aazhooding, meaning Cross Lake. The word Ponemah has always been the dominant reference to the village in English for government officials, missionaries, and local residents, but early government documents in particular have also interchangeably used Cross Lake as the village name.[58]

The school was built quickly in Red Lake, but in Ponemah it was not so simple. In Ponemah they had Nodin Wind. He was twenty-six years old now and starting a family of his own. He thought all the time about the world his children would live in. The government planned to build the new school at the traditional village site at Ponemah, on existing recent burial spots and Ojibwe home sites. Nodin Wind and the rest of the local population were furious. The residents were also very much opposed to the idea of any effort to assimilate their children through education. They promised to burn to the ground any building constructed and threatened violence if the plan proceeded. Captain William A. Mercer was acting agent for the Leech Lake Agency, which had oversight of Red Lake still in 1900. Mercer had Howell Morgan and Watson C. Randolph, the clerk and assistant clerk, develop a plan for construction of the school at Ponemah. Peter Graves was working for the Office of Indian Affairs at this time.

Mercer wrote: "There is a band of Indians known as the Cross Lakers, who live on the opposite side of the lake from the Government school, and who are not only uneducated but are uncivilized and are undoubtedly thoroughly wild Indians." Ignoring all warnings, Mercer sent contractors to Ponemah to start on the construction, but they were prohibited from doing their work by Nodin Wind and a large group of Ponemah men who threatened immediate bloodshed if they proceeded. Peter Graves explained to Mercer that the Red Lake village residents were not of the same opinion as those in Ponemah about the construction of schools, but that if trouble started, they would be more likely to stand by their brothers from across the lake than with the government.[59]

Mercer had no choice but to go to Ponemah and try to defuse the situation himself. He commissioned twenty-seven Red Lake residents as "special policemen" and had them hide in the hold of his boat as they approached the landing at Ponemah, where they saw a still sizable group of men keeping watch to prevent work on the school. The special policemen were Stands Forever as captain, Joseph Weaver as lieutenant, Joseph Thunder, Stands Quick (Gezhiiboogaabaw), Little Beard (Miishiidoons), Lone Cut (Nezhekiishkang), Stone Man (Asiniiwinini), Starting Ax (Maajii-waagaakwad), James Shears, Light of the Sky (Waase-giizhig), Fast Feather (Gegizhiigwaned), Flys Up and Around (Bebaa-ombii), Crosses the Sky (Mishagaame-giizhig), Reaching Over the Hill (Dedaakamaajiwind), Little Buck, Bazile Thunder, Baptiste Lawrence, Joseph Nah-gou-ub, James Fisher, John B. Pemberton, George Brunette, Joseph Martin, Joseph Bellanger, George Bonga, Joseph Sky, William Douglass, and James Anoka. The Ponemah Indians held their ground even against a well-armed police force, insisting that they would not tolerate the construction of a school to assimilate their children. Fearing immediate bloodshed or that his police would be overwhelmed by the more numerous village residents, Mercer threatened to call for a troop deployment to force the issue.[60]

Nodin Wind and the elderly chiefs in Ponemah held council three days later and offered a compromise. They would allow the construction of the school if the Office of Indian Affairs agreed to their terms. The Ponemah chiefs would choose the location of the school. The principal at the school had to be an Indian. The Ponemah chiefs had sole authority to appoint the principal. The construction of the school could not involve any land grants to the government or outside agencies as had happened in Red Lake for the construction of missions and schools. All the land and the school building itself would belong to the people of Ponemah and future decisions about the structure would be dictated by the chiefs of Ponemah.

Fearing a major bloody incident, Mercer acquiesced to all the demands of the council in order to keep the peace and build the school. And he followed through on the promises he made. The government built the school where the chiefs directed, on the north shore of Lower Red Lake, away from burial and home sites, and five miles from where most Ponemah families lived at the point. (Ponemah town demographics shifted to their present form slowly between 1900 and 1945.) The people of Ponemah owned the school. The chiefs appointed John G. Morrison Jr. as principal. And the school was run in a completely secular fashion, unlike most government schools, which included substantial cultural and curricular efforts to indoctrinate the children into Christian beliefs.

Construction proceeded quickly after that, and the new school opened on January 10, 1901. The influence of the Ponemah chiefs continued, and many of the largest Ponemah families were among the school's first employees: William Bonga (teacher), Margaret Nason (teacher), Josette Lawrence (seamstress), Mary Brun (cook), and Susan Sayers (laundress). By 1902, there were forty-two kids boarded at the school in Ponemah and more who attended school there during the day. By 1905, the school was boarding fifty-six children.[61]

By 1900, the Indian agents at Red Lake and Leech Lake were increasingly responding to the national Indian education policy. Many of the children on the Red Lake reservation were going to boarding schools in Ponemah and Red Lake. But many others were now being shipped across the country to other schools run by the Office of Indian Affairs at White Earth and Morris in Minnesota and Vermilion, Pierre, and Chamberlin in South Dakota. Most Red Lakers were sent to Carlisle (Pennsylvania), Haskell (Kansas), Tomah (Wisconsin), and Flandreau (South Dakota). The government also subcontracted with and paid for nine mission schools to run its assimilation program, a clear violation of the principle of separation of church and state. Various churches also paid for and ran another forty-five

Indian mission boarding schools. Almost all of them were run by the Catholic church, although the Episcopal, Lutheran, and Presbyterian denominations were all active in the Indian education business. St. Mary's was operated by the Catholic church under U.S. government contract.[62]

The Office of Indian Affairs and the missionaries focused their activities on the villages at Little Rock, Red Lake, Redby, and Ponemah. But there were still many Ojibwe living in enclaves at War-road and the Northwest Angle and scattered across the ceded lands between Lake of the Woods and Red Lake. Some of those families pursued traditional lifeways. Others voluntarily worked to assimilate with the settler population so they could stay where they were and seek prosperity in the new agriculture and timber economies. The government relentlessly pursued their children for inclusion in the residential school roundups. It didn't matter if the children were monolingual Ojibwe speakers or monolingual English speakers, if they wore buckskin or woolen dresses, if they looked white or very brown. If they were Indians and the government knew it, they were heading to residential boarding school. Such was the case for Lutiant LaVoye, a light-complexioned Red Lake girl living on a settlement farm with her family on ceded land at Roseau, Minnesota. Despite her high degree of integration into white society, her native roots eventually landed her at the Haskell Indian boarding school in Law-rence, Kansas.[63]

All across the reservation, the people struggled financially. The superintendent of Indian schools claimed that the education for assimilation program was working to civilize the Indians and bring them financial prosperity. In his 1900 report, he wrote, "76 percent of the pupils who attend school were classified as excellent, poor, or medium, and but 24 percent as bad or worthless. This speaks volumes for a system of education, which can in so short a time, develop from an uncivilized race 76 percent of men and women capable of taking their places in the body politic of this Republic."[64]

The success of the education was questionable. But even more important, the opportunity to economically advance was denied to Indians because of their race. Mercer wrote: "It may be interesting to the public to know how Indians manage to live during the cold winter months at a place where no rations are furnished . . . and where no working is going on by which they can be kept in employment. . . . Fish is their principal food and wild rice is next, while maple sugar and syrup are made by most of the families in sufficient quantities to last them nearly half the year. Some of them raise a few potatoes and a small quantity of vegetables. Berries are abundant in the summer months." The Red Lake Ojibwe actually had 275 acres of land under cultivation in 1900, raising more than 14,000 bushels of vegetables. But the primary source of food still came from the lakes. In spite of all efforts, the Red Lake Ojibwe were living by their own means in the same way their ancestors always had. They were just doing it on less of their original land and with more pressure on their land and resources.[65]

At the government school in Red Lake, enrollment continued to grow. By 1902, they had seventy-seven children boarded and sixteen in the day school, and total attendance increased to 111 by 1909. Some of the local residents were having better success at picking up jobs in the schools as well. A. Alvin Bear was hired as a teacher, Mary C. Brunette as an assistant matron, and Jane Saice as the cook. The government school soon eclipsed St. Mary's residential boarding school in Red Lake, which leveled off enrollment at around ninety children in 1909. With land loss and the declining access to natural resources, people had to look for jobs, alter their diet, and think about all available opportunities for feeding their children, even if it meant sending them to boarding schools.

The tribal population across Minnesota experienced a rapidly declining standard of living during the early settlement period. It is not the case that Indians were always poor and never climbed out of poverty. Indians were healthy and, by their own terms, wealthy until whites took the land and resources. Their children and subsequent generations paid the price and suffered the consequences. Poverty became pervasive.

In the 1930s, the Ojibwe at White Earth were destitute and sent a truckload of their children from White Earth to Red Lake, many crying with hunger, hoping that the people at Red Lake would better feed them. They were folded into the boarding schools at Red Lake before anyone at White Earth knew that the student dormitories at Red Lake were mere tarpaper shacks. Some of the White Earth parents learned this months or even years later.[66]

The residential boarding-school experience dominated education for Red Lake's children for generations. Change came slowly at first, but Red Lake was able to move from the residential model to day schools before most reservations did. The change began in 1907 with the establishment of a public day school at Redby. A lot of white families lived on the reservation, working for the Office of Indian Affairs, logging companies, and missions. The first school was designed to serve them, but also provided a welcome segue for the Red Lake kids, whose parents were eager to have them live at home. The Redby school was part of the Beltrami County school district system—Unorganized School District 118. William B. Stewart supervised school operations, and Stella Minton was the teacher for the inaugural class of twenty students. This was the first public school district on the Red Lake reservation. The new facility was completed in 1908. In 1924, Benjamin Bredeson of Bemidji was awarded a contract to build an expansion to the school at Redby. The work was completed by 1926.[67]

In 1926, the U.S. Senate Committee on Indian Affairs conducted an investigation of Ojibwe land and timber issues in Minnesota and held hearings at Red Lake and other communities for several days. Red Lake and the other Ojibwe groups petitioned the Senate for redress of many issues, including education policy. Especially disturbing was the government's diversion of tribal trust funds, intended for distribution to tribal members as partial payment for land and timber sales, to pay tuition for Indian children attending *public* schools. All children were to receive free public education. Indian children across the country had extra guarantees for their free education stipulated in many treaties, widely understood as an inherent part of their sovereign status. Yet the government was charging them for their imposed assimilation. The petition did not bring an immediate remedy, although some of the issues were incorporated into later litigation for successful redress.[68]

In 1912, Red Lake followed Redby's lead in the shift to public education. It established Unorganized School District 119. The government boarding school in Red Lake continued to operate, but the public school took over day-school operations, using one of the rooms in the same facility. The rest of the campus for the government boarding school was converted to use for the public school in 1923. A new two-room structure was built for the public school in 1922–23. Federal funds were appropriated to cover the cost.[69]

The children of the many white families living in the Red Lake area were sent to school at Red Lake with the Indian kids. Under Ethelyn Hall, the school employed some Indian teachers in the early years, including Vera May, Mildred Dickinson, and Helen Sather. An elementary school and a gymnasium were built at Red Lake in 1927. In 1934, the remainder of the campus for the Red Lake government boarding school was completely converted to day-school use. This marked the official end of federal government boarding-school operations in Red Lake. The Office of Indian Affairs built a new high school in Red Lake in 1935 and turned it over to Beltrami County for administration. In 1937, Red Lake graduated its first high-school seniors: Katherine Lou Bailey, Louis R. Caswell, Orvin Nelson, Alphid S. Selvog, and Kella H. Selvog.[70]

The public high school at Red Lake operated as a day school, but the curriculum was still designed for assimilation. The teaching was scripted to track the children of Red Lake to manual labor, domestic service work, or farming. In 1937, an overhaul of curriculum created three programs for students: industrial arts, home economics, and agriculture. Most of the teachers were white and lived at the school. When the high school and gymnasium burned down in 1940, they had to hold classes in the old boarding-school dorm, which now housed the teachers, an awkward arrangement that persisted until 1949 when a new facility was finally built. The delay persisted because most federal appropriations were diverted to the war effort in the 1940s.[71]

It took a long time for attitudes about Indian education to change. Criticism from Francis Ellington Leupp, commissioner of Indian affairs in 1907, and the Meriam Report, in 1928, brought greater awareness of the damage caused by Indian education policy. In the early 1930s, John Collier, the new commissioner of Indian affairs, was able to make major changes. At Red Lake, those changes accelerated in 1934, as the government boarding schools were converted to day schools. As they were folded into the county school district administration, the federal government divested itself of moral and

Katherine Lou Bailey, one of the first graduates from Red Lake High School.

financial responsibility. Like Redby, Ponemah and Red Lake developed public day schools. For the people of Red Lake, it meant that most of their kids were now living at home—a welcome change.[72]

In 1936, the Office of Indian Affairs (OIA) started to dismantle the residential boarding-school system nationally. The OIA contracted the state of Minnesota to assume management of all schools serving native communities except for Pipestone and mission schools. At Red Lake, the change brought consolidation of schools on the reservation. In 1936, the Redby school district, which had been independent since 1907, was subsumed by the Red Lake school district. The new entity was now Red Lake School District 119, and they shared one superintendent.

The evolution of public schools in Ponemah lagged behind the other communities because of entrenched resistance to assimilation efforts. In 1917, a public elementary school was built in Ponemah. It was expanded in 1921. Joseph Jourdain did most of the construction work. In 1936, when the Redby public school was subsumed by the Red Lake district, the school in Ponemah, still operated by the OIA, was also put under the administrative jurisdiction of Red Lake public schools. The schools at Redby and Ponemah now ran elementary education through grade six. Red Lake ran grades seven through twelve for the entire reservation. This brought some financial and administrative efficiency to the public education system at Red Lake, but also made for longer bus rides and less direct community control of the schools that served reservation high-school children.[73]

Local governance of the schools at Red Lake was enabled in 1942, when the system at Red Lake converted from "unorganized" to "organized," which meant local elections for school-board positions. Although many people from Red Lake had worked at the schools, they were administered through federal, state, or county auspices. Now the people of Red Lake would elect their own people to school-board positions. Tribal members serving on the school board successfully influenced the focus of the school to move from agriculture, industrial education, and home economics to a more diversified curricular approach with the addition of instruction in music, fine arts, and business as early as 1950.

The public school infrastructure on the reservation underwent several waves of improvement. The school at Ponemah was expanded

Unidentified schoolroom at Red Lake, 1941

and modernized in 1941, burned to the ground in 1951, and was rebuilt in 1953. The high school in Red Lake was expanded and modernized in 1950–51 and again in 1954–55. The Red Lake and Redby elementary schools were also consolidated in 1955. The General Council of the Red Lake Band of Chippewa Indians approved a quitclaim deed for nineteen acres for the school in Red Lake in 1955. The land grant to the school made it possible to get impact aid dollars designated for educational agencies financially burdened by federal activities from the legislature after 1950. Special appropriations outside of impact aid were not politically feasible at that time, so the General Council conceded the land grant to get the school.[74]

In 1956, a new apartment complex was built for nonnative people working at Red Lake. Throughout its history and to the present day Red Lake schools have employed an almost entirely nonnative teaching team. Now there is desire to hire Indians at the reservation schools, but the legacy of education for assimilation produces poor high-school and college graduation rates and low motivation among graduates to pursue teaching careers. Today, Red Lake residents call the house and apartment area for nonnative teachers and hospital workers "The Compound."

Most of the infrastructure improvements at Red Lake had to come from special legislative appropriation or the federal government—the Office of Indian Affairs, renamed the Bureau of Indian Affairs in 1947. Because the land at Red Lake is not individually owned, bonding bills and special tax assessments could not be used to drive school repairs or expansions. The special treaty status of Red Lake and the trust responsibility of the federal government to Indians for education still requires the government's responsible and timely response to school needs on the reservation today.

Undermining the Chiefs

Because of his long life, Nodin Wind witnessed nearly every major phase in the political development of Red Lake. The constant evolution of Red Lake's political landscape was heartrending at times, exhilarating at others, but always instructive. Steeped in Ojibwe tradition, Wind was a deep listener, cautious, and always intentional when it came time to act.

He knew that white folk wanted the land, the timber, and the very souls of his people. The Office of Indian Affairs was the tool they used to get it. The OIA was created in 1832 and housed in the Department of War. In 1849, it was moved to the Department of the Interior.

Nodin Wind saw the government's deliberate undermining of hereditary chiefs at Red Lake. The OIA created Red Lake's Court of Indian Offenses in 1884 and formalized its structure in 1890. Red Lake's first judges were appointed by B. P. Schuler, Indian agent: Joseph Charette, William V. Warren, and John G. Morrison Sr. They served at Red Lake and at White Earth. Through these courts, the Indian agents began to take over responsibilities that had been reserved exclusively for the chiefs. They became the law of the reservation. The Indian agents operated on directives or "circulars" from the OIA, some of which instructed agents to prohibit tribal members from participation in ceremony. The agents used the courts to try to convict people for anything from assault to participating in give-aways or ceremonial dances. Some Red Lake residents served long sentences for participation in the medicine dance.[75]

Indian agents had a lot of power at Red Lake in the late 1800s and early 1900s. They managed the Indian police and the Court of Indian Offenses, and they were the conduit between the chiefs and business interests. Often, powerful or ambitious businessmen became Indian agents because they were able to advance their own economic interests most successfully from inside the Office of Indian Affairs. George A. Morrison, for example, was Indian agent at the Red Lake subagency in 1899, but he also operated a hotel, a store, and timber businesses at Red Lake.

In 1905, an Indian police force was organized for Ponemah for the first time. Over the next fifty years, many of Ponemah's biggest families had people serve in the Indian police. It was one of the few paying jobs in the community, even though compensation was very low. The Indian police force in Red Lake village was even larger. Although getting a job with the Indian police meant money to feed one's children, it also meant enforcing the directives of the Indian agent on other tribal members. Often, it drove wedges between individuals and families in ways never seen before.[76]

Nodin Wind watched with mounting horror as the true effects of the Nelson Act, the fraudulent surveys, the timber boom, and the pace of white settlement encroached on Ponemah. The chiefs from his community had never agreed to a single land cession, had capitulated to no missionary, had remained steadfast and strong. But still they were enveloped by white settlers. White lumbermen harvested the big trees on Ponemah Point. White houses were going up at Waskish on the shore of Upper Red Lake. And nobody at Ponemah had agreed to any of it. Being strong, resistant, and isolated would not be enough to save Ponemah. The warriors of Ponemah had to fight back in the war on culture, but the new fight could not be won by military force. Victory required political power.

On the south shore of Red Lake, the chiefs worked hard to validate their positions and advocate for their people. On many other reservations, chiefs had been so thoroughly deposed and undermined that many tribal members didn't even know who they were. At Red Lake, the chieftainships were universally known and the chiefs successfully asserted themselves in challenging situations. In many ways, sovereignty was what they made of it.

In 1909, the chiefs decided to petition the government for a redress of grievances. Paul H. Beaulieu, at only twenty years of age, was asked by the chiefs to travel with them to Washington to interpret and advise. Beaulieu had made a living working for the government and in private business. He had the blood of French royalty and fur traders in his veins. But he was just as native as he was white, with a brown skin, a native family, and a heart that beat for the people of Red Lake. He was not a chief, but he was a leader at Red Lake, someone who led through influence.

Traveling with Beaulieu were the chiefs of Red Lake. Sufficient Sky (Debi-giizhig) was the head chief for the delegation. The other chiefs were Joseph Mason (Migiziins, or Little Eagle), Bazile Lawrence, Alexander Jourdain Jr. (Alex-eaince), Rattler (Zhenaawishkang), George Highlanding (Bebaami-giizhigoweshkang, or He Who Treads Across the Sky), and John English. Many of the delegates were chiefs or at least signatories to the Nelson Act, including Joseph Mason and Bazile Lawrence. None of them were from Ponemah.

Nodin Wind was at a crossroads. At thirty-four years old, he was still relatively young, but he had proven his worth in the ceremonial community at Ponemah. He showed grit in the face of conflict over construction of the school, on missionary visits, and in political discourse with the OIA. His influence was remarkable. Wind probably would have been content to live out his life in Ponemah without political ambition, but the whites would not leave Ponemah alone.[77]

Something was happening at Red Lake that had been building for many decades. The three villages on the south shore of the lake and many of the scattered families from Thief River Falls, Warroad, and elsewhere in the allotted or ceded lands were coming together. White Thunderbird, the Dakota boy adopted at Ponemah, symbolized and sparked political change that reverberated across the region. Moose Dung, from Thief River, was a tribal strategist who spread the changing culture of Red Lake across their territory. He Who Is Spoken To was a nation builder, pulling on the shared culture of the Red Lake people, navigating treaty negotiations and land cessions, fighting for the lake—north and south shore alike. A nation was rising—a native nation, a warrior nation. And Ponemah, while sharing the same culture in many respects and tied inextricably to the fate of their cousins across the lake, had stayed out of the formal political transformation. But going forward, Ponemah would never be left in isolation, and there was too much at stake to stubbornly pretend that they could weather the war on culture alone.

Nodin Wind must have gone through a lot of tobacco as he parlayed with the chiefs in Ponemah. He humbly shared his observations and fears—that they would do what they always did—stay away. But they were swayed by his passion and concern and they respected his position as an emerging leader in ceremony and community life. They gave their blessing for Nodin Wind to represent the village. He was one of the chiefs now.[78]

Nodin Wind put on his best shirt and beaded vest. He grabbed his otter-skin turban and porcupine-hair head roach, adorned with a long hawk feather and several small eagle feathers, every one of them earned by an act of service for the people. Then he paddled across the lake to Red Lake to join the 1909 delegation of chiefs for the Red Lake Nation. When warriors go into battle, they need allies.

Wind's influence rippled throughout Ponemah as he left. Every Wind (Endaso-onding) caught up with him to help represent Ponemah. King Bird, a reputable spiritual leader and by nature especially distrustful of people outside of Ponemah, was swayed by Wind's initiative and joined the delegation as well.

The last official Red Lake delegation to Washington DC, 1909. Seated: George High-
landing, Peter Everwind, John English, Nodin Wind. Top row: Joseph Mason, Paul H.
Beaulieu, King Bird (Ogimaa-bines), Bazile Lawrence, attorney John Gibbons, Alex
Jourdain Jr., Waiting Day (Baabii-giizhig), Curved Feather Man (Emiiwigwanaabe)

The delegation got few concessions in Washington in 1909. Most important, the section of land on Upper Red Lake that was illegally taken after the 1889 Nelson Act was not returned. But in the internal dynamics of Red Lake's polity, something significant was happening. As Wind traveled with Paul H. Beaulieu and Sufficient Sky, devout Catholics, he was building bridges across the lake, transcending religion, and finding shared culture and common political goals.

In 1918, Wind extended his effort to keep Ponemah part of the new nation at Red Lake. The General Council of the Red Lake Band of Chippewa Indians was created by Peter Graves and Paul H. Beaulieu that year. It was a move of political genius that formalized the Red Lake national identity and developed the first modern representative tribal government in the United States at the same time that it preserved the roles and functions of the hereditary chiefs. Nodin Wind was there, acknowledged by the entire reservation. He was not just a chief from Ponemah. He was now one of the seven formally acknowledged chiefs of the entire Red Lake Nation.

The war on culture was far from over. By some measures, it had really just begun. But something fundamental changed as Nodin Wind led Ponemah's defense. Ponemah was united with the villages on the south shore of Red Lake as equal partners in the growing Red Lake national identity and political culture. Chiefs from Ponemah have served on the General Council and in the contemporary council of hereditary chiefs ever since. Citizens from Ponemah have also been consistently elected as representatives in Red Lake's democratic elections, including to the top post of tribal chairman. Ponemah became, just as much as Little Rock, Red Lake, and Redby, a cornerstone of the common tribal nation.[79]

Nodin Wind lived for another seventy-two years after serving on the 1909 delegation. He kept horses at his family plot in Ponemah. He worked as a commercial fisherman and joined the Red Lake Fisheries Association, which put him in sustained business relationships with people from across the reservation. He continued his political representation of Ponemah and deepened his work as a spiritual leader for the region. Just before turning one hundred, he publicly retired from officiating medicine dances and funerals owing to the strain of the work and his advanced years. He pushed Dan Raincloud up as his successor and until age 106 still regularly attended ceremonies to support Raincloud, Leonard Hawk, and Thomas Stillday Jr., arranging for transportation during the last few years of his life when he moved to an elder care facility in Blackduck. Through his often-emulated example, the ethos of his status as a spiritual leader, the logos of his political disposition, and the deep pathos he displayed as a passionate Red Lake patriot, Nodin Wind also changed the culture of Ponemah. He didn't just put Ponemah into the Red Lake Nation; he put the Red Lake Nation into the hearts of the people of Ponemah.

Peter Graves, 1953

5

Peter Graves and the Modernization of Red Lake Politics

"In his very being were the forces destined to open
a new way for his poor and oppressed, and by his
masterful leadership, his unyielding perseverance
in the field of battle he was able to preserve the Red
Lake Reservation for the people to whom it rightfully
belongs. . . . The things for which he fought will live
forever in the hearts and minds of his people."

DAVID B. O'REAR *(Peter Graves Tribute adopted
by the General Council of the Red Lake Band
of Chippewa Indians, April 2, 1957)*

The Birth of Red Lake's Political Genius

Collins W. Oakgrove (Zhaawanoowinini, or Man of the South) was in
many ways a typical Red Laker. He was short in the legs but broad
in the shoulders, a full-blood, a member of the kingfisher clan, and a
direct lineal descendant of White Thunderbird. Oakgrove was born
in Red Lake on March 16, 1944, and raised mainly in Ponemah. His
family never had much money. He remembered packing a Mason jar
of tea and a lard sandwich and walking to school most days because
his family did not have a vehicle for many years. But he was happy,
quick to laugh, and proud of his family and place. In 1956, his parents
gave him a dollar to purchase a loaf of bread and a gallon of milk from
the store in Ponemah.

Thomas and Mary Spears clerked the Ponemah store at that time. The luxury of refrigerated food products was new in Ponemah. A small and unreliable diesel power plant had been built to power the school several years previously, but residential and commercial service elsewhere had been very rare until October 1, 1952. That's when the Rural Electric Association (REA) tied the village into the power grid and ran cable to Ponemah, bringing power to most of the village. The Ponemah store changed with the times, stocking less kerosene for the house lamps and more refrigerated food. Collins Oakgrove was hot and dusty by the time he made the walk to town. He stood in front of the milk refrigerator with a hand on the glass, cooling down. He was twelve years old.[1]

Oakgrove snapped to attention when Peter Graves walked into the store. Graves had a light complexion compared to most Red Lakers. But he was a tall man and had a commanding voice as he talked to Mary Spears, eloquently engaging her in Ojibwe, laughing, and nearly running right into Oakgrove, who stood staring. It wasn't just Graves's complexion or height that caught his attention. Graves was wearing a shirt with a button-down collar, a tie, a vest, a suit coat, slacks, and shiny dress shoes with just a hint of dust from the dirt parking lot outside. Everything about his appearance told Collins Oakgrove that he had money and power. With a gravelly laugh, Graves patted Oakgrove on the head and stepped past him to grab his milk and return to the clerk to pay. Reaching into his pocket, Graves produced a large wad of cash, too thick to fit in any wallet. He had paid Spears and turned to leave when Oakgrove, still standing in front of the refrigerator, asked, "Wow. Where did you get all that money? Does it grow on trees?" Graves erupted in raucous laughter and patted Oakgrove on the head again: "Don't be a fool, boy. Money doesn't grow on the trees. It grows *in* the trees." He winked and left.

Peter Graves was born on the south shore of Red Lake, by the water, just a half mile east of the Red Lake Indian agency. His official government birth record lists May 20, 1870, as his date of birth, but church records give the date as May 20, 1872, which Graves himself believed to be more accurate. Although he was Red Lake's most powerful political figure for thirty-nine years, it surprises many people to know that he claimed no blood from Red Lake. His mother, Lake Superior Woman (Gichi-gamiiwikwe), was from Leech Lake, a daughter of an Ojibwe chief there named Chaff (Mazaan, or Wild Rice Chaff). As a young woman, she fell in love with a man from Red Lake and moved there around 1860 to get married and start a family with him. Her husband was a younger son of Moose Dung. Together they had five children. But tragedies struck in rapid succession as she lost her husband and three of their children. She had to start over, and it was a painful struggle.[2]

Mary C. English, sister of William Whipple Warren, was a teacher at the new government boarding school in Red Lake. She was part of the very large Warren–Cadotte trading family and was a direct descendant of Richard Warren, who came to America as one of the original pilgrims on the Mayflower in 1620; Michel Cadotte, a famous French trader; and the head hereditary chief from the Ojibwe village at La Pointe, White Crane (Waabishki-ajijaak). Mary English was very knowledgeable and spent years informing and collaborating with Frances Densmore on her groundbreaking work *Chippewa Customs*.[3]

English took pity on Lake Superior Woman and, in an effort to help her rebuild, decided to give her an English name through a baptismal rite. Lake Superior Woman, a monolingual Ojibwe speaker with no English name, was christened Elizabeth Margaret Graves, named for a friend of Mary English who lived in Boston. The two namesakes never met, but from that simple act sprang the large and powerful Graves family at Red Lake. Elizabeth Graves eventually forged a new relationship with Joseph Truman Omen. Omen was a refugee from the Louis Riel Rebellion in Canada (1869–70). He came to Red Lake in 1871 and soon connected with Elizabeth Graves. Within a year their son was born. Elizabeth, who in spite of her baptism still largely followed traditional Red Lake Ojibwe religious beliefs and practices, sought out respectable community members to serve as namesakes for her son. At the ceremony, he was named Lone Feather (Nezhikegwaneb).

Omen was a white man. In spite of his connection to the Louis Riel Rebellion, he was not Métis and had no native or French ancestry, but was from pure Scots-English stock. Although Lone Feather had a bona fide Indian name, the Red Lakers seized on the identity of his father and called the boy Zhaaganaash, which meant Englishman. The name stuck. From 1872 to 1877, Lone Feather was usually referred to as Zhaaganaash.[4]

Joseph Omen never married Elizabeth Graves and didn't show much loyalty to his relationship with her. He had another son with another woman at Red Lake and named that boy Joseph Omen Jr. Elizabeth Graves turned to her old mentor, Mary English, who suggested the name Peter for her son and the surname Graves, after his mother. Joseph Omen exerted some influence on Peter Graves during his early years. At his insistence, even though Elizabeth still largely held on to traditional Ojibwe ways, Peter was baptized Catholic.

Omen left for a job with the railroad when Peter Graves was five years old and never returned to Red Lake. Peter was raised with his two step-siblings from his mother's marriage to the son of Moose Dung. He knew his half-brother, Joseph Omen Jr., but they never formed a close relationship.[5]

In 1877, at age five, Peter Graves was sent to the government boarding school that was established in Red Lake that year, as a member of its inaugural class of kindergartners. In 1884, at the age of thirteen, he was sent to Jubilee College, a secretarial preparatory school located in Dubee County, Illinois (near Peoria). After only ten months at Jubilee, he was transferred to the Lincoln Institute in Philadelphia, which Graves called the Educational Home. The school was industrial and he took several jobs as he progressed through the grades, working on a farm, doing construction work, and rolling cigars. When he was seventeen, he played professional baseball with the old Middle States League, based in Hazelton, Pennsylvania.

Graves was admitted to Princeton University on a baseball scholarship, but declined the opportunity because he believed that they valued him as a baseball player only and not for his brains. He left Pennsylvania on October 5, 1889, and returned to Red Lake. He arrived just after the most significant political development in recent memory at Red Lake—the negotiations for the Nelson Act whereby Red Lake ceded a vast swath of acreage around its now diminished reservation.

Graves struggled in his first few years back at Red Lake. He worked in a lumber camp during the winter of 1889-90, cutting timber and helping to boom logs on Lower Red Lake, which were towed to the Red Lake River outlet and then run on the river down to Crookston for milling. In the spring of 1890 he took a job as janitor and disciplinarian at the government boarding school in Red Lake. In 1891, he met Mary Fairbanks and fell in love. They were soon married and raising children—John (Wenji-gimiwang, or Cause of the Rain), Joseph (Baadwewidang, or Approaching Sound), Isabelle, Alice, William, and Rose.[6]

Graves never lost his command of the Ojibwe language in spite of spending twelve years away from his home community in English-only environments. His knowledge of English was exceptional. In the summer of 1890, he was hired by the Office of Indian Affairs to work at the Red Lake Agency as an interpreter. For the next thirty years he worked there in several capacities, serving under a Mr. Laird, Captain George B. Read, Captain J. C. Lawler, George A. Morrison, Daniel Sullivan, and Earl W. Allen.

In 1893, agent John T. Frater recruited twenty-one-year-old Graves to the Indian police. Within five years he was promoted to chief of police. The Indian police were the law-enforcement agency on the reservation, working for the nonnative Indian agent under the auspices of the Office of Indian Affairs. Graves quickly developed a reputation as being stern and fair. He was also exceptionally loyal to his supervisors in the OIA, and he took great pride in never criticizing them in his long tenure working for the U.S. government.[7]

Graves was put to the test soon after his promotion. On September 15, 1898, U.S. deputy marshal Robert Morrison and U.S. Indian agent Arthur M. Tinker arrested Leech Lake elder Hole in the Day for bootlegging. Several Leech Lake Ojibwe rescued Hole in the Day in a daring attack on Morrison and Tinker. Major Melville C. Wilkinson, General John M. Bacon, and a detachment of around a hundred soldiers from the Third Infantry Regiment boarded steamers and came to Bear Island on Leech Lake on October 5, 1898, to arrest Hole in the Day again. When they disembarked, one of the soldiers accidentally discharged his rifle. The Leech Lakers, hiding nearby, thought they had been discovered and fired upon. They fired back, killing one Indian police officer and six soldiers, including Major Wilkinson. Ten more soldiers were wounded. The Leech Lakers suffered no casualties. All of Minnesota was in an uproar. The Leech Lake Ojibwe were bracing for war.[8]

At Red Lake, the hereditary chiefs held council to decide if they should intervene and send warriors to fight with the Leech Lakers against the U.S. Army. Peter Graves, now age twenty-six and serving as chief of police for the past five years, politely asked to join the council. He was welcomed by the hereditary chiefs and entered the assembly, shaking hands, exchanging pleasantries, and reconnecting with Red Lake's leaders. But when the council formally began, Graves sat with a stern look on his face, listening intently to the discussion until he was unable to restrain himself any longer. He sprang to his feet and took over the meeting with a stunning assertion of authority. Here's his account in his own words:

> They were ready to go. I argued. I told them that anybody who would go to help the Leech Lake Indians must stay and belong to that band. We don't want no rebels from the Red Lake reservation. Whoever goes, I said, relinquishes their rights on Red Lake.... I said, "We're not going to war with the government." I said, "We know better." I said to one old man, I said, "Let me tell you something. You're an old man. You're the warrior; you're the veteran." He had been in battles with the Sioux. You couldn't do anything. That's what I told them. When I got through, they agreed with me. There was not a single one that went. They knew they'd be on the road; they wouldn't belong here if they went and fought with Leech Lake.

The venerated warrior that Graves confronted at the chiefs council was none other than Sun Shining Through, nicknamed Business (or Pus-se-naus). As soon as Graves had accomplished his objective, he defused the tension, telling Sun Shining Through, "All the government will do with you is keep tea away and you'll go crazy." Graves remarked, "He was a great tea drinker." Sun Shining Through burst into laughter, soon joined by all the other chiefs. The Red Lakers stayed home and let the Leech Lakers deal with fallout from the Battle of Sugar Point on their own.[9]

Before this, Graves had earned positions in large part because of his English-language skills, education, and connections with the OIA. After 1898, the eloquent, educated, light-complexioned, half-white, half–Leech Lake Indian became an established political force at Red Lake in his own right. From that day on, the hereditary chiefs looked at Peter Graves differently. They could have denied him access to the council in the first place, refused to let him speak once he got there, or dismissed his counsel as the words of a youngster, an outsider, or a usurper. Instead, they responded to his brash and unsolicited inter-

vention into the affairs of the chiefs with a firm, respectful validation. His position became theirs. From then on, Graves was ascending, and the hereditary chiefs sought to include and empower him
at every turn. Graves returned the respect. Rather than try to push
past them, he responded as a willing pupil and subordinate, though
he was never shy about sharing his own pointed opinions on policy.

Later in 1898, Graves considered enlisting in the U.S. Army when
the Spanish-American War broke out. He had a strong desire to distinguish himself on the field of battle. But the chiefs wanted him
to stay at Red Lake. He followed their counsel. Forty years later he
remarked, "I was very unfortunate in not having the opportunity to
enlist in the Spanish-American War. I was then, what I consider, in
my prime. Certain parties advised me not to enlist."[10]

Graves's relationship with the hereditary chiefs continued to
deepen in 1899 when he accompanied a delegation from Red Lake to
Washington, DC, as both interpreter and delegate. Captain Mercer,
agent at the Leech Lake Agency, insisted on his appointment as interpreter because of his well-established service as a U.S. government
employee and intermediary with tribal leaders. But the Red Lake
hereditary chiefs insisted that he also serve as a delegate for the tribe.

In 1902, when James McLaughlin came to Red Lake to negotiate
with the chiefs for the cession of the eleven western townships, the
government again wanted Graves to interpret. The chiefs wanted
him to help them. He did both. His influence was instrumental in
advancing the goals of the chiefs. He helped them prepare a petition
that articulated their position on critical issues—a new diplomatic
tactic that helped them negotiate better terms in the cession agreement. Graves also followed an interesting pattern in his employment. Instead of moving from one job to another, or ascending up
a supervisory command chain, he often kept his current positions
and simply added more. His ability to balance so many demanding
jobs simultaneously was a marvel. In government and police work it
sometimes earned him criticism as a dictator. There is no doubt that
he was accumulating political and material power through his stack-
ing of positions. On April 30, 1901, without stepping away from his
duties as chief of police, he also assumed the position of postmaster,
which expanded his influence.

In 1908, he again demonstrated the extent of his influence on

Red Lake delegation to Washington, DC, 1899. Front row, left to right: Red Robed, Two Skies (Niizho-giizhig), Blue Sky (Ozhaawashko-giizhig), Old Man (Akiwenzii), Sounding Light (Madweyaasang), Cut Ear (Giishkitawag), Across the Sky (Edawi-giizhig). Standing, third from left, Shining Feather (Waasegwaneb); fifth from left, King of the Sky (Ogimaa-giizhig). Photo by C. M. Bell.

tribal leaders even beyond Red Lake. In a striking display of trust, Leech Lake chief Hole in the Day, the central figure in the 1898 Battle of Sugar Point, came to Red Lake for Graves's advice and counsel. According to Graves:

> He sent word to see if I could see him. I sent word that he could come see me any time, so he came at 2 o'clock one night. He wanted to know what they were going to do to him. He was the *leader* of that fight, you see. He went to Canada and lived there for ten years or so before he turned back. He had trusted me, you see. Whatever I told him would be so. That is why he came to me. I told him that as long as he behaved himself . . . if he didn't, if he was arrested for drunkenness or anything, he'd be out. It would be put against him, and he'd have to be responsible for his actions in the past. That's what I told him.

Hole in the Day took his advice, prompting Graves to say years later, "I want to say that the old man was of very good character up to the time of his death."[11]

Graves's influence was growing in all directions—deepening his relationships with the Red Lake hereditary chiefs, expanding his sphere of influence in Indian country, and earning respect from his supervisors in the Office of Indian Affairs. After Hole in the Day's visit to Red Lake, Graves was promoted to assistant clerk for the OIA at the Onigum branch of the Leech Lake Agency. He accepted the position, which required his presence at Leech Lake. He maintained a steady back-and-forth between Leech Lake and Red Lake over the next several years.

Graves suffered a terrible setback in his personal life in 1912, when his wife Mary died. He did his grieving by pouring himself into his work for the OIA, receiving stellar reports from each supervisor he reported to: Major G. L. Scott, John T. Frater, J. F. Giegoldt, Karl F. Mayor, and Harvey K. Meyer. In spite of his career success, the next few years made for hard adjustments as he kept up his work at Leech Lake, parented his children alone, and worked hard to serve the community at Red Lake without an official position in which to do so. Graves was an attractive man, full of charisma and potential. In 1915, he attracted the attention of Susan Wright, fell in love, and wasted no time in marrying her the same year. Their blended family grew with new additions—Mary, Maude, Amy, Clyde, Mildred, and Doris.[12]

While Graves was rebuilding his personal life, forces were at work to undermine the land status of the Red Lake Ojibwe. Officials in Washington, DC, still hoped to allot the reservation, breaking the communal status of the land and enabling individual ownership. That in turn would enable land sales, tax seizures, and white commercial, timber, and agricultural development at Red Lake. Some Indians were willing to work with the government to make that happen.

Walter F. Dickens and Representative Halvor Steenerson met with the Red Lake chiefs to bargain for the commencement of allotments and further opening of timber at Red Lake for white harvest. Steenerson served in the U.S. Congress from 1902 to 1923 and was one of the primary advocates for timber exploitation at White Earth and Red Lake. His appropriation bill riders and legislative efforts were a large part of the enabling effort behind white timber harvests in Indian country. In fact, when Steenerson and Dickens met with the Red Lake chiefs in 1912, Steenerson had already included language in the appropriation bill to enable timber harvesting and the drainage of swamps at Red Lake.[13]

Nathan J. Head, a mixed-blood Ojibwe born in Winnipeg, was among those advocating for allotment at Red Lake. Head was roughly the same age as Peter Graves, having been born on March 20, 1875. In 1912, he wrote a sophisticated plan to allot and subdivide the lakeshore at Red Lake. On September 10, 1913, the commissioner of Indian affairs wrote to agency superintendent Walter F. Dickens, "Submit allotment matter to general council of Indians Sept. 22, and advise the Office here. Mail promptly the result." The chiefs of Red Lake never approved allotments, and this time was no exception, but the government was relentless in its pursuit of that goal.[14]

Ed Prentice and other Red Lake leaders traveled to Washington in April 1914 to voice complaints about timber and land issues. The delegates all received letters from the OIA that read: "Your applications have been filed and when the question of giving the Indians of the Red Lake Reservation allotments in severalty shall have been determined will be given consideration." Tensions between the government and its pro-allotment allies at Red Lake and the chiefs, who still opposed any form of allotment, were extremely high.[15]

Red Lake's trust funds from the sale of ceded lands and timber were being badly mismanaged by the federal government. Graves

saw a lot of the correspondence through his work for the OIA, and
he knew that something had to be done. In 1913, the money that the
federal government collected for sale of the land that Red Lake ceded
around Thief River was supposed to be transferred to the tribal trust
fund. The tribe expected the government to make a payment of $8.1
million, which was essentially the difference between the collected
sale value of land and its appraised value plus compensation for the
delay in paying the tribe. Graves worried about payments to Red
Lake being mismanaged or even redirected. He knew that the hereditary chiefs needed more structure and formalized power if they were
to be successful in protecting the land, water, and interests of the
Red Lake people.[16]

Peter Graves and Building the General Council, 1918-1957

Graves was now poised for one of the most critical and long-lasting
contributions ever made to the political evolution of Red Lake. In
1939, Graves humbly wrote, "I promoted their Council in its present
form in the year 1918." But he did much more than promote the General Council. He saw the need for Red Lake's government to evolve
and orchestrated the change.[17]

On most reservations across the United States, the Office of Indian
Affairs appointed Indian agents—white men—to rule the Indians.
The agents usurped the power of chiefs over time. When the government owed money to Indians, the money used to be distributed
to chiefs, who dispersed it to their people. That made chiefs powerful financial arbiters. But during the treaty period, the Indian agents
took over that duty, and the Indians lined up to get their payments
from white men. That took power from the chiefs and gave it to the
Indian agents. The agents ran the allotment process on most reservations. They had their own police forces in most places, and they even
had their own court systems.[18]

The critical powers and functions of chiefs were systematically
dismantled. As white land, mining, oil, and timber speculators
descended on reservations across the country, the Indian agents
enabled their predatory takings from Indians and usually were paid
handsomely for their service by both the government and private

business interests. The ability of chiefs to protect their people diminished with each passing year. Many tribal people lost the knowledge of who their hereditary chiefs were.

At Red Lake, the hereditary chiefs held on. In some ways, the OIA and private business interests did at Red Lake what they did everywhere else. But Graves acted as a counterforce. He was highly respected by his supervisors in the OIA and he used his relationship capital with them to support the empowerment of the hereditary chiefs. He had a knack for being diplomatic and firm at the same time when serving as an intermediary between the OIA and the chiefs.

The government lumped all Minnesota Ojibwe together for many financial transactions, including management of trust funds. Red Lake ceded more than half its remaining land and timber resources in the Nelson Act. By 1918, Red Lake was generating 80 percent of the revenue for land and timber sales but collecting 14 percent of the profits from the trust funds. The other bands, dominated especially by White Earth Ojibwe, developed an organization called the General Council of the Chippewas of Minnesota to manage relations with the federal government regarding the trust fund.

Red Lake was being marginalized and treated unfairly. Graves said, "The Red Lake Indians found at this time that these few men [who were running the General Council of the Chippewas of Minnesota] would control their affairs, would ask congress to pass laws to attain their ends." At a special presentation before representatives of the other Ojibwe bands and the U.S. Senate Committee on Indian Affairs, Graves directly told them, "They [the Red Lake chiefs] have decided to sever their relations to your Council [General Council of the Chippewas of Minnesota] and do not further recognize your said Council as a medium for the transaction of their tribal matters and affairs before the Indian Department and the Congress of the United States." Red Lake needed its own council. Graves summed up the development: "We asked fair play from the General Council of the Chippewas, but they would not give it to us, so we had to separate from them."[19]

As the white feeding frenzy on Indian resources, especially timber, was reaching a peak by World War I, Graves knew that more had to be done to strengthen Red Lake's right and ability to practice self-governance. He also knew that the Office of Indian Affairs could be pushed only so far. This knowledge made him a deft and dexterous creator of Red Lake's first modern governance structure.

In 1918, Graves invited the hereditary chiefs to a meeting and explained that they had to modernize their government and make it official to be properly recognized and legitimized by the OIA. He worked closely with Paul H. Beaulieu, who was not a chief but was a well-respected community and business leader. Together they drafted a constitution for the General Council of the Red Lake Band of Chippewa Indians and presented it to the chiefs for review. Otto Thunder, Spencer Whitefeather, and Alva Burns signed approvals from local village Indian councils for the new governing system. It was a unique structure in many respects and not without flaws, but it did serve to bridge the ancient Ojibwe leadership paradigm to a new age in tribal governance.

Article 1 of the constitution established the General Council, but Article 2 recognized the role and positions of the hereditary chiefs and empowered them to be the primary political agents at Red Lake. Red Lake had seven primary hereditary chiefs at the time, so the document named seven hereditary chieftainships and empowered each of them to appoint five fellow representatives to the General Council. Together, they were the voting membership of the General Council. Chiefs from villages outside of the diminished reservation at Warroad and other places were not formally recognized in the new structure. Ponemah had multiple chiefs as well, and not all were represented. But in spite of these shortcomings, the new constitution and General Council empowered most of the identified chiefs at Red Lake and had their full support.

Article 3 articulated the right of the General Council to appoint a chairman and other officers, although none of the appointed officers had voting power. Article 10 made it clear that each hereditary chief's position existed with successor rights by heredity. In other words, those positions were to pass from father to son. Essentially, the structure of the General Council preserved the power and positions of the hereditary chiefs, but gave it a formal organizational structure.

The addition of nonvoting officers to keep and record minutes and assist with financial record keeping did not reduce the General Council's powers but made the work easier. Eventually, it would enable them to supplant the documentary and fiduciary activities of the OIA on the reservation. The hereditary chiefs had a lot of faith in Graves and saw the proposed constitution as supportive of their power and positions. Although Red Lake had maintained hereditary chieftainships from 1760 to 1918 without any documentation, the change won approval. With the unanimous support of the chiefs, the constitution of the General Council of the Red Lake Band of Chippewa Indians became Red Lake's charter political document.

On April 13, 1918, the General Council held its first formal meeting under the new constitution. The seven formally recognized chiefs were King Mountain (Ogimaawajiweb), Sits Alone, Little Frenchman, William Sayers (Niigaanose, or He Who Walks Ahead), Red Feather (Miskogwan), Striped Day, and Nodin Wind. Most of the hereditary chiefs already had many decades of political leadership as a result of their positions. Sits Alone had been chief since 1864. His father, Little Thunder, died in Washington while serving as chief during the Old Crossing Treaty renegotiations. Sits Alone and Striped Day signed the Nelson Act in 1889 and the Thief River land cession in 1902. They were now seventy and fifty-two years old, respectively. Little Frenchman and King Mountain, at sixty-one and fifty-nine, were also signatories to the Nelson Act. Wind, one of the most respected spiritual leaders on the reservation, had served as chief in the Red Lake delegation to Washington in 1909. Red Feather was the son of Red Robed. Bazile Lawrence temporarily served as acting hereditary chief for a while after 1918. He was a signer of the 1889 Nelson Act at the age of twenty-two and a tribal delegate to Washington in 1909, but he was not a hereditary chief then. Half the hereditary chiefs at the time of the General Council's genesis signed by an X mark because they had no English-language literacy. They were powerful in Red Lake, and now Graves could use the General Council to further empower them with the U.S. government.[20]

The first job of the General Council was to appoint officers. Peter Graves was named treasurer and served in that capacity from 1918 to 1920. Then he was appointed secretary-treasurer and served in that role from 1920 to 1957. Joseph B. Jourdain was appointed chairman and John Graves secretary for the first two years. Both of the other officers deferred to Peter Graves, who was the primary authority figure and architect for the entire effort. Once the General Council was created, Peter Graves served for life without dispute. Anna

Gibbs reflected on his contributions: "Peter Graves created the Gen-eral Council. All the traditional chiefs were there and he honored them, but he also made the council like the United States of America government. There were white people just swarming all over the res-ervation before that. But once Peter Graves made the council, that's when the white people finally left Red Lake alone."[21]

Getting white people to leave Red Lake alone took much more than creating the General Council, but the new governance structure was a critical step. Red Lake was one of the first tribes in the United States to develop a modern representative constitutional governance structure. Most other tribes didn't even think about trying to do that until after passage of the Indian Reorganization Act in 1934. Even then, it took decades for most to develop the political and economic infrastructure to manage their own affairs. In Mille Lacs, for exam-ple, all business operations for the tribe were run by three white bankers from Onamia until 1954.[22]

Two tribes, inspired by Red Lake's success, tried to replicate the process for their communities. The Flandreau Santee Sioux Tribe and the Leech Lake Band of Chippewa Indians tried to develop mod-ern councils like Red Lake. But efforts in both places stalled because they did not have support from within the Office of Indian Affairs and because tribal leaders were not sufficiently unified to collectively advocate for themselves without dissension. The General Council of the Chippewas of Minnesota, which tried to represent all of the Min-nesota Ojibwe, broke up from internal division and excessive OIA control. Replicating Red Lake's success was difficult without some-one like Peter Graves to organize internally on the reservation and advocate with the OIA.

Red Lake's General Council breathed new life into the warrior nation. The General Council sent delegations to Washington, DC, to advocate for land and political issues affecting the tribe. Nodin Wind led one in 1920 that met with Senate and congressional committees, secretary of the interior John B. Payne, and commissioner of Indian affairs Cato Sells. Wind and Graves led another delegation in 1924, and Graves traveled to Washington several times alone to pursue Red Lake's political agenda.[23]

The constitution for the General Council underwent at least one significant amendment—Red Lake tribal members had to be born

to Red Lake parents. Residency was important for political participation at Red Lake. The Ojibwe had always freely moved from one
village to another. It had long been assumed that the new village of
residence, much more than history, defined political association.
The first chiefs at Red Lake were all born elsewhere. Peter Graves
had invoked the importance of residency over birthright in 1898 to
intimidate would-be participants in the possible conflict between
Leech Lake and the U.S. government. Throughout the treaty and
early reservation periods, Ojibwe people were moving and changing
associations. The U.S. government reinforced that with its efforts to
relocate people to White Earth. Elizabeth Graves, Nathan J. Head,
and many others had shown through personal example that you
didn't have to be born in Red Lake to be a Red Laker; but you did
have to live there.

By 1918, things were starting to change. Indians owned less land.
Annuities from land sales, pressure from white settlement, and
government policy made people more sedentary. This posed a real
challenge to prevailing assumptions about political identity. Roger
A. Jourdain recalled: "It was generally assumed that if you were born
in the Red Lake Hospital, built in 1914, you were a Red Laker. You've
got to understand that in those days not many people left the reservation, and if you decided to leave, you were on your own." The
General Council eventually adopted an amendment to dispose of the
requirement for birth on the reservation in favor of a looser defi-
nition of Red Lake citizenship eligibility—being born to Red Lake
parents. Blood quantum was not required at Red Lake until 1961.[24]

The importance of the General Council of the Red Lake Band of
Chippewa Indians has yet to be fully understood or appreciated outside of Red Lake. In the end, it enabled Red Lake leaders to finally
take control of their own reservation, prevented the intrusion of
state government into the policing of the reservation, protected the
integrity of the unallotted land base on the main part of the diminished reservation, and preserved a vital role for the hereditary chiefs
in the leadership of the reservation. Its creation was a prescient act
of political genius.

Peter Graves in Transition: Allotment, Segregation, and Land Claims

By 1919, Peter Graves saw his position in the Leech Lake Agency of the Office of Indian Affairs as a conflict of interest with his role as treasurer for the General Council at Red Lake. He could not in good conscience continue to represent Leech Lake, so he resigned his position with the OIA and moved back to Red Lake. For Graves, resigning from the OIA was bittersweet. He strongly felt that it was the right thing to do, but he loved the work, his white supervisors, and his role as an intermediary, respected by whites and Indians alike. He guarded his reputation carefully. Reflecting on the decision years later, he said:

> My real reason for resigning the Indian Service was that the Chippewas of Minnesota had started to make claims against the Red Lake Band. . . . I was opposed to those claims, and they accused me of taking this stand on account of my being a Government employee, and there was nothing else for me to do but to resign, for I strenuously objected to their claims, which would have meant a calamity, as I thought, for the Red Lake Band of Indians if the claims had been upheld by the Courts. I resigned from the Service without any hope or expectation of getting another position in which I could make a living, so I moved back to the Red Lake Reservation in May, 1919.[25]

Graves then unleashed a torrent of political action and advocacy to protect the land and interests of the Red Lake Ojibwe. The General Council rallied behind him with a unified voice for the separation of Red Lake from the other Ojibwe bands in financial settlements, in opposition to allotment, and for holding all tribal lands in common for the benefit of all tribal members. In 1919, Graves pushed the OIA to investigate treaty and land rights in Ojibwe country. All of the non–Red Lake Ojibwe in Minnesota wanted to handle their claims collectively. Most bureaucrats and politicians in Washington also wanted to lump all the Ojibwe together, quantify the damages owed to the Indians, and pay it off to settle all claims on a per capita basis. But Red Lake's interests were unique. It had ceded more than half its remaining land in the 1889 Nelson Act and the 1904 Thief River land cession. The other Ojibwe bands in Minnesota had legitimate grievances of their own, but Red Lake was making the overwhelming majority of the deposits into a joint account with the other bands for timber and land sales but only received a fraction of the payments.[26]

Graves knew that the egregious land and timber fraud at Red Lake and the unique set of circumstances with regard to the Nelson Act and the Thief River cession and the refusal of the Red Lake chiefs to accept allotments necessitated a special treatment. He correctly foresaw that the proposed settlement would divert money owed to the people of Red Lake to the other Ojibwe bands. He also worried that allotment would somehow spread to Red Lake. The Ojibwe at Mille Lacs were still receiving allotments in 1926. The main Red Lake reservation remained intact, but Graves wanted to make sure that they were not coerced into accepting allotments: "We have reasons why we do not want allotments. We cannot take care of them. We will sell them. We know our young men would do it."[27]

Graves wrote a culture-based environmental manifesto as a codified tribal political position connecting resistance to allotment with protection of the environment: "We believe it is our best interests to own our Red Lake Indian Reservation in common so that we may not be able to commercialize or destroy our home."[28]

This view proved prescient, not only with regard to preserving tribal ownership and control of the land, but also with regard to degradation of the reservation's ecosystems and natural resources. Many white land and business speculators wanted to develop Red Lake's shoreline into resort and cabin sites for white tourists and homeowners. Graves beat back every effort, frequently saying, "I want this paradise kept for my children and my grandchildren." There is a direct connection between Graves's anti-allotment environmental advocacy from 1919 to 1957 and the fact that today Red Lake is the cleanest aquifer in the state of Minnesota.[29]

In order to protect Red Lake's governing system and land, it was becoming more and more important to formalize Red Lake's separation from the other Ojibwe tribes in Minnesota not just with an independent political council, but in all legal matters. Red Lake's independent action in court cases was the first salvo of a new battle in the long war to keep Red Lake independent, unallotted, and sovereign. Graves doggedly pursued Red Lake's financial and legal claims through numerous court cases over nearly three decades.

In 1920, Peter Graves traveled to Washington, DC, to hunt for an attorney and initiate Red Lake's case. He commissioned Daniel B. Henderson, explained Red Lake's position, and put him to work. Henderson was capable, although not an Indian law expert, and Graves spent hours educating him in preparation for advocacy with the U.S. Senate, the OIA, and the Court of Claims. Graves's position as a loyal Red Lake patriot and a well-educated, articulate English speaker paid heavy dividends for the tribe long before the legal process was under way.[30]

On March 1, 1924, Graves testified before the House of Representatives Committee on Indian Affairs. He brought Henderson with him but did most of the speaking. He was self-assured and clear on the legal issues. He wanted a bill from Congress to pay out the funds from Ojibwe land and timber sales currently held in trust by the federal government and to separate Red Lake's share. He got traction with the representatives, and they recommended further work with the Senate. There too Graves succeeded in advancing Red Lake's effort, as the Senate established a special commission for field hearings in Minnesota.[31]

On August 26, 1924, Graves brought Henderson with him to Bemidji. Red Lake's financial claims from land issues were directly challenged by all the other Minnesota Ojibwe. A new Senate commission came to Minnesota to hear them out. Senators John W. Harreld, John B. Kendrick, and Lynn J. Frazier formed the commission, attended by commissioner of Indian affairs Charles H. Burke, several OIA officials, Ojibwe delegates, and attorneys. The atmosphere was adversarial and the senators tightly controlled the agenda and speaking time. The commission traveled to several Ojibwe communities and held hearings over the next several days. At the one in Bemidji, Graves displayed a consistently engaged, patient, forceful demeanor that had a real, tangible influence on the senators and ultimately shaped the political and legal position of all the Minnesota Ojibwe. Red Lake, of course, was the primary beneficiary of his representation.[32]

Graves kept Webster Ballinger, attorney for the Ojibwe bands, on the defense. He addressed Senator Harreld: "Mr. Chairman, you want correct information, of course, and you will never get it from Webster Ballinger so far as the Red Lake Indians are concerned." He carefully praised the OIA while pushing the government for action to release the trust funds and pay the people of Red Lake what they were owed for timber and land sales, and he evoked American ideals of rugged individualism to accomplish this goal: "They would starve to death. They cannot use the money if they cannot get hold of it. When you work you expect to be paid and pay your way."[33]

Timber and land-sale proceeds went into the fund in Washington, DC, but Red Lake could not access its own money while the other tribes demanded a piece of it and the government held all the controls. Graves gave a brilliant series of statements and rebuttals. He brought the hereditary chiefs with him to meet the senators and asked them to testify in Ojibwe. He corrected the government interpreters and clarified language and position issues. In the end, the entire Senate delegation was supportive of Red Lake's position. One OIA official wrote afterward, "Peter Graves is perhaps the most intelligent Red Lake Indian."[34]

Graves presented copies of the General Council's founding documents, citations for bills, quotes from critical pieces of the 1889 Nelson Act and 1904 Thief River cession legislation. Then he released the tribe's attorney to address the senators. Henderson's job was easy at that point. He told the senators: "There is specific, express and most positive legislative enactment now that compels that money to be paid to the Red Lake Indians, separately and apart from all the others. Until legislation to a contrary effect, there is no escape that the money is going to be paid; there is no escape in regard to whom it shall be paid."[35]

In 1926, the non–Red Lake Ojibwe bands in Minnesota sued the federal government over mismanagement of their trust funds from land and timber sales. Red Lake's land and timber sale money was tied up with that of the other Minnesota Ojibwe. Rather than join the suit, Graves counter-sued both the government and the other Ojibwe bands as intervener in the case. This succeeded in getting many of Red Lake's land and trust fund claims codified in a major lawsuit and brought before the U.S. Court of Claims. The case was pending for three years while affidavits and depositions were compiled. Graves had to find more lawyers, and eventually hired Fred Dennis, an attorney from Detroit Lakes, and retained him for decades. Multiple issues were on the table. The first argument was over compensation for land sold at Red Lake and for mismanagement of the tribe's trust fund. Graves initially asked for $5,469,698.20 in compensation to the tribe for land plus interest and an additional $800,000 for trust fund mismanagement.[36]

After further delays, the Court of Claims case received an initial hearing in 1930. Eventually, the Red Lake claims case was appealed to the U.S. Supreme Court. On October 14, 1935, the Supreme Court denied the petition of the other Ojibwe bands, essentially affirming Red Lake's independent status for trust fund administration and exclusive ownership of its own reservation. After that, Graves's work with the senators began to bear fruit and Red Lake had much less trouble protecting its independence.

Additional Red Lake land claim issues were allowed before the Indian Claims Commission by an act of Congress on August 13, 1946. The tribal petition was ultimately denied on September 17, 1951. Many of those claims are still unresolved.[37]

Red Lake did not win all of the arguments in all of its cases by any means, but much new and important information came to light. The Catholic priest from Red Lake, Thomas Borgerding, and a dozen Ojibwe participants in the 1889 negotiations provided depositions and testimony significant for the case and for documenting divergent perspectives on the Nelson Act. Borgerding was present for the Nelson Act negotiations and claimed that the official treaty log did not properly reflect the strenuous insistence of the Red Lake chiefs that they retain all of Upper and Lower Red Lake.

The government also wanted to lump all payments to all of the Minnesota Ojibwe together, but Graves strenuously objected. He felt that Red Lake's land and trust fund issues were unique and could not be treated in common with the rest of the Ojibwe population. He also felt that Red Lake was owed more because it had been more egregiously robbed and defrauded.

Perhaps even more important, he worried that a blanket treatment of all the Ojibwe would provide a legal precedent or justification for the future allotment of the reservation at Red Lake. On July 7, 1933, in the middle of the legal claims process, G. E. E. Lindquist, representing the Board of Indian Commissioners, wrote to Harold Ickes, secretary of the interior, to advocate for allotment of the Red Lake reservation. Red Lake won a partial but significant victory in its case. It did not get the lake back. It did not get the full compensation it had asked for. But it did avoid allotment, validate its independent position, and document timber and land issues for future action. In the end, it saved Red Lake more than $10 million.[38]

The other Ojibwe bands in Minnesota kept their financial claims consolidated with one another. They even built a new common governing body—the Minnesota Chippewa Tribe. Each reservation had independence over local governance, but tribal enrollment and many other issues were handled collectively through the Minnesota Chippewa Tribe's governing body. Again, Red Lake maintained its separate financial and political position.

The personal sacrifice Graves made in quitting his job with the OIA to serve Red Lake's interests in the land claim paid off for Red Lake. It protected Red Lake's unallotted reservation from further land loss. If not for Graves's intervention, Red Lake would likely be part of the Minnesota Chippewa Tribe today and could very well have been forced to allot its reservation. Graves's action also further cemented Red Lake's political cohesion and the respect that the OIA had for Red Lake's General Council. Red Lake was a sovereign force in its own right and everyone knew it. It also enhanced Graves's reputation as a strong and dedicated leader.[39]

When the tension over the settlement dispute subsided, Graves focused on rebuilding his personal homestead at Red Lake. He converted a small bedroom into an office, which was stacked with books and articles on Indian history, treaties, and U.S. government policy. He planted gardens, raised vegetables, and fished. He took a temporary job as field census enumerator for the Red Lake district in 1920. All the work he was doing to provide for his family as a hunter, fisherman, and gardener got him thinking about how to leverage those skills, widely shared by most people at Red Lake, into full-fledged commercial businesses.[40]

Peter Graves and the Timber Tycoons, 1918–1957

Graves opened a window into the timber business for Red Lake as soon as the General Council was established. It did produce results, generate jobs, and create a revenue stream for the tribe. But Red Lake was late to the party. Minnesota's timber business peaked in 1905, and by 1919, even the Mill City (Minneapolis) lumber mills were closed. It is not by accident, then, that Red Lake was finally able to assert control over the mill and timber business on the reservation as many of the wealthy timber tycoons abandoned the region and moved to the state of Washington to set up operations in the Columbia River Valley.

In 1917, the output of the Red Lake sawmill was doubled to 2 million board feet per year, with most of the cutting being done at Ponemah Point over the next several years. The General Council established itself and worked to expand operations immediately afterward. They focused on their independent tribal logging operations and expanding influence and control over federal timber contracts on the reservation. The U.S. Forest Service brought the first cars to Red Lake—a Ford car and a Dodge truck. The General Council often negotiated with the federal government on support and forestry analysis.[41]

Federal legislation in 1916 and 1924 allocated funds from Red Lake's trust accounts for the construction of a new mill on the reservation. In 1924, the General Council directed the expansion to take place at Redby. By 1925, the new mill was operating at capacity. It more than doubled the production of the previous mill to 5 million board feet per year. In 1926, legislation was passed to spend more of Red Lake's trust funds for further expansion of mill operations, including the addition of a planer operation and a box factory. The mill was busy, and sometimes eclipsed demand and infrastructure capabilities. In 1933, the mill was closed and the employees furloughed for three years while the supervisor worked to sell excess inventory.[42]

As the General Council got more involved in mill operations, the business started employing Indians through logging outfits to piece out the remaining sections of the reservation under supervision of a federally appointed superintendent. This formally replaced the mill operation at Red Lake. Initially, the entire operation was supervised by white men. A. C. Goddard operated the mill, built by Cyril Dickinson. Both were white men, as were 70 percent of the employees. That shifted as the mill operation evolved over the next fifteen years. They stopped floating logs in Red Lake in 1936, and trucked everything to the mill site. By 1950, operations moved to a new base camp at Little Pine Island with a 99 percent native labor force.[43]

Red Lakers loading logs on the reservation, about 1940

Red Lake was technically a closed reservation, meaning that it was never opened to white settlement or private ownership. No whites owned private land on the reservation except for a few parcels sold to schools and railroads, some of which did end up in private white ownership. In spite of that, Red Lake was overrun by whites. Fleets of boats operated in tribal waters from Thief River Falls to Redby to transport logs for the mill at Red Lake and in support of nonnative logging operations throughout the region. Red Lake was taking control of its own mill and lumber operations. At the same time, numerous nonnative timber operations were working major contracts throughout the ceded lands, and often by arrangement on Red Lake lands. In the summer of 1926, for example, the International Lumber Company laid fifty miles of logging railroad tracks, opened six new lumber camps, and cut 45 million board feet of timber on 19,000 acres. Once the timber was hauled out, they pulled up the tracks and moved to another area.[44]

The intense cutting at Red Lake produced a pattern of natural and human impact that continued to deplete the resources. The General Council pushed for a sustainable tribal harvest plan, reseeding, and capturing more of the value-added work through its mill operations. But every major nonnative timber business simply wanted to cut all the trees and leave. The harvest protocol of clear-cutting large amounts of acreage damaged soil fertility because of increased wind and rain erosion and salinization of the soil by water penetrating deeper into rock and mineral substrate and releasing salt. Every summer, seasonal strong winds and occasional storms became more and more catastrophic, as standing timber was exposed to winds without the natural buffers of a surrounding healthy forest. This weakened root systems, causing massive blowdowns every year.[45]

Compounding the soil and timber damage was the rate, size, and intensity of forest fires. The number of arson fires set in the late 1800s and early 1900s diminished when timber companies no longer needed to use the dead and down laws for access, but they did not end. There were fewer arson fires, but the fires that did occur were larger and much more intense.

Natural fires usually burned through the understory and left the tall timber unscathed. But when tall timber was clear-cut in many places, the understory and the blowdown timber burned completely. The fires raged so hot and intense that the partially decomposed pine needle duff burned clean, further depleting soil nitrates and topsoil depth. Dormant seeds in the decomposing soil were burned out and natural timber regeneration was impossible in many areas. In 1930, for example, a large blowdown felled 2 million board feet of timber on the reservation. Timber companies reclaimed just over half. Then a forest fire raged for days, engulfing three thousand acres of land on the reservation, destroying everything in the burn area from dormant seed to tall timber. More fires the same year at Ponemah, Redby, and the Sandy River burned an additional 13,000 acres.[46]

Charles H. Winton, one of the Minneapolis timber entrepreneurs, was thinking about ways to accelerate growth rates for continued harvest and so reseeded 230 acres at Red Lake. But when thousands of acres were burned, thousands cut, and hundreds reseeded on soil with depleted nutrient values and higher salt content, the results were understandably poor. Eventually, poplar, bur oak, and scrub brush became established in many places. Red Lake's vast pine timber resources, the awe and envy of timber tycoons for generations, were quickly becoming a thing of the past.

The entire American timber industry was soon to feel the full impact of its unsustainable environmental and economic practices and experience massive decline. Minneapolis was the largest lumber market in the United States in 1900, yet by 1919 there were no sawmills operating anywhere in the city. Duluth closed mill operations in 1926. Focus shifted to the state of Washington with the same unsustainable model.

Eventually, with all of the old-growth forests cut, a much lower rate of timber harvest took place across the country. For the people of Red Lake it produced mixed impacts. They got a reprieve from the intense feeding frenzy of the timber tycoons, and the pace of white settlement slowed. But the depletion of the timber resources greatly reduced the potential of the industry to alleviate poverty for Red Lake families. Some Red Lakers worked in the mill or cutting logs, but most of the real money went to white companies that employed primarily white folk.

The forests at Red Lake were permanently changed and diminished, producing a catastrophic cascade effect on animal populations. Woodland caribou, once plentiful at Red Lake, declined rapidly with deforestation. The Minnesota state hunting season for caribou was canceled after 1904. By 1915, Red Lake was home to the only surviving herd in Minnesota. By 1940, they were extinct. Minnesota's elk were almost annihilated by habitat loss and overhunting. By 1932, only a small herd survived in Red Lake's reclaimed ceded lands. The northwestern Minnesota moose herd declined later, as a lag effect from habitat loss, tick expansion, and climate change. Red Lake had to cancel its moose season at times in the 1980s and put a moratorium on hunting by the 1990s. The animal population declines made it ever harder for Red Lakers to live a subsistence lifestyle.[47]

Keystone species such as the timber wolf suffered tremendously as the big-game population around Red Lake imploded. Starving timber wolves increasingly hunted the feral horse herd in Ponemah, domestic livestock, and even fish. Frank Donnell recalled:

> In the winter it was kind of dangerous being out there on the lake. The wolves, they'd take off after you. Them timber wolves—Christ, they're as big as Shetland ponies. And if they didn't get no fish, they'd take off after you.

My dad, he used to haul mail across there, from Red Lake to Ponemah.
He used just a regular sled that he used to use hauling wood. They called
it a wagon box. They'd put that on there and throw the mail in there. He
said he could never go across that lake alone. He used to have two, three
teams with him. They'd get so far out on the lake and all the timber
wolves would take after them. See, they were starving. They were after
them horses.[48]

In the 1930s, Minnesota's timber economy nearly collapsed. Most
mills were closed, rail infrastructure was dismantled, and prices
plummeted. Stumpage prices (the standard value for standing timber measured as board feet per stump) in 1936 were about one-third
what they were just twenty years earlier. Red Lake stayed in the timber business in spite of the declining benefits. In the early 1900s, Red
Lake's mill was one of 554 northern Minnesota lumber mills and was
smaller than at least thirty of them, but by 1936 it was the third largest in the state. That did not happen because of Red Lake's expansion
so much as because everyone else had declined. The smaller margins
on the business were not the top concern for the General Council,
which was primarily interested in sustaining milling to keep Red
Lake families employed and in maintaining a range of healthy businesses to grow the local economy.[49]

Agricultural conversion of timberland was an abysmal failure.
County governments nearly went bankrupt trying to drain the
largest swamp in the state for farmland cultivation. In 1932, Beltrami and Lake of the Woods Counties converted several sections of
ditched land to state title for a game preserve as payment for ditching debts. In 1935, the OIA was still trying to get Indians to farm at
Red Lake. There were some successful tribal farmers on the west end
of Lower Red Lake, but in the swamp and timberland, farming was
not practical.[50]

In 1939, most of the timber was harvested, most of the white
farms had failed, the Crookston Mill went out of business, and the
Red Lake line was finally closed. The rails were pulled up and sold
off. The railroad right-of-way was sold for telephone lines rather than
reverting to tribal control. The tribe stayed engaged in the lumber
business. By the 1950s, Red Lake's lumber operation was grossing
$300,000 annually, all tribally controlled.[51]

On August 2, 1951, Peter Graves initiated major forestry litigation on behalf of the tribe with the Indian Claims Commission. It took fifty years to resolve, but eventually netted the tribe a settlement of $53.5 million. Graves was mainly responsible for both the legal action and the successful conversion of the reservation logging operations to Red Lake control.[52]

Peter Graves and the Red Lake Fisheries, 1918–1957

Graves had spent his teenage years in Philadelphia, and he traveled extensively. He knew that there was no way to go back in time or drive all the white folks away from Minnesota. But there was a way forward, and it did not require the cultural capitulation of the Red Lake people.

The people of Red Lake had always fished to feed their families. In 1900, Red Lake chief Praying Day filed formal complaints with the OIA about white encroachment on Red Lake waters at Lake of the Woods and Red Lake. In the early 1900s, some Red Lakers started to trade or sell some of their catch to white settlers. As Graves returned to subsistence living himself in 1920, he could see the value of helping all Red Lakers leverage the natural resources and their traditional fish harvesting skills into a new commercial enterprise. It became, and remains, one of Red Lake's most distinguished and successful modern cultural and economic accomplishments.[53]

Graves knew that for the idea to succeed he needed to have the chiefs and the General Council behind it, and he needed to chase the white folk away from Red Lake's fish. White businessmen were the primary beneficiaries of Red Lake's timber harvests. They had a lot to gain and a lot of experience in navigating the federal government, the state government, and entrenched powers in the OIA. They were ready to apply the same protocol and practice to Red Lake's fish resources. But things were different this time—thanks to Peter Graves and the General Council.

On September 12, 1917, as a temporary wartime measure, the Commission of Public Safety worked with white business interests to establish Red Lake Fisheries under Minnesota state law with the stated purpose of alleviating food shortages in Minnesota. John Lind, who was governor of Minnesota from 1899 to 1901, had a controlling interest in the Minneapolis, Red Lake, and Manitoba Railroad Company, which operated the rail line to Redby. Lind wanted to increase freight traffic on his railroad. He was also a member of the Commission of Public Safety, which authorized the state-operated commercial fishery in Redby. Lind's Minneapolis, Red Lake, and Manitoba Railroad was awarded an exclusive contract to transport all fish from Red Lake to market.[54]

The state-sanctioned operation at Red Lake also needed federal approval. Minnesota's state game and fish director, Carlos Avery, succeeded in getting the necessary permissions. Lind supported Avery's subsequent unsuccessful run for governor of Minnesota in 1924. In 1918, the fish plant in Redby shipped 500,000 pounds of walleye and whitefish throughout Minnesota. The fishery operated under a wartime contract until 1919.

At the close of World War I, white businessmen and state officials sought to maintain their control of Red Lake's fish beyond a wartime permit. The Minnesota State Game and Fish Department extended the commercial harvest and sale of Red Lake's fish by its own fiat, without further regulatory approval or consultation with Red Lake's new General Council. In 1921, it also removed the wartime restriction on sales only to Minnesota and began shipping Red Lake fish all over the country. In 1923, the Minnesota legislature approved funding to construct buildings for the Red Lake Fisheries plus a dam on

Red Lake Fishery, about 1915

Mud Creek to regulate water levels for the new hatchery. The funds approved were derived from the sale account for the fish harvest, which was managed by the state and had a significant surplus.[55]

Red Lake did not have exclusive control of proceeds from the fishing. The state shared in those proceeds, usually taking at least half of the gross revenue, and the buildings were constructed from the state's share. The marginalization of the Red Lake people in the fishery plant development and sale pricing was all the more maddening because Red Lake was supposed to be a business partner with the state and Indians did most of the work.

For typical Red Lakers trying to make a living from fishing, the process was aggravating. They had to supply their own boats and nets and do all of the labor for their harvest, but they could only sell their catch to the fishery at Red Lake. Red Lake tribal harvesters were routinely paid about 40 percent of the price garnered by white harvesters in the United States or Canada. S. A. Selvog, Minnesota State Game and Fish overseer for operations at Red Lake, wrote, "The price paid for the same quality of fish is much under that paid by private parties. . . . This in itself results in dissatisfaction on the part of the Indians." The artificial price suppression continued long after the end of World War I. There was no way for tribal members to directly sell or control the fruits of their harvest.[56]

In addition to having their compensation restricted by the state, tribal harvesters had to wait to be compensated until sale cycles were complete. When that happened, they received their deflated payment for their catch and, later, a small fishery royalty. Royalties that were paid to Red Lake for fish sales were distributed to the entire tribal population. The state provided no labor, no materials, and no insurance for the operation. But they collected half of the profits and controlled all of the sales, pricing, and revenue distribution. Tribal harvesters had been fishing with nets for generations, but the state viewed their fishing rights as a new gift from the state exercised at the government's pleasure. Minnesota State Game and Fish commissioner James F. Gould avidly enforced the state's controlling position. He wrote, "The Indians have no legal right to fish commercially in the waters of Red Lake . . . and the moment they fish in the waters of Red Lake and attempt to or do transport fish produced by them outside the confines of the Indian reservation . . . both the seller and

Lloyd and Rufus Johnson fishing

the purchaser subject themselves to prosecution." The state also reg-
ulated net mesh sizes and equipment specifications.[57]

Peter Graves's son, John Graves, traveled to Grand Forks to sell
fish in the spring of 1926. He was arrested and charged with poaching
and sale of fish without a permit, both violations under state game
laws. The arresting officer said that since Indians became citizens
in 1924, they were subject to all state laws. That was patently false.
Tribal sovereignty was not impacted by the Indian Citizenship Act.
Peter Graves wrote to OIA officials for remedy or intervention and
received none. He paid a sixty-dollar fine and left the issue alone,
even though he probably could have won in court had he pursued it.[58]

Political approval for expansion of state fishery operations at Red
Lake was easy to get at this juncture because it involved no tax burden and all of its advocates were well-established white business
interests. John B. Hanson, a Redby merchant, was one of the primary advocates who pushed for legislation to continue the commercial fishery after World War I. He obtained a special order vesting
the rights for commercial harvest of fish at Red Lake in six people,
only two of whom were Indians. These four whites and two Indians
had permission to net fish themselves or buy fish from Indians. So
the first sanctioned commercial fishermen at Red Lake were mostly
white men. The bill also did not require them to buy fish from Indian
fishermen. Some white men, such as Art Allard, held jobs at the Red
Lake fishery plant from 1918 to 1929.[59]

State Game and Fish Commissioner Gould knew that resistance
was building to state control of the Red Lake commercial fishing
operation. He wrote a flurry of letters to various officials, investigating the possibility of allotting the Red Lake reservation, creating a
state or national park, or finding another legal means to enable continued white control of Red Lake's fishing. In spite of the growing
power of the General Council of the Red Lake Band of Chippewa and
Peter Graves's hawkish eye on the commercial fishing arrangement,
Commissioner of Indian Affairs Burke wrote back to Gould: "Allotments will be made at as early a date as possible. . . . There will still
remain approximately 200,000 acres of tribal land after the Indians
now eligible are allotted." High-ranking state and federal officials
were still working on a way to carve up the Red Lake reservation
even in the 1920s.[60]

The people of Red Lake were not pleased with the maneuvering of outsiders to get at their fish resources. Their understanding was that they owned all of the fish in both Upper and Lower Red Lake. The first large commercial net strung across the narrows was cut on the Ponemah side and irrecoverable. Graves hired attorney Edward L. Rogers to investigate the issue of pricing and control of sales in 1926. Some of the Red Lakers started to sell whitefish in Red Lake Falls, hoping to receive a citation that would result in a test case.[61]

It soon became abundantly clear that some concessions would have to be made to the people of Red Lake. The authorization bill was rewritten with terms providing for an exclusively tribal harvest. For Peter Graves, the lesson was clear: sovereignty was what people insisted upon. When they didn't, it was systematically eroded. The legislative change enabled all Red Lakers to fish for the commercial operation. But as with logging, that in no way guaranteed that the profits would flow to the Indians. Almost 850,000 pounds of fish were harvested in 1925, but the majority of the profits were still going to the state, which collected all money from the sale of fish, controlled the price markup, issued sales receipts, and banked the proceeds, keeping most for the state and distributing the rest to a trust fund for the tribe.[62]

In 1927, private businesses tried to derail commercial fishing at Red Lake. An attempted injunction failed. Then Michael Lapinski, a white commercial fisherman, brought a lawsuit against the state of Minnesota for operating a commercial business enterprise, a violation of state law. Because the state was trying to supersede the tribe and take control of the fish business, it never asked Red Lake to join the suit or make arguments about its sovereign immunity. That might have endangered the state's intervention and control of the fish at Red Lake. Lapinski won his court case. The state was ordered to close the fishery.[63]

Red Lake was in a tough spot. The Red Lake people wanted to fish, needed the money, wanted a fair price, and desired to control the fruits of their own labor. The state wanted the fishing to continue, which put the tribe in alignment with the state on that critical point. But the state also wanted to capture most of the revenue, and that did not sit well with tribal members. Recent state efforts to build infrastructure for the commercial operation left the state feeling entitled to the profits. The fishing business was getting complicated. Many nonnative agencies and individuals were playing chess with the Red Lake people's livelihoods.

Graves again used his political and legal acumen, his official function as secretary-treasurer for the General Council, and his knowledge of state and federal political processes to advance Red Lake's agenda. On February 19, 1927, Graves arranged a special meeting with Theodore Christianson, governor of Minnesota, and State Fish and Game Commissioner Gould. Joseph B. Jourdain and Roy A. Bailey also represented the interests of the General Council. Recent legal developments put the state in violation of its own laws and the entire fishery operation was in limbo. The General Council passed a resolution supporting Roy A. Bailey's nomination for superintendent of the fishery, although the state resisted the idea.[64]

Graves proposed that the state of Minnesota amend state law in order to enable the state to engage in commercial fish operations as a temporary measure. Such a law would likely be ruled unconstitutional in court. As soon as legislation could be arranged and before there were further legal challenges, he proposed transferring title of the fishery from the state to the federal government, which would then lease the buildings back to the state. That would keep the state in the fishing game—a win for Gould and Christianson. But it would reduce state micromanagement and its ownership stake in the fishery and allow the tribe to strengthen its control.

Graves's plan was an incremental shift to tribal control of the fishery—from state to federal, and then from federal to tribal management. He promised to support this phased action if a price structure more favorable to the Red Lake Ojibwe could be negotiated. The temporary measures proceeded, but tensions remained high for two more years as the state jockeyed for a way to maintain control of fishing at Red Lake and Graves countered with legal action.

In 1928, the General Council contracted with attorneys Robert C. Bell and Fred Dennis to pursue all aspects of the Red Lake case, including its power as a sovereign nation. The legal battles and appeals they won confirmed that the state of Minnesota could not operate or partner in the operation of a commercial fishery at Red

Lake. That gave the General Council a means of taking control of the fishery operation, which now had to be managed under the auspices of the sovereign tribal government.

On February 15, 1929, the Minnesota legislature introduced legislation to authorize the lease of state fishery buildings to the federal government on behalf of the Red Lake Ojibwe. The phased and incremental process by which Red Lake asserted control over the fishery must have seemed agonizingly slow to those who made their living on the lake. But a faster or more revolutionary approach would have surely failed to generate the necessary support for state legislation, federal legislation, and cooperative arrangements with all the agencies that already had a stake in the business. Graves's ultimate success in liberating the fishing industry from the state and keeping it alive is to this day one of his most appreciated accomplishments at Red Lake.[65]

On March 27, 1929, the General Council and the state of Minnesota executed a legal agreement, with the state giving Red Lake exclusive control of the fishery and of maintaining the enterprise. The state of Minnesota had spent considerable money—all earned through the sale of fish caught by underpaid Red Lakers—in building fishery infrastructure at Red Lake. Under the new agreement and with legal hurdles successfully cleared, the fishery plant was leased to the federal government, which assigned use rights to Red Lake.[66]

The change orchestrated by Graves in 1929 enabled Red Lake to use tribal values to guide the fishery operations. Instead of highly competitive individual business practices, the men and women who fished Red Lake formed a business cooperative. It was organized as the Red Lake Fisheries Association on March 27, 1929. Within three days they had an approved corporate charter, operating under tribal, state, and federal law. Graves was elected secretary-treasurer for the Red Lake Fisheries Association in 1929 and was reelected annually for the next twenty-eight years. John Wind, Peter Sitting, Simon Stately, and Benjamin Littlecreek joined Graves on the first Red Lake Fisheries Board in 1929. In order to create and manage a sustainable fish harvest without state intermediaries or legal complications, the General Council named the Red Lake Fisheries Association the only legal conduit for Red Lakers to get fish to market.[67]

It took a long time for Red Lake to assert full control over harvesting in its own lake. From 1927 to 1934, there were still eighteen white fishermen commercially harvesting on Lower Red Lake, which was seven percent of the harvester labor force. While Indians had to sell their fish through the Red Lake Fisheries Association, white commercial fishermen at Red Lake were selling independently and at a better price. In 1933, the white fishermen filed a lawsuit against the Red Lake Fisheries Association in state court, arguing that their exclusion from the Red Lake Fisheries Association was illegal. Their primary concern was financial. If they were part of the association, they would receive the band members' royalties from the fishing operation, which captured five percent of the gross sales. The U.S. district attorney in St. Paul joined the federal government to the lawsuit because of its established interest. This time America's sovereign immunity (not the tribe's) got the case dismissed. After 1934, all of the commercial harvesters were Ojibwe.[68]

As the state was slowly pushed out of its controlling position at the Red Lake fishery, it continued to meddle and attempt to undermine Red Lake's sovereignty and control of the resource. In 1935, the state used monies from its Red Lake fish harvest trust fund to purchase land in the village of Waskish and by the Tamarac River. Those parcels were among the most contested titles in the region because the people of Red Lake understood them to rightfully belong to the tribe after Henry Rice promised all of Upper and Lower Red Lake and a mile of land in all directions around them to the tribe at the Nelson Act councils in 1889.[69]

Now the state of Minnesota was buying sections of that land, denying access to the tribe, and doing it with money from the sale of fish harvested by the Indians of Red Lake. The activities of the state were an extension of the long-standing practice of pushing Red Lakers off of Upper Red Lake and protecting white access. The state claimed to need the property and buildings for a new fish hatchery, but that was an elaborate smoke screen. The state's ownership of fishery buildings did not entitle it to acquire land and restrict Ojibwe use of the land. In 1936 the state's own solicitor clearly stated, "Exercise of the Indian right of fishing is subject to Federal and not State regulation and control." The state's action was both morally wrong and inconsistent with the State Game and Fish Commission's mission of public access, conservation, and sustainable resource use. The new tribal attorney, Fred Dennis, wrote to Minnesota governor Harold Stassen: "It was the most extravagant, wanton, and uncalled for expenditure of funds of the State that could have been made."[70]

Peter Graves always had a fire in his belly, but the state manipulations around Red Lake land stoked it red hot. In 1939, Graves wrote to Harry E. Speakes, the new state game and fish representative:

> So far as I am personally concerned you may come and take your buildings which we are occupying at any time you so desire. The state of Minnesota owns the buildings acquired by unlawful methods, as I understand, as found by its own court, of which you must be aware. These buildings were built from profits of the Red Lake Fisheries, most of the money being earned by the Red Lake Indians as not one penny of Minnesota taxpayers money went into these buildings. . . . It appears that as long as you are dealing with an inferior race of people there should be no consideration given regardless of conditions. You may come and take over your buildings just as soon as you please since showing your attitude, but I hope you do not write me any more letters.[71]

Graves had a simple agenda: the return of Upper Red Lake and pushing the state out of the Red Lake fishing business. Raymond H. Bitney, superintendent of the Red Lake Indian agency, was persuaded. In 1939, he wrote:

> That portion of Red Lake in the northern end of it which was taken away from them in the Treaty of 1889 and should be restored to them, and in addition to that portion of Upper Red Lake which is not inside the shore of the lake be given to the Indians and become part of their reservation. In addition to the exclusive control of the lake and the restoration of the lake to the reservation, it would be well to ask the State of Minnesota to turn over to the Red Lake Cooperative Fisheries Association or to the Red Lake tribe the fisheries building, fisheries lease, and the hatchery at Redby.[72]

As Graves gained more political traction in getting Upper Red Lake back, he pressed harder for a remedy. Bitney was supportive of his efforts, as were a number of politicians in St. Paul and Washington. Graves wanted to work out a land exchange whereby the state would swap its parcels in the disputed area for federal lands elsewhere. The federal government would repatriate them to the tribe and appropriate funds to slowly buy out willing private landowners within the originally agreed-upon boundary for the reservation.[73]

At Graves's request, Representative Richard T. Buckler, whose district included the land in question, introduced a bill in 1935 to enable the land swap at the federal level. Buckler immediately began getting loud complaints from white constituents. The main objectors to the legislation included the Bemidji Civic and Commerce Association, the Beltrami County Board of Commissioners, and the Bemidji American Legion Post. They claimed that the county had spent millions trying to drain the swamps in the land proposed for retrocession and that they had a financial interest in keeping them; they also complained that Red Lakers would kill off the woodland caribou, moose, and deer.[74]

Graves found it both maddening and amusing that whites in Beltrami County were worried about Red Lakers killing off the game they had maintained sustainably for nearly two hundred years. He did not argue, but went to work with the General Council and soon sent Buckler and all objecting parties copies of a tribal resolution to declare all retroceded lands a game preserve, free from hunting or trapping by either whites or Indians. He asked for a meeting with the objectors and various political figures, including the Beltrami County auditor, the Beltrami County attorney, the county commissioners, and the secretary of the Civic and Commerce Association. He brought Fred Dennis, the tribe's attorney, who laid out the entire history of the taking of the lake. Then the real reasons for the objections came to the surface. Beltrami County Commissioner Tyrene said, "People are objecting to the Indians acquiring all of the lake and not permitting anyone to fish therein."[75]

Graves was not surprised, but he was certainly disappointed. Nobody at the meeting questioned the validity of Red Lake's claim to be rightful owners of all of Upper Red Lake. They simply wanted to fish there too; and nobody in Washington had the stomach to tell them no.

Graves knew when and where to fight political battles. He had to abandon the push for major federal legislation, and turned his attention to the state, with some success. The Minnesota state senate passed a bill to allow Graves's proposed land swap process on

February 20, 1939. It was a safe move for the legislature, but it was enabling legislation and, ultimately, the federal government would have to set up a process and appropriate funds to do it.

The OIA surveyed land parcels and improvements to calculate an appropriation and recommend federal legislation to push the plan forward. The OIA favorably reported on the intended bill to the U.S. Congress but struck the appropriation recommendations out of the legislation, leaving Red Lake responsible for purchasing back the land that had been stolen. The political wind behind a remedy for the theft of the lake died shortly after that. Through the tribe's attorney, Fred Dennis, Graves did persistently push for land reclamation in state court condemnation proceedings throughout the 1930s, with some success; regaining the lake would have to be a continuing battle. But Graves came close to getting the lake back.[76]

Graves regarded the effort as a personal failure and it haunted him for the rest of his days. The people of Red Lake still see it as a valiant effort, and one that illuminates the possibility and paves a political path that might yet get the lake back in Red Lake's sovereign domain. They walk that path every day.

Graves continued to push for the return of Upper Red Lake and exclusive Red Lake control of the fishery. He got a breakthrough on fishery management. The commissioner of Indian affairs refused to sign a renewal of their agreement with the state when it expired on July 1, 1938. That forced the state to cooperate in the final transition of fishery operations to the tribe. In 1943, ownership of the remaining fishery buildings was transferred from the state of Minnesota to the federal government, and Red Lake assumed control of the trust land and buildings without further need for agreements or leases. The state was finally off the tribe's back.[77]

The entire fishery operation was a tribal enterprise. It paid royalties to all enrolled tribal citizens and patronage payments to fisheries members. The state and federal governments never subsidized the Red Lake Fisheries Association or any part of the operation, as it was and remains a self-sustaining business.

With a sustainable harvest of fish and a generous restocking program through the Redby Fish Hatchery it was anticipated that the Red Lake Fisheries would be able to support, through gainful employment, as many as two hundred families or more in perpetuity. The

Hanging nets to dry, about 1935

propagation of walleye and whitefish proved reasonable, and the fishery thrived for many decades. By 1950, more than two hundred Red Lake men and women were employed through the fishery, with a direct impact on six hundred families. More than $3 million was paid to tribal members as royalties from fishery operations. The Red Lake Fisheries Association had 240 members at its highest point.[78]

The Red Lake Fisheries Association managed the tribe's fish resources and finances responsibly, but in the 1990s faced an unforeseen crisis. A combination of illegal harvesting by tribal members for unsanctioned sale and increasing white sport fishing on Upper Red Lake resulted in an overharvest of walleye, the staple fish resource and the economic driver for fishery sales. In 1987, Byron Dyrland of the Minnesota Department of Natural Resources (DNR) caught Red Lake tribal member Bill Lawrence with ten thousand fillets of Red Lake walleye. The fish was not harvested for sale through Red Lake Fisheries, but was on its way off the reservation for illegal sale. The confiscation was the largest ever in the history of the Minnesota DNR.

The marine ecosystem at Red Lake is a complicated one with multiple trophic levels. When the walleye population collapsed, the crappie population exploded, as the two species are on a population teeter-totter at Red Lake. In a gut-wrenching decision, the Red Lake Fisheries Association called a moratorium on commercial fishing from 1997 to 2006 so the walleye could recover. The tribe and state conservation enforcement agencies stepped up oversight on illegal harvesting and sale. The walleye recovered and the association resumed business with a careful management plan for sustained harvest.[79]

The development of the Red Lake Fisheries Association was a major contribution to Red Lake's cultural continuity as a nation of fish harvesters and warriors. It strengthened Red Lake's political empowerment and cross-village cohesion. Peter Graves's legacy with the fishery was one of sustained cultural endurance and a financial bridge to success in the larger economy.

When it came to the pace and direction of change, Graves was both pointed and patient, saying, "I wish to state that I do not believe in trying too rapidly to enforce the white man's civilization on the Indians, but rather that they be given plenty of time and all the necessary assistance in learning." The fishery provided a sustainable venue for the people of Red Lake to test and sharpen their financial and business acumen in a new economic reality. Graves dismissed concerns about the emerging financial management skills of the people and defended the sovereign right of the Red Lake people to run their own affairs and businesses. He said, "Give the Indian time. If there's any money, hand it to him if it's his. That's good education. The experience will teach you. But if you don't get that experience, how are you going to know anything about it?"[80]

He added: "The only salvation for any people—the Indians, and anyone else—is if they can get enough education to compete with the way of life in which they are living. . . . If a young man is educated, he can compete and make a proper living." In a formal position drafted and vetted through the General Council on March 11, 1950, Graves stated, "Our children must be educated as far as possible that they may be able to compete in the methods and ways of the present civilization. Education, we believe, is the only real salvation."[81]

Sovereignty Ascendant, 1934-1957

Peter Graves was fighting for control of the Red Lake fishery during the Great Depression. At the same time a major change in federal Indian policy was brewing that had the potential to greatly help or greatly harm Red Lake's sovereignty. The political pendulum in Washington swung to the left as a vast array of New Deal programs started, including Social Security and the Civilian Conservation Corps. John Collier, who served as commissioner of Indian affairs from 1933 to 1945, wanted to make an Indian New Deal. His guiding philosophy was to make the OIA an advisory agency to tribes rather than a supervisory one. He wanted to recall the Indian agents and let tribes govern themselves. That was a welcome thought in Indian country, but the destruction of so many tribal governments through the treaty period meant that a lot of work was required to build new ones.

The cornerstone of Collier's plan was the Indian Reorganization Act (IRA). It became law on June 18, 1934. The IRA created a template for tribes to reorganize, but the template was fraught with problems, including cookie-cutter constitutions that did not reflect tribal culture, customs, or values and usually had very little separation of powers. The law did have a provision whereby tribes had to decide if they wanted to reorganize or not via a referendum vote.

Red Lake already had a representative governing structure that empowered its ancient chief system and it seemed to be winning important battles on fishery and land issues. Graves worried that reorganizing under the IRA could weaken the Red Lake system or impose a foreign one. Even so, he supported bringing the issue to the people of Red Lake for a vote. On May 3, 1947, the people rejected the revised constitution (229 for and 266 against). It ultimately failed over fears that the changes might undermine the authority of the hereditary chiefs and put too much power in the hands of the OIA, because the proposed revised constitution was an IRA reorganization. While the other tribes in Minnesota accepted the IRA, Red Lake again struck out on its own.[82]

Even though the General Council rejected reorganization, it used the political climate in Washington and the reorganization process in place across Indian country to further legitimize the General Council as the governing body and to increase its influence. Graves pursued every opportunity to strengthen Red Lake's sovereign power. First and foremost, Article 3 of the IRA provided: "The Secretary of the Interior, if he shall find it to be in the public interest, is hereby authorized to restore to tribal ownership the remaining surplus lands of any Indian reservation heretofore opened, or authorized to be opened, to sale, or any other form of disposal by Presidential proclamation, or by any of the public land laws of the United States." The new legislation would not change the reservation boundaries, but there was a lot of public land in the territory that Red Lake had ceded in 1889.[83]

Graves soon had the tribe's attorney, Fred Dennis, and Red Lake OIA Superintendent Raymond H. Bitney writing a flurry of letters and legal briefs to repatriate Red Lake's "undisposed" ceded lands now in public possession because of tax forfeitures and failed farms. Much of the ceded land north of Red Lake, opened for white settlement after 1889, was swampy, and the drainage projects had failed. Many of the white farms and homesteads were abandoned and went into tax forfeiture.[84]

After twenty-seven years of advocacy, secretary of the interior

Harold L. Ickes finally responded to the petitions of the General Council and Graves's relentless efforts. On February 22, 1945, Ickes issued an order to "restore to tribal ownership all those lands of the Red Lake Indian Reservation which were ceded . . . and which were opened for sale or entry but for which the Indians have not been paid and which now are or hereafter may be classified as undisposed of." Abandoned white homesteads in Nelson Act territory with titles assumed by county, state, or federal agencies had to be returned to the tribe. The General Land Office presented a list of lands for repatriation to William A. Brophy, commissioner of Indian affairs. The impact was monumental, with 156,698 acres of ceded land returned to tribal control.[85]

The land repatriation was highly contested. Some white landowners and hunters feared being denied use of reclaimed parcels. Some government officials were in principle opposed to land going from the government to Indians when they had been trying to engineer land transfers from Indians to the government for most of their careers. In addition, a large section of 32,000 acres by Baudette was inadvertently excluded from the transfer order.[86]

Many title issues became evident as the transfer process got under way. Although the land transfers were valid, they were never formally added to the federal register because of all the title questions, prompting extended delay and investigation. The 1945 list of lands for repatriation was replaced by a new one in 1988 that omitted some from the 1945 list and added many others. The total repatriation acreage on the 1988 list was now 186,533 acres. After a long legal pursuit by the tribe's attorney, Marvin J. Sonosky, the 32,000-acre parcel in Koochiching County was officially transferred to the tribe on January 8, 1989. A new list was developed in 1997 and many parcels remain unresolved. Today, most titles have completed transfer to the tribe, but the review process is ongoing and open.

While Peter Graves pursued Red Lake's legal and financial claims with the government and worked on building Red Lake's fishery business, he was also supporting development initiatives in many other areas on behalf of the tribe. The General Council successfully undertook to work the emergent federal government grants system as well as the legislative appropriation process. It successfully peti-

tioned for funds in 1937 to improve the roads from Red Lake to Highway 2 and along the lake to Ponemah. In 1948, Red Lake established a
revolving loan fund to support tribal member business and personal
property development. It was enabled by tribal trust fund reserves,
with an initial set-aside of $100,000. As loans were repaid, the tribe
kept granting more.[87]

Graves also convinced the General Council that it needed a
communication strategy and the power to share information. A
local newspaper, the *Red Lake News,* had been established in 1912.
It failed in 1920, but through support from the General Council it
was relaunched and has successfully continued ever since. Today the
tribe maintains an electronic newsfeed, Red Lake Nation News, as
an extension of the communication platform adopted by the General
Council during the Peter Graves era.[88]

Public Law 280 and the Pushback against Tribal Sovereignty

The General Council was having success in many simultaneous political battles, but its work was usually accomplished through adversity.
The Office of Indian Affairs was renamed the Bureau of Indian Affairs in 1947. That was a tiny part of a larger effort to make the agency
more advisory and less supervisory. Red Lake was able to slowly diminish the agency's controlling position on the reservation. Not everyone supported the waxing power of the tribal government. Many
nonnative citizens and politicians were adamantly opposed to tribal
sovereignty. The state of Minnesota was especially distrustful of Red
Lake after it lost the long battle over control of the fishery.

The political pendulum that swung left in 1934 for the Indian Reorganization Act swung far to the right in 1953. The federal government
passed legislation that year to give state governments more jurisdiction over criminal affairs on Indian land. The effort had been developing for many years. Criminal matters in the United States were
considered almost entirely under state law. In 1883, the court case *Ex
Parte Crow Dog* ruled that due to the sovereignty of tribes, state governments had no jurisdiction over Indian crime on Indian land. Only
the federal government could take actions that affected tribal sovereignty. In 1885, in response to that court case, the federal government

passed the Major Crimes Act, which established a mechanism for the federal government to assume jurisdiction in Indian cases of murder, manslaughter, rape, assault, arson, burglary, and larceny. In 1953, the federal government wanted to transfer that power back to state governments. The proposed legislation, called Public Law 280, would affect Indians in several states, including Minnesota.[89]

In 1953, most tribes in Minnesota were just starting to organize reservation business committees and develop modern governing structures under the Indian Reorganization Act. When the new law was proposed, they were not in a political position to fight it, but Peter Graves was. He wrote letters on behalf of the General Council to his connections in the Bureau of Indian Affairs to influence the legislation. Red Lake's well-established political presence was impossible to dispute. There was simply no need for further state jurisdiction at Red Lake, especially when it was obviously not welcome. Public Law 280 passed into law on August 15, 1953. Red Lake was exempted. The Minnesota Supreme Court later explained, "the exclusion of the Red Lake Reservation from Public Law 280 was done out of deference to the wishes of the Red Lake Band of Indians."[90]

There were legal tests after the legislation passed. Red Lake's exclusive jurisdiction over all civil and criminal matters except for those explicitly covered by the Major Crimes Act was affirmed by ruling of the Minnesota Supreme Court in *Sigana v. Bailey,* where the state was denied jurisdiction in a civil suit because of Red Lake's inherent sovereignty and exemption from Public Law 280. *State v. Holthusen, State v. Lussier,* and other cases further affirmed Red Lake's unfettered exclusion from state interference. Legal arguments had to be made. Lawyers had to be hired. Sovereignty was not unassailable; but it could be protected with consistent effort. Red Lake maintained a higher degree of political and legal independence as a result of its exemption from Public Law 280 than most Minnesota tribes were able to. In 1973, the Bois Forte Band of Chippewa in Minnesota also got an exemption. Today, most of the tribes in Minnesota are trying to develop their courts and police infrastructure so they too can be free from state control over criminal matters.[91]

Judicial Arbiter: Peter Graves
and the Development of Red Lake Courts,
1936-1957

The greatest affirmation of the faith the people of Red Lake placed in Peter Graves is evidenced in his role as the primary reformer of the reservation's justice system. At the very beginning of the treaty period, Indian agents began to assume controlling positions on reservations across the country. They ran political affairs, usurping the power of chiefs. They had their own police forces in many places. They also ran the Court of Indian Offenses to administer justice and enforce restrictions on tribal religion and culture. To change this system, Graves again had to apply all of his skills as an insider with the General Council and with the government.

Indian agents customarily appointed judges to the Court of Indian Offenses they administered on the reservations. Sometimes they appointed themselves. Usually, a government official, fur trader, or business leader was chosen to assume the duties. Sometimes the judges were of native descent, but usually they were of mixed heritage and were more integrated into the nonnative business and political community than the Indian community.

Graves was in a unique position at Red Lake. By 1936, it had been eighteen years since he had worked for the OIA, but he was still deeply trusted by white officials. He communicated in English and in their way, with letters, formal notices, and position papers. The fact that Graves was also a man of the people, an Ojibwe speaker, and a Red Lake partisan might have excluded him from consideration for a job as judge in most places, but his relationships with white government officials and his service to the government overshadowed his tribal status in their eyes and persuaded them to trust him. Graves was appointed judge for the Court of Indian Offenses at Red Lake and served from 1936 to 1943.

Being trusted by whites got Graves the job as judge, but being trusted by Indians enabled him to shape the judicial climate on the reservation. He held court only one day each week, always on Saturdays at 10 AM. For most of his tenure as judge, he worked in tandem with Charles C. Harkins, who served as chief of police. Although careful not to have any miscarriages of justice, they moved with incredible alacrity. One time they disposed of thirty-three cases in two and half hours.

As judge for the Court of Indian Offenses, Graves had a great deal of procedural freedom, including determining the need for juries. He always offered the accused the opportunity for a trial by jury but, in a stunning testament to the faith that the people had in him, every defendant in the more than five thousand cases he presided over declined the right to trial by jury and instead elected to have Graves be the sole arbiter of their fates. There were no exceptions. "I know them all," Graves said. "They are my people. I know their reputations, good or bad. They can have a jury if they want one, but they never do."[92]

Graves was given this deference because of his fairness, not because of his leniency. He had little tolerance for those who violated Red Lake's liquor laws in particular. "Outlaws and anarchists, I call them," he said. "All our troubles come from liquor." He unabashedly discussed alcohol problems on the reservation and consistently advocated that Red Lake remain a dry reservation.[93]

For several years, Graves was secretary-treasurer for the General Council, secretary-treasurer for the Red Lake Fisheries Association, and judge for the Red Lake Court of Indian Offenses. He was a man of great power. For some Red Lakers, he was also beginning to be seen as a man with considerable conflicts of interest. Paul H. Beaulieu brought the issue to his attention in private, and Graves listened. In 1943, Graves resigned his post as judge and used his considerable influence to get Paul H. Beaulieu appointed to the position. Graves knew that the most effective way to avoid accumulating enemies was to keep them as friends. Beaulieu served as judge from 1943 to 1955 and was equally firm and fair.[94]

Graves then worked to empower the General Council in making official endorsements of judge selections on the reservation. The important power vested in the Indian agents to make these decisions was now being transferred to the indigenous governing body for the reservation. It was a significant transformation. At the same time, Graves strongly advocated keeping the state government out of Red Lake's jurisdictional hair. His success at fending off Public Law 280, combined with his own service as a judge and his sustained advocacy for and leadership of the General Council, helped to successfully

shape the Court of Indian Offenses—originally a powerful assimilation tool—into a cornerstone of Red Lake's indigenous political
power base.

End of an Era, Rise of a Nation

Graves came a long way over his many years on earth. From a small
"half-breed" with no sustained father figure and no special favors to
the height of his power, he proved himself again and again: he was
resilient in the face of forced assimilation, diplomatic under pressure, firm in his values. In 1900, he earned $240 per year, which
was 20 percent of the average wage for whites working for the OIA.
By the time he died, he had retired as postmaster and judge but still
served as secretary-treasurer of the General Council and secretary-
treasurer of the Red Lake Fisheries Association. He had enemies,
but they were too afraid to fight him openly. He had many friends,
both white and Indian. He also had a very large family. At the time
of his death at age eighty-four, he had fifty-one grandchildren and
seventy-six great-grandchildren. Today his descendants number in
the hundreds.[95]

Graves reflected on his life: "I have never belonged to any clubs
or societies, except church societies. . . . I have no special hobbies.
Baseball was my greatest enjoyment when I was playing in the games.
Hunting wild game, not for the fun of it, but for actual necessity, is
my other hobby." Graves was never elected to any position or inherited any title. But he was the most powerful political leader on the
Red Lake reservation for many decades.[96]

People often asked Graves how he built and maintained his position. Red Lake was a nation of warriors, and nobody on the reservation submitted to anyone without a fight. He offered a simple, blunt
answer: "I was more pushy than anybody else. I always acted in the
interest of these folks on many occasions." He elaborated: "You know
just how stubborn I am in doing things for the Red Lake Indians
that I am absolutely sure are for their benefit." Graves valued honor,
integrity, and humility as well as forward thinking: "I didn't want to
lie to anybody if I could possibly help them, because if I got caught
lying, everybody would be laughing at me. If I'm not positive about
anything I'll tell you."[97]

Graves worked hard at politics but saw his role as more than political. He had to look out for his people. During the Great Depression, he used to take horse-drawn wagons through the communities of Little Rock, Red Lake, Redby, and Ponemah with Christmas packages, purchased at his own expense, and distribute them to needy families. When he saw a legal threat or intrusion on the tribal nation, he mounted a vigorous defense.

There were weaknesses in the governance structure at Red Lake, and Graves could see them. He did not blindly defend the system he worked so hard to build. He tried to help it evolve. In 1942, he proposed changes to the tribal constitution, but the people rejected them. He was able to implement some incremental changes to Red Lake's political structure, but he knew that more had to be done. Still, he could not move faster than his people or his chiefs. He was a team player in that sense, even though he was perceived as more of an autocrat.

In 1940, Graves received the Indian Achievement Medal at the Indian Council Fire in Chicago. Although he was exceptionally self-assured, he carried on work in an often adversarial environment that left him short on appreciation and affirmation. He was especially proud of that medal and the acknowledgment it represented.

It is hard to overstate what Peter Graves did for Red Lake. He Who Is Spoken To pulled the chiefs of the villages at Red Lake together in an emergent national identity. Nodin Wind catalyzed that effort and pulled Ponemah into the Red Lake nation. Peter Graves grew, strengthened, and formalized Red Lake as a tribal nation. He modernized and evolved the political structure. He also fought off major intrusions into Red Lake's sovereignty and numerous efforts to allot its land. He coalesced the power of individuals and hereditary chiefs to create a common institution—the General Council. It allowed Red Lake to act as a united political entity. Even though he was an appointed officer and served at the pleasure of the hereditary chiefs, his self-sacrificing service, force of personality, and political acumen led the General Council to give him undisputed power to wield for the Red Lake people. Ultimately, Red Lake paid the price for the structural weakness of that arrangement, but it benefited greatly from his wisdom, foresight, and capability as a leader of the warrior nation.

Peter Graves had a way of getting things done. It was awe inspiring at times, and deeply offensive at other times. He worked with the U.S. government, never against it. It made him effective in many different ways, but the pace of change was sometimes too slow for the people. The OIA built a mess hall for agency employees in 1910 and continued to operate it until 1955. The IRA of 1934, the shift from supervisory to advisory agency, and the change of the Office of Indian Affairs to the Bureau of Indian Affairs in 1947 all offered entry points for reducing agency personnel and pushing the U.S. government out of Red Lake. Graves never used a heavy hand with the government, however, even though he and the General Council outlasted the government's role. Without bloodshed or a reduction in government support, Graves eventually saw the Indian agents and personnel recalled, the mess hall closed, and Red Lakers retaking control of Red Lake.[98]

Graves usually worked with rather than against white folk at Red Lake. At his urging, the General Council approved the white-owned and -operated Red Lake Summer Resort Association to lease land at the Narrows on Red Lake and run tourist resorts there for white vacationers. For at least thirty years the General Council granted annual permits for white duck hunters to hunt on the reservation at Red Lake. Special fishing privileges were extended to white employees of St. Mary's Church, the school, and tribal programs.[99]

Graves was a fighter, and he would take on anyone, native or white, in any political battle. But he accomplished most of his work not in opposition to the OIA but in collaboration with it. He spent most of his working years as its employee. And in running the affairs of the General Council, he struck a steadfastly cooperative position. In a policy statement made through the General Council, he wrote: "The General Council sincerely believes that the office of Indian Affairs, which is under the immediate supervision of the Secretary of the Interior, should not be abolished as it has and is now doing wonderful work in the advancement of the Indian Race in the United States." In the same document he also wrote: "The Red Lake Band of Chippewa Indians suggests, most solemnly, that their consent first be obtained to dispose of any of their tribal affairs and property." When speaking to the U.S. Senate Committee on Indian Affairs, he said, "We do not wish to go on record that we are blaming the Indian Bureau for anything. Everything is blamed on the Indian Bureau, but it doesn't all belong there. It originated from some other place." He reported that during his entire tenure with the OIA, "I never had any trouble with any of the officials that I have worked for during my career in the Government Service."[100]

Graves was an intimate friend of Senator Knute Nelson, the man He Who Is Spoken To had dubbed Chipmunk because he was so annoying. Graves looked past Nelson's personality defects and his role in drafting the legislation that engineered Red Lake's large land cessions in 1889 and 1904. Graves remarked, "I have often wondered why Senator Nelson liked me—because I was just as stubborn as he was."[101]

Graves wielded his relationship with the federal government like a double-edged sword. His connections and friendships with numerous white officials usually served the people of Red Lake well. When he needed to take a firm stand with the government, as he did with the development of the Red Lake Fisheries Association, those relationships and that trust made all the difference in the world.

The double-edged sword cut the other way too, particularly when Graves stepped out of sync with the will of the people at Red Lake. Especially late in his tenure with the General Council, that became more common. By the time he died, almost every appointed officer and nonhereditary authority figure on the General Council was an immediate family member of his. Graves never directly countermanded the hereditary chiefs, so the issues before the General Council did not divide him and the chiefs. He had protected their positions and power, and they accommodated his requests for family members to be appointed to positions with the General Council.

When Collins Oakgrove saw Peter Graves come to the Ponemah store with a large wad of cash in 1957, Graves felt no need to hide the fact that he had obtained the cash from timber sales. Because there was no private ownership of land at Red Lake, the money could only belong to the people of Red Lake. Graves used it to buy his milk. It was a small thing, but part of a larger pattern that undermined support for him and faith in the integrity of the General Council.

Eventually, divergent views on tribal policy tested Peter Graves as never before. He always passed the tests of his power, but increasingly he had a hard time passing the tests of his ability to diplomatically unify political factions on the reservation. In 1952, the General Council gave permission to the Minnesota National Guard "for the use of a portion of the Red Lake Reservation as a bivouac area and firing range." They also extended permission to the U.S. Air Force and the U.S. Navy to test ordnance (including two-foot bombs and rockets) and do bombing and strafing runs north of Upper Red Lake. The air traffic and explosions were a constant annoyance and were even terrifying for some tribal residents.[102]

The General Council also allowed uranium prospecting in the Northwest Angle. In 1956, it approved separate uranium prospecting permits for one-thousand-acre parcels of tribal land for Alyce Modahl and Louis J. Glick. Test drilling went on for at least four years. Ultimately, no uranium was found, but if it had been, it could have been a real environmental and health crisis. When the people found out, they were furious.[103]

Increasingly the people wanted their legally closed reservation to be, in a practical sense, closed to white management and intrusion. They wanted someone to stand up to the federal government too, and Graves was not that man.

In the 1940s, Graves worked with Bazile Lawrence to sign off on the construction of a dam on the Mud River in Redby by the U.S. Army Corps of Engineers. It had the potential to support the fish hatchery in Red Lake, a stated objective. But many others saw the development differently. Roger Jourdain, the protégé of Paul H. Beaulieu and for many years a student and an admirer of Graves, was so furious that he began to politically organize in opposition to the General Council. The Ojibwe across Minnesota were devastated when the government built dams at Pokegama, Leech Lake, Lake Winnibigoshish, and the Rum River in prior decades because the flooding they caused permanently damaged wild rice and lowbush cranberry resources. In Mille Lacs, tribal members actually destroyed the dam when it was first built across the Rum River.[104]

Jourdain felt that Graves and Lawrence had lost touch with the primary mission of the Red Lake people—to keep the land and water intact and under tribal control. Surrendering control to the federal government in an action detrimental to the environment that served no financial benefit to the people was unforgivable to Jourdain. Over the next decade his organizing against the General Council grew more formidable, attracted more adherents, and eventually prompted Jourdain to say, "Their day of retribution is at hand."[105]

Jourdain was on the move, but Graves paid him no heed. On December 1, 1954, the Bureau of Indian Affairs consolidated its agency at Red Lake with Leech Lake and White Earth in a new office in Bemidji. In 1956, the Department of the Interior entered into a long-term agreement with the University of Minnesota to provide extension services throughout the state. The General Council did not advocate for Red Lake to be exempted or given control of program funds to administer on Red Lake's behalf. The actions of the agency and the development of the extension program heightened the growing sense at Red Lake that the government was marginalizing the tribe. It added extra fuel to the fire that Jourdain was stoking: the General Council was losing touch with the people as well as its effectiveness in advocating for them in Washington.[106]

Peter Graves was visiting his grandson, Peter Strong (Bebaamibatood, or He Who Runs Around), and other family members in late January 1957. The Strongs had a young, spirited colt, less than a year old. Graves went out to see the animal, patting his head and talking to him. The horse was playful and even a bit tempestuous at times. He grabbed Graves by the collar of his coat and started to pull him around, accidentally toppling the elderly statesman over. Graves's head collided with the frozen ground. Family members rushed to his aid, but the damage was done. Internal bleeding from his head injury put pressure on his brain, and the old man never recovered.

He lay in a coma for more than six weeks. Many friends and family members came to see him. His political adversaries and allies watched with awe—and some with barely bridled ambition—as Peter Graves slowly slipped away. The moment finally came at 7 PM on March 14, 1957. Peter Strong clearly remembered Charlie Smith standing in the room, asking repeatedly, "Is he dead yet? Is he dead yet?" When Graves drew his last breath, Smith donned his coat and drove straight to the home of Roger Jourdain to tell him, "Now. Now we can move." Strong recalled, "But now looking at it, Christ, how much power that old man had, totally unconscious for nearly two months, and they still couldn't do anything."[107]

Erwin F. Mittelholtz, who worked for the Beltrami County Historical Society and worked closely with the General Council on a major tribal history project, memorialized Graves: "Peter Graves (sometimes called "Chief") was perhaps one of the greatest leaders and spokesmen that the Chippewas of the Red Lake Indian Reservation will ever know or remember. He ruled firmly, sometimes with an iron hand, yet he was a statesman and guardian for the rights and protection of the Red Lake Chippewa Indians for more than half a century. In all, he gave over 65 years of rewarding service to the cause and betterment of the Minnesota Chippewas through his leadership and guidance." Jay Edgerton, who often reported for Minnesota newspapers on Red Lake politics, wrote in the *Minneapolis Star* after Graves died: "The grand old man of Red Lake may have been the greatest Indian of our time." Raymond H. Bitney, Red Lake OIA superintendent, worked with Graves for years. He wrote: "Peter Graves has always been interested in the welfare of his people from an unselfish standpoint, and at all times has been opposed to any move to exploit them or their interests. He is a great orator and has a very strong and forceful personality and thinks things through very carefully before arriving at a decision."[108]

Hundreds of people came to pay respects to Peter Graves as his body was interred at St. John-in-the-Wilderness Episcopal Church cemetery in Red Lake. They were overwhelmed not just by what they had lost with his passing, but by what they had gained because of his coming. As they shared stories and reminisced, they were stunned to find that during his last year of life he had privately bequeathed a final message to each of his children and many of his grandchildren. It was not about his undying love for them or what he had done with his life. It was about the lake.

In spite of all his amazing accomplishments, Peter Graves spent the last year of his life obsessing about not getting the lake back. It burned in his heart as the greatest wrong visited upon the Red Lake people in their history and the one thing he could not successfully rectify in his lifetime. The final message he left to his family is that he would never stop trying: "Even when I am dead, I will haunt the shores of these waters. My spirit will never be at rest until all of the lake is back in the hands of my people." For his many progeny and the citizens and leaders of Red Lake today, there is every reason to believe that that is exactly what happened.[109]

Roger Jourdain, about 1970

6

Roger Jourdain
and Self-Determination

"[Roger Jourdain is] the Elder Statesman and Dean of Indian Politics. He's not a radical. He's trying to make things work. . . . He has unbelievable stamina and energy. He's one of Minnesota's extraordinary people."

WALTER MONDALE

Red Lake's New Political Patriarch

Roger Jourdain was an imposing figure. He was five feet seven inches tall, but built like a buffalo bull at 230 pounds. He was a direct lineal descendant of Mississippi Ojibwe chiefs Broken Tooth (Bookwaabide) and Hole in the Day and had as many relatives at White Earth as he did at Red Lake. He embodied the quintessential attributes of the Red Lake people. He was the descendant of accomplished diplomats, large and devotedly loyal families, and warriors. He channeled those experiences and attributes in everything he did. He was hilarious and charming, but he was also a hard man—the kind who made you feel safe when he was standing by your side, fighting for your land and political rights, and the kind who made you very uncomfortable when you stood in his way.[1]

Like his ancestors, who had to wage war to establish the Ojibwe communities at Red Lake, fight and fend off waves of white political and financial assaults on their resources and land, and preserve Red Lake's political patrimony in the face of incredible pressure, Roger

Jourdain was all backbone and brain. He had a photographic memory and could dazzle anyone with total recall of names, faces, politicians, their committee assignments, voting records, and anything related to Red Lake history. He was smart and studious, always assessing and evaluating, thinking and preparing, reading everything of even tangential relevance to his mission. He told his fellow Red Lakers, "This is the golden rule of Indian politics: You can be friends with the white man but you can never trust him." He was impossible to intimidate, no matter the odds or who the opponent. At age forty-five, Jourdain succeeded Peter Graves as the dominant political figure at Red Lake, but his mettle was forged first by a painful experience in forced assimilation and then through years of service and tutelage with Paul H. Beaulieu, Graves, and Red Lake's hereditary chiefs.[2]

Roger Alfred Jourdain was born on July 27, 1912, to Joseph Jourdain (1881-1938) and Margaret Johnson Jourdain (1892-1988), in the tribal village of Little Rock on the Red Lake reservation. John Strong performed a ceremonial adoption and naming ceremony for him when he was six days old, giving him the name Golden Eagle Flying on the Wind (Giniwgwaneyaash). Other namesakes called him Boy (Gwiiwizens). He did not receive his English name until his father filed papers some weeks after his birth. He had no brothers and three younger sisters—Ruth, Gladys, and Alice.[3]

Roger was a special favorite of his grandmother, who forced his uncles to teach him how to drive at age eleven in a Model T Ford. He needed a booster seat to see over the dashboard, but when instruction was complete, she made him drive her around Red Lake. She always sat in the back seat and gave a nonstop soft-spoken train of cautionary instructions. Jourdain said he was often tempted to laugh at her but knew he would probably get the worst beating of his life if he did.[4]

Ojibwe was his first and primary language, although his mother taught him English at home as well. Jourdain reflected, "I learned to speak English from the hymns that my mother taught me." He mastered English and used it with great eloquence in running affairs of the tribe with the outside world. But when in the presence of Ojibwe speakers, he always preferred Ojibwe, and ran tribal council meetings in the language until there were new members who had not mastered Ojibwe. Both of his parents were enrolled at Red Lake as half

Indian. Jourdain was identifiably native, but lighter than many of his peers. Both of his parents also had some education. Margaret went to school at St. Mary's in Red Lake and Flandreau, South Dakota. Joseph went to school at Fort Totten, North Dakota, and then at Haskell in Lawrence, Kansas.[5]

Joseph, Roger's father, was a seminary prefect as a teenager but a fighter by disposition. As a young adult he got into a fistfight with the Red Lake Indian agency superintendent over control of a pair of horses. He knocked the superintendent to the ground and took off in the carriage, later explaining to Roger that the Office of Indian Affairs was always trying to "establish their authority over the Indians." The experience left an indelible impression on young Roger.[6]

Joseph, a skilled carpenter, was employed for his entire adult life in the profession except for several years as a school disciplinarian when Roger was very young. Shortly after Roger was born, Joseph took a job at White Earth, but the family returned to Red Lake before Roger started elementary school at St. Mary's Catholic Mission School. Roger's mother, Margaret, was a devout Episcopalian, but Joseph insisted that Roger be baptized Catholic. Roger served as an altar boy at St. Mary's Catholic Church in Red Lake. He spent three years at St. Mary's. Jourdain reflected, "I got more darn lickings than I ever got in my life." Joseph Jourdain's employment at the government school in Red Lake was terminated in 1922 because he kept quarreling with the principal, Chester C. Pidgeon. In the middle of a dispute resolution with the superintendent, Joseph threw a stool at Pidgeon. He was transferred to the school at Ponemah as punishment.[7]

Roger was nine years old when the family moved across the lake to Ponemah. His father worked as the school disciplinarian and his mother worked in the dormitory there as a matron. One hundred percent of the Ponemah kids were fluent in Ojibwe and none of them were Catholic. At first, Roger found himself besieged with negative assumptions about who he was and what he knew. For two years he had playground scuffles, but he fought back, and when it was known that he could hold his own both in schoolyard fights and in verbal banter in Ojibwe the pressure eased, and he was eventually accepted by his peers. For the descendants of warriors, the experience of triumph through adversity built mutual trust. Nearly forty years later it made all the difference with his political ambitions.

In 1925, Roger's parents agreed to send him to residential board-ing school in Tomah, Wisconsin. After five years in Red Lake and Ponemah, he left the only community he knew and boarded the train for Wisconsin alone. He was twelve years old. In 1991, in a compelling interview with the *Lakota Times,* he reflected on his boarding-school days in Tomah:

> We were issued some cut-down, old Army clothes, had dinner, and went to bed early. Right after lights out I heard the most lonesome sound I had ever heard. Somebody was playing Taps on the bugle.
>
> Off in the distance I could hear a train whistle. Some of the kids in the dormitory started to cry. It sure was a lonesome time, my first night away from home.
>
> I later found out that the kid who blew Taps every night was from Ponemah. His name was Greeting Spears.

Roger struggled at Tomah. He was stubborn and recalcitrant by na-ture. But there was something about the environment of forced as-similation that hardened his determination. At St. Mary's Catholic Mission School in Red Lake, and now especially at Tomah, his lan-guage and culture were marginalized. That just made him dig deeper, turn more inward, and vow to do something about it.[8]

After a year at Tomah and many letters petitioning his parents, they succeeded in getting him returned to Red Lake. His father took work in Red Lake village as a carpenter and later as a mechanic, so Roger was not returned to the school in Ponemah, but instead to St. Mary's. It brought some relief to be back in Red Lake, to hear the waters lapping and churning on the south shore of Lower Red Lake rather than bugle songs and train whistles. He still chafed under the yoke of the nuns at St. Mary's, so in 1927 his parents again agreed to try another course and sent him to Flandreau Indian School in Flan-dreau, South Dakota (not far from Pipestone, Minnesota).

For Roger, Flandreau was an even bigger test than Tomah. Roger was isolated from his family and home community. The numer-ous moves and continued bombardment of English and education for assimilation were taking a toll. He got into trouble with school authorities at Flandreau when the school did community service work at the reservation next to the school. He had to serve out gov-ernment rations of flour, tea, and lard. One elder woman asked for two scoops and he obliged her. But all the other people in line saw and he ended up giving everyone two scoops. He couldn't understand being punished for fairness and generosity.[9]

In the summer, Flandreau kept kids who underperformed academically. Roger made a pact with his good friends Jimmy Brun and Nathan "Scan" Head, both from Red Lake, that anyone who got held back would run away and the others would help him. As it turned out, Jimmy Brun got held back, so Scan and Roger helped him run away. They stowed away on a train for three days and nights. Roger recalled: "It was a pretty miserable time. After the first day, we spent most of the time giving Jimmy hell. We called him all kinds of names and talked about how dumb he was. He cried a lot. Hell it was me and Nat who were dumb, we could have been riding the cushions [traveling via paid fare in the coach]." The kids were only thirteen years old when they ran away from Flandreau the first time. The trip home was over two hundred and fifty miles.[10]

Roger had many stories from his two years at Flandreau. Some were hilarious. Most were painful. He severely burned his leg from a gasoline spill and fire in the school shop. Compounding his anger with the school was the peer experience at Flandreau, where most students were Dakota and Nakota (Sioux). A short Ojibwe boy looked like an easy target. For two years he got into fistfights on a daily basis. One time Roger, Jimmy Brun, and Nathan "Scan" Head got jumped on the Flandreau football field by three Dakota boys in a bloody rumble, eventually broken up by Amos Jumping Eagle, another Dakota boy. Disgusted with everyone at the school, Jourdain finished his last fight, ran right out the school door, and didn't stop until he had walked the entire two hundred and fifty miles back to Red Lake. Nobody bothered to try to send him away again after that.[11]

He spent the next two years at St. Mary's Catholic Mission School in Red Lake. Among his classmates there were Hap Holstien, Simon Howard, and David Munnel. High-school years were sometimes wild for him. He had a reputation as a great dancer, a slick dresser, and a ladies' man. For a number of years he was called "Shieker," on account of his dating history, but the label fell off soon after he married. He loved to play and coach baseball and basketball. He once got a legendary public beating from his maternal uncle Phillip Johnson for siphoning gas from his truck.[12]

Roger married Margaret Beaulieu on November 12, 1932. Margaret was the daughter of Paul H. Beaulieu, who was not a chief but was a political force in his own right. Roger was nineteen years old when he married, and together he and Margaret struggled to care for their young family. They were deeply devoted to each other. In their teens and twenties, Margaret stayed with Roger as he took jobs working on logging and road construction crews in Red Lake, Canada, and Alaska. When she could not go with him, he deposited his entire check into a shared bank account and she freely provided for their family with the funds. Jourdain noted, "We had an understanding second to none."[13]

Jourdain contemplated higher education and even applied for and received a loan for $180 to attend Wahpeton School of Science in 1933. The loan acceptance form required that each student take out a $1,000 life-insurance policy and name the commissioner of Indian affairs as the beneficiary in order to collateralize the loan. Even as a young man, Jourdain had no tolerance for ridiculous bureaucracy, especially from the Office of Indian Affairs. He refused to make a government agent the beneficiary and his loan application was rejected. "They didn't want us to get educated," he said. "They just wanted to keep us at a certain level."[14]

He went to work instead. He started out in the logging camps at Red Lake, where he was paid $29.50 per month in 1934. But he progressed to shift manager and was making $43.20 per month before he left the logging business, having acquired skills operating skidders and bulldozers.[15]

In September 1935, he took out a loan, enrolled in the Minneapolis Technical School, and completed a course in heavy equipment mechanics. After that he immediately found work as a master mechanic with the St. Paul firm Carl Bolander and Sons, then worked in Underwood, North Dakota, and finally was with Bechtel Corporation in St. Paul for a number of years. During World War II, his employment included civilian service on Canol, a top-secret project supervised by Lieutenant General Brehon Somervell, head of the U.S. Army Source of Supply Command. Jourdain had to work heavy equipment in brutally cold temperatures to build pipelines and infrastructure to bring Canadian oil to supply depots in Alaska. He was injured on the job, severely enough to prohibit his being drafted or enlisting in the army during World War II, as many of his peers from Red Lake did. He and Margaret moved back to Red Lake in 1947.[16]

Jourdain recognized the value of character but also the importance of outfoxing the white man at his own games. To that end, he developed a habit of voraciously reading every document related to Red Lake and every organization that intersected or communicated with the tribe, from U.S. government employment regulations to legal briefs to historical records. It must have consumed countless hours, but over and over it paid dividends to him personally and to the people he represented for more than three decades.

In 1947, he read the employment regulations for the U.S. Post Office and learned about the residency requirement for anyone serving as postmaster. Red Lake's postmaster was not a reservation resident. Jourdain issued a formal letter of complaint to Congress and sent copies to every sitting Minnesota representative. One congressman tried to dismiss his complaint, saying, "Any goddamn fool can run that post office." But congressmen were supposed to follow the letter of the law and usually avoided bad press unless there was something to gain. The postmaster was fired. Jourdain soon assumed the position of postmaster at Red Lake himself and served from 1953 to 1955. It was a lesson for him about who to complain to and how.[17]

Jourdain's entrance into tribal politics and economics was perhaps inevitable. At the age of nineteen he began to take his father-in-law, Paul H. Beaulieu, to meetings of the hereditary chiefs and to the formally assembled General Council of the Red Lake Band of Chippewa Indians. He reflected: "He [Beaulieu] fought against the whole bureau. He was a very compassionate, charitable guy. He'd give you his last 25 cents. I took him and others to council meetings. I kept the fires going, the water buckets filled. Unknowingly, I was absorbing all that. The traditional people were all admonishing the younger people, 'Don't forget. Pay attention to what we're saying. Don't forget what we're doing.' I didn't know I was listening."[18]

Here he saw tribal politics in action, as well as a clash of personalities and ideas. He marveled at Peter Graves, who always projected strength of character to achieve political results. Graves made close friends and strong enemies. By his own admission, Graves was "more pushy than anybody else." Jourdain was cut from similar cloth and it didn't take him long to learn leadership skills and strategies from

Graves. In American politics, power revolved around political parties, the flow of money, and compromise (or the lack of it). But in tribal politics, especially at Red Lake, it was all about relationships. Personality, integrity, character, oratorical ability, ancestry, and family were far more critical to political position than campaign funds, political parties, or voting records.[19]

For the next twenty-five years, Jourdain watched, waited, and listened. This was not a passive period in his life, but rather one in which he was continually evolving, strengthening, and deepening his abilities and personal relationships. Even though he was not a formal political representative of Red Lake in the early 1950s, he developed deep relationships with Senator Leonard R. Dickinson and Representative John McKee and after three years of advocacy persuaded them to introduce legislation to create the Minnesota Indian Scholarship Program in 1955. Although the program began humbly with an appropriation of $5,000, it was the start of a more concerted state effort to address the educational needs of native students. That Jourdain was the primary tribal advocate for the legislation and wasn't even a formally elected tribal politician at that time says a lot about his political astuteness and success both inside and outside of Red Lake. By the time he ended his political career, the scholarship program had a budget of $1.8 million, and Jourdain considered it one of his proudest accomplishments.[20]

Jourdain observed the success of Peter Graves and his ability to maneuver within Red Lake's political system. He learned about what to do, but also what not to do. Graves made many concessions to enable tribal control of politics at Red Lake. That served the people well in many cases, but it also sometimes put Graves into cozy relationships with white politicians and businessmen that did not serve everyone's interests equally well. Throughout Graves's tenure, more and more of the decision-making power shifted from the hereditary chiefs to the officers of the General Council—especially to Peter Graves. Graves had always done so much good that it was next to impossible to fault him for whatever was not. And with the Graves family controlling so many of the political and economic operations of the tribe and with his being such a forceful presence, it was not practical to directly oppose his leadership.

On April 8, 1955, Roger Jourdain's political aspirations received a major jolt when his longtime mentor and father-in-law Paul H. Beaulieu passed away. Beaulieu and Jourdain were cofounders of the Red Lake Tribal Business Association, which worked on economic development but increasingly also served as a watchdog on the General Council. It exposed and sometimes condemned the council's actions, and even called for referendum votes on some issues. For twenty-four years Beaulieu was also Roger Jourdain's family, mentor, adviser, and teacher. Jourdain felt he owed a great deal of his good fortune and potential to him. Beaulieu had a vision for Red Lake, and as his health failed, he bequeathed that vision and a profound sense of civic responsibility to his protégé. Roger Jourdain wore that mantle for the rest of his life.[21]

Jourdain organized Red Lake's Young Men's Committee and used it as a platform to mobilize Red Lake's next generation. He was building his political skills and relationships. He did not use the Young Men's Committee to directly oppose Graves, but he was thinking many moves ahead of potential rivals for the time when Graves would be gone. He was ready to initiate permanent changes to Red Lake's leadership structure and the people who were calling the shots. It would have been rude to make a move while Graves lay in a coma after his horse accident, but Jourdain knew that the end was inevitable. Charlie Smith was a loyal supporter of Jourdain in the early years, and when Graves passed away, he rushed to Jourdain's house, saying, "Now we can move." Jourdain grabbed his coat and hat and stepped out the door.

Assuming the Mantle of Leadership

Red Lake's political power was waxing. Peter Graves had built the first modern representative governance structure in a tribal community in the United States in 1918. In 1934, the Bureau of Indian Affairs (BIA) had become more advisory than supervisory. In 1954, the BIA consolidated the Red Lake Agency with Leech Lake and set up a regional office in Bemidji. Every decade Red Lake broke more of the shackles that hindered their free exercise of political power. While white timber, mining, and land interests swarmed over all tribal communities, Graves used the General Council of the Red Lake Band of Chippewa Indians to increase tribal control over policy and economics. On the one hand, he empowered the hereditary chiefs to exert more control than whites at Red Lake and, at the same time, vested more of their power in the General Council, which he increasingly controlled. Red Lake was becoming top-heavy as a result of the daunting and powerful leadership of Peter Graves. It was poised for change.

The Graves family moved quickly to fill the void left by his passing, determined to preserve their power and legacy. On April 28, six weeks after his death, a special meeting of the General Council was called to order. August King, one of Red Lake's hereditary chiefs and a member of the General Council, advocated for adherence to the rules of the General Council and greater shared power among the council's thirty-five members. He wanted to keep and strengthen the General Council, which had served Red Lake for many years, but he was concerned about the waning power of the hereditary chiefs. Graves family members occupied many of the officer and voting council positions; fearing resistance from King, the council voted to dismiss him as one of the hereditary chiefs even though they had no formal authority to do so under the tribal constitution. Peter Graves's son Joseph was named a hereditary chief in the place of Bill Lawrence, who was very ill and passed away on June 13, 1957. Joseph Graves was also appointed chairman of the General Council.[22]

Peter Graves had never claimed to be a hereditary chief. It only followed, of course, that Joseph Graves had no hereditary chieftainship rights, so the move to name him as a chief inflamed many of the true hereditary chiefs. At the same meeting, Rose Graves, Joseph Graves's aunt, was named secretary-treasurer for the General Council. Hereditary chiefs William Sumner, Jacob Ricebird, and James Whitefeather all walked out of the meeting with their roster of councilmen, repudiating the decisions at the meeting and the validity of the General Council itself.

Sumner, Ricebird, and Whitefeather met with August King, John F. Smith, and Robert Smith, who had direct lineal descent from other Red Lake chiefs, and formed a new council called the Hereditary Chiefs Council. On November 23, 1957, Joseph Graves died. There was no effort to reconcile the Hereditary Chiefs Council with the General Council. Instead, on the night of the wake for Joseph Graves, a special meeting of the General Council was called and Joseph Graves's position was filled by his son Byron, who was appointed chairman of the General Council and, instead of hereditary chief, was named "head chief" in his place. No such position had existed before.

The General Council then made numerous appointments to fill vacancies left by the political defections and deaths. Membership now included Byron Graves, William Smith, Joseph Johns, Len Hill, Louis Yellow, Ted Rosebear, and Charles Jourdain. The turmoil continued when Alex Everwind resigned from the General Council and joined the new Hereditary Chiefs Council on January 23, 1958. Dan Raincloud, who carried a lot of clout at Red Lake through his chief lineage and his position as one of the primary spiritual leaders from Ponemah, also joined the Hereditary Chiefs Council and was soon named chairman. Still loyal to the General Council was the entire Graves family and several other respected community members, including Alfred Lussier, Francis Lussier, Elsie Fuller, Verna Lepper, Harvey Strong, and Thomas Cain Sr. (Meskokonayed, or Red Robed).[23]

Once the council divisions at Red Lake were finalized, the political fire was fully stoked, and now Roger Jourdain entered the fray to strike while the anvil was at maximum temperature. For twenty-five years, he had worked with Red Lake's political leaders, and he understood the importance of honoring tradition and the positions of the hereditary chiefs. Emerging from his first meeting with their full support, he moved to

Dan Raincloud, about 1970

strengthen and legitimize the new Hereditary Chiefs Council at Red
Lake and in the eyes of the U.S. government.[24]

Jourdain was fully empowered to speak on behalf of the Hereditary
Chiefs Council. He did so as a spokesman and never as an officer or
a hereditary chief. This unique combination of humility and bravery
and his experience with people in Ponemah from his school days—as
well as with everyone on the south shore of Lower Red Lake—helped
him move sure-footedly. Soon he made so much headway gathering
support from the Red Lake people that the disempowerment of the
General Council was all but certain. Numerous community meetings
were scheduled, and the number of people turning out and the content of the discussions soon mobilized the entire reservation.

Jourdain was much more than a dissident. He was trying to build
something and serve his people. In the middle of the tension and
brewing battle between the General Council and the Hereditary
Chiefs Council, he ran for school board and handily won a seat. He
stayed on the school board through the entire political transformation of Red Lake that followed, serving for eight years, some of it as
chair. In 1957, he was joined on the board by his old classmate and
friend Nathan "Scan" Head. The irony that they had both run away
from Flandreau together and were now trying to keep kids in school
was not lost on them. But what they really wanted to do was trans-
form the educational experience on the reservation into a positive
one so Red Lake children would not have to suffer as they had. It
worked. During Jourdain's eight years on the school board, he developed an early-childhood program for all children on the reservation
and used his school-board position as well as his eventual political
office to build new schools at Red Lake and Ponemah. From 1956 to
1958, he also served as superintendent of the Red Lake Road Department. He used that position to expand his network and advance economic development ideas.

Graves family members knew that Roger Jourdain was now the
most substantial political force in opposition to the General Council, and they moved to counter him, but blundered. At a community
meeting in Redby, Jourdain was arrested by tribal police and charged
with disorderly conduct. He was presented with a formal complaint
signed by tribal member Roman Sigana on February 2, 1958. An
arrest warrant was signed by William Blue, the tribal judge, on Feb-

ruary 7. Royce Graves, brother of Byron Graves, was police chief in Red Lake at the time.

The Hereditary Chiefs Council was assembled inside the community building at Redby. When they were alerted to Jourdain's arrest, they poured out of the meeting and into their cars. As Jourdain was escorted toward the jail in Red Lake, some five miles distant, several cars full of chiefs and supporters closely followed the police car. Halfway to the jail, another police car intercepted them, stopped the convoy, and curtly told the other officers, "This arrest has been canceled." Rather than retreating to the meeting hall in Redby, Jourdain insisted upon an immediate trial, right there in the middle of Highway 1 between Red Lake and Redby, in full view of the Hereditary Chiefs Council and many community members. There was so much scrutiny that his request was granted. Roman Sigana appeared and testified about his complaint against Jourdain, saying "He quarreled at me and called me names." Jourdain entered a plea of not guilty, and the case was quickly dismissed by Judge William Blue for lack of evidence. The entire event bolstered Jourdain's growing reputation as a fearless man of action. His position as a leader was already beyond question.[25]

With the Hereditary Chiefs Council gaining ground politically at Red Lake, Jourdain now reached out to the U.S. government, a critical step if the council was ever to control political and financial interactions with groups outside of Red Lake. Jourdain petitioned the Department of the Interior for validation of the Hereditary Chiefs Council. The Department of the Interior assembled an investigatory panel and sent it to Red Lake to find out what was happening and recommend steps for a just intervention. The committee consisted of Newton Edwards, M. W. Goding, and George Robinson, all whites. They took evidence at numerous meetings in Red Lake, Redby, Little Rock, Ponemah, and Bemidji. The BIA reported a substantial attendance of a hundred people in Ponemah, a hundred fifty in Redby, and two hundred fifty in Red Lake, as well as interviews with ninety tribal members.[26]

Both the Hereditary Chiefs Council and the General Council appeared willing to accept the results of the investigation. That was significant in and of itself because for the next thirty-two years Roger Jourdain proved resistant to almost every decision coming from the

Department of the Interior and the BIA. But for now, he needed their support to get rid of the General Council.[27]

Many chiefs and citizens presented evidence and testimony at the investigatory panel meetings. Otto Thunder testified, "After the constitution was formed in 1918, we found there was something wrong in the council. We had no voice in government. We could not borrow money from the Tribal Credit Association to acquire higher education. There is a saying, 'If you have a starving Indian you can handle him easily; if he is not hungry you can't handle him.' We want to make this reservation a paradise for everybody, not just for a small group."[28]

The Red Lake Tribal Business Association backed Jourdain's position and claims at all meetings. To discredit it, Tom Cain Sr. produced an old editorial from the *Minneapolis Journal* dated June 15, 1953, in which Jourdain's old mentor Paul Beaulieu said, "I am certainly in favor of resorts on the reservation. The fishing industry is profitable and a few white fishermen at Red Lake would not hurt the fishing any." Any proposal to further open Red Lake to outsiders usually amounted to political suicide, but there were plenty of accusations flying in all directions. Byron Graves defended the General Council, saying, "This is not a question of which council has the right to rule, but a question of breaking up your reservation." He worried not just about losing power but about the BIA having so much power to arbitrate the decision.[29]

The Hereditary Chiefs Council elected Jourdain as secretary and he was firmly established as its primary spokesman. The General Council of the Red Lake Band of Chippewa Indians kept Byron Graves as chairman and primary spokesman. Xavier Downwind, Dan Raincloud Sr., Dan Raincloud Jr., Ona Kingbird, and Elizabeth Hardy all testified in support of Jourdain's request for recognition of the Hereditary Chiefs Council. Ted Rosebear and Tom Cain Sr. spoke in support of the General Council.

The investigation took a lot of time, and much of the testimony was presented in the Ojibwe language. Xavier Downwind was pictured on the front page of the *Bemidji Daily Pioneer* translating for Dan Raincloud Sr. at a public hearing in Ponemah attended by more than a hundred community members and representatives from the Department of the Interior. Downwind, speaking on his own behalf, told the gathering, "The hereditary chiefs should rule, and Rose Graves seems to have chiefs dismissed or appointed whenever she wishes." Tom Cain Sr. said, "I follow the present recognized council because I believe it to be the most stable one." Cain was pressed on his reluctance to support an elective council, and responded, "I'm afraid I'll get in there with people I don't like and can't work with."[30]

There was a heated discussion of the dismissal of August King as hereditary chief from the General Council because he spoke in favor of the Red Lake Tribal Business Association, which was feuding with the General Council over development ideas. Cain was asked, "You mean there's no room for opposition on your council?" Cain replied, "Not to the extent where he was trying to tear down the council." Dan Raincloud Sr. objected to closed General Council meetings and the appointment of Byron Graves as hereditary chief on the night of the wake for Joseph Graves without public notice or discussion.[31]

The BIA called a special meeting on March 19, 1958, at Red Lake to share the investigation findings. Secretary of the interior Hatfield Chilson formally announced on March 20, 1958, that Red Lake would have to hold new elections to determine tribal leadership going forward. Rather than pick sides, the BIA decided to put it to the people of Red Lake. There would be a new constitution, ratified by the people, and new leaders elected by the people. The BIA report said that the 1918 constitution provided for seven chiefs and thirty-five councilmen, but that power had effectively shifted from the council to the officers. This happened in large part because of the expertise and leadership skills of the officers, but in the end it served to weaken the structure in their own constitution, rendering the governing document ineffective. Because of chief removals, resignations, and reappointments, one family effectively controlled the resources and all day-to-day operations of the entire Red Lake Nation.[32]

The report said that the 1918 constitution did not provide for the removal of chiefs or appointment of new ones. In fact, the 1918 constitution did have a provision for the temporary appointment of people to vacancies but not the power to name chiefs or break the hereditary rights of succession. The report also noted that over the previous year the council had made eight changes to the seven chief positions. Hatfield Chilson said, "The custom of chieftainship as a self-perpetuating office following hereditary lines has been repudiated by these recent actions of the council." He also said, "The hereditary chiefs have not acted entirely on their own in forming a rival council and seeking recognition by this department. Rather, the conflict between rival 'councils' masks a struggle for control of the tribal government by rival aspirants to the council offices. Claims of legitimacy of the lines of chiefs by one side camouflage a struggle which would not be relevant if the council had operated in its proper constitutional role."[33]

The Hereditary Chiefs Council had representation from some hereditary chiefs, but certainly not all, and it held community meetings but had no governing body, document, or structure for the Department of the Interior to legitimize. In the end, the investigation concluded, "Neither of the rival councils is properly organized and constituted in accordance with the constitution adopted by the members of the Band in 1918."[34]

The Department of the Interior determined not to recognize or legitimize either council, but instead recommended the formation of a constitutional committee, the membership of which would be elected by the tribal population at large. That committee would draft a new constitution and present it to the tribal population for ratification and then BIA approval. The report further laid out options of a council of chiefs only, a democratically elected council only, or both. In the end, the people of Red Lake wanted the hybrid option of democratic governance and hereditary chiefs. Until the new government was organized, the BIA took control of Red Lake. The bureau assumed the civic functions of the reservation pending the adoption of a new constitution and the election of officers.

The transition of Red Lake to a new governing structure was firmly established, even though the General Council continued to try to assert control over the next few months, creating a new, mirrored council called the Red Lake Closed Reservation Committee and electing Byron Graves, Tom Cain Sr., Adolph Lussier, and Jane T. Beaulieu as officers. They also exercised substantial influence in the election of officers to the Red Lake Fisheries Association, where many (but not all) officers were supporters of the General Council. Xavier Downwind, Byron Graves, Edward Holenday, Joe Johns, and William Smith were elected to one-year positions.[35]

The effectiveness of the General Council and the Red Lake Closed

Reservation Committee was overwhelmed by the new constitutional process, which quickly proceeded with an election for the constitutional committee on May 22, 1958. Dan Needham Sr., hereditary chief and grandson of Sun Shining Through, was elected chairman of the new committee, and Tom Cain Sr., Roger Jourdain, and Byron Graves all served as secretaries. All factions would build the new governing structure at Red Lake together. They hired the law firm Hoag, Gruber, and Lindquist to advise them on constitutional law and had Rex Quinn from the BIA working with them at all meetings.[36]

Roger Jourdain was featured prominently in the work of the constitutional committee. He also appeared at separate meetings unrelated to the constitutional work where the interests of the band were under discussion, including ones at Bemidji State College. The sooner Red Lake's new government was organized, the sooner the BIA would quit running the affairs of the tribe. Time was pressing. The Indian Claims Commission, which had judicial oversight over most tribal land claims in the country, had a major case pending involving the Red Lake and Pembina bands, and since the tribe wasn't organized, the BIA was controlling the decision-making process regarding their own government's obligations. In a move that would be almost unheard of today at Red Lake, the BIA had the tribe delegate to its law firm the decision-making authority over whether or not to appeal its entire Indian Claims Commission case after it was ruled that compensation should be forty-five cents per acre.[37]

The constitutional committee labored diligently to produce Red Lake's new governing document. The hereditary chiefs would be included and empowered as regular participants in every aspect of Red Lake's political process. Decision-making authority, however, would rest in the elected leadership of the new tribal council. Indian Reorganization Act draft constitutions served as a framework for the committee, but ultimately Red Lake's governing structure was uniquely its own.

In 1959, Red Lake was finally ready to hold elections for leadership on the new Red Lake Tribal Council. The BIA managed the elections with local representatives and BIA supervisors in each district. Absentee ballots were sent directly to the BIA district office in Bemidji. Commissioner Glenn L. Emmons was directly involved in all facets of the electoral process. The election was truly historic, but the battle was won in the relationships Roger A. Jourdain had forged and strengthened over the preceding decades. In a landslide, he was named Red Lake's first democratically elected tribal chairman.[38]

Modern Warrior: Roger Jourdain and Termination

Cornelia "Coya" Knutson was Minnesota's first female congress-woman, elected in November 1954 and assuming office on January 3, 1955. She was also the only Democrat elected in the ninth district after World War II. The district itself was eliminated in 1963 as part of a major redistricting effort in Minnesota. Knutson was a real po-litical force—a liberal meteor in a libertarian conservative place, a powerful woman in a man's world, and someone who could both rock the boat and get things done.[39]

When Peter Graves was still the nexus of political power in Red Lake, Roger Jourdain was building relationships. He supported Knut-

Administering the oath of office to the new Red Lake Tribal Council, 1959

son's first campaign and her reelection. Jourdain's photographic memory for faces and names was an asset, and as Red Lake's political participation in mainstream American politics grew, his value to Knutson did too. Her first two congressional campaigns were successful, though by thin margins. Jourdain's help was crucial to her success in getting as many as two thousand Indian votes.[40]

On August 1, 1953, the U.S. Congress passed concurrent resolution 108, which enabled the policy of termination. The plan was to dissolve the sovereign status of federally recognized tribes one at a time and fold tribal citizens further into the American political and economic mainstream. There had been several other experiments with terminating tribes starting in 1940, but in 1953 the policy was implemented nationally. It was a disaster for the 109 tribes that were terminated, which included the Menominee, Klamath, Ponca, Paiute, and Alabama-Coushatta. Tribal businesses collapsed, land became taxable and was lost in forfeitures, and tribal citizens became even more impoverished. During Knutson's second term, some members of Congress were pushing for termination of tribes in Minnesota.[41]

In 1955, Senator Edward Thye introduced a bill to terminate all four of the Dakota tribes in Minnesota. It died in committee, but remained a topic of discussion within the Minnesota caucus. Jourdain contacted Knutson to appeal to her good sense and ask for a return of favors. He wanted her to block any effort to terminate Minnesota tribes, especially Red Lake. Knutson refused to take a strong stand, and even voiced support for some of the proposed legislation. Jourdain felt betrayed, and although he was a staunch Democrat, he pulled his personal support for Knutson and went on the attack.

Jourdain never took a half-hearted approach to politics. When he went after Knutson, he gave it everything he had. He paid for advertisements against her campaign. He made hundreds of phone calls, wrote letters, and gave speeches. He talked to everyone at Red Lake, but also campaigned against her in St. Paul and Minneapolis. Knutson had other political problems in 1958, including a political betrayal by her husband, who publicly requested that she not seek another term, which her Republican rival inflated with sexist vitriol, urging her to "be a good woman, go home, and cook for her husband." Jourdain's opposition cost her vital support in her home district and divided the

Democratic base. She lost by 1,390 votes of just over 93,400; a switch of 696 votes could have made the difference. Jourdain may have cost her the election.[42]

Jourdain had shown himself to be a political force as a regular citizen, winning the first fight against termination before his election as chairman. But termination was still the dominant policy of the day. During Red Lake's dispute between the Jourdain and Graves factions, the BIA had run the day-to-day operations of the tribe. Now, a new constitution was in place and a new chairman was elected to face the challenges of U.S. Indian policy. The Peter Graves administration had never fought the BIA, and it had many friends in Washington. But Jourdain was more interested in tribal sovereignty than in pleasing white bureaucrats. His election as tribal chairman triggered a backlash in Washington. Officials in Washington decided to seize the opportunity to attack Red Lake's sovereignty and maintain control over the reservation. They wanted a formal termination of Red Lake's status as a sovereign nation.

As soon as election tallies came in, BIA officials moved to block Jourdain's assumption of power and to push for termination of Red Lake. They closed the Red Lake hospital and froze Red Lake's federal funds. The BIA underestimated Jourdain, because there was nothing like a good fight to motivate Red Lake's consummate warrior.

Jourdain went into action, calling his good friend Hubert H. Humphrey and scores of other politicians, bureaucrats, and bankers. Within twenty-four hours, the Red Lake hospital was open for business again, and Jourdain had unrestricted access to Red Lake's financial records and accounts. The BIA was reeling from a torrent of public outcry in the press, from Minnesota's leading political figures, and from Jourdain, who blasted the BIA as "the first instance of organized crime on the reservation."[43]

The BIA retreated from meddling in Red Lake's politics or attacking its sovereignty. Coya Knutson tried to run for Congress again, but she was defeated by a wide margin. Her political career was over. None of Minnesota's congressmen dared to voice support for termination again. Jourdain's hard stance on the issue and his efficacy in influencing elections put him in a powerful position—all demonstrated even before he became tribal chairman, and strengthened afterward. Most tribal leaders in Minnesota since the 1950s have little idea how greatly their uninterrupted sovereign status was made possible by the political skills of Roger Jourdain.

Fighting the BIA

Jourdain's political career was born in a cauldron of fire, but the BIA's attempts to shut down the reservation and terminate the tribe were only the beginning. Major changes were being made nationally during Jourdain's rise to power. Some people in Washington felt that reservations were negative places and that getting Indians off of reservations was a public service to Indians. On July 1, 1951, the U.S. government passed legislation to encourage Indians across the country to move off of reservations and settle in urban areas. This new relocation policy ultimately transformed tribal communities, including Red Lake. Participants in the relocation program received one-way transportation to urban areas like Chicago, Milwaukee, and Minneapolis, financial assistance for the first month's rent, and job placement advice. In 1953, a white social worker at Red Lake named Alfred Loktu began to push for tribal citizens to move to cities. By 1955, Dennis G. Ogan was hired by the BIA to move Minnesota Indians to urban areas. As soon as Jourdain came into office as chairman, he had to contend with the legislated relocation of his citizens and a wide array of BIA and social-service employees working hard to implement the policy.[44]

Jourdain saw Red Lake as more than home. It was a cultural and political sanctuary. He saw the effort to remove the people from their sanctuary as personal and political warfare and vowed: "The Red Lake Band of Chippewa will never agree to voluntarily give up our sovereignty and permit federal or state intrusion into our affairs." He was singing a very different song from Peter Graves, who usually worked cooperatively with the federal government, even when he fought the state over the fisheries. Jourdain was not afraid to upset bureaucrats. His power rested in conviction and the affirming vote of his people. About the BIA, he quipped, "The sovereignty of tribal nations has been under attack since 1492."[45]

Jourdain worked three angles to slow the movement of people from the reservation. First, he worked with alacrity and success to improve the standard of living on the reservation. Then he kept up a constant barrage of communication to show people at Red Lake how they were best served by maintaining strong connections with their home reservations. He never shamed those who moved, and eventually opened an urban outreach office for the tribe in Minneapolis. Finally, and most important, he brought the BIA to heel.

In 1962, Jourdain used his political connections outside of the BIA to force it to focus its attention where he needed it to be. Politicians responded with surprising speed to his demands. The BIA subagency at Red Lake had been closed and folded into a combined agency with Leech Lake and White Earth. Jourdain demanded that it be reopened so he could directly communicate with the agency when he needed to without driving to Bemidji or writing letters to Washington. In a matter of months, Jerome F. Morlock, Red Lake's new agency superintendent appointee, showed up at Jourdain's door, briefcase in hand, ready to establish direct liaison with the tribe.

Jourdain played Morlock and his later replacements like a warm hide drum at a summer powwow. The Red Lake Tribal Council asserted control over the police force and the court. Jourdain worked on compact after compact to convert various state and federal programs into tribally administered programs with state or federal funding. The tribe took over most social-service programs incrementally over a period of several years. It also asserted control over Red Lake Indian Mills, the primary tribal logging enterprise, even bringing court action to demand accountability, establish control, and push back the BIA.[46]

In 1967, Jourdain battled the BIA over land rights. The BIA was busy writing and disseminating rules for right-of-way easements on the reservation as it did in many other tribal communities. Jourdain took the BIA to court and won an important battle affirming the sovereign right of the Red Lake tribe to make decisions over land use on the reservation.[47]

Jourdain pushed back hard against the BIA for bringing a host of nonnative people to Red Lake to tell Indians how to run their own government. The paternalistic position of the BIA was offensive, but white guys getting good-paying jobs on reservations for work that Indians were at least as competent to perform was intolerable. In 1976, Jourdain spearheaded a push for new national legislation to create TERO (Tribal Employment Rights Ordinance). It established an Indian-preference employment policy and training protocol for reservations across the country. Red Lake was among the first to be funded. The legislation created jobs at Red Lake, but, more importantly, it empowered Jourdain to indigenize the workforce at Red Lake in a way never seen before. By the time Jourdain was done with the overhaul, there wasn't a single white worker at Red Lake who did not firmly believe that his or her employment was not a right but a privilege that existed at the pleasure of the tribal council.[48]

The tribe still hired white folk in certain positions. At the hospital and the school it was necessary because so few native people had the credentials to get the jobs. But Jourdain's work tracked hundreds of Red Lakers into gainful employment. Today the people of Red Lake could not imagine nonnative people acting like they own the place, but often forget that it was Jourdain who sculpted and enforced the Indian-first employment policy there. Not just at Red Lake, but across the nation, tribal governments owe much to Red Lake's first chairman for the legislation that enabled Indian preference and tribal control over employment on reservations. Fairness would never be given; it would have to be made. Jourdain emphasized hawk-like vigilance: "We have to keep them honest all the time. There's a constant battle—we have to be watching and watching all the time."[49]

The Boycott

On October 24, 25, and 26, 1966, public relations and publicity director for the Bemidji Chamber of Commerce Robert Kohl gave a trio of live radio broadcasts on KBUN in which he went on a series of offensive classist and racist rants. Kohl was the owner and operator of Kohl's Last Resort on Turtle Lake, north of Bemidji, and a former candidate for Congress.[50]

Kohl had visited the homes of several welfare recipients off and on the reservation at Red Lake, and his personal observations fueled his comments. Before Kohl's visit to Red Lake, BIA superintendent Reginald Miller cautioned him "not to embarrass the reservation or the Indian people." Kohl was extremely conservative and harbored strong racist feelings; he was not capable of following Miller's advice. Kohl described Red Lake homes as "indescribably filthy." He said that the people he saw "are so low on the human scale that it is doubtful they will ever climb upward. Their satisfaction level is so low that it corresponds to that of the most primitive of earth's animals. . . . Perhaps we should never have lowered our sights to this level, perhaps we should have let nature take her course, let disease and malnutrition disrupt the reproductive process and weed out those at the very bottom of the heap." He went on to ask: "Is it any less heartless to sacrifice physically and mentally healthy young men in Viet Nam or Korea to make the world safe for our political philosophy than it is to sacrifice these hopelessly morally and mentally indigent for our economic philosophy?" And he continued: "With our welfare dollars, we provide a little food in the belly, some kind of primitive shelter and a place to reproduce, and this is all that is wanted, all that is needed, and all that is desired."[51]

Kohl broadcast his experience visiting a welfare home at Red Lake where the kitchen had been swept

> in anticipation of our coming, swept into a pile in the corner. But the kitchen table has not been washed in weeks, the flies are thick, the floorboards rotten, the two beds and two chairs and derelict davenport . . . the only furniture in the shack . . . are filled with kids into the teenage bracket, sitting, just sitting. The yard, of course, looks like a tornado dumped the nearest trash heap into it. And it is perfectly obvious that little responsibility for anything is wasted in this environment. The scene is typical . . . dirt and filth, cats and dogs and flies, lots of kids . . . some retarded, some with emotional problems of a serious nature, but more in proportion than any families off the reservation, a banged-up, usually partly assembled radio and sometimes a television set, and a yard full of junker cars run until they quit and then too much trouble to repair.[52]

His remarks provoked the wrath of Roger Jourdain, who mobilized the tribal communities of northern Minnesota in ways never seen before. Indians did half of the shopping in Bemidji and had virtually none of the jobs. On October 25, the same day the radio broadcasts began, Jourdain called a special meeting of the Red Lake Tribal Council. They immediately passed a resolution calling for a boycott of all Bemidji businesses: "Urge residents of Red Lake to patronize those business communities that do not harbor or make possible such ancient prejudices or inflammatory broadcasts." Jourdain sent letters to Walter Mondale, Hubert Humphrey, and Lyndon Johnson, enclosing copies of the broadcasts. He filed a complaint against the radio station with the Federal Communications Commission. He called other tribal leaders. The Leech Lake Tribal Council passed a resolution to join the boycott of Bemidji on October 28, 1966. White Earth followed suit on October 29, 1966.[53]

There was an outpouring of demands that Kohl be fired and formal apologies issued. Several Bemidji merchants withdrew advertising from KBUN. Local clergy members Steven Bergstrom, Walter Ellingson, and Vernon Nelson voiced support for the boycott. Hundreds turned out at community meetings in Red Lake in a strong show of support, including White Earth and Leech Lake tribal leaders, BIA personnel from Bemidji, and BIA superintendent Miller. Support for the boycott was broad and deep. The Leech Lake Tribal Council voted to withdraw $1.25 million in assets from Bemidji banks. Red Lake planned to withdraw the $500,000 it held in Bemidji as well.[54]

The entire tribal population from Leech Lake, Red Lake, and White Earth began shopping at Grand Rapids, Detroit Lakes, and Thief River Falls. The *Bemidji Daily Pioneer* editorialized: "The boycott has been so effective and so thorough that over the week, for the first time since Bemidji became a community, Bemidji's streets have been practically devoid of Indians. This is a deplorable situation and one that cannot be allowed to continue. Bemidji cannot long withstand the harmful effects of a strict boycott."[55]

There was a barrage of letters to the editor and commentary in the opinion section of the *Bemidji Daily Pioneer*, most of it in support of an effort to heal the wounds. Jourdain started it off: "We do not consider ourselves as sub-human, as animal like, or 'morally and mentally indigent.'" He referred to Kohl's disposition as a "hate-the-Indian complex" and issued a call for action: "It is unfortunate that such a broadcast would be made; it would be even more unfortunate if it were allowed to pass unchallenged." But some unabashedly defended Kohl. Bemidji resident Jim Daman wrote: "I was perplexed at the immediate indignation shown by the Indians of this area after Bob Kohl's candid appraisal of local welfare conditions. Was this a case of the shoe fitting only too well?" Another local resident, David E. Umhauer, wrote: "I hope that those Indians offended by the broadcast do boycott Bemidji. If they do, it will be a cleaner town."[56]

Politicians scrambled to disassociate themselves from Kohl as fast as the business community had. Minnesota gubernatorial candidates Harold LeVander and Karl F. Rolvaag sparred publicly over their previous associations with and backing of Kohl. Kohl's support was slipping.[57]

Kohl and the KBUN manager, James Hambacher, tried to defend Kohl's statements, saying that he only commented on what he saw. But their defense only strengthened the boycott. On November 3, 1966, Kohl drove to Red Lake with Hambacher and Bemidji Chamber president Carl Olson to appear before the Red Lake Tribal Council. Their visit was arranged in advance and there was no way to keep it quiet. More than two hundred fifty people attended the meeting.

Kohl made what must have been a very uncomfortable statement of regret. Hambacher said that Kohl would not be announcing for the Commentary Program series but that he would remain on the station payroll. Olson said that Kohl would remain with the Chamber of Commerce as public relations and publicity director. That received a cool reception from the crowd, and the Red Lake Tribal Council rejected the parlay efforts. The boycott would continue until Kohl was no longer working for the Chamber of Commerce and the radio station. Kohl, Hambacher, and Olson were unwilling to make any further concessions and left the meeting.[58]

On November 4, 1966, Bemidji mayor Howard Menge used his influence to attempt a reconciliation. Kohl was forced to resign as a part-time commentator for the radio station and as public relations and publicity director for the Bemidji Chamber of Commerce. He was removed from the payroll for both organizations. Menge personally delivered to Jourdain copies of Kohl's resignations. Kohl's letter of resignation from the radio station was defensive: "It has become painfully obvious that reason without retribution is an impossibility." But the effect was the same—Kohl was gone. Hambacher aired an apology on the radio as well.[59]

Afterward, the Red Lake Tribal Council met with officials from Beltrami County and the city of Bemidji. A joint resolution by the Beltrami County Board of Supervisors, the Council of the City of Bemidji, and the Red Lake Tribal Council established a community relations commission "for the purpose of promoting and safeguarding equal opportunity, mutual respect, full employment opportunities, and pursuit of happiness of all the residents of the communities." Roger Jourdain, Howard Menge (Bemidji mayor), and Walter Fenske (chairman of the Beltrami County Board of Supervisors) were the first appointees.[60]

After that the Red Lake Tribal Council called off the boycott. It did not retract its formal complaint to the Federal Communications Commission. It permanently reallocated some of its bank funds to institutions outside of Bemidji. Realizing the importance of his native patrons, Joseph Lueken, owner of a local grocery chain in Bemidji, instituted an affirmative-action employment policy after the boycott as well. It was the first of its kind in Bemidji. Ever since, Lueken's has had native employees and tracked many into management positions. Prior to his death on July 20, 2014, Lueken attended numerous powwows at Red Lake and elsewhere and was called out by tribal members on a number of occasions to receive an honor song for his handling of the boycott.[61]

Racism dies hard. More than twenty-five years after the boycott, in 1992, Kelliher resident Lyle Daken told the Beltrami County Board that the people of Red Lake "should not be allowed to vote, they are not taxed, and they should not receive welfare benefits from our country." Although residents of the Red Lake reservation do not pay real-estate taxes because they do not own the land there (it's held in common), they do pay federal income taxes. Welfare payments are block-granted from the federal government to states. Red Lakers pay into the pool of taxes that fund welfare the same as everyone else. In addition, Red Lake provides ambulance and fire service, plows the roads, and provides police protection for everyone of all races who drives across or spends time on the reservation. By some measures, Red Lake actually provides more in-kind support and public service for white citizens than it receives.[62]

The thought that the people of Red Lake should not be allowed to vote or receive welfare is just another example of thinly clad racial vitriol. Such thoughts are still pervasive in the white communities around Red Lake, although they are not universally held. Even today, Kohl's words echo in everyone's ears. But Jourdain's response is also burned deeply into people's minds. In Bemidji, the nonnative community treads more carefully, thinks more critically about hiring practices, and usually chooses words more judiciously.

The Indians receive a little less marginalization and a little more respect—and they stand a little taller too.

Reclaiming Space

Roger Jourdain proved his power as a political warrior over and over during his early years in office. At the same time, he was shrewd and deliberate as he marshaled Red Lake's tribal council to repatriate land inside and outside the reservation. He was remarkably effective. Peter Graves had doggedly pursued the return of Red Lake's 1889 ceded lands. His success established the legal process and right of Red Lake to claim public lands lost through tax forfeiture within Red Lake's pre-1889 territorial boundaries. Jourdain finished the process, including repatriation of a massive 32,000-acre parcel in Koochiching County. He pursued every opportunity available, no matter how large or small.

On September 14, 1960, Jourdain pushed through a tribal resolution to restore land inside the reservation that had been granted to Independent School District 45 during the Graves administration. The school district cooperated with a memorandum of understanding to enable the land transfer. Jourdain then turned his attention to several parcels of land in the village of Redby. They had been pieced out of the unallotted land base to railroads and churches after the Nelson Act. Some were now in private ownership. Others were forfeited to state or county offices for tax delinquency. Jourdain could not convince county officials to give the land to the tribe, so he worked with the tribal council to appropriate funds from the tribal timber business to buy the land back in 1966. He used the same process to purchase property for the band on the Redby town site owned by the Church of Christ.[63]

Roy and Catherine Bailey had acquired a private parcel within the Redby town site from the section granted to the Minneapolis, Red Lake, and Manitoba Railroad. When the railroad went out of business, it sold the parcels, creating private plots on the reservation which otherwise was closed to private ownership of land. Catherine Bailey was a Red Lake tribal member, Redby postmaster starting in 1928, and owner of the Redby General Store and Restaurant. She was a respected community member, and her daughter, Katherine

L. Bailey, became the first high-school graduate in Red Lake in 1937. In 1966, Jourdain reached out to see if the Baileys wanted to grant their private parcel to the tribe and take a homestead assignment from the tribal council. Roy Bailey was white. Worried that their descendants might not be eligible for tribal enrollment or homestead assignments, they declined. They were willing to sell their plot to the tribe for a fair price. Jourdain made the arrangements and pushed through a resolution to authorize the purchase.[64]

The numerous small land transactions began to add up. Jourdain was incrementally decolonizing Red Lake's sovereign territory. The Red Lake Nation was reclaiming its land—an inspiring exercise in political power.

Red Lake's Housing Boom

Roger Jourdain established strong ties with the Minnesota AFL-CIO, politicians, educators, and health officials. He constantly sought to deepen his connections, and served on numerous boards and committees. He had no particular love of traveling, but service built relationships, and relationships made the capital he needed to get things done. When presenting, he had the ability to wear people out through sheer exhaustion, but normally he was dynamic, cogent, entertaining, engaging, and sometimes electric.[65]

Jourdain often had Minnesota's politicians and BIA officials walking on eggshells. They needed his support, and when they got it, it made all the difference in the world. He produced results for them in the voting booth, in the polls, and in the halls of government. But when they did not step in line with his agenda, he was capable of brutal, venomous attack. And when he attacked, he did not simply vent hot air. He could recite long lists of political missteps and BIA wrongdoings. He remembered political voting records for everyone of importance who could affect his agenda for Red Lake, and he never hesitated to remind the world about that when it served his purpose to make politicians uncomfortable. He worked the carrot and the stick with equal skill.

In the early 1960s, Jourdain was ready to push for a major housing initiative at Red Lake. It was a top priority for him and the rest of Red Lake's first democratically elected officials. Tribal members had a hard time getting financing for houses because no individuals owned land at Red Lake and there was nothing to collateralize a loan. Jourdain knew that he needed political support for funding and he needed motivated allies in Washington, DC, to get Red Lake prioritized for housing requests from the BIA. He went on a public-relations tour to line up support.

In Fergus Falls, he made a presentation to a women's group: "For a hundred years they have oppressed our people and held us down. They've taken our land and timber. Housing is so substandard that most people live without running water or indoor toilets. Life expectancy is barely forty years. How would you like to live like that, and when you tried to do something about it, be told you couldn't, or shouldn't, or mustn't?" Over the course of a year he was covered in most of the local newspapers in northern Minnesota. Local politicians read the papers and heard about the issues from their *white* constituents. BIA officials heard about the need for housing at Red Lake from elected *white* politicians. When Jourdain then asked for an audience with BIA officials to share solutions, they were ready to move on requests for road and infrastructure improvement, a new sawmill, and a major expenditure for housing at Red Lake.[66]

On January 8, 1964, Lyndon B. Johnson announced America's War on Poverty, the cornerstone of his Great Society. Congress soon passed the Economic Opportunity Act and created the Office of Economic Opportunity. Jourdain was waiting. The new programs created funding opportunities to redress poverty, and Jourdain helped Red Lake beat everyone to the grants and congressional budget line items. It amounted to a massive influx of money and a great deal of new construction business at Red Lake.

In most places, successful grant recipients started hiring contractors and building houses. Red Lake established its own construction company and hired it to build the houses. The goal was to have the dollars circulate in the tribal community through the creation of jobs, the construction of houses, and the expenditure of income. Jourdain said, "In the past when the BIA built something our unemployed stood around and watched while outside contractors and their help did the work. We'll build our houses ourselves."[67]

Jourdain pieced together support from local banks where Red Lake had deposited funds, new federal grant programs, and special appropriations to build an impressive array of financial support for infrastructure and housing work. When they were finally ready to start construction, one of the inspectors for the federal grant agencies ordered a halt to the work. All other War on Poverty housing appropriations required construction in designated development zones. Most of this was happening in urban areas. It was a classist restriction, designed to keep the poor from integrating into well-to-do neighborhoods. A development zone on the reservation didn't make much sense.

Jourdain had invested too much effort to be controlled by an unthinking bureaucrat. He fumed publicly and privately at the Office of Economic Opportunity (OEO). He pulled a team together at Red Lake and did a cost-effectiveness analysis, proving that scattered housing in the traditional lots where Red Lakers were accustomed to living was just as cost effective as development zones and enjoyed far greater community support. The OEO still refused to release the funds.

At the next tribal council meeting, Jourdain pushed through a resolution to create a development zone at Red Lake, included a legal description, and enclosed a beautiful map of the reservation. The OEO finally released the funds, and construction began immediately.

The efficiency with which the construction commenced was a marvel. Excavation crews opened the sites, immediately followed by the cement contractors, and then the construction crews. They built thirty-five houses the first summer, even with the delayed start caused by the embargoed funds. Over the winter, the expanded sawmill milled timber nonstop, and construction crews prefabricated modular units and roof trusses. Jourdain ordered private loan and tribal monies to extend the work until the next cycle of federal funds came in May of 1965. As the houses were filled, new funds cycled into the program and the work continued.

The OEO inspector finally came to Red Lake for a site visit. After driving around for half a day, he came storming into Jourdain's office, yelling, "You lied to me! Those houses are built all over the place! They're not in clusters!" Jourdain gave him a wry smile. "They're all built in the Redevelopment Area. We even sent you a map! Can't you read a map?" Jourdain held out a duplicate map and a copy of the legal description for the entire 640,000-acre diminished reservation.[68]

To this day, Red Lake's HUD housing development area takes in the entire reservation. They built houses all over the reservation with no fetters on the tribe's sovereign control or jurisdiction. The BIA might have felt tricked, but in the end it supported and advocated for passage of the legislation, so there was no more resistance. Chagrined, the OEO official retreated to Washington, with no choice but to release the rest of the funds. Over the next decade, Jourdain's efforts saw the construction of houses for five hundred families at Red Lake.[69]

After the boycott of Bemidji ended, Jourdain used the supportive sentiment among Minnesota's politicians to leverage political action on housing and poverty. He started with tribal resolutions and public statements of thanks to supporters. He traveled tirelessly, speaking on the issues and arranging private meetings with political leaders. He corresponded frequently with Walter Mondale and Hubert Humphrey. He worked his connections with the press. The *Minneapolis Tribune* ran the full text of tribal resolutions expressing thanks, detailing progress in housing and poverty, and advocating further action. He sent detailed antipoverty progress reports and tribal resolutions to every member of Congress in the midst of the boycott and repeatedly afterward. He invited film crews to Red Lake to document economic development and antipoverty work. Then he went right back to Washington and asked for more money. Red Lake became a national leader in tribal economic development.[70]

Economic Development

Jourdain's political and financial momentum was unstoppable. For thirty-two years, he was reelected to the top political post at Red Lake. The citizens of the reservation had modern houses, electricity, and economic opportunities barely imagined before he took office.

He was an innovator, not just a politician. Red Lake had timber resources and a mill. He bent the mission of the mill to serve Red Lake's housing needs. Then he pushed the tribal council to establish a wood fence manufacturing plant with Red Lake timber and employees. In 1963, the tribal council improved the sawmill from steam-operated machinery to electric. That created greater efficiency in the business and higher profit margins. In 1976, he pushed to expand Red

Lake's construction capabilities with a new tribal modular-housing construction company—Red Lake Builders. Over the years it manufactured numerous buildings and homes and created many jobs.

A new fisheries building was erected in 1976. The equipment was upgraded. The Red Lake Fisheries Association was soon reporting more than 2 million pounds of processed fish every year.

A new gas station and store was built in Ponemah. In 1986, the Red Lake Trading Post created a new financial hub on the south shore of the lake. It remains one of the tribe's most important businesses today. Jourdain wanted jobs for his people and he wanted the money people earned at Red Lake to be spent in Red Lake for whatever people needed. In a healthy economy, a dollar will circulate seven to nine times in a community, and that's what Jourdain was trying to engineer. That remains a goal of the tribal council today.

The Health Crusade

It is stunning to compare the longevity of the Red Lake people in recent years with that of its earlier leaders. Nodin Wind and John KaKayGeesick lived more than one hundred years. Moose Dung, He Who Is Spoken To, Sun Shining Through, Peter Graves, Rose Graves, Jane Graves, Joseph Nedeau Sr., and Roger Jourdain all lived beyond the normal life expectancy for whites or Asian Americans. But for most Red Lakers, health and longevity have been elusive for five generations.[71]

The traditional Ojibwe diet was cyclical, vitamin-rich, high in protein and fiber, but extraordinarily low in fat. Wild rice, berries, fish and wild game (boiled, not fried), and (starting in the 1800s) cereal crops and garden vegetables dominated Red Lake diets. People were active, fit, and hardworking. Anything else was a recipe for starvation.

After the Old Crossing Treaty in 1863, pressure on the traditional Ojibwe lifestyle increased. People had less land on which to harvest and fewer available food resources. They had to compensate for the shortage caused by land loss with the rations and annuities from the government they received as partial payment for the land sold. Those foods included flour, lard, salt, and salted pork. The diet changed quickly. Red Lakers began to fry their fish and meat and then to purchase more commercially processed food. As the Red Lake economy

evolved into a wage-based structure with some employment opportunities in timber and service industries, Red Lakers increasingly
spent their money on food in stores, and that food transformed their
diet, and not in a good way. By the time Roger Jourdain took office
as tribal chairman, Native Americans (at Red Lake and elsewhere in
Indian country) had the highest rate of diabetes in the world. Living
standards and life expectancy dropped dramatically.

Compounding the diet-based health problems at Red Lake was a
lifestyle that was more sedentary. People were restricted more and
traveled less. New diseases such as smallpox, still active at Red Lake
in the 1900s, killed many people. Others, such as tuberculosis, spread
rapidly in the crowded conditions of residential boarding schools.[72]

There was also a dearth of proper medical care and treatment. If
someone had a heart attack in Ponemah after World War II, there
was no electricity, no running water, no telephone service, no ambulance, and no help. If someone had a serious accident in Red Lake,
friends or relatives had to transport the injured person to the hospital themselves. If they did not own a car, they had to borrow one or
carry the person on foot. A small hospital had been built at Red Lake
in 1914, but it was not equipped for twenty-four-hour emergency-
room care. In 1955, a few years before Jourdain's first election as
tribal chairman, administration of the hospital transferred from the
Bureau of Indian Affairs to the Indian Health Service. It still lacked
many basic service capabilities.[73]

The rapid pace of cultural change, brought on by missionaries
and government assimilation programs, had an effect on health
too. There were fewer traditional healers. Those who did have such
knowledge were shamed by government officials and missionaries
and were increasingly persecuted and sometimes jailed.

Having money or health has never been a guarantee of happiness,
but the absence of those things can make one miserable. Jourdain
wanted to do something about this situation. His plan involved a
fundamental overhaul of health infrastructure and services on the
reservation, and a concerted (and still ongoing) effort to change the
food culture on the reservation.

He started with the hospital. The day he was voted into office the
BIA tried to shut it down in a power-control move. Jourdain won that
fight. He then worked systematically to convert as many health ser-

vices as possible to tribal control in order to limit further interference from the BIA. Simultaneously, he poured countless hours of time into fund-raising and advocacy to increase the services themselves.

In the mid-1960s, Jourdain recruited Margaret Seelye to his staff. She was an employee at Leech Lake's health education program, which was administered through the Community Action Program (CAP) there. CAP was developing a variety of service and outreach programs in many tribal communities. Seelye, an enrolled member of White Earth with a nursing degree, was in her early twenties, bright, and passionate about health in Indian country. Jourdain had her start writing grants. Right away she hit on a big $500,000 grant for comprehensive health services. It made Red Lake the first and only reservation in the country to take over its own health delivery and administration. Red Lake could now control programs for the well-being of its people.[74]

Seelye became director of the new comprehensive health program. Through the program, numerous Red Lake members were trained in emergency health delivery and triage. Red Lake developed tribal programs for occupational therapy, physical therapy, and dentistry. The entire program was up and running within six months, and it grew from there. Within a few short years, there was an ambulance bay at the hospital and a fleet of ambulances.

Many BIA and Indian Health Service (IHS) administrators felt threatened. If Red Lake took over all of the health jobs and delivery, the administrators might become obsolete. They pushed back professionally and sometimes competed directly for funding. A cultural transformation was in progress in the delivery of health services at Red Lake, but it took a long time to implement.

The first person trained as a comprehensive health aide at Red Lake was Susan Johnson. She was a young Ponemah full-blood, Ojibwe speaker, and dynamic health advocate. Her first emergency intervention under the new program involved a man from the main village at Red Lake who was having a heart attack. She performed emergency triage, stabilized the patient, and helped transport him to the hospital in Red Lake. She rushed up to the IHS emergency room and demanded immediate help to transport him from the gurney to the emergency room. "He's having a heart attack," she said. The nonnative nurses looked at her and sighed. "How would you know if he's having a heart attack?" Johnson's Ponemah accent, dark skin, and youth played into the cultural resistance from IHS staff to the comprehensive health expansion at Red Lake. Johnson insisted, patient but firm, until the hospital staff came to the gurney to investigate. They immediately realized that she was right about his condition. He was rushed inside. Incredulous, the nurses looked at Johnson in a whole new light: "You just saved his life." It was the first of many such incidents.[75]

As the stories of helpful interventions and life-saving treatments made possible by the new comprehensive health program poured in, Jourdain got more and more fired up. He worked to expand the staff for comprehensive health and modernize the equipment at the hospital. He pursued government grant dollars and bonding funds. Then he obtained funding to hire staff and get emergency medical technicians (EMTs) on the ambulances. Sick or injured tribal members no longer had to transport themselves to Bemidji or Blackduck for care or wait an hour or more for help to arrive from out of town. This saved hundreds of lives.

With an impressive record of health delivery, statistical analyses of program efficiency, and lots of powerful anecdotal evidence, Jourdain then descended on Capitol Hill. He met with politicians and health officials. He brought Seelye and other health staff to Washington to describe what was happening at Red Lake. By the time his political blitz was done, he had won a permanent line item in the federal budget through the IHS to sustain the Red Lake comprehensive health effort.

Jourdain and a growing staff of native medical professionals and administrators at Red Lake also worked hard to move other state and federal health programs under tribal oversight: Women, Infants, and Children (WIC), a health and nutrition program run through the U.S. Department of Agriculture, Supplemental Nutrition Assistance Program (SNAP), run through state human services agencies, immunization drives, and dental programs. This created jobs for tribal members. But it also created an expansive array of health and nutrition programs to meet the needs of tribal members and slowly reshape the dietary culture on the reservation. The long-term goal was prevention and cure.

Over the course of his long tenure in office, Jourdain kept pushing for more ideas and more resources for the health crusade. He got telephone service established in Ponemah and fire stations to serve each community on the reservation. He advocated for and built youth recreation programs, which changed with the times from baseball to basketball, which is still the most popular sport on the reservation.

Jourdain also tapped into his personal relationships to get support for line items in bonding bills. As a result, Red Lake was able to open an expanded modern hospital on March 14, 1981. In 1990, Red Lake opened the Jourdain-Perpich Extended Care Facility, a modern assisted-living and eldercare facility. Rudy Perpich was governor of Minnesota, and Jourdain convinced him to make Red Lake's facility a top priority in his political platform. Jourdain campaigned for Perpich and got both of their names on a building, but most important for both Perpich and Jourdain, they built something that served a critical need and higher purpose. The Jourdain-Perpich Extended Care Facility was named one of the highest-rated eldercare facilities in the state of Minnesota by *Consumer Reports* in 2006.[76]

The life expectancy for the people of Red Lake went from forty-three to sixty-five during Jourdain's tenure as tribal chairman, and it was the result of intentional political action. That was an increase of one year for nearly every year Jourdain was in office.[77]

Red Lake Trailblazing

In 1976, Jourdain traveled to Philadelphia for the commemoration of America's two hundredth birthday. Governors, senators, and presidents were in the lineup of speakers for the celebration. His good friend Wendell Chino, chairman of the Mescalero Apache, sat with him. Chino was a Baptist preacher in addition to being chairman at Mescalero, but he had a raucous sense of humor and loved to tease. As the speeches droned on and on, Chino goaded Jourdain relentlessly to go up to the podium and grab the microphone and tell everyone how things really were. Jourdain was not an invited speaker. Chino was, of course, trying to embarrass him, but finally the Red Lake chairman had had enough.[78]

Jourdain reached into his briefcase and grabbed the Gideon Bible that he had swiped from the hotel room that morning, stormed up to the podium, and took the microphone. His voice echoed throughout

Roger Jourdain and Wendell Chino, 1989

the building: "You have two constitutions here in the United States. You've got two. You've got this, and you've got the written constitution. You've got this Bible and you've got the written constitution, and you've never lived up to either one of them. You've broke the writing and the things that are included in this Bible and the U.S. Constitution with the American Indians." Then he held the Bible high over his head and slammed it down on the ground with a loud bang and stormed off the stage.[79]

Jourdain was baptized and raised Catholic, and his mother was a devout Episcopalian, but he detested the role of churches in undermining tribal sovereignty, language, and culture. He frequently visited Jimmy Jackson at Leech Lake for spiritual guidance as he got older, and he considered Jackson a friend, mentor, and brother. Roger's son, Roger Paul "Rod" Jourdain, said, "He believed in listening to the elders and believed in our Indian culture. . . . His basic beliefs were the Indians' beliefs and teachings." One time he was brought before the Senate Select Committee on Indian Affairs and refused to place his hand on a Bible and be sworn in. They accepted his testimony regardless.[80]

Jourdain was a living manifestation of sovereignty. And he always backed up the bravado with action. On January 16, 1974, Red Lake became the first tribe in the United States to issue tribal license plates. Jourdain saw no need to get permission from a state government to drive a car. The state litigated its objection in *Red Lake Band v. State,* but Red Lake emerged victorious in the legal battle. The tribe eventually negotiated a compact with the state to bring Red Lake's registration system into sync with state and national databases for greater ease of law enforcement. It was important to Red Lake for the state and federal governments to acknowledge its sovereign authority. The compact was the fastest way to guarantee that recognition in perpetuity. More than one hundred tribes in the United States followed Red Lake's lead. Today, Red Lake's tribal license plates show a picture of the lake, the clans of the original hereditary chiefs, and the clan of the car owner. There are thousands of plates in circulation now in a public declaration of sovereignty and cultural affirmation.[81]

Soon after, Jourdain worked with the tribal council to develop Red Lake Nation tribal passports. He planned to use them to travel internationally. He also wanted to require entry visas and passports from visitors to Red Lake. The visitors' passports read:

> The Supreme Court case of Chippewa Indians v. United States (1937) 301 U.S. 358, held that the Red Lake Reservation belongs to the members of the Red Lake Band of Chippewa Indians for all purposes and that no other Indian or person has any right therein. The U.S. Circuit Court of Appeals for the Eighth Circuit relied upon the Supreme Court decision and reaffirmed the status of the Red Lake Reservation in its 1974 bald eagle decision, U.S. v. Jackie White. In keeping with this Supreme Court decision, when the Revised Constitution and bylaws of the Red Lake Band of Chippewa Indians was adopted in 1958, Article VI, Section 4, vested in the Tribal Council authority to remove from the reservation persons not legally entitled to reside therein and whose presence may be injurious to the peace, happiness or welfare of the members of the Band. Article II, Section 1, of the bylaws states the Chairman shall see that all resolutions and ordinances of the Tribal Council are carried into effect.

The visas, or visitor passports, were provided to each nonmember visitor, "as a guest of the Red Lake Band of Chippewa Indians to visit the aboriginal lands and lakes of the Red Lake Band."[82]

Red Lake Leading Tribal Solidarity

Jourdain also saw Red Lake as a vital member of a larger league of native nations. His leadership extended far beyond the borders of the Red Lake reservation, and it put both him and Red Lake in the national spotlight.

Jourdain visited all of the tribes in Minnesota and built consensus to form a commission to speak to the governor and state legislature with a unified voice. In 1962, this effort was formalized as the Minnesota State Indian Affairs Commission. Jourdain served as chairman of the commission for many years. The name evolved over time to the Minnesota Indian Affairs Inter-Tribal Board; today, it is the Minnesota Indian Affairs Council (MIAC). It remains the primary vehicle of communication between the tribes and the governor's office. The effort was so successful at influencing legislation and protecting sovereignty that tribes in other states began thinking about similar organizations. Jourdain traveled to Wisconsin on several occasions to advise the tribes as they launched the Great Lakes Inter-Tribal

Council and fought a heated battle with legislators over termination policy. In 1985, he withdrew Red Lake from the MIAC over a political fight with the state, but rejoined when the political climate was more receptive to Red Lake interests.[83]

The Minnesota State Indian Affairs Commission successfully advocated for a tribal culture-focused residential alcohol treatment center in Minnesota. Jourdain said, "That darn liquor is the downfall of mankind." Fond du Lac tribal chairman William Houle was a primary advocate for locating the facility at Fond du Lac. Jourdain wanted it to be at Red Lake, but in the end agreed to support Houle. He could not resist some brutal humor when it came up for a vote with the commission: "I would like to voice my strong support for Bill Houle's recommendation to build the facility at Fond du Lac. An alcohol treatment program for Indians should be located where the highest concentration of drunk Indians is." Employees for the governor's office and all the Indian commissioners erupted into laughter, and the resolution sailed through without further debate.[84]

Jourdain saw the need for direct communication between tribal chairs across the country, and worked with many of them to form the National Tribal Chairman's Association (NTCA). The Department of the Interior funded initial efforts, hoping the voice of the NTCA would eclipse the growing Indian activism of the 1970s. They worked on joint strategies and legislative efforts. They supported one another through many tough internal and external political battles. Jourdain was elected vice president of the organization, and it was at the front line of Indian policy during the Nixon and Ford administrations.

Jourdain also brought Red Lake into the National Congress of American Indians (NCAI). The NCAI was formed in 1944, and worked to generate solidarity and cooperative political action among the many federally recognized tribes in the United States. Jourdain's presence at NCAI was electric. He had a vision of tribal sovereignty that was not just aligned with other tribal leaders, but full of many examples of how it could and should be wielded and strengthened. He catalyzed the efforts of the organization, and within a short period of time was elected as vice president.

Jourdain built personal and political relationships effortlessly, but always paid close attention to nurturing them. His service to the MIAC, NTCA, and NCAI put him in regular contact with many of the most powerful people in Indian country. He was especially close friends with Wendell Chino (president of the Mescalero Apache Tribe), Arthur Gahbow (chairman of the Mille Lacs Band of Ojibwe), Joseph De La Cruz (chairman of the Quinault Nation of Washington), and Newton Lamar (chairman of the Wichita Tribe of Oklahoma). Hundreds of other well-known tribal leaders and advocates considered him a friend and political ally. He had their backs, and everyone owed him political favors.

Red Lake Leading National Indian Policy

Roger Jourdain applied the same force of personality and political grace under pressure in the nonnative political arena. He had deep, friendly relationships with Hubert Humphrey, Walter Mondale, and Ted Kennedy. He even gave Humphrey an Indian name (Ogimaa-niigaanigwaneb, or Chief Leading Feather) and made him an honorary member of the tribe. He also named Mondale for one of Red Lake's founding chiefs—He Who Is Spoken To (Medwe-ganoonind). Jourdain stayed at the White House several times during the Carter-Mondale administration, often visiting for long hours beyond the normal call of business.[85]

Getting things done in Washington was tricky business for everyone regardless of race. Jourdain learned the game quickly, and he knew how appreciative politicians could be when they received support for their agendas. He delivered the goods for them over and over, and the reciprocation elevated him and empowered his political agenda. He always paid it forward in politics, and he was paid back in kind. Usually, he supported Democrats, but any betrayal or tepid posturing on Indian issues usually earned politicians not just a denial of support but vigorous backing for their political opponents.

Jourdain met every U.S. president and worked with every top official in the Department of the Interior and the BIA for thirty-two years. In 1976 and 1984, the years Walter Mondale ran for vice president and then for president, Jourdain served as a Democratic delegate to the Electoral College. Jourdain was a member of the Minnesota State Human Rights Commission and the United States Commission on Civil Rights (USCCR). His work with the USCCR put him in regular contact with most of the prominent civil-rights advocates

Chief August King, Senator Walter Mondale, Roger Jourdain, and band member Bill Dudley at the Bemidji airport, 1967

in the United States and brought him into both activist work and government outreach on issues of voting rights, segregation, justice, and economic equity. He was also a delegate to the Pan-American Conference in Mexico, where he was able to represent Red Lake at a gathering of nations focused on trade and political cooperation.[86]

Jourdain kept up a steady schedule of public speaking, private and public meetings, letter writing, and phone calls. Everyone knew Red Lake's business and political goals. On smaller, local stages, he gave just as much effort, speaking to Rotary clubs, schools, and chambers of commerce. He even agreed to give the commencement address at Flandreau in 1983. He struck a balance between challenging the assimilation platform that led him to run away from the school as a student nearly sixty years earlier and encouraging the students to forge their own destinies.

Jourdain had a profound sense of civic duty to the American nation, but it all channeled into his primary mission of serving Indian country and Red Lake in particular. No tribal leader before or after him has had as great an impact on national legislation for Native Americans. Hubert Humphrey was a force in politics from the height of the civil-rights movement in the 1950s through the era of Indian activism in the sixties and the tribal self-determination era of the seventies. Few U.S. politicians had greater influence. Humphrey served as senator from Minnesota from 1949 to 1964, vice president of the United States from 1965 to 1969, candidate for president against Richard Nixon in 1968, and again as senator from 1971 to 1978. When it came to Indian policy, Humphrey said, "Before we act on Indian legislation, we must first check with Chairman Jourdain."[87]

Jourdain's most significant political gift to all of Indian country came in the form of the 1975 Indian Self-Determination and Education Assistance Act, which enabled tribes to assert direct control over their business and political activities instead of working through the BIA. It took nearly fifteen years of steadfast advocacy to bring it to fruition. Jourdain worked both behind the scenes and in front of the lectern to make it happen. He never missed an opportunity to push for greater tribal self-rule. He wanted to get the BIA off the backs of the tribes and let tribes run their own affairs. This is common practice in Indian country today, but in the 1960s it appeared radical. He was slowly winning over politicians, Democrats and Republicans. His appointment to Richard Nixon's National Council of Indian Opportunity in 1970 unleashed his influence on the Nixon administration. Within just six months, his regular consultations with the president and his staff galvanized a new line of thinking about Indian policy.[88]

On July 8, 1970, Nixon gave a historic address, usually referred to as "Message from the President of the United States Transmitting Recommendations for Indian Policy." Nixon formally repudiated the policy of termination, which had devastated more than one hundred tribes and Indian communities and caused deep resentment of the government across Indian country. Nixon said that the government would stop trying to control and ultimately eliminate tribes. Instead, the government would seek new ways to strengthen tribes and remove the oppressive shackles of government control. Tribes would be encouraged to rule themselves and determine for themselves the best directions and methods for their own improvement. The Indian Self-Determination and Education Assistance Act would make that happen.[89]

Jourdain knew many of the staff members at Health, Education, and Welfare (HEW) and the Office of Economic Opportunity (OEO) who helped draft the language for the Indian Self-Determination and Education Assistance Act. Some, such as Robert Treuer, had spent years working in Red Lake. Jourdain's relationships and political influence affected even the most minute details of the legislative effort.[90]

Nixon had his hands full with the Vietnam War and Watergate, and resigned the presidency in 1974. Gerald Ford signed the Indian Self-Determination and Education Assistance Act into law on January 1, 1975. The act allowed the secretary of the interior and the secretary of HEW to give grants to and execute contracts directly with tribes. Prior to this legislation, funding for Indian programs was directly administered by the BIA on behalf of tribes. The BIA was not always responsive to tribal leaders. It usually hired nonnative people to fill government program positions on reservations. Jourdain was having success getting the BIA to both back off the control levers and listen more to tribal positions, but he always wanted direct control of the programs and resources. He got exactly what he wanted. The new legislation specifically stated that "the employees and administrative control of an otherwise federal program are transferred to the tribal government."

At first the BIA pushed back hard against its loss of control over who to hire and how to spend money on reservations. Jourdain again had to fight to hold bureaucrats accountable to their own laws. He called on his colleagues in the National Congress of American Indians (NCAI) to generate a broad base of tribal support. He called in favors with mainstream politicians as well. As Senator Humphrey and Vice President Mondale pressured the BIA to change its way of doing business, the bureau eventually relented. Jourdain (and all

other tribal leaders in the United States) were now free to take control of the programs, hire Indians to do the work, and direct spending according to self-stated tribal needs. Jourdain even influenced
the appointment of BIA commissioners. Red Lake tribal member
Bill Hallett served in that position from 1979 to 1981. Pushback on
the law did not fully die until a major Supreme Court case, *Cherokee Nation of Oklahoma v. Leavitt,* affirmed the self-determination
provisions of the contract process in 2005. By then, it was already
inconceivable to have anyone from the BIA tell Red Lake leaders how
to spend tribal program funds.[91]

Jourdain did not support the Indian Civil Rights Act, which passed
over his objections in 1968. He felt that the law, which focused on the
individual rights of tribal members across the country, did so blindly
and actually undermined the emerging strength of native nations.
He also probably worried that his own power could be undermined
through the legislation. The primary means of recourse for individual
Indians under the Indian Civil Rights Act was through action in federal courts. Jourdain supported individual Indian rights, but wanted
to strengthen tribal courts as the primary vehicle for protecting the
people. Tribal governance structures often had weak judiciaries. His
plan would take time and meet significant resistance externally from
the BIA and internally from tribal members opposed to constitutional reform. It is still an ongoing battle.

Jourdain's political accomplishments were not linear. He did not
work one issue and get something done and then move to another.
He pushed on multiple fronts simultaneously. While advocating for
the new self-determination policy and legislation, he also moved to
increase funding for Indian education. Through cooperative work
with other tribal leaders, Jourdain helped get the Indian Education
Act (IEA) passed into law on June 23, 1972. The IEA created the Office
of Indian Education and the National Advisory Council on Indian
Education. All representatives on the council were native, and Minnesota was always well represented, starting with the first chairman,
Dr. Will Antell—an enrolled tribal member from White Earth and
personal friend of Jourdain. There were several amendments to the
act and reauthorizations over the next twenty years; Jourdain was
involved in every one of them.[92]

Jourdain testified before Congress so many times that even politicians with committee assignments completely removed from Indian issues got to know him well; among them was Senator Daniel K. Inouye from Hawaii. Inouye served in the U.S. Senate from 1962 to 2012, a long tenure of fifty years. He began his career there with a focus on military and intelligence issues, but soon found himself drawn to Jourdain's mission. In 1984, Inouye introduced legislation to create the National Museum of the American Indian. Inouye, who served on committees on commerce, Watergate, and appropriations, was eventually elected president pro tempore of the Senate. He could have chosen to chair any committee he wanted, and he chose the Senate Select Committee on Indian Affairs. He later remarked on Jourdain's political career: "Chairman Roger Jourdain was one of the greatest Indian leaders of his time—he was a mentor and a courageous warrior who always put the protections of the rights of his people before all else. He will be remembered with great respect by all those who had the privilege of knowing him. He is truly revered in all parts of Indian country."[93]

Native religious freedoms were another issue Jourdain got involved with. Members of the Native American Church, which fused the pre-Columbian use of peyote with Christianity, formed an alliance with traditional native healers to push for greater religious freedom in the 1970s. Newton Lamar, who was elected chairman of the Wichita Tribe of Oklahoma in 1976, advocated for legislation to protect Indian religious freedom. He was already fast friends with Roger Jourdain and in a short matter of time they were in agreement about legislative action.

Native and nonnative power brokers coalesced in 1978 and put together a landmark piece of legislation—the American Indian Religious Freedom Act. It is both sad and ironic that the First Amendment to the U.S. Constitution was insufficient to protect the religious freedom of the first Americans. The new legislation, which passed into law on August 11, 1978, protected Indian access to sacred sites, freedom to worship, and tribal rights to possess and use sacred objects. The law lacked any enforcement mechanism or remedy for those whose freedoms were still being violated, but it did produce significant changes in practice and perception. Nodin Wind, now 103 years of age, had fought for the religious freedom to practice the medicine dance at Ponemah for many decades through great adversity and pressure. It must have brought some satisfaction to know that his tribal chairman now had the power to really protect it.[94]

Jourdain was at the center of Indian politics in the United States during the Carter administration, and he never stopped fighting for Indian rights and tribal sovereignty. In 1966, he said, "I work seven days a week, 24 hours a day. My only enjoyment is my work. When I don't get things done, I really get into a depressed state." The flurry of legislative action he was pushing for in the 1970s reached a crescendo with the Indian Child Welfare Act (ICWA) in 1978.[95]

For over fifty years there had been a truly horrific problem in adoption and foster care of native children. Approximately 35 percent of native children in the United States were removed from their homes and many directly from the hospitals in which they were born by involuntary adoption or foster-care proceedings, usually orchestrated by county social service agencies across the country. In Minnesota, as much as 25 percent of the infant Indian population was being placed for adoption, and Red Lake had the highest removal rate among tribal populations in the state. Minnesota's Indian out-of-home placement rate was five times that of nonnative children. More than 90 percent of the placements were with non-Indian families. Numerous parents were disempowered in the raising of their own children. Generations of native youth were disconnected from their families, reservations, and culture. Adoption and foster care was, like education policy, simply another front in the long war on tribal culture.[96]

Social-service agencies did not have the procedures, personnel, or training to equip them to work with Indians. Most of the native kids were removed from their homes without a social worker ever seeing them. Racial bias was pronounced. Many Red Lakers were afraid of losing their children merely because they were Indian. Something had to be done.

This was an issue close to the hearts of many tribal leaders. Native women in North Dakota started national advocacy, and Jourdain was an early, loud, and persistent voice in the legislative effort. Washington politicians soon saw that a real miscarriage of justice was being perpetrated on native families every day. ICWA was the first attempt to find a solution. It mandated state courts and county social-service agencies to place children who were removed from their homes according to the following priorities: (1) preference of the child and parent, (2) extended family, (3) other tribal members, and (4) other Indians. Agencies had to notify tribes of cases affecting their members, and tribes could intervene in their children's welfare.[97]

There was broad political support for ICWA in Washington, but some adoption and church groups fought provisions that would weaken their efforts to track native kids to white families. In spite of some blowback, the biggest obstacle to the legislation was apathy. Jourdain and other tribal leaders had sent such a long list of legislative needs through the pipeline that politicians were feeling Indian policy fatigue. Jourdain needed constituents to rally to get the legislation out of committee and into the law books. He hit the lecture circuit again, traveling tirelessly, speaking to community organizations and schools. He focused on young people, sensitized to issues of inequity from the civil-rights movement and Vietnam War protests. In Wisconsin he spoke to a group of students at the Clyde Memorial Institute about the Indian Child Welfare Act. John Red Horse recalled:

> Roger sort of stiffened up . . . and he said, "You know there are only three things tribes have to be concerned about." The students were getting on the edge of their seats. They were waiting for these magical pieces of wisdom to come out, and Roger said, "Sovereignty, sovereignty, and sovereignty." You could just see the passion in him as he started talking about the trust responsibility, the abdication of trust responsibility, the role of tribes in the United States, and the treaty rights that have been withdrawn many times. The single-minded passion of a national leader. You begin to understand why Red Lake . . . successfully avoided removal down to White Earth. . . . That passion . . . led to that rush of legislation in the 1970s that organized and restructured and brought to the surface where we are as nations in this country. That passion is part and parcel of the Indian Child Welfare Act.

The legislation passed, and again Jourdain's sworn testimony in Washington and his relentless advocacy were instrumental in making it happen.[98]

ICWA was a welcome change, but it was far from perfect. There were no fines, sanctions, or punishments for failure to comply. Caseworkers often did not know if a child was Indian or what tribe to contact. Social workers knew little about native culture, history, language, or the ICWA. Social-service agencies were and remain grossly under-funded. Even years after the ICWA, only a small percentage of the Indian foster-care removals had a site visit. Often tribes received late notice or none at all. By the time they tried to intervene, the affected children had already been removed from their homes for years.

Jourdain worked at Red Lake to create a solution by developing the tribe's human services programs and staff. Even today, among all Minnesota tribes, Red Lake is the most consistently involved in child welfare cases affecting their children. It sends social-service workers to CHIPS (Children in Need of Protective Services) hearings every time it receives notice. Today, Minnesota social-service agencies must develop permanency plans within one year of initiating litigation such as a CHIPS petition, and communication between Red Lake and Beltrami County has greatly improved. Some state and tribal governments signed memoranda of agreement that obligate states to pay for foster-care placements ordered by tribal courts. Today Red Lake's consistent intervention in Indian child welfare politics and social service program development continues to help strengthen native families.

In 1999, Minnesota passed the Minnesota Indian Family Preservation Act, which sought to strengthen and expand ICWA provisions in the state. Minnesota saw a 92 percent decline in Indian adoptions and a 66 percent decline in Indian foster-care placements during the first two decades after passage of the ICWA. There is still a long way to go. Indians still have the highest out-of-home placement rate of any racial group in the United States. Jourdain was instrumental in developing the legal tools to address these issues, and Red Lake leaders and social-service staff have been using those tools to pursue justice and family health for their people ever since.

Ronald Reagan proved far less receptive to Indian legislative efforts than Eisenhower, Kennedy, Johnson, Nixon, Ford, or Carter. The pace of Jourdain's legislative accomplishments slowed, but not their depth. He continued to develop and sustain his political relationships and advocacy through the 1980s.

One of the most powerful impacts of tribal sovereignty was that tribes had direct relationships with the U.S. federal government that superseded state authority. In 1981, the Seminole in Florida tested the waters on Indian gaming and won a landmark case in *Seminole*

Tribe of Florida v. Butterworth. The entire country was trying to figure out what that meant when a 1987 case in California, *California
v. Cabazon Band of Mission Indians,* made it clear that Indians could
operate bingo and casino operations regardless of state laws or the
intrusion of Public Law 280, which gave states criminal jurisdiction
on many reservations.[99]

After that, the federal government passed landmark legislation
that affirmed the court-validated right of tribes to operate casinos,
but it required them to negotiate compacts with the states in which
their reservations were located. The law was called the Indian Gaming Regulatory Act, and it passed in 1988. Jourdain supported tribal
gaming but he was adamantly opposed to the legislation, presciently
predicting that states would abuse the compact process to get at tribal
revenues. He viewed that as not just another case of outsiders digging
into Indian pockets, but a real compromise of sovereignty. The fervor
around tribal gaming pushed the legislation straight through.

Jourdain filed suit against the law after it was passed. Wendell
Chino had the Mescalero Apache join the suit. Although Jourdain did
not win that fight, his opposition produced a substantial result in
Minnesota. Governor Rudy Perpich and other Minnesota state politicians feared a backlash, and ultimately pushed through some of the
most liberal gaming compacts in the country. One of the most significant issues is that they do not have sunset clauses. That means that
tribes do not have to constantly renegotiate with the state or have
their business operations held hostage or chiseled down by revenue-
sharing agreements.[100]

In 1988, Jourdain spearheaded a reauthorization of one of his signature legislative accomplishments—the Indian Self-Determination
and Education Assistance Act of 1975. The new legislation did more
than reauthorize the self-determination legislation. It made BIA
schools eligible for new funding and gifted and talented programs.
Several key programs such as natural resource management and
child care would also be transferred from BIA control to direct tribal
control.[101]

The legislation had special language about honoring broken treaties. This was a broad effort, but at the forefront of Jourdain's mind
was the issue that had plagued all Red Lake leaders since 1889—the
return of the lake to Ojibwe control. He wanted the section that had

been cut off from the reservation on Upper Red Lake to be restored to the tribe. The legislation did not explicitly make that happen, but he hoped it might help pave the way for it.

The legislation passed in 1988, and a special transfer of jurisdiction ceremony (from the BIA to the tribe) was scheduled at Red Lake in 1989. Ever the statesman with a mind for proper spectacle, Jourdain timed the signing to coincide with the one hundredth anniversary of the Nelson Act. Jourdain arranged the transfer agreement to be signed at the Pike Creek outlet where He Who Is Spoken To signed consent for the Nelson Act with Henry M. Rice a century earlier. Red Lake did not get the lake back that day, but it pushed the BIA one step further away from its previous controlling position at Red Lake. Sovereignty again was affirmed, and it was growing.

Jourdain was an extremely successful politician—earning respect, favors, and power, and then asking, demanding, and negotiating Red Lake's agenda of and with the rest of the world. Most Indians across the country paid little attention to American politics in the 1950s and 1960s, but Red Lake was different. Jourdain knew that the key to motivating politicians was not explaining the legitimate needs of the Red Lake people but showing them that the Red Lake people had something the politicians needed—votes. He had great success with this at Red Lake and then took the effort national.

Jourdain led many voter registration drives to sign tribal members up to vote in American elections. In 1983, his national voter registration drive signed up 32,000 Indian voters. Today, Red Lake's voter turnout consistently exceeds the national average. Jourdain's home village of Little Rock on the reservation has sometimes turned out 100 percent of its registered voters. In close political contests, Red Lake's voter participation makes a huge difference. Red Lake's votes made up the winning margin in Al Franken's close election to the U.S. Senate in 2008. The state representative seat is heavily influenced by the Red Lake vote, as are Beltrami County races. The Red Lake Political Education Committee was formed in recent years to try to get more Indians elected in county races, and it succeeded in electing Sandra King, Quentin Fairbanks, and Tim Sumner to the Beltrami County Board. Jourdain's influence on the political culture at Red Lake continues to pay dividends for the reservation today.[102]

Red Lake Burning

With the incredible mystique and experience Roger Jourdain had as Red Lake's premier political warrior, it is ironic that the greatest test to his leadership came not from any enemies outside the reservation, but from within. Like Peter Graves, Jourdain had a reputation as a hard man. He was a warrior, not a people pleaser. But as he increased the programs and funding for Red Lake, the people he did not please had more and more ammunition for counterattacks. He was always right about self-determination and tribal sovereignty, but it was the small battles and the methods he employed to win them that began to alienate some of the people at home.[103]

Jourdain's first meaningful political opposition came during the 1967 chairman's race. Leon F. Cook, a young, handsome, educated, and highly charismatic Red Laker, had lots of support both on and off the reservation. He came from one of Red Lake's biggest families, and he was a great campaigner. In the end, Jourdain pounded on Cook about everything from alcohol policy to authenticity and eked out a win in the general election. The win was an important one for Jourdain, but some of the family divisions the election stirred up stayed with him after that. Because it was a close election and Red Lake had a long history of "strong man" politics from the Graves and Jourdain eras, allegations of nepotism, dictatorial politics, and election fraud began to be voiced. Jourdain only had one son and had not pushed family members into jobs, but he certainly did groom supporters and worked hard to help them in campaigns for tribal government.

Many tribal residents were losing faith in the integrity of tribal programs and the people running them. In 1979, Jourdain lost an unrelated court case over his personal income taxes. He claimed to be exempt from federal taxation because of Red Lake's sovereignty, but the court did not see it that way. In *Commissioner of Taxation v. Brun,* it was established that tribal members living on tribal land who obtained all of their income from the tribe were exempt from state income taxation but not federal income tax. Jourdain's political opponents saw it as another case of his using his position for personal aggrandizement. Red Lake had seen much improvement in housing and health, but poverty persisted for tribal members. A fundamental fissure was developing between tribal leadership and the people.[104]

Jourdain's sway mattered a great deal, but never amounted to control, especially in 1977, when one of his loyal supporters, Alvin R. "Lummy" Oliver, lost his election bid against Stephanie Hanson for treasurer. Stephanie Hanson was young, charismatic, and ambitious. As treasurer she had a great deal of authority over Red Lake tribal accounts and policy, but she was at odds with Jourdain from her first day in office. Eventually, she overstepped her constitutional authority and started to manipulate the accounts without approval from Jourdain or the tribal council. The tribal council censured her for violating constitutional protocol and filed a restraining order on her husband, Harry, in 1978, citing his willful intimidation of tribal employees and elected officers. In 1979, the council became aware that Hanson planned to eliminate the council-sanctioned tribal sawmill project and had new undisclosed plans for the $1.3 million appropriated for that project. On May 18, 1979, the council decided to remove Hanson as treasurer by a quorum vote.[105]

The next day, on May 19, 1979, Hanson's husband, Harry, and a group of armed Red Lake men took two BIA officers, a police dispatcher, and two BIA jailers hostage at gunpoint and held them in jail cells at the tribal law enforcement complex. Robert McMullen, a white man, had supervisory authority over Red Lake's tribal police as head of BIA law enforcement at Red Lake. He called FBI agent Robert Erwin for help. McMullen then approached the jail to parlay for the return of the hostages, but was fired upon by Hanson and his accomplices. McMullen retreated. Bemidji police chief David Simondet and Beltrami County sheriff Thomas Tolman responded to calls for assistance. McMullen refused to intervene or to delegate his authority to manage the police response. Agent Erwin made it to Red Lake and assumed command.

Erwin pulled all law enforcement back to a grocery store off the reservation and ordered no further intervention. With no police on the reservation, Harry Hanson lit the jail on fire with all of the hostages locked in cells inside the burning building. Delwyn and Mildred Holthusen were driving by the jail when it was set on fire and heard the screams for help. Delwyn Holthusen was a BIA police captain on physical disability leave at the time. He broke into the jail and used a steel bar to eventually pry the jail cell doors open, freeing the hostages before Hanson returned and the building was completely engulfed in flames. He drove the hostages off the reservation, and the jail collapsed shortly afterward.

The BIA, which had long been Jourdain's punching bag and the primary recipient of his pushback to assert self-determination, refused to countermand Erwin's order to retreat or to otherwise intervene at Red Lake. The FBI had claimed jurisdiction over major crimes at Red Lake, including arson, ever since the passage of the Major Crimes Act in 1885, but it rejected all calls for help. Erwin stayed put. State and county agencies had no choice but to follow the lead of the FBI. They all just let it burn. Red Lake was on its own.

Hanson's mob and various rioters took over Red Lake, unimpeded by law enforcement. Rumors of outside agitators from the American Indian Movement instigating trouble on the reservation were false; the rioters were Red Lake residents. On the evening of May 19, Hanson's mob burned several buildings west of the creek in Red Lake, including tribal program buildings, a tribal warehouse, Francis Brun's house and laundromat, and many vehicles. Then Harry Hanson and his entourage attacked Roger Jourdain, Margaret Jourdain, and Elaine Johnson at the Jourdain residence. All three had to lie on the floor while bullets whizzed overhead. Jourdain's frantic telephone calls for help eventually got a couple of BIA officers to respond, and they escaped with their lives. Jourdain's house was burned to the ground. Johnson and the Jourdains weren't hurt, but when Margaret escaped she said she would never live in Red Lake again. She kept that promise.

Throughout the evening of May 19 and the day on May 20, rioters carried on unrestricted throughout Red Lake village. There was no meaningful law-enforcement response. Local fire crews were overwhelmed and unable to save the buildings. Nobody was willing to intervene to prevent further arson, looting, and public displays of aggression. There were two deaths. Both happened when several young reservation residents ran through the village of Red Lake with loaded guns. One of them tripped and accidentally killed himself. Another was shot and killed in crossfire from a friend. Both of the fatalities were teenagers. No charges were filed. Two other individuals were wounded by gunfire. One was shot in the nose and the other in the leg. In addition to the human casualties, more than $4 million worth of private and public buildings burned to the ground.

Ponemah residents refused to participate in the riots. Twenty-five village veterans from Vietnam, Korea, and World War II, including Eugene Stillday, built a barricade at the Battle River bridge. They manned it for four days and three nights. Their spouses and other village residents brought them food and coffee. Eugene Stillday was selected as their leader, although he was humble and refused to be acknowledged or even to speak to reporters at the time.[106]

Stillday set up four-hour shifts to rest the Ponemah sentries simply because he was used to four-hour shifts on his navy ship when he was in the Korean War. The Ponemah sentries turned back three groups of rioters from Red Lake village at the barricade. The leader of one group directly challenged Stillday when he was told that they would not be allowed to drive to Ponemah. Stillday told him, "You won't get past these guys." The man brandished a sidearm and told Stillday, "Well, we'll see." He stepped past Stillday toward the barricade. Several of the Ponemah sentries cocked handguns and chambered shotgun rounds. He turned right around, hopped in his car, and sped away.

In the aftermath of the event, Harry Hanson surrendered to authorities, and there was eventually a formal investigation. Hanson was sentenced to twenty-six years in prison by U.S. district court judge Edward Devitt, for "leading a revolution of blatant lawlessness." Devitt called Hanson's conduct "shocking to the mind and conscience" and said that Hanson "visited disgrace on the Indian people."[107]

After the riots, Jourdain was understandably worried about his personal safety. He temporarily froze Red Lake funds, issued press releases, and pushed outside agencies to move on the investigations. Ten years after the riots, federal courts found the FBI negligent (because it had jurisdiction and refused to intervene) and awarded the tribe $700,000 in damages and Jourdain $100,000 for the loss of his home and vehicles. In the intervening years, however, there was a big question about who would now lead at Red Lake and how.[108]

Jourdain was as brave as he was stubborn. Honoring Margaret's resolution, the Jourdains bought a house in Bemidji. He replaced his vehicle and drove back to Red Lake, knowing that someone could take a potshot with a rifle or walk into his office with a gun at any time. He set up a temporary tribal headquarters and began to rebuild everything at Red Lake, from physical structures to his political base. Most of the people were still behind him. He won reelection many times afterward. The divisions, discord, and resentment that boiled over in 1979 never fully dissipated, but it took more than bullets and burnings to stop Roger Jourdain.

When Warriors Lead

The biggest difference between the Roger Jourdain administration and that of Peter Graves was that Graves unabashedly used his position to support and reinforce the policies of the Office of Indian Affairs (renamed the Bureau of Indian Affairs in 1947). But Jourdain was one of the first and loudest advocates of sovereign power and used his position to reduce the oversight and interference of the BIA. During his time in office, almost every program and resource that used to be controlled by the BIA was converted to tribal control and management. The process was piecemeal and was often resisted in Washington, but it accumulated into a monumental achievement. And Red Lake paved the way for others to follow suit. Today, tribal sovereignty is a mantra preached by all elected tribal officials across the country. Jourdain's revolutionary approach transformed tribal politics and remade the Red Lake nation. He ruffled a lot of feathers in the process. When warriors lead, someone usually gets bloodied.

Jourdain's legendary reputation for pushing back outsiders extended from big national policy changes to tribal affairs at every level. In the early 1960s, a group of Mormon missionaries came to Red Lake hoping to establish a mission and church. They voiced a belief that lack of racial pigmentation reflected moral virtue—the darker the skin, the darker the soul. Although that view is not universal among Mormons, all they succeeded in doing was offending Jourdain and most of the tribal council. The council passed a resolution banning the Church of Jesus Christ of Latter-day Saints from the reservation. Jourdain instructed tribal police to escort them off the reservation and tell them to never come back.[109]

In 1971, the Ridge Mining Company wanted to do aerial geological surveys at Red Lake. Jourdain had no faith in the company's motives. He flatly denied the request. Then he made sure to pass a tribal resolution prohibiting aerial surveys and sent copies to Ridge and other mine prospecting businesses.[110]

The first time an airplane flew over Red Lake in the 1930s, some tribal members thought it was a giant thunderbird and ran down to the lakeshore with tobacco wrapped in cloth to make offerings for protection. But the planes kept coming back. The Graves administration gave permission for military ordnance testing on tribal land, and the repeated bombing runs always annoyed and sometimes terrified reservation residents. Everyone had a problem with the thousands of fish killed by military ordnance. Jourdain's administration reauthorized the bomb and rocket testing by the U.S. Air Force and U.S. Navy in 1959, but soon saw no benefit for the tribe in continuing the arrangement and put a stop to it in the 1960s.

On May 4, 1978, Jourdain got a resolution passed forbidding not just ordnance testing, but any flyover by military aircraft. Then he called the U.S. Air Force command center in Grand Forks, North Dakota, and told them that "as Chairman I had full authority over this land and the next time they flew over, we'd be waiting with our 30-30s and shoot your plane down." The air force colonel in charge of the bombing runs called tribal attorney Red Edwards Sr. and asked: "Do you think Jourdain would shoot down our plane?" Edwards replied, "You're darn right." The air force ceased its ordnance testing protocol on the reservation and has rerouted its flight paths around the reservation ever since.[111]

Red Lake had a long history of permitting white duck and goose hunters to access Red Lake land and water during the Peter Graves era. Jourdain continued the courtesy, but established a fee-based system to generate revenue for the tribe. In the 1960s and 1970s, he also established a moose season for white hunters on Red Lake land in the Northwest Angle and other designated parcels. Eventually, the money generated was outweighed by his vision for total tribal control and exclusive access to tribal-owned land, and the tribe quit issuing permits to white hunters.[112]

Following the passage in 1982 of the Nuclear Waste Policy Act, which placed stringent restrictions on the disposal of nuclear waste, many nuclear power companies solicited tribes for permission to establish nuclear storage facilities, hoping that tribal sovereignty would protect them from federal regulation. Jourdain proactively moved to protect Red Lake's land and water from the pressure to house nuclear waste. The tribal council adopted a formal policy statement forbidding any nuclear waste on the reservation, the lease or sale of any land for storage purposes, and any action that had the potential to endanger Red Lake's land, water, or people. Nuclear energy companies relentlessly pursued nuclear storage contracts with Prairie Island in southern Minnesota and several tribes in the Southwest, but they knew that Red Lake would never be an option.[113]

In 1986, Jourdain tore into BIA officials who advocated opening the Red Lake reservation to white business development. The BIA pushed back and the *Minneapolis Star Tribune* ran a negative newspaper article about Red Lake's tribal courts. Instead of defending tribal policy or firing back at the newspaper, Jourdain pushed through a new tribal resolution requiring all tribal lawyers and judges to operate the court in the Ojibwe language. If anyone wanted to analyze tribal court proceedings, they would have to do it in Ojibwe. That practice was not continued indefinitely, but long enough to make a critical demonstration of tribal sovereignty. William Houle, Fond du Lac tribal chairman, knew Jourdain well. He said, "He's taken on the BIA, the Department of the Interior, congressmen and senators in hearings throughout the country, and I don't think he's ever lost a battle."[114]

One former Jourdain staff member wrote: "Jourdain's personality and occasional public outbursts are awe-inspiring. Denver International Airport lost his luggage once, and Jourdain exploded in an imperial tantrum in the middle of the lobby until reassured it had been located and would be sent to his hotel before the day was out. This is not pique; it is a method that gets results. He is a counterpuncher, abrasive, aggressive, persuasive by turn; he expects much from himself and others and fumes at slipshod performance—bordering on compulsiveness." Jourdain shared his deep knowledge freely but sometimes had a hard time delegating to others. Trust had to be earned, and he was careful with his confidences. Sometimes he turned against younger people, such as Leon Cook, if he deemed them a threat or potential challenger.[115]

The constant political battles were not always pretty, but the message was clear and consistent. "We are an aboriginal Indian nation,"

Jourdain said. "Our ancestors never gave up this land. They had to surrender large tracts until only this was left, but this remainder has always been Indian. It is not a reservation set up for us, but what we always had. By treaty with the United States we are a sovereign nation." This unflinching vision and Jourdain's political acumen enabled him to play a key role in federal legislation under ten U.S. presidents.[116]

Jourdain's overbearing demeanor took a toll on his support during his last twelve years as chairman. Accusations of voter fraud raised during Leon Cook's 1967 campaign for tribal office still haunted Jourdain's standing on the reservation. His tax case left an unfair impression among many that he was in office simply for himself. The riots in 1979 exposed deep division and dissatisfaction. Litigation from the riots wasn't resolved until 1989. The settlement to the tribe was well justified, even too small. But there was also a settlement to Jourdain personally, and even if that was justified, it did not sit well with his people. Jourdain won the battle with the FBI and the BIA, but he lost standing at home. Many Red Lakers had had enough. He was politically vulnerable. The vote margins in elections for Red Lake chairman were narrower with each new election. Jourdain did not evolve in response; he stiffened and hardened, and it cost him in the end.[117]

Tribal members like Bill Lawrence and Susan Hallett scrutinized tribal elections ever more closely. Hallett was one of the most respected elders in Red Lake, and when she asked to be election auditor for the reservation even Jourdain could not refuse. The chairman's race in 1990 was a hot contest, with Jourdain and Gerald "Butch" Brun (Asiniiwinini, or Stone Man) both campaigning hard. Brun's platform was not radically different from Jourdain's, but his calls for accountability and transparency were eroding Jourdain's normal support. The election was close, but Brun came out on top.[118]

Jourdain demanded a recount. Susan Hallett locked up the ballot boxes and refused to turn them over to Jourdain's office. For days there was a tense standoff. Jourdain contested the election result in tribal court. The judge was Margaret Seelye Treuer, who had worked for Jourdain in the 1960s to build Red Lake's comprehensive health program, went on to become the first female Indian attorney in the state of Minnesota, and was now Jourdain's judicial appointee.

Bill Lawrence, a tribal member, political dissident, and journalist, petitioned the tribal court for dismissal of Jourdain's case. Lawrence argued that Jourdain was not a resident of the reservation. He had moved to Bemidji after the riots in 1979. The tribal constitution had a strong residency requirement in order to run for office, established by amendment to the tribal constitution in 1978. No matter what was in the ballot boxes, Jourdain should not have been certified in the first place. Jourdain did not contest the residency question. To him, it was a law that nobody paid attention to, like the ones still on the books in some states that say it's illegal for Indians to ride on horseback after dark. They are there but nobody enforces them. But this wasn't a minor and obsolete statute. Election law at Red Lake was laid out in the tribal constitution. Treuer had no choice but to validate the Lawrence petition. Jourdain's dispute of the election was dismissed. Butch Brun would be Red Lake's new tribal chairman.[119]

Jourdain had some hard choices to make. He must have felt horribly betrayed by the voters, Judge Treuer, and Bill Lawrence. He could have appealed the ruling, fired the judge, and fought back. But in the end he loved the Red Lake Nation too much to destabilize it. He stepped down and cooperated in a smooth transition of power to Brun.

Jourdain touched many lives, and he was often honored in return. Walter Mondale considered nominating Jourdain for a Nobel Peace Prize in 1970. The city of Bemidji formally proclaimed April 1, 2003, as Roger A. Jourdain Day. Jourdain's accolades and awards included American Indian Heritage Foundation Man of the Year (1987), Minneapolis Star Tribune Most Influential People of the Millennium (1991), Minnesota House of Representatives Commendation for Distinguished Service to Indian People, and NCAI Outstanding Indian Leader of the Year (1991). When Jourdain received his 1991 award from the NCAI in Arlington, Virginia, Wayne Ducheneaux, Cheyenne River Sioux and NCAI president, said, "You have demonstrated an ability to command the respect of national leaders and push them into action, which is an invaluable asset in Indian country."[120]

As a civilian, Jourdain focused first on his family. In the twilight of her life, his wife Margaret suffered a debilitating stroke, and Roger, in spite of his own health limitations and advanced age, nursed her day and night until she passed away in 1992. He continued to travel, speak, and advocate. He appeared at many public forums. He made peace with old political opponents and even Margaret Treuer. He charmed everyone, speaking at funerals for Don Allery and others. He still never missed a chance to talk about Red Lake history or the importance of sovereignty.

Jourdain passed away on March 21, 2002. His funeral was a notable event. Senator Paul Wellstone, Minnesota Senate majority leader Roger Moe, and many other dignitaries attended.[121]

There is nothing like a critic to flesh out a deeper understanding of a public figure, and Jourdain had a career-long critic in Red Lake tribal member and journalist Bill Lawrence (1939–2010), who wrote scathing editorials about Red Lake's tribal government and played a significant role in ending Jourdain's tenure in office. Jourdain was actually Bill Lawrence's godfather, but the constant vitriol from Lawrence once prompted Jourdain to say, "I should have dropped him in that baptismal font." But even Lawrence, who pulled no punches, remarked when Jourdain passed away, "We had our differences. But I realized that he was a consummate politician. He brought home a lot of programs. He also established a strong tribal government and worked tirelessly toward self-determination."[122]

In all his travels, Roger Jourdain had made hundreds of trips by car to St. Paul, and almost invariably went to Cass Lake and down Highway 371 rather than through Akeley and Motley, which is several minutes faster when traveling from Red Lake or Bemidji. On nearly every trip, he stopped in Walker at the city park, which has a spectacular view of Leech Lake. He always got out of the car and made any travel companions disembark as well to take a long and nostalgic look at the lake. He wasn't simply admiring the scenery. He was reminding himself and anyone else within earshot that Red Lake could have been just like Leech Lake—its natural splendor interrupted by white sport fishing, vacation homes, gates, fences, and landscaping. It was a way to remind himself of how lucky they were at Red Lake to have had ancestors, chiefs, and leaders who unflinchingly worked to keep the entire land base in common ownership for the benefit of all tribal members. And it was also a reminder that the fight was never over. Someone would always be coming after Red Lake's land and water, trying to do to it what had been done at Leech Lake. But now it was his watch, and he had to be vigilant. Red Lake still needed warriors, and to his dying day, that's exactly what Roger Jourdain was.

Anna Gibbs, 2015

7

Anna Gibbs and Red Lake Shaping Indian Country

"They can't persecute a man for following his dream. Everybody knows that."

ANNA C. GIBBS

The Bombing

The house shook so violently from the explosion that the rafters shuddered, raining down dust on the kitchen table. The window-panes rattled for more than a minute from the force of the detonation and then reverberated again as the ice across Upper Red Lake cracked and whined from the impact and sound waves bounced off the tree line and back to the house. Dempsey, Irene, Frank, Warren, Paul, Francis, Violet, Sarah, and Rose were huddled together under the kitchen table. Rose was crying quietly, rocking back and forth. Dempsey, the baby, was inconsolable, tears running down his cheeks, howling in uncontrollable fear.[1]

Anna was standing at the kitchen sink, next to her mother, Helen Greenleaf. They were both staring out the window of their house on Ponemah Point. Anna had both hands wrapped around her mother's waist. It was spring of 1953; she was nine years old. Anna had just received her first pair of eyeglasses. Between the dark, wavy locks of her hair, which seemed to have a mind of their own, and her glasses, it might have seemed like there wasn't space on her face for anything else. But there was room enough for a look of sheer terror as the drone of U.S. Air Force plane engines crescendoed overhead.

The floorboards started to shake; then it happened again. Anna could see the long line of flares on the ice and the ordnance dropping from the planes. There was a split second of silence. Then the explosions started all over again. She watched trees topple on the far shore, massive plumes of dirt shooting into the air. Then the windowpane rattled again; dust fell from the rafters. Dempsey's screaming reached a new pitch.

Anna heard the sound of breaking glass and turned to see the family's prized picture of a kingfisher fall from the wall. That was their clan. Anna was a direct descendant of the Dakota boy who brought that clan to Ponemah when the first generation of Ojibwe people settled there. Anna's family was especially spiritual. At age nine, she saw the picture falling as a bad omen.

The ice cracked and moaned again, then the blast echo bounced back. Anna looked at her mother's face, hoping for reassurance. But her mother's gaze was anxiously fixed on the sky, on the path of the airplanes, circling back around for another bombing run. Anna slipped away.

She grabbed her coat and boots, tied a scarf around her ears, and slipped on her mittens. She popped the door open and stepped outside into the cool, damp spring air. There were still a couple of feet of snow on the ground, but it was starting to melt. The air was warm, moist, and filled with the distinct smell of spring in the Red Lake woods—musty tree bark, damp leaves, and light gusts of wind off the still-frozen lake. She took a deep breath, releasing some of her fear and tension.

She glanced at the ponies. They were prancing around in their enclosure, nervous and agitated. The Greenleaf family had kept ponies at Ponemah since the early 1800s. Anna's great-grandparents had ridden them throughout the Red River Valley for buffalo hunting, trade, and occasional war excursions against the Dakota. They couldn't go there now because white settlers claimed the hunting grounds and killed all the buffalo. But they still had the ponies. They used them to travel, haul supplies to the sugar bush, and till the gardens in Ponemah.

The buzz of the airplane engines grew louder. The ponies were tossing their heads as they trotted around the fence line. Anna ran over to the gate and called to Bagaskin (Tight Hide). Bagaskin was her favorite, a dapple mare, a little shorter than the others. The pony loved maple candy as much as Anna did. She opened the gate just long enough for Bagaskin to come through. There was no time for a saddle. Anna was short in the leg at age nine, but she was strong. She flipped over one of the pails they used to haul water from the lake for cooking and climbed on, using Bagaskin's mane to pull herself up.

"Apa'iwedaa iskigamiziganing!" ("Let's escape to the sugarbush!") Bagaskin didn't need any more encouragement than that. They took off down the driveway, west on the Ponemah Point Road, and then into the woods. They followed the muddy trail Anna's dad, Henry Greenleaf, had cut to access the family sugar bush. They didn't stop until they made it all the way to the sanctuary. It was six miles from the house. The sound of the airplanes and explosions was distant now.

Anna slipped off of Bagaskin's back and patted her pony on the head. The family had opened the sugar bush the week before. It was just the two of them there now. Anna walked around and peeked in the buckets. Nothing yet. Bagaskin was nibbling at the dogwood buds, content. She thought of her mom and brothers and sisters. "I should pray for them," she thought. But in her haste to escape, she forgot her tobacco. You couldn't pray without tobacco.

She sat by the woodpile and let the tears roll down her cheeks. There were many cords of wood already. Her dad was a hard worker. They always made enough sugar to last for the year and to sell some for extra grocery money and a special family trip to Bemidji. Boiling down forty gallons of sap for every pound of sugar required a lot of wood, and the Greenleafs made a lot of sugar. She leaned back against the piled tree bolts and closed her eyes. The sun was shining on her face now, and she fell into a deep sleep.

Anna dreamed about the gift of maple sugar. She saw an Ojibwe man who had barely made it through a very hard winter. He was out of food, hungry, desperate. Running through the woods, he tripped over a root and thought he might not have the strength to ever rise again. Looking up he saw a massive sasquatch (misaabe) with a long knife, raised high in the air. The bigfoot swiped the knife in a downward motion, and the man cringed and averted his eyes, taking the action for an attack. Instead, the bigfoot cut his own leg; blood ran down his hairy limb. When the man looked up, the bigfoot was gone. In his place stood a massive maple tree with a gash in its trunk. Pure maple syrup was flowing out. He reached up and touched it, bringing the nourishing goodness to his mouth. The man was stronger now, and he rose to his feet to share the remarkable gift with the people.

When Anna woke up, the sun was high in the sky. She must have slept for hours. Bagaskin was still there. Something was different, though. Anna could hear the sound of water dripping and plinking in hundreds of buckets all around her. The sap was running. She grabbed one of the galvanized pails they used for hauling and poured a little sap into it from several of the closest buckets. The first taste of pure maple sap was a high prize, a spiritual energy drink full of life.

Then Anna saw movement on her periphery. She turned her gaze and saw people coming through the woods. It was her sister Rose, with Dempsey on her back. Relief washed over her as she realized that they were okay. Her brothers were coming too, poking each other with sticks and laughing. Her mom, Helen, was on the other pony behind them. His name was Tony. Helen glanced at Bagaskin and gave Anna a deep stare. Anna smiled sheepishly as she held up the pail, "The first maple sap." Her mother got off the pony, and everyone closed around Anna to look inside. Anna grabbed her mom's hand, "Asemaa na gidaawaa?" ("Do you have tobacco?") Her mother handed Anna a pouch of tobacco. "For the bigfoot," Anna said, as she put some of the tobacco by the maple tree. She grabbed the bucket and raised it to her lips, the faint smell of galvanized tin and musty trees eclipsed by the cool rush of sweet sap—the taste so familiar, but never sweeter.

Waasabiikwe: Anna C. Gibbs

Anna Gibbs's appearance defies description. She hobbles with a walker, necessitated by a lifelong disability. One of her legs is shorter than the other and lacks a hip joint. She is only four feet eight inches tall. She has soft, dark, leathery skin, huge Coke-bottle Indian Health Service eyeglasses, and a mass of thick, curly black hair with a few gray streaks, usually held in place with bobby pins and liberal applications of hair spray. She always wears a skirt over her pants, holding fast to a traditional Ponemah teaching that a skirt is a critical attribute of the spiritual identification of women in the eyes of the creator. Her eyes are bright, kind, filled with secrets, and her beautiful, cackling laugh is one of the most contagious in all of Indian country.[2]

Anna's physical stature may be small, but her emotional and spiritual stature is truly grand. When she walks into a room, people flock over to help her with the numerous bags she always brings with her—separate ones for her pipe, her smudge dish and sage, her snacks and gum, her personal items, her purse, and at ceremonies, various drums, rattles, and medicines. People surround her to help, but also to make sure that her very strict ceremonial protocol and customs are carried out to the letter.

Anna wants every ceremony and meeting to be perfect, free from mistakes, and worthy of recognition and help from the many spirits continually in her company. She needs strike-anywhere farmer matches—not other wooden matches, paper matches, or lighters—when she lights her pipe. And her voice rises in volume, intensity, and frequency until those matches are in her hand. It is the same for the setup of the chairs, tables, food, tobacco, ceremonial items, and people she intends to help. Throughout Minnesota people are accustomed to her strict ways and demeanor, and she in turn is used to being respected, listened to, and accommodated in her every request. Her paradoxically strict yet mirth-filled way of being makes powerful medicine. She is one of the most beloved, revered, and respected elders in Ponemah today.

Anna Gibbs, whose Indian name is Waasabiikwe (or Waasabiik, for short), was born on December 17, 1944. Many years later, after a ceremony in Ponemah in 1999, she had people drive her way out to the Point. They pulled into a small sandy lake access and saw the moon, full, bright, and low on the horizon, shining off the water in myriad sparkles, shimmers, and beautiful, eerie, iridescent lights. "That's my name," she said. And whenever people think about her or hear her name, it is that image they often see, rather than the words used to describe it—Moonlight Shining on the Water. Anna is as beautiful as she is tough. It's just one of her many secrets.

Anna is more than seventy years old now, and over the course of her life she has grown from a ceremonial attendant to a central figure in Ponemah religious life, and she is now the primary ceremonial leader on the Red Lake reservation. Her story is one of triumph through adversity. She had a hard life as a child. Her scars come from much more than the repeated bombing of Red Lake by the U.S. Air Force in the 1950s. Even as a young mother, she struggled. But when

she straightened out her path and committed herself to Ojibwe ceremonial life, she had a breadth of personal experience that has been a
bastion of strength for her and for many other people.

Anna credits the late Thomas J. Stillday Jr. as her primary source
of ceremonial knowledge. She does things his way. Anna is the first
female ever to run a medicine lodge and officiate at traditional Ojibwe
funerals. She is sought out in part because the number of people who
know enough to officiate at those kinds of ceremonies is shrinking.
She carries a great deal of very rare knowledge, and that knowledge
is desperately needed. Yet she is also sought out because she has a
special gift with people and spirits alike. As much as anything else,
it is her deep knowledge and high spirit that call others to her and
bend even ancient customs (such as keeping ceremonial leadership
exclusively male) to the greater good.

At the same time that Anna is a well-respected religious leader,
she is also a character so funny and idiosyncratic that she must be a
close relative of Nenabozho himself. She owns no car and does not
drive. Yet she travels fearlessly throughout Minnesota, Wisconsin,
Michigan, North Dakota, Ontario, and Manitoba. The sight of her
little brown thumb sticking in the air over the tall grass in the ditches
on area roads is common. She hitchhikes often and carries a thick
black book full of names and phone numbers for everyone who owes
her a favor. Whenever she needs a ride, a place to stay, supper, help
cashing a check, someone to take her shopping and bring presents
to her grandchildren or to help at ceremonies, she works her phone
lists, and she never fails to achieve her desired outcome. She has a
persistent charm and puts forth a relentless effort—and everybody
owes her something because she spends her life helping others.[3]

Since she quit smoking in the mid-1990s, Anna has chewed gum
with a vigor that should earn her shares in the Wrigley Company.
And she leaves a trail of it everywhere she goes. There are thick wads
of it under most of the benches in the Ponemah Community Center, where she puts it while officiating at wakes and funerals. One
time she ran out of gum and reached under the bench in front of
her and broke off a chunk that had been stuck there long ago. People
gasped in horror while she shoved it into her mouth. She just laughed
and said, "What? It's probably mine from the last time." Once when
smoking her pipe, she had no bench on which to stick her gum, so she

shrugged and placed the wad on the end of her pipe, and giggled when she was seen doing it.

Anna's "rezzy" demeanor has been a source of much mirth. One time, during Bemidji Crazy Days, when store vendors put their merchandise on racks in the street and mark everything on sale, Anna was shopping for hours in the heat and finally walked into Gene's Bar (now 209 Bar) to get a drink of water. But between the heat, humidity, and shopping, her hair was wild, curly, and flying all over the place. She was sweaty and somewhat wild-eyed when she entered the building. The sight was so dramatic that the bartender told her, "Hey, lady. Stop. That's it. I'm cutting you off." And she hadn't even been drinking.

In the spring of 2006, Anna had an especially arduous stretch of work. There were funerals every few days throughout the area. Thomas Stillday had been sick frequently during that period, and Anna got most of the calls to officiate. The strain was wearing on her energy, stamina, and disposition. She was happy to help, but funeral work is stressful on the officiator's emotions, not just because of the loss but because the officiating crew takes responsibility for directing the departing soul to the spirit world without mistakes so that it doesn't get lost. It's a hard job. The officiant sacrifices days of her time to prepare the family and to speak at the wake and funeral and feasts afterward. The officiating crew usually receives no money, so the work can involve a significant financial sacrifice, with time away from work, family, and other duties. Anna vowed that when things lightened up she would take a break and go to the movies.

In May 2006, things did finally ease up, so Anna gathered up more than a dozen of her namesakes, called in some favors, and was taken to the movie theater in Bemidji. She loves spending time with namesakes. They went to the movie *X-Men 3: The Last Stand*. It turned out to be quite an adventure. The X-Men movies are about mutants with special gifts of flight, strength, extrasensory perception, and the like. Her namesakes figured that Anna would be able to relate them to spiritual gifts and follow right along. But some things just don't translate.

In the X-Men movies, the mutants are persecuted by humans and usually try to disguise their special gifts. So, the opening scene begins with one of them, named Angel, cutting off his wings to avoid detection and persecution. The entire audience was quietly watching the film when Anna started yelling in her high, lilting Ponemah accent:

"What's he doing?"

"He's cutting off his wings."

"What?" She looked incredulous.

"He's cutting off his wings so people won't be mean to him."

"Why?"

Other moviegoers were turning around with annoyed stares as Anna shoveled popcorn into her mouth and fired off more questions at top volume. Her namesakes slunk down in their seats as one tried to answer her questions in hushed tones.

About two-thirds of the way through the movie, she bellowed, "What's a mutant?"

The entire audience abandoned their fixation on the movie and annoyance with Anna's questions and laughed. Unaware, Anna continued through to the final scene, where Angel spread his wings in proud acknowledgment of his gift and flew away. Anna smiled.

"Wow. That was a good movie," she said. "We should go again."

In her everyday life, in her work on Ojibwe-language publications, when she is officiating at ceremonies, Anna continually reminds her people that there needs to be a balance between serious and fun, spiritual and practical. The journey is every bit as important to her as the destination.

Leading the Way in Healing: Thomas J. Stillday to Anna C. Gibbs

Anna Gibbs will be the first to say that traditional Ojibwe religion does not belong in a book. It is often hard for outsiders to understand this, especially when Ojibwe people at Red Lake and elsewhere are facing unprecedented language and culture loss. To outsiders, writing about traditional Ojibwe religion seems the easiest way to preserve, protect, and teach such important things to future generations; for Gibbs, there is a better path.

Something profound is compromised when Ojibwe oral tradition is textualized. In Ojibwe culture, most spiritual matters are not shared for anthropological purposes, for the curiosity of outsiders, or for intellectual enrichment. They are shared as part of a spiritual experience. Songs, legends, and intricate and highly symbolic spiritual practices are shared to heal, help, and guide—to help people live healthier and more meaningful lives. Access to such teachings cannot be gained outside of their religious context. In other words, if people want the songs, they cannot just turn on a tape recorder or go to a ceremony. They have to go *through* the ceremony. That experience involves someone who knows the teachings taking the songs out of his or her soul and directly transferring them to another, where they become a permanent part of who someone is. To give someone a way to circumvent the use of tobacco and the spiritual process is to strip the music, legends, and teachings of their authenticity and power. Ojibwe cultural carriers today do not allow others to circumvent their elders or avoid the proper protocol or commitment needed to carry out sacred teachings. Ceremonial knowledge must be paid for— and not with money, but with tobacco, food, culturally appropriate gifts, and time.

Frances Densmore and others who found a way to record some of these things struggled to explain their deeper meaning and failed to realize that their work held no real value for Ojibwe people because it could not be used for ceremonial purposes. They probably didn't care, and that's also part of the problem. Red Lakers have been defrauded by academicians, anthropologists, and government officials many times. The process has often obscured the true identities of the people who knew the material to begin with—recorded as nameless "informants."

For many decades, Anna Gibbs has devoted her life to keeping Red Lake knowledge and Red Lake ways of knowing alive for the benefit of Ojibwe people everywhere. On March 3, 2004, she traveled with Thomas J. Stillday Jr. to Bena, Minnesota, to officiate at the wake for Michael Matthews Sr. At the wake, Michael's brother, Bobby Matthews, remarked, "This is the first time in decades that there has been a traditional funeral in the Matthews family. But it won't be the last. Anna and Tom did something truly beautiful." Tom and Anna had a way of igniting passion about Ojibwe culture, and this was just one of many similar stories about how they touched the lives of people, families, and whole communities. They were fire starters and much, much more.[4]

Anna was a protégé of Tom Stillday in ceremony and in life. Even her raucous humor evolved through her tutelage from him. After the Matthews wake was over, Tom shuffled into the passenger seat of a Subaru wagon. It was brutally cold and snowing, and he shivered as he gingerly slid into his seat. Anna sat behind the old man.

Their young driver had the seat warmers turned up high and the heat cranking out at maximum to ease the coldness. They pulled out of the parking lot and onto Highway 2, and then Tom began to tell a long story. Tom was a consummate storyteller—smart, witty, and with a penchant for details and deadpan humor. He had had a double stroke several years earlier that left him with a partial speech impediment, so his long narrations were sometimes strained. His listeners had to be patient and attentive, but they were rewarded with his humor and deep knowledge.[5]

His story that evening was about stereotypes of cowboys and Indians: "You know how they say that Indians used to capture cowboys and tie them up upside down? And then they made a fire and they cooked him alive?" Anna nodded her head in agreement as the story droned on for nearly twenty minutes. "Well," he said, "they say that they built that fire right under his upside-down head and cooked him until his head just burst open. That's how my nuts feel right now."

Anna burst out in uncontrolled laughter as their driver smacked every button on his control panel until the seat warmers and heat were turned off. Tom could have simply said, "Turn off the seat warmers" and in twenty seconds saved himself twenty minutes of thorough cooking. But he wouldn't be Tom Stillday if he took a quick, impatient path that wasn't loaded with humor. Anna learned from the best.

Thomas J. Stillday, whose Indian name was Wezaawibiitang, was born on February 20, 1934, and died on October 14, 2008. Sometimes his name has been translated as Yellow Water. His explanation was less grandiose: "You know when the waves are coming in from the lake and they make that foam that kind of looks like puke? That's my name." His parents were Thomas Stillday Sr. and Lucy (Johnson) Stillday, and the family lived in Ponemah. His father was one of his great teachers, although by his own admission Tom was not groomed for a position of spiritual leadership. He was a regular attendee at ceremonies but not a leader and not from a family of leaders. Community pride and cohesion are strong in Ponemah.

When there is a funeral, all families cook food and bring it to the service—not just because they usually knew the deceased, but because they are part of the same community. Tom was frequently in the company of great men in Ponemah such as Dan Raincloud Sr., Nodin Wind, and Leonard Hawk.[6]

Tom served in Korea toward the conclusion of the conflict, in the Army Corps of Engineers. He used his Ojibwe language there proudly with other Ojibwe servicemen. However, he was not an Ojibwe code talker as has sometimes been claimed. That honor was unique to the Navajo servicemen during World War II and in some less-developed army experiments with Lakota and Choctaw.

Tom worked in many professions, from education to commercial fishing. He graduated from high school, but that was his highest academic achievement. He served on the board of the Red Lake Fisheries Association for seventeen years, the Red Lake school board for five years, and the Red Lake Tribal Council for eight years. He was invited to serve on many other boards and panels by institutions including the Minnesota Historical Society, the University of Minnesota–Duluth, and numerous health organizations.

He married Mary Lou Thomas in 1973, and as accomplished as he was, he would have been lost without her. On August 1, 1996, a driver picked him up to bring him to Balsam Lake, Wisconsin, to officiate at the wake and funeral of Archie Mosay, a renowned medicine man. Mary Lou was away that day, and Tom packed his own bag. Without her help, though, he ended up officiating at the funeral (with more than two thousand in attendance) wearing a tattered braid, sweat pants, his diabetic shoes, his son Dexter's AC/DC T-shirt, and a man purse.

As time went on and many of Ponemah's great spiritual leaders passed, Tom did something that very few others have done. When the going got tough and people were worried about who could continue the work and preserve the knowledge of Ponemah, Tom stepped up. His colorful younger days were hard for some of his peers to forget, and he often recited the adage that no man is a prophet in his own town. But Tom had integrity, experience, and spirit in abundance. He gave Indian names and officiated at funerals, medicine dances, and many other ceremonies. He never claimed a title or position, but people kept asking him, over and over again.

Tom also broke with a long-standing tradition among the Ojibwe people. Where customarily the knowledge of ceremonial practice was kept in families and guarded very closely, Tom actively worked to teach all who would learn. He knew that the Red Lake Ojibwe were in for the fight of their lives to keep their language and culture going, so he reached out. As a result, he is single-handedly responsible for the fact that Ponemah still has a medicine dance today. One of his best students, Anna Gibbs, learned all of her critical ceremonial knowledge from him, and that would have been impossible if he had decided to share it only within his family. Tom intentionally sought out Anna Gibbs because of her command of Ojibwe, skill at working with people, and profound spiritual gift with dreams.

As testament to their widely recognized spiritual gifts, Tom and Anna have advised ceremonial drums in several communities, from Oak Point on the Leech Lake reservation to Ponemah. They have both officiated at funerals in nearly every Ojibwe community in Minnesota and Wisconsin. They have even had white people ask for spiritual help, guidance, and healing, including Minnesota's senate majority leader Roger Moe. Tom was also the first Indian to be named chaplain for the Minnesota state senate.

Throughout his life, Tom Stillday was a legendary comic. Sometimes he didn't even know how funny he was. One time he traveled to Lac Courte Oreilles to officiate at the funeral for Marilyn Benton. His blood-thinner medication gave him terrible nosebleeds at that time, and he had one right in the middle of the service. A woman came up and helped him push the end of a paper towel in his nose to stop the flow, telling him that she was a nurse. The paper towel stuck out sixteen inches from his face. His ceremonial assistants told him that he could tear the end off so it wasn't in the way, but he said, "No. That lady's a nurse." He conducted the entire funeral with the paper towel in his nose. The family would be mourning and sad, but then they would look up at Tom, start smiling, and put their heads down again. He had no idea that his nose was mitigating their hurt.

Sometimes, Tom purposely entertained. On August 7, 1996, he flew with a group from Bemidji to Minneapolis and then on to Toronto for a conference on writing systems for the Ojibwe language. In Minneapolis, he walked up to a kiosk and abruptly said, "Hey. Get me one of them golf carts. I'm a cripple." He showed them his cane.

"Right away, sir," came the response.

A young woman drove the cart up to the kiosk and then he said, "My friends too." And he motioned for everyone from the Bemidji delegation to hop onto his golf cart.

The machine groaned under the weight and the entire entourage couldn't help smiling as the woman asked Tom, "Are you all Native American or something?"

"Yeah."

"Do you all live in teepees?"

What followed was classic Tommy J. Stillday: "Yeah. This morning we got up in our teepees. And we walked two miles to where the horses are stabled. Then we rode horse for another twelve miles to the canoes. We got in those canoes and paddled twenty-three miles to the railhead. Then we took the train here."

The woman soaked it all in. "Really? Wow." Tom never even cracked a smile until everyone got off the cart. In typical fashion, his telling took the entire time he spent on the ride.

Every year, the American Indian Resource Center at Bemidji State University has a banquet to honor graduating Indian seniors and academic achievement among the native student population. The keynote speaker is usually an academician, politician, or educational leader. In 2001, however, Tom Stillday got the honors. The Beaux Arts Ballroom was packed with graduates and their families, deans, professors, tribal leaders, and university presidents. Tom broke every rule about graduation banquet speeches (which are supposed to be short and focused on the students). He spoke for an hour and a half about Ojibwe culture—all in Ojibwe. When he was done, he said only one thing in English: "All you people who study Indians, study that!" Ojibwe speakers in the audience were laughing to themselves about the glazed eyes of the university officials, but reflecting on the contents of his speech and his eloquent language, many were thinking: "That's advice we all should take."

In 2005, there was a terrible shooting at the high school in Red Lake. Jeffrey Weise killed the school guard and ten students. Every family on the reservation was affected by the event. Media attention on Red Lake was uncomfortable on good days, but after the shooting it became unbearable. Every one of the dozen American school shootings before Red Lake's involved white shooters killing white

kids, and the country seemed to look at such events as isolated tragedies, easily attributed to the mental illness of the shooters. But when
one happened at Red Lake, some people seemed to think it was an
"Indian thing," attributed to the perceived dysfunction of Red Lake.
One reporter wrote, "Weise's acts were simply an expression of profound nihilism. And it is a sad fact that Red Lake, like other reservations in Minnesota, has become a breeding ground for such feelings."
The search for answers included investigations of Weise's classmates
that went far beyond a fact-finding mission. To many people at Red
Lake it seemed like the outside world was blaming the entire reservation for what happened to the victims.[7]

The people at Red Lake were really grieving. In addition to the
individual tragedies and the losses that their families faced, there
was a profound sense of collective loss and sadness. Stillday and
Gibbs used their prestige as spiritual leaders to effect healing on the
reservation. They joined community healing events, helped smudge
down the school, and performed pipe ceremonies. They officiated at
the funerals and counseled many of the families.

In Ponemah, traditional funerals customarily had a two-night
wake. The first night was for wake services—feasting, legends, songs,
and preparation of the departing soul for his or her journey. The second night was reserved for open visitation and was much less formal. Tom and Anna decided to use the second night for open singing
of ceremonial music. Every attendee was encouraged to share songs
of life with the bereaved families. Hundreds of people came to the
funerals, and the change in protocol seemed to help. Ever since,
every traditional funeral on the reservation has been conducted the
same way.

All across Ojibwe country a battle is raging to keep the language
and culture alive. In that effort there are pockets of strength and
areas of widespread loss. The increasing numbers of Ojibwe people
looking to their ceremonies have to look to those pockets of strength
for their healing and learning. That brings them to Ponemah. Since
Tom passed away, that brings them to Anna.

Anna Gibbs carries on the great endeavor of Tom's life—a spiritual
healing and renewal for all Ojibwe people. Tom inherited that quest
from Nodin Wind, Dan Raincloud, and Leonard Hawk. Ponemah has
always been a bastion of strength for the people—keeping the lan-

guage and culture alive when others succumbed to pressures of a pernicious history and colonial experience. And Anna is a consummate warrior, leading the charge to fight for Red Lake's most precious gifts. She is looking for others to muster the courage and the will to renew this effort with the many tools the ancient ones left at Red Lake—the people, the language, the drum, the pipe, and the place.

Home of the Ojibwe Language

In 1918, Indian country was under siege. The effects of land loss were inescapable. The Indian residential boarding-school system was engulfing most reservation youth at Red Lake and across the nation. White Indian agents were supplanting tribal chiefs as the power brokers in tribal communities. Everywhere, native people were wrestling with oppression—externally, internally, and laterally. Many tribal people were beginning to doubt the need for or importance of their own cultures and languages—but not at Red Lake.

At Red Lake, something exceptional was happening in 1918, the year that the constitution for the General Council of the Red Lake Band of Chippewa Indians and the first modern representative governance structure in Indian country were created. The entire tribal population at Red Lake was fluent in Ojibwe at the time. And rather than give up sovereign power, culture, or tribal language, they endorsed a genuinely indigenous perspective on native nationhood. Peter Graves developed a sophisticated validation of Ojibwe language use for the tribe in a twenty-page policy statement titled "Language Policy for the Red Lake Band of Chippewa Indians." The most poignant section reads:

> The Chippewa language is the indigenous language of the Red Lake Band of Chippewa Indians. Since time immemorial, the Chippewa language has been, and will continue to be, *our mother or native tongue,* which is our natural instrument of thought and communication. The Chippewa language is the *national* language of the Red Lake Band of Chippewa in a political, social, and cultural sense. The Chippewa language is the *official* language of the Red Lake Band of Chippewa Indians of the Red Lake Reservation and may be used in the business of government— legislative, executive, and judicial. . . . We declare that the Chippewa language is a *living* and vital language that has the ability to match and

even surpass any other in the world for expressiveness and beauty. Our language is capable of lexical expansion into modern conceptual fields of politics, economics, mathematics, and science. Be it known that the Chippewa language shall be recognized as our *first language.*

On April 27, 2010, the tribal council reaffirmed Ojibwe as the official language of the Red Lake Nation.[8]

A sign on the road to Ponemah reads "Home of the Ojibway Language." The people there are proud of their culture, heritage, and language. Even those who are not fluent speakers are proud that it is a living part of their community. Everyone knows how important it is. At the same time, everyone knows how threatened it is. The Ojibwe language will definitely still be alive one hundred years from now, mainly because there are regions in Canada where all of the people speak Ojibwe. But all of the dialects on the U.S. side of the border are in trouble. In Michigan, Wisconsin, Minnesota, and North Dakota, the language is spoken primarily by elders. Everyone among Anna Gibbs's generation is a speaker in Ponemah, and a scattering of good speakers are younger than she. Among the Ojibwe communities in the United States, Red Lake is the strongest, and most of its Ojibwe speakers live in Ponemah.

Across the Red Lake reservation, the elders want to share what they know. Young people want to learn. The main impediments to making the connection between them and revitalizing the language are that those who want to teach and those who want to learn don't spend enough time together. Those raising children are no longer speakers, so the intergenerational transmission of the language has been interrupted. If language use has to begin in the home, it will never begin. Future vitality of the language is not certain, but it is possible. When it comes to the Ojibwe language, never underestimate a Red Lake warrior.

Anna Gibbs, Tom Stillday, Rose Tainter, Rosemarie DeBungie, Elizabeth Kingbird, Collins Oakgrove, Darrell Seki, Vernon Whitefeather, Jack Kingbird, Don Kingbird, Margaret Porter, Murphy Thomas, Ona Kingbird, Rose Barstow, Margaret Sayers, and Eugene Stillday are among a dynamic cadre of Red Lake Ojibwe speakers who have risen up to face the challenges to the future health of the Ojibwe language. Tom Stillday was among the delegates to an important conference in Toronto in August 1996 that adopted the double-vowel writing system for Ojibwe. He advocated developing literary traditions for this oral language. It is a powerful way to preserve words, grammar, stories, and teaching tools beyond the welcome contributions of early academic and missionary writings about Red Lake Ojibwe dialects by Sela Wright (1862) and Josselin de Jong (1905). Ponemah elders cannot do all of the teaching needed in Ojibwe country, but they have created a wide range of materials to help students and teachers across the region.[9]

Some of the earliest Ojibwe language revitalization work was done by Red Lakers. Tom Cain Sr. published word lists and a book of Ojibwe stories. Rose Barstow and Angeline Northbird worked on Ojibwe curriculum publications with Tim Dunnigan (a white anthropological linguist) at the University of Minnesota in the 1970s. Ona Kingbird, also from Ponemah, published Ojibwe teaching tools and curriculum for several schools in the Twin Cities. In the 1980s, Margaret Sayers worked with Rick Gresczyk to publish books and audio material in Ojibwe. All of that was largely grassroots, driven by the passions of Cain, Barstow, Northbird, Kingbird, and Sayers. Soon the Ojibwe preservation efforts of Red Lakers grew into a series of important academic, educational, and community efforts with increasing institutional support.[10]

Anna Gibbs, Rose Tainter, and especially Eugene Stillday have been recording Ojibwe vocabulary and grammar material with linguists John Nichols and Michael Sullivan. Nichols and Sullivan have been adding the audio files to an online dictionary for Ojibwe called the *Ojibwe People's Dictionary*, a free, Web-based, talking dictionary. Users can look up words in Ojibwe or English and see the translations, click on the words, listen to audio from naturally recorded speech, and usually pick from a variety of speakers, male and female, speaking different dialects. Red Lake dominates the entries in the dictionary because of the weighty contributions of its speakers, but Mille Lacs and Ontario dialects are also widely represented. It is already many times larger than the largest print dictionaries for Ojibwe, and new entries are being added regularly.

Anna Gibbs, Eugene Stillday, Rose Tainter, Tom Stillday, Collins Oakgrove, Darrell Seki, and Rosemarie DeBungie have also been part of a growing team of Ojibwe first speakers who have been producing books, movies, and radio material in Ojibwe. Darrell Seki, Red

Lake tribal chairman, has for years recorded Ojibwe-language radio spots encouraging Ojibwe people to vote in American elections. Collins Oakgrove has a large collection of stories published bilingually in Ojibwe and English in *Living Our Language: Ojibwe Tales and Oral Histories.* Anna Gibbs has been recording public-service announcements for the Affordable Care Act in Ojibwe and a new animated video of Ojibwe stories called *Wenji-dakwaanowed Makwa.*[11]

Gibbs, Stillday, Tainter, and DeBungie have been working with a team of scholars to produce monolingual children's books in Ojibwe as well. The series, published by Wiigwaas Press, has been a tremendous success and includes the titles *Awesiinyensag, Naadmaageng,* and *Wiijikiiwending.* Gibbs, Tainter, and Eugene Stillday also helped write *Aaniin Ekidong: Ojibwe Vocabulary Project,* an important Ojibwe word resource project to develop terminology for new technologies and concepts in the modern world. Gibbs, Tom Stillday, Eugene Stillday, Oakgrove, and Vernon Whitefeather have all contributed to the only academic journal of the Ojibwe language, the *Oshkaabewis Native Journal.*[12]

Many young people, inspired by the work of their elders, have joined the effort in recent years as well. Nate Taylor, Sam Strong, and Marcus Kingbird have contributed in different ways to the birth of an Ojibwe early childhood education program at Red Lake, where the tribal language is the medium of instruction rather than a subject of study. Ponemah speakers Elizabeth "Pug" Kingbird and Frances Miller teach there every day. Sadie Kingbird and Emily Bellanger are mentored by the elder speakers on language use and teaching skills. Elizabeth Strong and Liz White help coordinate the program and do community outreach. Taylor helps teach. A couple of non-band members assist with the program as well—Brian Smith and Zac Mitteness.

Taylor has also been building up his own knowledge of the language through participation in the adult Ojibwe immersion program Ojibwemotaadidaa Omaa Akiing. The Ojibwe advisory council for the new early-childhood program wants to grow the effort every year until it is a full-fledged Ojibwe-medium immersion school all the way through high school. The advisory council includes twenty Red Lake speakers and cultural carriers—Susan Johnson, Eliza Johnson, Mary Lou Stillday, Violet Patterson, Rose Cloud, John Barrett, Carol

Barrett, Frances Johnson, Robert Kingbird, Carol Schoenborn, Donald Iceman Sr., Anna Gibbs, Murphy Thomas, Elizabeth Kingbird, Frances Miller, Eugene Stillday, Greeting Spears, Arnold Kingbird, Lee Whitefeather, and Roberta Major.

Rose Tainter was a founding member of the first Ojibwe-language program in the world, Waadookodaading, located in Reserve, Wisconsin, on the Lac Courte Oreilles reservation. More than one hundred children have come through the program, learning her words and ways. After she passed away, her legacy endured in the ongoing work of the school and all the materials she helped develop. Twin Cities Public Television won an Emmy for its documentary on the work of Red Lake's language warriors titled *First Speakers: Restoring the Ojibwe Language,* which profiles Red Lake speakers Susan Johnson, Larry Stillday, Eugene Stillday, Rose Tainter, and Anna Gibbs.[13]

The influence of Anna Gibbs and other Ponemah speakers on Ojibwe revitalization efforts is profound. Their determination is heroic, and is finally showing some results. For the first time since the 1950s, there are new first speakers of Ojibwe. Nobody could have done that without the Red Lake language warriors.

Academic Powerhouse

Red Lake's leadership in Ojibwe-language revitalization is only the beginning of the people's contribution to intellectual and academic pursuits. Peter Graves and Roger Jourdain were both exceptional students of Red Lake history. Most of their successors in tribal government have been just as avid researchers and teachers of tribal history and politics. Many Red Lake citizens have fundamentally shaped the fields of linguistics, history, gender studies, politics, and tribal sovereignty.

Kathryn "Jody" Beaulieu, niece of Roger Jourdain, spent years building the tribal archives at Red Lake. She successfully advocated for space in the tribal government complex and organized a wide range of archival collections: press clippings and journalism on Red Lake history and current events, three major oral history projects, archival materials on tribal history, political correspondence, genealogy, tribal resolutions, information on tribal litigation and land issues, photographs, and art. She pulled in family collections and materials from Harlan Beaulieu, Donald "Dude" May, Anna Gibbs, and others. Beaulieu was eventually elected secretary for Red Lake nation, and the archival work shifted to Gary Fuller. Today, Red Lake's tribal archives are a critical resource for band members and researchers on the history of Red Lake. Beaulieu has a passion for advancing knowledge about native people at Red Lake and through-out Indian country. Her service has included advising the Minnesota Historical Society on best practices, cultural competence, and areas for future research and publication.

The tribe developed the Red Lake Nation College in 2001 to meet the career and college needs of tribal members, build an academic home for higher education on the reservation, and accelerate Red Lake's academic impact on the rest of the world. Dan King, who was appointed college president in 2012, has overseen an expansion of facilities and accreditation through partnership with the Leech Lake Tribal College. King, who served as Red Lake treasurer from 1998 to 2001, has a master's degree in public administration from the John F. Kennedy School of Government at Harvard University.[14]

Many Red Lakers have made important contributions to academic work on Indian identity and activism through their scholarship and writing. Adam Fortunate Eagle authored *Heart of the Rock, Pipestone*: *My Life in an Indian Boarding School* and *Alcatraz! Alcatraz!* Francis Blake wrote *We Have the Right to Exist.*

Brenda Child is an influential voice in the field of native his-tory. Her seminal work on residential boarding schools, *Boarding School Seasons: American Indian Families, 1900–1940*, was a major award-winning piece of scholarship. It spawned a vibrant academic and social discussion about America's Indian education policies. Today, it is still often cited in academic work, equity discussions, educational program development, and even Canada's truth and rec-onciliation work on its residential boarding-school system for First Nation peoples.

Child's more recent works, *Holding Our World Together* and *My Grandfather's Knocking Sticks*, have opened up a new subfield in his-tory on Ojibwe women's studies. In addition to providing a detailed narrative on the Auginash family, she has illuminated the role of women in historic Ojibwe economies and political systems with groundbreaking research and a fresh perspective. It is helping historians in many other parts of the field to rethink missing narratives and the role of women.

Political Juggernaut

Red Lake is still a hard place to lead. The distinct libertarian culture there makes people tolerant of new and innovative ideas but reluctant to make them their own, and resistant to being controlled. When great leaders have emerged in Red Lake they have usually been so exceptional that they led for many decades. Such was certainly the case for Moose Dung, He Who Is Spoken To, Nodin Wind, Peter Graves, and Roger Jourdain. After Roger Jourdain's thirty-two-year tenure as tribal chairman, political careers have often been shorter, although the tenor of leadership is no less extraordinary.

Red Lake has had only six tribal chairmen in its history. Roger Jourdain was unseated by Gerald "Butch" Brun in 1990. Brun was well supported but found the chairman's job extremely stressful and decided not to run for a second term. Bobby Whitefeather won the subsequent election in 1994. He was the first person from Ponemah to hold the office. Whitefeather was from the kingfisher clan, a fluent speaker, and well respected. Political tension still ran high in Red Lake, and Brun challenged Whitefeather in the 2002 election and won back the chairmanship. Brun died in office in 2003, and his brother and hereditary chief George William "Billy" King was appointed chairman. Floyd "Buck" Jourdain, the grandson of Roger's first cousin Patrick Jourdain, won the next election, becoming chairman in 2004 and staying in office until 2014, when Darrell Seki emerged victorious in the tribal election.[15]

Through the efforts of each successive tribal chairman, Red Lake has continued the successful repatriation of "submarginal" land parcels from the 1889 land cession. In 2001, Red Lake reached a settlement in its forestry litigation with the government. Peter Graves began the legal proceedings in 1951; the settlement ultimately netted the tribe $53 million. The tribe has put the money to work with a 50,000-acre reforestation program on the reservation and the reclaimed ceded lands. Each chairman has also continued the effort to regain Upper Red Lake. Some political objectives are so deeply rooted in the hearts of the people that they rise to the top of the agenda for all tribal leaders at Red Lake.[16]

Outside its boundaries, Red Lake has produced many pivotal leaders in national Indian issues. After Leon F. Cook lost the tribal chairman contest to Roger Jourdain in 1967, he turned his attention to advancing Indian interests nationally in both politics and economics. Cook was appointed director of economic development for the BIA in 1971 by Louis R. Bruce. He worked internally to reform the BIA and advocate for tribal interests. Sometimes the bureau got too cozy with business interests, and Cook soon had to fight entrenched powers to protect the tribes. He resigned in protest over the bureau's treatment of tribal sovereignty, and explained his decision: "Morality goes by the boards as pressure develops from vested business interests who see the Indian water and land as booty." Afterward, Cook served as president of the National Congress of American Indians (1971-72). He has remained engaged in tribal politics and national issues ever since. An able administrator and fund raiser, he held many administrative appointments, including his service as the first executive director of the American Indian Resource Center at Bemidji State University.[17]

Red Lakers have long had a powerful impact on state and regional elections. In 1996, Sandra King was elected Beltrami County commissioner, the first Indian elected to a county board in the state. She was succeeded by two fellow Red Lakers—Quentin Fairbanks and Tim Sumner. In the Beltrami County commissioner races, Red Lake's large population impacts the results, but successful Red Lake candidates are also bridge builders, representing county citizens of all races, and winning their votes.

Red Lake member Holly Cook-Macarro has been a peerless influence on national politics, especially within the Democratic Party. She has a master's degree in business administration from the University of St. Thomas and has spent most of her life working at the intersection of business, law, and politics, always with an eye on the best benefit to Indian people. Cook-Macarro distinguished herself as a staff member of President Bill Clinton's White House Office of Intergovernmental Affairs (1997-98). She worked at Holland & Knight Law Firm (1999-2001), and that connected her even more to important political figures such as Lynn Cutler, who served as senior staff to President Clinton on intergovernmental affairs.[18]

Holly Cook-Macarro worked as a staffer with the Democratic National Committee, and along with her husband, Mark Macarro, chairman of the Pechanga Band of Luiseño Indians, has campaigned for several prominent Democratic candidates, exerting significant influence toward their success. Since 2001, she has been a partner at Ietan Consulting, doing lobbying and fund-raising. Cook-Macarro's service has elevated native issues with many key policy makers.

Many other Red Lakers have had an impact on state and national politics. Since 2006, Annamarie Hill has been executive director of the Minnesota Indian Affairs Council. It puts her in a powerful position, working with all eleven tribes in Minnesota to advance their interests and communicate with the governor. Thomas Cain Sr. was one of the creators of Red Lake's 1958 constitution. He wrote books on the Ojibwe language and also led through influence in his interactions with key national native organizations such as the National Indian Education Association and the National Congress of American Indians. William E. Hallett served as commissioner of Indian affairs (position renamed assistant secretary of the interior for Indian affairs during his tenure) from 1979 to 1981. In that position, he was able to fundamentally shape national Indian policy.

Red Lake's Business Drive

Red Lake has a long history of tribal economic development, including Red Lake Fisheries, Red Lake Builders, Red Lake Nation Propane, Red Lake Nation Fuels, Red Lake Farms, Red Lake Nation Foods, Red Lake Trading Post, Ponemah Market, and casino operations in Red Lake, Thief River Falls, and Warroad. Peter Graves and Roger Jourdain provided most of the impetus and leadership for developing early Red Lake tribal businesses, but the base of dedicated and competent Red Lake business developers has grown exponentially over the past few decades.

Some of the developments have been contested, such as wild rice cultivation and peat mining. The tribe has experimented with both in recent decades. Some tribal members and other tribes have objected on environmental grounds, and the tribe has responded to those concerns with an evolving business plan designed to promote traditional values and economic advancement. Red Lake continues to explore new ideas and innovations with the customary Red Lake warrior work ethic, drive, and determination.

William E. Hallett was especially well known for his advocacy for Red Lake business development. Hallett grew up and was beloved on the reservation. He was a Red Lake High School graduate in 1960 and a Bemidji State University graduate in 1965. He served as director of housing and economic development at Red Lake (1967–68) and then took his talent to Washington to shape economic policy for Indians. He worked as director of economic development for the National Congress of American Indians (1968–70) and then as regional administrator of Housing and Urban Development until 1979. President Jimmy Carter appointed Hallett as BIA commissioner (1979–81) on the recommendation of Roger Jourdain. Eventually, he returned home and was appointed tribal economic developer in 1990. While working at Red Lake, he coauthored the Red Lake Band of Chippewa Indians Economic Development Act in 1991 and formed the Red Lake Economic Development Commission. The idea behind the commission was to separate the political and economic activities of the tribe so that election cycles and political motives could not disrupt business development. It remains a continuing success. Hallett died in 1992.[19]

Many Red Lakers have also built successful independent private businesses or taken important positions in established corporations. Marvin Hanson worked as vice president of Grand Casinos for many years. In 2013, he launched a restaurant in Bemidji called the Marvelous Fish House, which featured Red Lake walleye and wild rice. The restaurant, which closed its doors six months after opening, was not as successful as his corporate career, but he was a source of pride for people at Red Lake and Bemidji for branching out beyond the reservation in the business world. Dennis Johnson, who serves on the Red Lake Economic Development Commission, is also the chief financial officer for Ho-Chunk, Inc., which is widely respected as one of the most successful tribal business venture firms. James "Dino" Garrigan built Northern Engineering and Consulting, Inc., which runs engineering contracts across several states. Andy Wells, chief executive officer of Wells Technology, Inc., sells aeronautic, robotic, and automation technology to fifty-four countries. Wells runs most of his manufacturing from his private plant adjacent to the reserva-

William E. Hallett, about 1970

tion so he can recruit and retain Red Lake employees while carrying out his business mission.[20]

Innovation and the Law

In 2006, Anna Gibbs was asked to testify at Red Lake Tribal Court. The defendant had shot a moose in violation of the tribal conservation code. He argued that he needed to take the animal for spiritual reasons, to carry out instructions he had received from the spirits in a dream, and that the tribal conservation code violated his traditional religious rights. Anna was summoned to court to testify about the reliability of the defendant's claim that there could be a spiritual need for shooting the moose. In typical fashion, she started barking orders as soon as she entered the courtroom, and the bailiff helped with her walker as attorneys for both sides scurried around to see that she was properly escorted to the stand, was given a glass of water, had her walker set aside, and was made comfortable. She then began, in her thick, lilting Ponemah Ojibwe accent, to yell at the judge.

"This man had a dream," she said. "You can't persecute him because of his dream. What kind of court is this? He's an Indian, and this is an Indian court. The spirits told him to a kill a moose. Do you know more than the spirits? I don't think so."

In record time, the case was dismissed without prejudice. The attorneys, defendant, judge, and bailiff stood for a moment in stunned silence, batting their eyes at the charged atmosphere, and then Anna started laughing her loud, contagious laugh until the whole room erupted into guffaws.

"Well, they finally did the right thing," she giggled. "Even if I had to yell, at least they listened. They can't persecute a man for following his dream. Everybody knows that."[21]

Anna Gibbs's appearance in tribal court was not just a humorous interlude. It was a real case of grassroots power, indigenizing the legal process. Peter Graves and Roger Jourdain had both made powerful statements about the right and need to have tribal courts reflect tribal values and operate in the Ojibwe language.

The tension between Ojibwe thought and the legal process came to a head at Red Lake later in 2006. For years, trucking companies routinely violated the speed limit when carrying freight on Highway 1, right through Redby, Red Lake, and Little Rock. One tribal resident was killed in a hit-and-run, and the driver was never apprehended. Residents had had enough. The tribal council responded, and tribal police stepped up traffic enforcement. Almost immediately after the increased scrutiny was announced, truckers Chad D. and Dennis Nord, speeding on Highway 1 on the reservation, collided with Red Lake member Donald Kelly. Tribal police responded to the accident. Red Lake ambulance service transported Kelly to the Red Lake hospital. The Nords were determined to be at fault and charged in tribal court with a traffic violation.

The Nords were not happy about their ticket and even less happy to have to deal with the Red Lake Tribal Court. They lost their case and appealed the decision, petitioning the court for dismissal because they felt that Red Lake should not have jurisdiction in the matter.

Aloysius Thunder, Verna Graves, and Garnet Comegan served as appellate judges.

Aloysius Thunder, a good speaker of Ojibwe, wrote the opinion of the court—in Ojibwe. The Nords were told to hire a translator if they had trouble respecting Red Lake's sovereign authority or wanted to pursue further legal action. Roger Jourdain started the systemic use of Ojibwe in the Red Lake courts, and Aloysius Thunder advanced that effort. The Nords won a subsequent appeal to the federal district court on January 31, 2007, and the tribe did not appeal. The Nords have driven the speed limit on the reservation ever since.[22]

The Nord case might seem like a small one, but it speaks to a much bigger issue. Red Lake has been showing the rest of the world the meaning of tribal sovereignty for a long time. In some ways, sovereignty is what tribes make of it. Tribal rights have consistently been trod upon, so keeping those rights has required constant vigilance, careful strategy, a strong cultural foundation, and an understanding of the law.

Aloysius Thunder was one of many Red Lake members protecting tribal sovereignty and showing the rest of Indian country new ways to do it. Red Lake tribal members Shirley Cain, Leah R. Sixkiller, and Stacey Thunder, all with law degrees, have often worked with not just the tribal courts and the tribal council at Red Lake but many other agencies and venues to teach what tribal sovereignty is all about. The results have been impressive.

The Navajo Nation runs its courts in their tribal language. The Crow Nation and other tribes with strong language communities have also looked at Red Lake's examples and explored ways to use tribal law, language, and culture to evolve their court systems. Mille Lacs uses an elder advisory council to infuse traditional cultural beliefs into its legal structure. Red Lake member Stacey Thunder serves as its legal counsel. A great deal of innovative work is happening now in tribal courts. Red Lake is not responsible for all of it, but Aloysius Thunder, Shirley Cain, Leah Sixkiller, Stacey Thunder, and other Red Lake legal experts have generated an important and consistent ripple of waves from Red Lake that has helped strengthen the status of tribal sovereignty everywhere.

The Warroad Challenge

In 1889, when the Nelson Act was signed, about fifty Ojibwe people were living in a village at Warroad and another fifty at Roseau. Their chief, John KaKayGeesick, his brother Sturgeon Leaf, and Little Raven spent years trying to affirm their right to stay in their ancestral villages. They never consented to the land cession in 1889, and they were peaceful and self-sufficient. It seemed unfair to make them move without their consent. In 1905, the government accommodated them by giving them allotments in the Northwest Angle and at Warroad. For many years, the white villages at Warroad and Roseau grew around the Ojibwe villages. Over time, many of the Ojibwe residents moved to Red Lake, and some to Buffalo Point First Nation in Canada. Several families stayed at Warroad, and their descendants are still there.[23]

John KaKayGeesick's descendants at Warroad today have had a sometimes strained relationship with Red Lake. They are one of the few native families in the entire country that kept their original allotment and passed it down through the generations even while a sea of nonnative financial interests besieged them. All of that is greatly admired by many tribal members at Red Lake. The stresses have come because some of the family members are not bona fide Red Lake tribal members. Some do not meet the blood quantum threshold for enrollment at Red Lake. Others pursued membership status in Buffalo Point First Nation in Canada. John KaKayGeesick signed Treaty Three with the British government in Canada on October 3, 1873, even though he lived on the U.S. side of the international border and took an allotment there. Those who stayed at Warroad and Roseau pursued every political effort imaginable to keep the land and community at Warroad in Ojibwe hands. They won some of those battles, but for a few of them it came at the expense of their Red Lake citizenship.

In 1973, Mary K. Angus offered to give Red Lake an estate gift of her land inheritance from John KaKayGeesick. The tribe accepted the land transfer, but it was blocked by probate of her estate and the objections of other heirs. The BIA refused to act on the request of Angus and the tribal council. The KaKayGeesick allotment stayed in the hands of the chief's heirs for another thirty years.[24]

In 1999, the Warroad allotment came back into question. Donald KaKayGeesick and his siblings ran into struggles with the Mary K. Angus heirs and the tribe. The Angus heirs wanted to sell the property to the tribe. The tribe wanted to buy the property from them. Red Lake has very little land around Warroad, and white residents were not willing to sell in order to accommodate the tribe's planned casino expansion. The tribe needed the room to expand and found themselves in the awkward position of asking the only remaining Red Lake allottees who had held on to their allotments to give them up. The tribe offered an olive branch and made a generous offer to purchase the acreage and compensate all Angus and KaKayGeesick family members.[25]

The Donald KaKayGeesick family wanted to stay where they have always been. Some of the KaKayGeesicks were so upset that they wanted to politically separate from Red Lake, but their numbers are small, most are not enrolled members, and there is little legal precedent for such an undertaking. Donald KaKayGeesick and his family lost the legal and political arguments with the tribe and with the Angus family in probate court. They lost the land, too, for which the tribe paid a generous $1 million. The Angus heirs offered to include the KaKayGeesicks in distribution of the funds, but the KaKayGeesicks refused. Subsequent legal efforts have been unsuccessful.

The bigger question for the tribe and the KaKayGeesicks is how to heal the rifts. Those rifts include the political status of Warroad, which has a distinct political tradition and community leadership structure but now finds itself a minority part of a larger Indian political entity. Red Lake members at Warroad vote in Red Lake tribal elections but do not have a community representative in the current political system, where the villages of Little Rock, Red Lake, Redby, and Ponemah do. The divisions also include the touchy subject of tribal enrollment. Although many things remain unresolved, awkward, and sometimes tense, the challenge from Warroad may help the entire Red Lake Nation to better grapple with the critical issues of identity, citizenship, and place. There is potential for Red Lake to once again blaze a path for the rest of Indian country as they navigate similar troubled waters.

Leading in Media

Over the years, Red Lake has generated numerous talented media personalities. Early tribal politicians Peter Graves and Roger Jourdain were experts at communicating with the rest of the world, and growing up in that environment was formative for entire generations of Red Lake citizens. Prominent among them was Bill Lawrence, Roger Jourdain's godson. Lawrence created and ran two newspapers, the *Ojibwe News* and the *Native American Press.* He was deeply concerned with any exercise of authority that countermanded the traditional Red Lake libertarian ideal, and he used his professional life to try to speak truth to power. Sometimes his papers were filled with anger and even voiced conspiracy theories to the point where some people started to call the *Native American Press* the *Native American Inquirer.* Even today, Lawrence's legacy usually inspires strong reactions at Red Lake both in support and in condemnation of his work.

Lawrence and Jourdain frequently sparred in the media—Lawrence through his papers and Jourdain through editorials in the *Bemidji Pioneer,* the *Minneapolis Star Tribune,* and tribal publications. But when Jourdain passed away, Lawrence spoke in admiring terms of his contributions to the tribe; and when Lawrence died, people from most reservation families paid respectful tribute. This was not just a case of public decency. Both men were warriors who fought for the people of Red Lake. They just saw the battlefield differently. Their ability to see themselves as brothers in arms at the end said much about the greater good they both fought for.

Stacey Thunder, whose legal expertise and influence at Red Lake and across Indian country were well established soon after law school, has also emerged as a powerful voice in the media. She has anchored several programs, usually aired through public television: *Indigenous, Common Ground,* and *Native Report.* She also received a best actress nomination from the American Indian Film Festival for her role as Elsie in *The Jingle Dress,* a 2014 William Eigen film.

While Thunder's media and legal career continues to impress, she also devotes substantial time to philanthropic work in Indian country. Her primary service in that regard is through her role as a board member for the N7 Fund, an independent affiliate of Nike Corporation that grants money to tribes and programs that serve tribal people in the United States and Canada in order to promote health and wellness through sports and exercise.

A group of young comics called the 1491s have been making a huge splash in the comedy world over the past few years. Tito Ybarra, a Red Lake band member, is an occasional collaborator. Migizi Pensoneau, who is an enrolled member of the Ponca Tribe of Oklahoma but the son of Red Lake member Renee Gurneau, helps anchor the comedy troupe that also includes Dallas Goldtooth, Sterlin Harjo, Ryan Red Corn, and Bobby Wilson. They have become more than a YouTube sensation with their satirical video shorts such as *Slapping Medicine Man*. They have also appeared on the *Daily Show* with Jon Stewart to address the use of Indians as mascots in sports and media. Through comedy, some of Red Lake's youngest voices have been among those with the greatest national impact.[26]

Incubating Activism

The people of Red Lake have resisted external control and oppression both on their home reservation and throughout the country. Adam Fortunate Eagle (born Adam Nordwall) was an early American Indian civil-rights organizer and activist. In 1969, he partnered with Richard Oakes to plan the takeover of Alcatraz. It was a seminal event in Indian activism that inspired many subsequent efforts to focus national attention on issues of justice for native people.

Red Lake citizen Francis Blake helped organize the American Indian Movement and served as treasurer for AIM from 1971 to 1973. He grew disillusioned with AIM afterward but continued to advocate for Indian rights. In 1975, he campaigned for Jimmy Carter and helped Bill Lawrence create and promote the tribal newspapers *Ojibwe News* and *Native American Press*. Keith Lussier and other Red Lake tribal members supported many AIM activities in the 1970s and afterward. The takeover of Alcatraz in 1969 and AIM activism in the 1970s were bigger than any one tribe, but Red Lake people were always there. More recently, many Red Lake citizens have joined efforts to challenge disrespectful appropriations of native imagery in sports and media.[27]

Warrior Sports

Basketball is the most popular sport on the reservation, and the Red Lake High School Warriors have made it to the state tournament many times. Even the local games fill the stands. Anna Gibbs is usually there, along with elected tribal officials, tribal employees, and families of the athletes. At home games, the national anthem is given in the form of a powwow flag song. You know you are in a native place, and it can be quite intimidating for opposing teams. Increasingly, Red Lake's success on the court has forced state officials and other teams to make cultural accommodations, and powwow music has been a regular feature at the state tournament when Red Lake's team is in contention for a title. Star basketball players from other tribal communities have sometimes moved in order to attend Red Lake High School just so they can try out for the team.

Red Lake hockey players have often dominated the sport in the Olympics and the National Hockey League. Henry Boucha, a tribal member from Warroad, played professional hockey for the Detroit Red Wings, the Minnesota North Stars, the Kansas City Scouts, and the Colorado Rockies from 1971 to 1976. He played a decisive role in the 1972 Olympics, helping the United States bring home a silver medal. Boucha was inducted into the U.S. Hockey Hall of Fame in 1995.[28]

Boucha's cousin, Gary A. Sargent, also played professional hockey, for the Los Angeles Kings and the Minnesota North Stars from 1975 to 1983. Sargent was a talented defenseman and was an NHL All-Star in 1980. After his professional career came to an end, he worked as a talent scout for the Kings for several years. Sargent's younger brother, Earl Sargent, was drafted into the NHL but never played in the league. He had a successful career in minor league hockey, and eventually returned to Minnesota and worked for the Minnesota Indian Affairs Council.

Red Lake's hockey greats also include Henry Boucha's cousin Timothy "T. J." Oshie. Oshie was drafted by the St. Louis Blues in 2008 and continues to play for them. He also made the 2014 U.S. Olympic Team.

Red Lake has had an unforgettable impact on professional wrestling as well, through Charlie Norris. Norris is six feet seven inches tall and weighs 285 pounds. He was a force in the ring from 1989 to 1996, wrestling for World Championship Wrestling (WCW) and claiming the Pro Wrestling America heavyweight title five times, starting in 1989. He also twice won the PWA tag team title with Sam Houston and Derrick Dukes. Norris had a falling-out with the WCW in 1993 and ended up filing a racial discrimination lawsuit against the league. He wrestled for the American Wrestling Foundation from then until he retired from the sport.

Red Lakers have always had a special appreciation for endurance sports. Many citizens there run marathons and participate in intertribal commemorative running events and belong to Red Lake's Native Thunder long distance running club. After Floyd "Buck" Jourdain ran around the lakes, an eighty-two-mile run, Ponemah elder Elizabeth Kingbird named him Niigaanibatoo (Runs in the Lead). In the 1970s, Henry "Stretch" Sumner ran from Red Lake to St. Paul to invite the governor to the Red Lake powwow, covering distances from twenty-eight to forty-two miles each day until he completed the trip. The governor never came to the powwow, but the run inspired great pride in Sumner's fellow Red Lakers. Even today there are copies of the press coverage for the event posted on the wall of the tribal council meeting room.[29]

Making Artists

Artistic talent and tradition at Red Lake run deep. Red Lake has been the home of many famous birchbark canoe makers, basket weavers, and bead workers. Dan Needham Sr., grandson of Sun Shining Through, used his knowledge of traditional crafts as his primary means of providing for his family. He ran a traditional arts and craft store at Red Lake for many years and used it to support not just his work but that of many other Red Lake artists.[30]

Patrick DesJarlait (1921–72) was Red Lake's most nationally prominent artist for many years. He was raised at Red Lake and went to boarding schools at Red Lake and Pipestone. His career had an ironic launch when he won the bid to animate a commercial for Hamm's Brewery and created the Hamm's beer bear. He also took commercial contract work and created the Land O' Lakes butter maiden. Desjarlait joined the Walt Disney staff to make films for the U.S. Navy during World War II.[31]

Once DesJarlait was established, he was able to innovate and focus on his true passion and talent. His signature paintings used watercolor, which he applied directly to canvas rather than through a wash. He produced hundreds of paintings, which have adorned dozens of book covers and hang in countless museums. His work has not only a defined, distinctive style but a profound focus on Red Lake lifeways. About his work he wrote: "I have always wanted to show others the interest and pride that the Chippewa take in their families, their ceremonies, and their environment."[32]

Patrick's son Randy DesJarlait has carried on the family tradition. He is currently a widely respected painter whose works have received broad acclaim. The tribe hired him to refresh all of the reservation welcome signs and many program logos at Red Lake.[33]

Samuel English was an early Indian civil-rights activist in 1968. He struggled as a young man, but in 1981 he made a commitment to sobriety and artistic expression. Since then, his work has been featured in art magazines such as *New Mexico* and *Winds of Change*. The book *Sam English: The Life, Work, and Times of an Artist* was a finalist for the National Indie Excellence Awards. Inspired by the success of Dan Needham Sr., Patrick DesJarlait, and Sam English, many other Red Lake artists have had successful careers and great impact in the field, especially in painting. Active and respected Red Lake artists today include Wes May, Gordon Van Wert, and Robert KaKayGeesick Jr.[34]

Leading in Music

Keith Secola is an accomplished rock-and-roll fusion musician, writer, and singer of "NDN Kars" (Indian cars), inductee to the Native Music Hall of Fame, and winner of seven Native American Music Awards. He is from Red Lake, and his work has included several songs written in Ojibwe. Secola has done a lot of collaborative work with other musicians and maintains a tireless travel and production schedule. In contemporary and ancient music, Red Lake is an unforgettable and transformative voice.

Red Lake is home to many of the best-known singers and dancers on the modern powwow circuit. The powwow is a relatively recent cultural phenomenon in Indian country. Many tribes in the Great

Lakes and Plains have ancient warrior societies and ceremonies that gave birth to the powwow. Different styles of dance come from those ancient ways—traditional and grass dance in particular. In the 1910s, an Ojibwe man dreamed about the jingle dress, and it proliferated at Red Lake and then spread to the rest of Indian country.[35]

In the 1970s, powwow customs evolved further to include traditional community powwows and contest powwows, where dancers compete against one another in numerous styles of dance. Red Lake's singers were some of the first and most influential: Kingbird Singers, Ponemah Ramblers, Black Bear Crossing, Red Lake Singers, and East Red Lake. Johnny Smith, Royce Kingbird, and many other famous Red Lake singers led the way for the growth of powwow culture.

In more recent years, Young Kingbird, Ogidaaki, Battle River, Mahnomen Creek, and Eyabay have taken home countless singing titles, created thousands of songs, and transformed powwow from local community events to a world stage. Lee Lussier Jr., Darryl Kingbird, Keveon Kingbird, Mark Kingbird, Roger White, Don Kingbird, and many other talented Red Lake singers are household names across Indian country and an inspiration to generations of tribal singing talent everywhere.

The Struggle

Red Lake faces many challenges today. The unemployment rate there is 38 percent, the lowest it has been since employment records were kept. Although many members subsistence hunt, fish, and gather to help support their families, financial strain and unemployment put a lot of pressure on residents to seek work away from home, which challenges community cohesion. Although Red Lake has done much to stabilize and revitalize Ojibwe, language and culture loss are undeniable. Substance abuse remains a scourge on the people. Crime and law-enforcement issues are major concerns. There are ongoing crises with physical health and suicide. Forced assimilation, religious oppression, and attempted government control did a lot of damage. Historical trauma is real. Red Lakers are sometimes hard on themselves and one another—a manifestation of internalized and lateral oppression. Red Lakers today see these problems, and many have devoted their lives to addressing them. But as overwhelming as it can be to think about all the challenges the reservation faces, every one of the problems can be fixed by what is right at Red Lake.

The Kingfisher

When she is not on the go, Anna Gibbs is often sitting in her living room at the Red Lake Senior Apartments. Her bed is in the living room because the bedroom is full of blankets given to her for officiating at ceremonies. She eventually gives them away to people who need them. A giant picture of a female kingfisher hangs on the wall. Her fridge is full of paper plates with leftover food from feasts, all carefully covered in aluminum foil. Anna remembers what it was like to go in want, and she never lets anything go to waste. People often visit her for advice, help, and assistance in understanding their dreams.

A man came to see her about a dream. In his dream, he was standing by the shore of Upper Red Lake and it looked like a wasteland. Every tree had been cut down; not a trunk was standing around the whole lake. There was slashed brush everywhere, bulldozed into half-buried piles. Some were smoldering, as if someone was trying to burn it all but couldn't quite make it happen. There was no hint of animal or human activity. The lake was still there, and it was calm, with a few light waves rippling to shore. He felt sick and fell to his knees, covering his eyes. How could they do this? How could anyone sleep at night knowing this was done?

Then he sensed movement in the air. Opening his eyes, he glanced at the lake. Kingfishers were hovering over the water, diving down for fish, and fluttering all around him. He could hear the whoosh of their wings in every direction. Then he heard another sound, like wind in the pine trees. Turning around, he saw that the barren, desecrated landscape was gone. Instead, there were pine trees all along the shore—ancient, tall white and red pines. The wind was whistling through their needles as far as the eye could see. He felt small, humbled and amazed at the height of the trees. And the kingbirds—there were thousands of them, not just hovering over the water but sitting in the trees, flying from branch to branch.

"What does it mean, Anna?" She looked at him through her large, dark-rimmed glasses. She wrapped her short, leathery fingers around his offered tobacco pouch and pulled it close to her on the table: "The kingfisher, that's one of our clans here on the Red Lake reservation. That's my clan." She spoke slowly, deliberately, with a penetrating gaze. "The first part of that dream, where all the trees were gone and everything was destroyed—that's how it was when the white people first got a hold of Red Lake. They tried to kill or take everything, even the trees. The second part of that dream, the good part, that's how it's gonna be in the future. War only lasts for a while—the war against the trees, and the war against us. But the lake is forever; and the water heals everything. Dreams are how the spirits talk to us. We have to pay attention to our dreams. The spirits love the Indian people, the Indians' clans, and the land. They're still watching over us. That's the power of dreams. Every time they tried to bury us, they didn't realize that we were the seeds."

Warrior Nation

There are only two reservations in the United States that are closed, where all of the land is owned collectively by the entire tribe. The Confederated Tribes of the Warm Springs reservation (Wasco, Pai-ute, and Warm Springs Tribes) in Oregon is one. Three different tribes were confederated there, and the reservation was a designated relocation point for many people in the massive ten-thousand-acre land cession in 1855 that created Warm Springs. Red Lake is the other closed reservation. Although Ojibwe people from numerous villages across the Red River Valley concentrated at Red Lake, it was not a relocation reservation like Warm Springs. Red Lakers kept their land under communal ownership because their leaders insisted on that arrangement time after time over one hundred years of sustained pressure to cede and allot their reservation. Considering that no other tribe in the United States was able to accomplish that and the incredible efforts exerted to take everything from the people of Red Lake, this achievement is monumental.

Keeping Red Lake's land status closed was miraculous enough. But that was one of a hundred impressive accomplishments achieved by dynamic leaders at Red Lake. Red Lake kept land on three of the six largest lakes in Minnesota (Lake of the Woods, Upper Red Lake, and Lower Red Lake). In 1918, it created one of the first modern representative tribal political structures in the country. In 1953, it avoided

WARNING

THIS IS RED LAKE INDIAN LAND

No Trespassing

No Fishing, Hunting, Camping, Snowmobiling, Berry Picking, Peddling or Soliciting
Without Authorized Permit From Red Lake Tribal Council Office. Violators and Trespassers
Will Be Prosecuted and Their Equipment & Firearms Will Be Confiscated.
Unauthorized Flights Over the Reservation Are Also Prohibited.
Under Federal Law 86-634

ALL AREAS PATROLLED

Chairman, Red Lake Tribal Council

Red Lake Indian Reservation

state jurisdiction over criminal affairs and maintained its own court and police systems. It created and still maintains a sustainable commercial fishery, bringing ancient knowledge forward to sustain its people in modern times. It has the cleanest aquifer in the state of Minnesota. It refused to legalize alcohol throughout its entire history. It has the highest tribal language fluency rate in the Great Lakes or Northern Plains. It is one of two Ojibwe tribes that never lost the medicine dance (the other is St. Croix in Wisconsin).[36]

In countless arenas of tribal politics, economics, and culture, Red Lake has not just shown the world the way but has trod the path with its own moccasins until it was a veritable highway of flowing thought and political action for everyone else to follow. Greatness is not made from complacency or by going with the flow. Greatness is made by those with the audacity to dream, with a vision for the future, and with the leadership to see it become a reality. Red Lake leaders have consistently done that for generation upon generation since their arrival in Red Lake. Fundamentally, that is what makes Red Lake a truly great nation. Since the first Ojibwe settled at Red Lake, the people there have strategized, built, united, reformed, revolutionized, and dreamed. These are the actions of true warriors, and Red Lake has always had warriors in abundance.

From scattered villages with an emerging libertarian ideal, they forged a nation; they made it and remade it over and over again. White Thunderbird symbolized and sparked cultural change. Moose Dung was the strategist for mitigating pronounced loss. He Who Is Spoken To was the nation builder. Nodin Wind was the uniter. Peter Graves was the reformer. Roger Jourdain was the revolutionary. Anna Gibbs is the dreamer. All are warriors.

There were numerous great leaders throughout Red Lake's incredible history. In recent years, many more have risen to distinguish themselves and their proud native nation in politics, business, law, sports, academics, linguistics, art, and music. Red Lake is generations of astonishing human history still in the making. It is ancient and modern. The people there have roots deeper than the lake itself. They have wings too, and Red Lake is, as it has always been, going somewhere. Red Lakers are not simply victims of history or its survivors. Every woman, man, elder, and youngster is not simply the descendant of warriors but a living, unconquered warrior. Collectively, with hearts still beating to the sound of the drum, they are the warrior nation.

Acknowledgments

THIS WORK WOULD NOT HAVE BEEN POSSIBLE without the assistance of numerous Red Lake citizens, elders, tribal leaders, and cultural carriers and many other Ojibwe and Dakota people who contributed their knowledge about this amazing story: Dora Ammann, Joseph Auginaush, Erika Bailey-Johnson, Thomas Beardy, Harlan Beaulieu, Kathryn "Jody" Beaulieu, Edward Benton-Banai, William Blackwell Sr., James Clark, Melvin Eagle, Anna Gibbs, Charles Grolla, Lawrence Henry, Susan Jackson, Fannie Johns, Nancy Jones, Floyd Jourdain, Ona Kingbird, Winona LaDuke, James Loud, Adam Lussier, William May, Archie Mosay, Collins Oakgrove, Earl Otchingwanigan (Nyholm), Margaret Porter, Mary Roberts, Carolyn Schommer, Daniel Seaboy, Vincent Staples-Graves, Eugene Stillday, Thomas Stillday Jr., Aloysius Thunder, Margaret Treuer, Robert Treuer, Walter White, Vernon Whitefeather, Angela Wilson. Thank you to Jessica Wike, Michelle Gonzales, Cooper Blackwood, and Caleb Waggoner for help with copies and filing. Thank you to Erika Bailey-Johnson, Dan Karalus, and John Swartz for help with photos. Thank you to Mark Anderson for help with audio and video conversions of the oral-history and Ojibwe-language archival material. Thank you to Michael Meuers and Kent Nerburn for sharing videos and notes on Red Lake history. Thank you to Kelli Carmean for research assistance on archaeological sites and Thomas Peckham for help with legal research. Thank you to Harlan Beaulieu, Vincent Staples-Graves, Floyd Jourdain, and James Loud for help with genealogy. A big thank you to David Katz for countless hours digging material out of the Minnesota Historical Society for this project. Thank you to Floyd "Buck" Jourdain, Samuel Strong, Justin Beaulieu, Harlan Beaulieu, and Donald "Dude" May for the impetus to create this book; and thank you to all members of the tribal council under the

Jourdain and Seki administrations for believing in me to do it. Thank you to Margaret Treuer, Harlan Beaulieu, Justin Beaulieu, David Thorstad, Heidi Stark, and especially Ann Regan for editorial advice. Thank you to Shannon Pennefeather, Dan Leary, Judy Gilats, Lisa Himes, Matt Kania, and Mary Russell for excellent work on production of the book.

Special thanks for support to Dora and Brooke Ammann, Dustin Burnette, Alfred Bush, Brenda Child, Collette Dahlke, Heid Erdrich, Louise Erdrich, Sean Fahrlander, Henry Flocken, Anna Gibbs, Thomas Goldtooth, Charles Grolla, Renee Gurneau, Daniel and Dennis Jones, Richard and Penny Kagigebi, Lisa LaRonge, Cary Miller, Mark, Mike, Melonee, Midge, and Frank Montano, Leonard and Mary Moose, George and John Morrow, Keller Paap, John Patrick, Monique Paulson, Mark Pero, Skip and Babette Sandman, Thomas Saros, Robert Saxton, Eugene Stillday, Mary Lou and Thomas Stillday Jr., Michael Sullivan, and Isadore Toulouse.

I am also always forever indebted to my family—my parents Robert and Margaret Treuer, my siblings David, Derek, Megan, Micah, Paul, and Smith Treuer, my children Jordan, Robert, Madeline, Caleb, Isaac, Elias, Evan, Mia, and Luella, and my wife, Blair. You all sacrificed a lot of time with me to make this book possible.

APPENDIX 1

When the Dakota Ruled Red Lake

"The Master of Life has given to all the Indians the land to live on in peace, but unhappily, we are all foolish."

BEAR HEART (NOKE-ODE')

Dakota Migration to Red Lake

Red Lake was not always in Ojibwe hands. The region was completely covered in ice during the last ice age, which ended around ten thousand years ago. The retreating ice sheets created a massive proglacial lake called Lake Agassiz, which covered much of Saskatchewan, Manitoba, northwestern Ontario, North Dakota, and Minnesota. Lake Agassiz was so massive that when the Hudson Bay ice sheets finally melted, triggering the drainage release of Lake Agassiz, global sea levels rose as much as nine feet. That flooded huge areas of land on most continents, dramatically reduced ocean temperatures, and triggered a climactic shift that enabled the birth of the world's agricultural age.[1]

The movement of glaciers prior to the big melt scraped much of the topsoil off of the Canadian Shield and deposited it in the Red River Valley's tallgrass prairie. The drainage of Lake Agassiz left massive lacustrine deposits along the Red River Valley, compounding the glacial movement of topsoil and making it the most naturally fertile agricultural region in North America. Lake Winnipeg, Lake Manitoba, Lake of the Woods, and Upper and Lower Red Lake are in fact the relicts of Lake Agassiz. This natural phenomenon enabled Upper and Lower Red Lake to become the region's most productive fishery and the surrounding land to support an unparalleled diversity and abundance of animal and bird populations. The water was clear, the topsoil was deep and black, the grass grew taller, and there were more buffalo per square mile than anywhere else on planet Earth. It's what made the Red Lake region paradise for Indians.

Many different tribes called Red Lake home after the drainage of Lake Agassiz. The Hidatsa, Arikara, Cheyenne, and A'aninin (Gros Ventre) all settled at Red Lake at different times after it became habitable by humans. The A'aninin developed a unique style of dwelling—a wooden lodge much like the hogan of the Navajo, but entirely covered with earth. Although labor intensive to build, these lodges provided excellent protection from the elements and enemy attacks. They also last a very long time. Lewis and Clark observed uninhabited earthen lodges in Minnesota in 1804. In the 1840s and 1850s, many A'aninin earthen lodges were noted by traders, explorers, and writers throughout Minnesota, even though the A'aninin themselves had already by then been driven out of the region to the Northern Plains by the Dakota. Those observations help us date the Dakota migration to Red Lake and their military dispossession of the A'aninin.[2]

That process may have begun as early as 1600 but was not complete until around 1700. William Warren personally observed A'aninin lodges in the 1840s and 1850s at Rice Lake, Sandy Lake, Mille Lacs, the Pine River outlet on the Mississippi River, and Gull Lake in central Minnesota. He also collected extensive oral histories from Red Lake chiefs and Ojibwe people throughout the region at that time in which many Ojibwe identified the locations of A'aninin lodges in the Red Lake and Red River Valley areas.[3]

The Dakota vastly outnumbered the A'aninin, and although precise dates are not certain, they definitely dispossessed them across northern Minnesota by around 1700. At Mille Lacs, the Dakota moved their families into the earthen lodges of their A'aninin predecessors and maintained those dwellings as Dakota homes for many years.

At Red Lake, the Dakota flourished for half a century. The fish, rice, and animal abundance sustained a large and rapidly growing population. The Ojibwe had been slowly on the move, as part of their great migration from the eastern Great Lakes toward the Minnesota rice beds, for hundreds of years already, but the Dakota had no fear of the Ojibwe. They were nearly as numerous as the Ojibwe, and they were also in a friendly trade and military alliance with them.

Ojibwe–Dakota Alliance

From 1641 to 1701, the Iroquois Confederacy (Mohawk, Seneca, Cayuga, Onondaga, and Oneida) warred with the Three Fires Confederacy (Ojibwe, Ottawa, and Potawatomi). This conflict was part of a larger and even longer war between the British and the French, who were using their Indian allies to wage economic and military war between their respective empires. The conflicts were terribly debilitating for all of the tribes involved.[4]

By 1650, Iroquoian-speaking Hurons and numerous Algonquian peoples were displaced from their eastern villages along Lakes Huron, Erie, and Ontario and sought refuge far to the west at Lac Courte Oreilles, Lac du Flambeau, Black River, and Lake Pepin, deep in Dakota territory. In 1653, some even took refuge west of the Mississippi River. In 1659, Claude-Jean Allouez saw more than four thousand Ojibwe, Potawatomi, Ottawa, Kickapoo, Illinois, Sac, Fox, Cree, and Dakota settled at Chequamegon Bay, with even more at Keweenaw Bay and Sault Ste. Marie. Eventually, the Dakota could no longer peacefully tolerate the war refugees harvesting most of their resources, and they drove them out.[5]

As the Ojibwe gained the upper hand in the Iroquois Wars, the Ojibwe and Dakota became the most powerful tribes in the western Great Lakes, with roughly 60,000 people each. With the Huron, Ottawa, and Potawatomi war refugees out of the way, the Ojibwe and Dakota found themselves in an unprecedented situation. The Ojibwe were the linchpin of French military defense and trade and were kept well supplied in muskets, kettles, and other European trade goods. But they needed new areas to hunt and trap in order to meet French dependence on them for furs. The Dakota held a huge territory with an abundance of furs, but they were too far away to actively and consistently engage the French in trade.[6]

In 1679, the Ojibwe and Dakota held a large peace conference at the St. Louis River outlet into Lake Superior. French traders Daniel

Greysolon, Sieur Du Lhut, and Nicolas Perrot observed the event. The Dakota approached each Ojibwe delegate and, according to Perrot, "began, according to their custom, to weep over every person they met, in order to manifest the lively joy they felt in meeting them; and they entreated the strangers to have pity on them . . . [thanking the Great Spirit] for having guided to their country these peoples. [The Dakota] loaded them with endearing terms and showed the utmost submissiveness, in order to touch them with compassion."[7]

Ultimately, the Dakota offered the Ojibwe the right to hunt and settle much of their territory east of the Mississippi River. La Pointe, Chequamegon Bay, Keweenaw Bay, Lac Courte Oreilles, Lac du Flambeau, and Fond du Lac became undisputed Ojibwe possessions. In return, the Ojibwe became middlemen in Dakota-French trade, keeping the Dakota well supplied with guns, knives, kettles, and other trade goods. By 1682, Ojibwe traders frequently traveled more than one hundred fifty miles into Dakota territory to pick up Dakota furs at Red Lake and deliver European trade goods. By 1680, more than a thousand Ojibwe were settled at La Pointe on Madeline Island and many were spreading out over the Chequamegon Bay area and deep into the interior of Wisconsin. Many Ojibwe and Dakota families arranged marriages between the tribes to further cement their peaceful connection with each other.

The Ojibwe-Dakota alliance was not good for many of the other tribes around Lake Superior, Rainy Lake, and Lake of the Woods. The Fox, Ottawa, Potawatomi, Cree, and Assiniboine were upset. The two most powerful tribes in the region were friends with each other and the French, but not always with these smaller tribes. As the Ojibwe-Dakota relationship deepened, the Ojibwe-Cree relationship suffered. Dakota hostilities with the Cree and Assiniboine soon enveloped the Ojibwe, who were now obligated to prove their friendship with the Dakota as military allies.[8]

The Cree made a deft series of diplomatic maneuvers to improve their position. In 1682, the Cree traveled to Hudson Bay to establish trade with the British at Fort Nelson. Then they told the French that they would sever their British trade relationship and show the French how to get to the Pacific Ocean if the French would establish direct trade with the Cree at Rainy Lake and Lake of the Woods. It worked. The French soon built new trading posts in Cree territory.[9]

Even though the Cree were now enemies of the Dakota and some-times even the Ojibwe, the Dakota intentionally established direct trade with the French as well. In 1695, the Dakota and Ojibwe both sent representatives with Pierre-Charles Le Sueur to Montreal and negotiated the opening of a French trading post on Isle Pelée (present-day Prairie Island, Minnesota). By 1700, the French built Fort L'Huillier in Blue Earth, Minnesota. The new posts ensured that both the Dakota and the Ojibwe could keep trade constant while reducing the risks of travel across Fox territory. From 1698 to 1734, Fox conflict with the French and their Ojibwe and Dakota allies was ferocious and eventually genocidal to the Fox.[10]

From 1679 to 1736, the Ojibwe–Dakota peace endured dramatic population shifts, external military pressure, and a transformation of tribal economies through engagement in the fur trade. Intermar-riage, adoptions, and joint military ventures had strengthened their relationship, but that was all before the French saw Red Lake.

Red Lake and the French Fiasco

Ojibwe chief Bear Heart said, "The Master of Life has given to all the Indians the land to live on in peace, but unhappily, we are all foolish." That statement proved prescient in 1736 when a series of economic changes, military events, and French manipulations shattered the fifty-seven-year peace between the Ojibwe and the Dakota.

All the trouble really started with one man, and he wasn't even Indian. Pierre Gaultier de Varennes, Sieur de La Vérendrye, was the first agent of New France permanently stationed west of Lake Supe-rior for an extended period of time. La Vérendrye was ordered to expand French fur trade networks westward and find a passage to the Western Sea (Pacific Ocean). The 1713 Peace of Utrecht affirmed exclusive British control of Hudson Bay to the north and their Amer-ican colonies to the south. The French were getting squeezed in the middle, making La Vérendrye's efforts a top priority.[11]

In 1729, La Vérendrye met a Cree man at Grand Portage, Minne-sota, who drew him a map on birch bark showing the route to the Western Sea. Although it is conceivable that the Cree man misunder-stood La Vérendrye, it is more likely that he drew the map (extending through all of the major lakes in Cree territory) in order to entice La

Vérendrye into Cree lands. La Vérendrye took the bait, establishing Fort St. Pierre on Rainy Lake (Cree territory) and Fort St. Charles on Lake of the Woods (Cree and Assiniboine territory), and bringing literally tons of French trade goods to the Cree and their Assiniboine allies. Fort St. Charles became his primary base of operations. It is located on Magnuson Island in Minnesota's Northwest Angle, and much of the fort area is today Red Lake reservation land.

In the 1730s, the Indian world in Minnesota was at war. The Ojibwe and Dakota were allied against the Cree and Assiniboine. In 1733 and 1734, La Vérendrye observed several Assiniboine–Cree war parties, some with as many as eight hundred warriors, massing at his post to prepare for attacks against the Dakota and Ojibwe.[12]

The Cree brilliantly manipulated La Vérendrye to meet their needs. They used information about travel routes to the Western Sea, tales of vast gold deposits to the west, British trade contacts at Hudson Bay, and Spanish trade contacts on the Missouri, which vexed La Vérendrye and spurred him deeper into Cree lands and influence. He had to pursue his mission with no more than two dozen French *engagés* and officers in the Lake of the Woods district. There were more than three thousand Cree in the immediate vicinity, forcing him to adapt to Cree political protocol in trade and exploration.[13]

The Cree asked La Vérendrye if they could adopt his son as their relative. Among most tribes, adoption and marriage were common practices used in cementing agreements and binding nations. La Vérendrye saw this as an opportunity to further his mission. In 1733, the Cree adopted Jean-Baptiste de La Vérendrye, his eldest son. Jean-Baptiste was soon entrusted with great responsibility in helping La Vérendrye, including oversight of the construction of Fort Maurepas in the Lake Winnipeg district the following year.[14]

In 1733, the Ojibwe and the Dakota carried out a series of attacks against the Cree and the Assiniboine, killing several people, including the son of a prominent Cree chief. The Cree prepared a response. They approached La Vérendrye and said that their new adopted relative, Jean-Baptiste, must join them.[15]

La Vérendrye had no choice but to handle the request according to Cree custom. He learned and sang a Cree war song. Then he attended the war council and responded to their request. He was in a very precarious position. He wrote of his decision:

I was agitated, I must confess, and cruelly tormented by conflicting thoughts. . . . On the one hand, how was I to entrust my eldest son to barbarians whom I did not know, and whose name even I scarcely knew, to go and fight against other barbarians of whose name and of whose strength I knew nothing? Who could tell whether my son would ever return. . . .

On the other hand, were I to refuse him to them, there was much reason to fear that they would attribute it to fear and take the French for cowards, with the result of their shaking off the French yoke. . . . [T]hey have not fully accepted it.

In this dilemma I consulted all the most intelligent Frenchmen of my post and those best able to give advice. They were all of the opinion that I should grant the request of the savages, and even pressed me to do so. They said that my son would not be the first Frenchman who had gone with savages to war. . . . [M]oreover, my son was passionately desirous of going.

The war party assembled in the spring of 1734 with Jean-Baptiste and twelve hundred Cree and Assiniboine warriors. Their target was the Dakota village at Red Lake. La Vérendrye asked the war chiefs to have Jean-Baptiste go only as their "counsellor and witness to their valour." [16]

As the attack commenced, the Dakota at Red Lake called out, "Who is killing us?" to which the Cree and Assiniboine responded, "It is the Frenchman." That was not a truthful reply, but it had a disastrous effect. [17]

The Dakota were friends with the French and even had French trading posts in some of their villages; the Cree did too. The tribes fought one another but never fought the French. Jean-Baptiste's involvement and the Cree's response gave the impression that the French had orchestrated and led the attack on the Dakota at Red Lake.

The Dakota had to develop an appropriate response to an attack from their Cree and Assiniboine enemies and an unprovoked attack from their French allies. We do not know the substance of Dakota war councils, but it was obvious that they did not want to lose trade with the French. At the same time, they could not allow anyone to attack them with impunity.

Their response was calculated to deliver a powerful message. They would attack the French located in Cree territory but leave the French in Dakota territory unmolested. The Dakota knew that the French position in Cree country was still tenuous. By attacking the French there, it was possible that the French would be forced to abandon the entire area in order to ensure the safety of their supplies and people. That might disrupt the Assiniboine-Cree weapon supply in addition to teaching the French a lesson. By making a major assault at Lake of the Woods, the Dakota could weaken both their French and their Cree attackers.

The Dakota were still in firm alliance with the Ojibwe, and the Ojibwe stood in the middle of the French trade routes. This had the potential to insulate the Dakota from any escalation of hostilities with the French to the east and south. Even so, the Dakota knew that attacking the French was risky. They took precautions, including inviting Ojibwe warriors to help them against the French at Lake of the Woods. They also made a truce with the Fox. All of this took time, so the Dakota response to the 1734 Cree-Assiniboine-French attack did not come for two years.[18]

In June 1736, the Dakota sent a small war party of one hundred thirty warriors from Red Lake up the Warroad River to Lake of the Woods. They immediately encountered René Bourassa, a French agent from Fort St. Charles on Lake of the Woods. The war party captured him, his crew, and his female Indian slave. The Dakota apparently planned to torture Bourassa, but the slave interceded, telling the war party, "My friends . . . if you want to be avenged for the attack made on you, you have only to go further on and you will find twenty-four Frenchmen, amongst whom is the son of their chief, the one who slaughtered us."[19]

The war party left Bourassa's entourage in peace and followed the directions of the Indian woman. Jean-Baptiste de La Vérendrye, Father Jean-Pierre Aulneau, and nineteen French soldiers and voyagers had just begun a trade voyage from Fort St. Charles to Michilimackinac. They camped on an island in Lake of the Woods on the evening of June 5, less than twenty miles from Fort St. Charles.

The next morning the Dakota and their Ojibwe allies attacked. All twenty-one Frenchmen were killed. Monsoni Indians investigating the incident about a week later found abandoned canoes stained with blood and a couple of bodies at Muskeg Bay, which suggests that the Indian warriors suffered casualties in the attack. The reports of both French and Indians who saw the dead suggest that the French died from arrow and musket fire and from hand-to-hand combat, with visible wounds from knives and war clubs. The bodies of Jean-Baptiste de La Vérendrye and Father Jean-Pierre Aulneau were mutilated. Jean-Baptiste was found "lying on his face, his back all scored with knife cuts, a stake thrust into his side, headless, his body ornamented with leggings and armpieces of porcupine." All of the Frenchmen were decapitated. Most were scalped. The heads were wrapped in beaver skins and neatly arranged in a semicircle as if holding council. The Dakota were sending a message: the French decision (made in council) to have Jean-Baptiste attack the Dakota had this attack as a direct consequence.[20]

On June 22, 1736, La Vérendrye heard about his son's death. He immediately fortified Fort St. Charles against possible further attacks and dispatched a group of French soldiers and officers to investigate the site. The island on which the bodies were found was renamed Massacre Island. It still bears the name today. The bodies of Jean-Baptiste and Jean-Pierre Aulneau and the heads of the nineteen crewmen were brought back to Fort St. Charles and buried at the chapel there. In 1908, an archaeological team used these remains as evidence to locate the exact position of the long-abandoned fort.[21]

The successful war party went home. Victory celebrations were held at the Dakota village on Lake Pepin and an Ojibwe camp at Lake Vermilion. At Lake Pepin, one of the Dakota had a French medallion taken from Jean-Baptiste's party. A French officer at the Lake Pepin post ripped off the medallion and part of the Dakota man's ear. The Dakota burned down the palisade and destroyed the garden.[22]

Cree and Assiniboine chiefs and La Vérendrye immediately reacted to the event at Massacre Island. Cree and Assiniboine warriors came by the hundreds to Fort St. Charles. The French were in a precarious position. They now had to depend on the Cree and Assiniboine to protect them. French–Dakota friendship and trade were in jeopardy. If the French could not be certain to reach Rainy Lake and Lake of the Woods in relative safety, they might have to withdraw from their posts in the area. The Cree might have to make the sixty-day round trip to Hudson Bay to trade with the British or be at the mercy of Ojibwe middlemen. The Cree also told La Vérendrye, "You forbade us to go to the English and we obeyed you, and if we are now compelled to go there to get guns, powder, kettles, tobacco . . . you must only blame your own people." The Cree played a deft hand, protecting the French, threatening their trade, and deepening French dependence on them.[23]

The French had themselves to blame as much as the Cree for the events that led to the killing of Jean-Baptiste de La Vérendrye, Father Jean-Pierre Aulneau, and their companions. But they held the Dakota solely responsible. The French had a lot to lose. The prospect of Dakota hostilities threatened every trading post and fort from the Missouri River to Lake Michigan. Hundreds of French traders and missionaries were exposed, many in Dakota territory.[24]

La Vérendrye was the highest-ranking French official in the Lake of the Woods district and the most powerful voice in shaping the French response, which was unfortunately more personal than professional. He recalled all of the French traders, missionaries, and fort staff from Dakota territory by 1737. He wrote that he was contemplating putting himself at the head of a Cree–Assiniboine war party to attack the Dakota. Instead, he encouraged the Cree and the Assiniboine to bring the fight to the Dakota. He made arrangements for weapon and ammunition resupply in Montreal and entreated the Cree and Assiniboine to "keep the road open and clear of the enemy." He wrote of the Cree: "They told me that they were weeping incessantly day and night, they their women and children, for the death of my son whom they had adopted as chief of the two nations; and they were all ready to move against the enemy, and asked me for vengeance. I made the same reply, and they went back . . . quite satisfied." La Vérendrye agreed to finance and supply all Indian allies with guns, powder, ball, and knives if they were willing to attack the Dakota, saying, "I want to sing the song of war with you." He pledged each tribe twenty fathoms of tobacco for a promise to wage war against the Dakota. He also wrote to Charles de la Boische, Marquis de Beauharnois (governor general of New France), that he wanted the French to support his call for vengeance for the attack.[25]

La Vérendrye could not immediately commit French troops to the campaigns because he had such a tiny garrison, but he promised to confer with his superiors to get reinforcements. His official report to the government of New France declared that he had promoted peace and tried to discourage campaigns against the Dakota. However, his

other correspondence and journals clearly show that he was the primary advocate for war against the Dakota. He was obviously trying
to preempt the potential wrath of Beauharnois over his bungling
and escalation of tensions in the economically critical areas west of
Lake Superior. La Vérendrye received mixed signals from some of
his higher-ups in Montreal. With their blessing he returned to Lake
of the Woods to wage a war against the Dakota and continue his primary mission—the quest for the Western Sea.

Breaking the Ojibwe–Dakota Peace

The French and the Cree now reached out to the Ojibwe for support.
The Ojibwe were allied with the Dakota and the French and had close
political, military, economic, and family ties with both through numerous intermarriages and adoptions. Now they had to choose sides.
The Cree made the choice as easy as they could for the Ojibwe, offering them the right to settle in some of the disputed territory on
the edge of the Dakota-Ojibwe-Cree boundary lines between Lake
Vermilion, Thunder Bay, and Grand Portage, extending west along
the Pigeon River.[26]

The Ojibwe were in an extremely difficult position. In the end,
their economic relationship with the French was more important
than their economic relationship with the Dakota, especially after
their middleman position was undercut by French trading posts in
Dakota lands—Fort Beauharnois in 1700 on Lake Pepin and Fort
L'Huillier in 1727 at Blue Earth. The charter of the Fort Beauharnois
trading post explicitly provided for a separate sphere of influence
from the Chequamegon post, the nucleus of the Ojibwe population.
The French mandated that the Dakota trading at Lake Pepin not go to
Chequamegon to trade. According to the charter, "The [Dakota] shall
not trade or hunt in the direction of Point Chagoamigon." Ojibwe-
Dakota trade was stymied by the French. The economic glue in the
Ojibwe-Dakota peace lost its strength. Social and political connections kept the peace, but after the killing of his son, La Vérendrye's
pressure was too much to bear.[27]

The Ojibwe decision was also shaped by their other Indian alliances. They could maintain their close friendships with the Ottawa
and Potawatomi only if they sided with the French. They also stood

to convert two enemy tribes—the Cree and Assiniboine—into fast friends by siding with the French.

Ojibwe-Dakota relations were still generally strong, but there were some notable intertribal stresses over domestic issues by 1736. William Warren wrote:

> A quarrel . . . happened between an Ojibway and a Dakota gallant, respecting a woman they both courted. The woman was a Dakota, and the affair took place at a village of her people. Of her two suitors, she preferred the Ojibway, and the rejected gallant, in revenge, took the life of his successful rival. This act, however, did not result in immediate hostilities; it only reminded the warriors of the two tribes that they *had once been enemies*; it required a more aggravating cause than this to break the ties which . . . years of good understanding and social intercourse had created between them.

Warren also reported of a series of Dakota-Ojibwe murders at Mille Lacs, causing a fundamental fracture of the intertribal friendship. These developments compounded in the context of French and Cree pressure to shatter the Ojibwe-Dakota entente.[28]

Strategically, the Ojibwe would have the element of surprise if they attacked the Dakota. But everyone knew that even though the Dakota had been slowly expanding their territory westward because of abundant buffalo on the prairie, there was no way they would give up their woodland homes without a fight. Once the decision was made to break the peace with the Dakota, the Ojibwe planned for a decisive blow.[29]

In concert with the Cree and Assiniboine, the Ojibwe planned a series of offensives on three fronts. The Assiniboine were going to attack the Dakota via the Red River. The Cree would attack the Dakota via the Big Fork River. The Ojibwe would attack the Dakota via the St. Louis and Mississippi Rivers at Sandy Lake and Mille Lacs and via the Chippewa River at Lake Pepin. All attacks would happen simultaneously from different directions, hopefully pushing the Dakota back, even forcing them to evacuate their northern villages. La Vérendrye depleted his personal funds in addition to government resources to support the effort. He himself made a trip to Montreal in 1736, in large part to garner support and supplies for the war against the Dakota. The odds greatly favored the Ojibwe and their allies.

In the fall of 1736, the Lac Courte Oreilles, Lac du Flambeau, and Fond du Lac Ojibwe attacked the Dakota at Lake Pepin. The French traders had not yet abandoned Fort Beauharnois and were present to observe the attack, although they closed the fort and departed immediately afterward. Now the Dakota knew that both the French and the Ojibwe were enemies. They immediately sought to secure a stable trade through the Fox. They were furious at the betrayal by their Ojibwe allies, and thousands of Dakota warriors mobilized in response.[30]

The Assiniboine and Cree also attacked the Dakota at Red Lake, Lake Winnibigoshish, Cass Lake, and Leech Lake. But their attacks were unexpectedly much smaller than originally planned. At the last minute, La Vérendrye tried to delay the offensives, mainly in response to criticism from Montreal that he was wasting time and money that should be focused on the search for the Western Sea. Even more important, the Cree and Assiniboine were both devastated by a wave of smallpox in 1736. The effect was catastrophic. Entire Cree villages at Lake Winnipeg were wiped out. La Vérendrye's second son, Chevalier, reported, "Those who escaped the plague . . . threw into the river all beaver, lynx, marten and other furs that belonged not only to the dead but to the living. The shores and portages were full of them, all of them going to waste because no one would dare touch them." In addition to the devastation to the native populations in the region, the loss of furs and fur trappers crippled the Assiniboine-Cree economy and caused the French a serious setback. It took years for the French and Indians to recover economically, and to this day the native population has not fully rebounded from the epidemic.[31]

The Dakota responded to the attacks with a furious counterassault. Because the Cree and Assiniboine did less damage to the Dakota and the Ojibwe attacks came as a surprise and betrayal, the Dakota vented all their anger on the Ojibwe—with devastating effect. The Ojibwe village at Fond du Lac was abandoned. Some Ojibwe quickly took advantage of the Cree promise to open the Arrowhead region to settlement and established new villages at Lake Vermilion, Grand Portage, and Thunder Bay. These new villages sprang up almost overnight as refugee centers. Once established, the villages remained in Ojibwe hands, even up to the present day.[32]

La Vérendrye got the approval of Beauharnois in Montreal for war against the Dakota. Beauharnois explained to the Indian representatives present with La Vérendrye that "he would avenge the blood of the French whom the Sioux had killed, and that meantime the Indian tribes were free to continue their war with them." The Cree adopted La Vérendrye's son Chevalier in 1737. The French even recruited the Winnebago, who were almost invariably loyal to their Dakota brethren, to join the Ojibwe in an attack on Lake Pepin in May 1737. The war was on.[33]

For ten years the Ojibwe had to retreat because of repeated ferocious Dakota attacks. By the mid-1740s, however, the Ojibwe and their allies made major breakthroughs and put the Dakota on the defensive, systematically dispossessing them from Sandy Lake and Mille Lacs, and over the next decade from Leech Lake and Red Lake. The Cree and Assiniboine vacated the region by then, pushing further west and north.[34]

La Vérendrye was forced to resign in 1744 for his failure to advance French goals in pursuit of the Western Sea. He died five years later. His passing marked the last of the prominent anti-Dakota leaders among the French. His successors were charged with trying to restore trade and peace between the French and the Dakota. The old French trading post at Lake Pepin was rebuilt, and the French were once again giving guns to both sides of indigenous war campaigns. The French didn't last much longer in the Great Lakes, and ceded their territorial claims to the British at the end of the French and Indian War in 1763. They left behind their people and a painful colonial legacy, but the conflict they engineered between the Ojibwe and the Dakota lasted off and on for another hundred years.

APPENDIX 2

Red Lake Reservation Post Offices

IN 1875, RED LAKE ESTABLISHED THE FIRST POST office in Beltrami County, before the county was even formally organized. The construction of a road linking White Earth to Red Lake in 1874 enabled overland mail routes, and Red Lake was a major political and economic hub in its own right, as well as a resource target for white timber speculators. The combination of tribal requests, white land and timber speculation, and the efforts of the Office of Indian Affairs created sufficient demand to open and staff the post office. Laura Pratt was appointed as Red Lake's first postmaster. Allen Jourdain ran the postal route between Red Lake and White Earth, and Stands Alone (Nazhikewigaabaw) was the first mail carrier. In 1882, the post office went through four different postmasters and temporarily closed the office, but aside from that the Red Lake post office has been a model of consistent operation. In 1894, William R. Spears was reappointed postmaster and moved the Red Lake post office to his store. In 1902, a second post office was opened on the reservation at Ponemah. John G. Morrison Jr. was appointed the first postmaster and Joseph C. Roy was contracted to run the first mail route there. A post office was eventually opened at Redby in 1907 and Westley O. Newman was appointed postmaster. Red Lake's first two postmasters were women and around a third of all postmasters at Red Lake have been women. While not a perfect record for gender equity, it certainly was far more progressive than the overall appointment rate for women in the U.S. Postal Service during the same time period across the country.[1]

RED LAKE POSTMASTERS

1875	Laura A. Pratt	1912	Louisa Beaulieu
1878	Adelia A. Allen	1915	John G. Morrison Jr.
1879	Jonathan Taylor	1926	Brete H. Dooley
1881	Clement H. Beaulieu	1928	Frank Gurneau
1882	R. R. Wenworth	1930	Paul H. Beaulieu
1882	Hattie R. Smithies	1930	Mary M. Beaulieu
1882	John H. Wilson	1942	Ella Skime
1882	William R. Spears	1942	Robert E. Lee
1885	J. R. Hollowbrush	1952	Leon "Scotty" McNeal
1886	S. M. Rowell	1953	Roger A. Jourdain
1886	Jeremiah Sheehan	1955	Roman Sigana
1888	Roderick McKenzie	1956	Frank W. Gurno
1892	Ida Rowe	1962	Ralph J. Thunder
1894	William R. Spears	1963	Barbara A. Gurno
1895	John G. Morrison Sr.	1964	Norbert Henry Colhoff
1898	Nathan J. Head	1974	Marion M. Beaulieu
1901	Peter Graves	1989	Beverly M. Bailey
1906	Susan Meley	2003	Paul Mankus
1907	John G. Morrison Jr.	2003	Karen F. Cobenais
1910	A. D. Perry		

PONEMAH POSTMASTERS

1901	John G. Morrison Jr.	1951	Edith Y. Sigana
1902	Margaret Nason	1960	Anna Belle Fast
1905	John G. Morrison Jr.	1961	Evelyn Spears
1907	George C. Davis	1962	Susan L. Spears
1911	Oliver L. Breckner	1978	Carol J. Barrett
1936	Thomas Cain	1999	Tyrone A. Bird
1939	Edward M. Knelman	2001	Joyce M. Brown
1942	Dorothy A. Henry	2008	John E. LeBlanc
1944	Tom C. White	2009	Betsy A. Brugueir
1944	Arthur Unrau	2012	Vivian R. Freeman
1945	Mary A. Spears		

REDBY POSTMASTERS

1907	Westley O. Newman	1945	Datus M. Arnold
1926	John G. Morrison Jr.	1967	Claude Harold Beaulieu
1928	Catherine Bailey	1988	Walter R. Gross
1934	Rose Graves	1988	Floreen Graves
1935	Datus M. Arnold	1991	Bridget Auginaush
1944	Seline Arnold	2014	Babar Bhatti

Red Lake Place-Names

Bagley	Mashkimodaaching
Bagley	Mashkimodaang
Battle River	Gaa-danapananiding
Bemidji	Bemijigamaag
Big Field	Chi-mashkikiwaaning
Big Field	Gaa-mashkosiwikaag
Big Field	Gichi-mashkosing
Big Foot Crossing	Gaa-aazhooshkaad Misaabe
Big Stone	Chi-asini-ziibi
Blackduck	Gaagaashibi-zaaga'igan
Blackduck River	Gaagaashibi-ziibi
Buffalo Lodge Lake	Bizhiki Endaad
Clearbrook	Asinagoojiing
Frog's Bridge	Aazhoogan
Gonvick	Okanibiig
Grand Forks	Gichi-gabekanaang
Gully	Babiikwadinaang
Hay Creek	Mashkode-ziibi
Holthusen Driveway	Gichi-madaabiikana
Island Lake	Gaa-minisikaag
Johnson's Place	Basadinaang
Kelliher	Moozoo-zaaga'igan
Little Rock	Gaa-asiniinsikaag
Mahnomen Creek	Manoomini-ziibi
Mahnomen Creek	Gaa-manoominikaag
Medicine Lake	Mashkiki-zaaga'igan

Miquam Bay . . . . Mikwami-wiikwedong
Miquam Bay . . . . Bagida'wewin
Mosquito Creek . . . . Niminamoowining
Narrows . . . . Gaa-maaboombaashiing
Narrows Point . . . . Agaami-obaashiing
Nebish . . . . Aniibiishiwi-zaaga'igan
Neptune . . . . Omakakiinsing
Pembina . . . . Gaa-aniibiiminikaag
Pickerel Lake . . . . Gwaaba'igan
Ponemah Bay . . . . Wekwaagaam
Ponemah Cliff . . . . Gaa-giishkadinaang
Ponemah Point . . . . Obaashiing
Ponemah Village . . . . Gaa-biisisiniinsikaag
Ponemah Village . . . . Aazhooding
Precipice (by White Sand) . . . . . Negawajiw
Rabbit Point . . . . Waaboozoo-neyaashiing
Red Lake . . . . Miskwaagamiiwi-zaaga'igan
Red Lake Village . . . . Ogaakaan
Red Lake River . . . . Miskwaagamiiwi-ziibi
Red Lake River Outlet . . . . Zaagiing
Red River . . . . Misko-ziibi
Redby . . . . Madaabiimog
Redby Chief's Village . . . . Ondatamaan
Round Lake . . . . Gaa-waawiyegamaag
Sandy River . . . . Metaawangaag
Saum . . . . Oshki-adaawewigamig
Shevlin . . . . Gwaaba'igan
Sisseton . . . . Ogimaa-wajiw
Sucker Creek . . . . Gaa-namebinikaag
Tenstrike . . . . Midaaching Bakite'igaadeg
Thief River . . . . Chi-madaawang
Thief River . . . . Gimoojaki-ziibi
Thief River Falls . . . . Gaa-gimooditagweyaag
Turtle Lake . . . . Mikinaako-zaaga'igan
Warroad . . . . Gabekanaang
West End . . . . Bikwaakwaang
White Sand Dunes . . . . Chi-waasadaawangideg

Red Lake Hereditary Chiefs: Succession Lines

All titles transferred father to son unless otherwise noted in square brackets.[1]

He Who Is Spoken To (Medwe-ganoonind)
Perpetual Wind (Gabe-noodin)
George King (Ogimaawajiweb, or King Coming over the Mountain)
August King (Giniw, or Golden Eagle)
Archie Royce King
George William "Billy" King [son of August King]

♦

Moose Dung (Moozoo-moo)
Red Robed (Meskokonayed)
Red Feather (Miskogwan)
William Sumner
Joseph K. Sumner [son of Red Feather]
George Sumner
Gary Sumner
John Sumner Sr.

♦

Crooked Arm (Gaawashkweniked)
Striped Day (Beshi-giizhig)
Ben Ricebird (Gegiishigwaneb, or Split Feather) [son of Crooked Arm]

Jacob Ricebird

Alvin R. Neadeau [grandson of Jacob Ricebird]

Johnson Loud Sr. [stepson of Ben Ricebird and half-brother of Jacob Ricebird]

James Loud

◆

Nodin Wind (Noodinoons, or Little Wind)

Alfred Wind (Waabizheshiins, or Little Marten) [adopted son of Nodin Wind]

Spencer Whitefeather [acting chief by nomination of Alfred Wind]

James Whitefeather

John Greeting Spears Sr. [son of Alfred Wind]

John Greeting "Gus" Spears Jr.

◆

Sits in Deliberation (Na'etoowab)

John J. Spears [grandson of Sits in Deliberation]

Robert Spears

Leonard Spears

Gerald Spears

◆

Praying Day (Anami'e-giizhig)

Little Frenchman (Wemitigoozhiins)

John Day (Wemitigoozhiiwakamig, or French Land) [son of Praying Day]

John F. Smith (Wiindigoowab, Sitting Windigo) [nephew of John Day]

Sam Smith [son of John F. Smith and grandson of Praying Day]

Henry Sutton [nephew of Sam Smith]

◆

Leading Feather (Niigaanigwaneb)

Last Standing (Gebegaabaw)

William Sayers (Niigaanose) [acting chief by family nomination]

Charles Jourdain [acting chief by family nomination]

George "Sandy" Gillespie [grandson of Last Standing]

Alexander Gillespie

Notes

NOTES TO "BATTLE RIVER"

1. Thomas Stillday Jr. interview (1998); Anna Gibbs interview (2012); White-feather, "Gaa-danapinaniding," 16–19; Warren, *History of the Ojibway People*, 185, 289; Mittelholtz, *Historical Review*, 7, 16. The Battle River fight was not the only major military event between the Ojibwe and the Dakota at Red Lake. There were a number of battles at several other river outlets and village sites, especially at the Sandy River outlet, where even today residents regularly find arrowheads and war club stones.

2. Thomas Stillday Jr. interview (1998); Anna Gibbs interview (2012); Benton-Banai, "Indinawemaaganag"; Warren, *History of the Ojibway People*, 76–94; Benton-Banai, *Mishomis Book*, 74–78. Eugene Stillday claims that the word *Obaas-hiing* is actually a derivation of *ombaasin*, meaning "updraft," because of the wind current across the narrows (interview, April 13, 2015). See also Warren, *History of the Ojibway People*, 185, 289. The oral history of Fannie Johns (September 26, 1909–January 5, 2005) is obtained from Fannie Johns interview with Charles Grolla (April 7, 2004). Her Indian name, Ogimaakwe, is variously translated as Queen, Female Chief, or Boss Lady. She was from the bullhead clan (owaasisii). Johns was raised by her grandmother, Ikwezens (Girl), who lived to be 102 years old and was alive during the time of conflict between the Ojibwe and Dakota at Red Lake.

3. Benton-Banai, "Indinawemaaganag"; Benton-Banai, *Mishomis Book*, 74–78; Mann, *1491*; Josephy, *500 Nations*; Leustig, *500 Nations*.

4. On emergence of the Ojibwe as a distinct people, see Warren, *History of the Ojibway People*; Pinker, *The Language Instinct*; Campbell, *American Indian Languages*; Copway, *Traditional History*; Kohl, *Kitchi-Gami*. Information on the evolution of the Ojibwe language, dialect variance, and its relationship to other Algonquian languages is based on Treuer, *Living Our Language*; Nichols and Nyholm, *Concise Dictionary*; Valentine, *Nishnaabemwin Reference Grammar*; Rhodes, *Eastern Ojibwa-Chippewa-Ottawa Dictionary*; Bloomfield, *Eastern Ojibwa*.

5. The Leech Lake communities of Inger, Ball Club, Bena, and Squaw Lake (who comprised most of what the U.S. government would call the Winnibigoshish Band) speak northern Ojibwe—no use of the suffix *jig* in participle formations, no initial vowel change on long *aa* vowels in participles, and differentiated use of *gaa* in place-names and conjunct tense markers. The Leech Lake communities of Oak Point, Bear Island, Sugar Point, Onigum, and Boy River (who comprised most

of what the U.S. government would call the Pillager and Mississippi bands) have more in common with the dialects of Mille Lacs and St. Croix than they do with the northern communities on the Leech Lake reservation.

When François Dollier de Casson and René de Bréhant de Galinée traveled to Sault Ste. Marie during the winter of 1669-70, they made a telling observation of the skills of Ojibwe fishermen: "The river forms at this place a rapid so teeming with fish, called white fish, or in Algonkin *attikamegue,* that the Indians could easily catch enough to feed 10,000 men. It is true the fishing is so difficult that only Indians can carry it on. No Frenchman has hitherto been able to succeed in it, nor any other Indian than those of this tribe." See "The Journey of Dollier and Galinée, 1669-1670," in Jameson, *Early Narratives,* 207. Ojibwe fishing skills proved to be exceptional, and necessarily so. Everyone else who tried failed. And when the Ojibwe came to Red Lake, failure at fishing, even in the most dangerous circumstances, meant starvation.

6.   The Dakota creation story says that the Dakota were created and placed on the shore of the sacred water. The late Dale Childs from Prairie Island, Minnesota, has shared the Dakota creation story many times, including in a textualized version included in Waziyatawin, *What Does Justice Look Like,* 18-20. In most versions of that story a specific place is not directly mentioned, although Waziyatawin and many other Dakota people believe the sacred body of water referenced in that story was Bdote, at the confluence of the Mississippi and Minnesota Rivers near present-day Fort Snelling. Other locations referenced by Dakota people include Mille Lacs Lake or another lake elsewhere in northern Minnesota. Although the physical location of the creation place of the Dakota is a subject of some internal debate in the Dakota tribal community, nobody questions the fact the Dakota were in Minnesota long before the Ojibwe. Archaeological evidence, oral history, and the direct observations of Dakota, Ojibwe, and French occupants and travelers in Minnesota support that conclusion. But the archaeological and oral records also support the conclusion that the Dakota were not the first occupants of Minnesota's lake country. William Warren reports personally observing the remains of earthen lodges in Mille Lacs County (present-day Kathio State Park) that were customarily built by the A'aninin, or Gros Ventre (Warren, *History of the Ojibway People,* 161, 178-80). The types of lodges occupied definitely fit the precise description of the lodges A'aninin people lived in throughout the period of early contact between that tribe and the French, British, and Americans. The Dakota did not customarily build the same types of dwellings. These observations suggest that the Dakota may have forced out the A'aninin and occupied the A'aninin lodges at Mille Lacs. Other archaeological findings in Minnesota support these conclusions about the presence of A'aninin people in Minnesota antedating the Dakota settlement of the region. See Juneau, "Indian Education"; Parkman, *LaSalle;* Ojakangas and Mastch, *Minnesota's Geology;* Streiff, "Mille Lacs Kathio"; Lloyd A. Wilford, "Field Diary and Notes," unpublished manuscript, 1933, Minnesota Historical Society; Wilford, "Prehistoric Indians of Minnesota"; Wilford, "Revised Classification"; Gibbon and Caine, "Middle to Late Woodland Transition"; Gold, "Archaeological

Investigations at Petaga Point"; Hennepin, *Description of Louisiana;* Hiller, "Reminiscences"; Johnson, "Cultural Resource Survey"; "Kathio State Park Archaeology"; Mather, "Archaeological Overview"; Bleed, "Archaeology of Petaga Point"; Brower, *Memoirs;* Buffalohead and Buffalohead, *Against the Tide;* Cooper, "Archaeological Survey."

The linguistic connections between the Cheyenne (Algonquian language family) and Ojibwe and the likely migration route of the Cheyenne make it probable that they occupied Minnesota before or contemporaneously with the A'aninin.

7.   The connections between these names and their Ojibwe counterparts (Zaagiing and Gaa-danapananiding) are obvious to speakers or those who peruse Ojibwe dictionaries. For reference and further reading, see Nichols and Nyholm, *Concise Dictionary;* Vogel, *Indian Names;* Cutler, *Brave New Words;* Upham, *Minnesota Geographic Names; The Ojibwe People's Dictionary,* http://ojibwe.lib.umn.edu/. Thomas Stillday Jr. interview (2003); Mittelholtz, *Historical Review,* 15. The earliest written cartography of Red Lake as Red Lake appears in the form of a 1737 French map, which charts the place as Lac Rouge (Red Lake). Jean-Baptiste de La Vérendrye observed Dakota people living at Red Lake in 1734. See Lawrence J. Burpee, *Journals and Letters,* 210. These references suggest that the Dakota, Ojibwe, and French all referred to the lake as Red Lake long before the Battle River fight, when the Dakota still occupied all of Upper and Lower Red Lake. From that we can deduce that the common story about how Red Lake got its name gave the words "red lake" new meaning rather than its formal name in Ojibwe (or any other language). See also Kavanaugh, *La Vérendrye;* Crouse, *La Vérendrye;* and Combet, *In Search of the Western Seas.* The Vérendrye maps and 1755 French map also refer to the lake as Red Lake.

NOTES TO CHAPTER 1: THE SPARK

1.   Opening quote, Warren, *History of the Ojibway People,* 356. The primary sources on White Thunderbird throughout this chapter are Whitefeather, "Waabibines," and Anna Gibbs interview (2001). The U.S. government called the band the Red Lake Band of Chippewa Indians. Although the Ojibwe called themselves *anishinaabe* (meaning "the people") or *Ojibwe* (a term used to refer specifically to the Ojibwe people rather than to all Indians), the French mispronounced and variously wrote the word *Ojibwe* as Ojibway, Ojibwe, Jibwa, Chipwa, Chippewa, and the morphed word stuck. The formal name the U.S. government wrote into treaties with Red Lake was *Chippewa.* The word was never repudiated by Peter Graves, Roger Jourdain, or other Red Lake leaders in the 1900s because they all spoke Ojibwe and it seemed natural to them that English-speaking people (such as those in the U.S. government) would have a different word for Ojibwe people. Graves, Jourdain, and others used English when speaking to outsiders, so they used Chippewa when talking to them. Today, tribal leaders and educators have been teaching others to use tribal words of self-reference, and *Ojibwe* and *anishinaabe* are winning out in the terminology discussion. Mittelholtz, *Historical Review,* 10; Warren, *History of the Ojibway People,* 356–67. Jean Baptiste Cadotte Jr. came to

Red Lake in 1796 and left a member of his party behind. In 1852, Red Lake chief Feathers in Different Directions (Wewanjigwan) told William W. Warren that the Dakota never mustered sufficient strength to challenge Ojibwe control of Red Lake afterward. The 1807 Meriwether Lewis map shows Red Lake and Thief River Falls as Ojibwe territory. The map and Warren references help validate the timeline for Ojibwe control of Red Lake.

2.   Keating, *Narrative,* 2:169. See also Hilger, *Chippewa Child Life,* 34.

3.   Mittelholtz, *Historical Review,* 135.

4.   Ona Kingbird interview (1993). Ona Kingbird said that her maternal grandmother was a full-blooded Cree woman. Language was learned most actively on the maternal side, and even in the late twentieth century, Kingbird said that her Ojibwe had a few Cree influences.

5.   James Lileks, "My Minnesota: Artist Proud of Red Lake Nation Flag Design," *Minneapolis Star Tribune,* November 30, 2013; Brill, *Red Lake Nation,* 9; *Medwe-ganoonind Times* 1.2 (March 23, 2004): 1.

6.   James, *Narrative;* Kohl, *Kitchi-Gami;* Warren, *History of the Ojibway People,* 35, 42, 50–52, 87, 141–53; Copway, *Traditional History,* 140–50; Copway, *Life, Letters;* Benton-Banai, *Mishomis Book,* 74–78.

7.   In fact, it has been so long since the clan system disintegrated among the Dakota that some Dakota doubt that they ever had a clan system. But early European contact records and Dakota oral history affirm that they did. Daniel Seaboy interview (1999).

8.   Whitefeather, "Waabi-bines"; Archie Mosay interview (1992); Vernon Whitefeather interview with David Treuer (1995); Warren, *History of the Ojibway People,* 165.

9.   James, *Tanner Narrative;* Kohl, *Kitchi-Gami;* Warren, *History of the Ojibway People,* 35, 42 50–52, 87, 141–53; Copway, *Traditional History,* 140–50; Copway, *Life, Letters;* Benton-Banai, *Mishomis Book,* 74–78. Thomas Stillday Jr. interview (1996); Anna Gibbs interview (1994); Archie Mosay interviews (1992, 1994). The word *doodem* comes from the morpheme *de,* meaning "heart or center." The relationship between the words *ode'* (his heart), *oodena* (village), *doodem* (clan), and *dewe'igan* (drum) has caused considerable confusion among some scholars, who have claimed that one of these words was derived from another when in fact they simply share the same root morpheme *de.* The heart is the center of the body (*ode'*). The village is the center of the community (*oodena*). The clan is the center of spiritual identity (*doodem*). The drum is the center of the nation, or its heartbeat. The drum is put in the center of the dance area for most Ojibwe ceremonies, and dancers move clockwise around it in recognition of this understanding. Although *de* means "heart or center," *we* pertains to sound, giving the word for drum the compound meaning of "heartbeat." The English word *totem* is derived from the Ojibwe word *doodem,* or clan. The word *doodem* is given in its independent form. However, it is more commonly used in its dependent (possessed) forms *indoodem* (my clan), *gidoodem* (your clan), the obviative *odoodeman* (his or her clan), and other dependent forms. This helps explain the variety of divergent spellings found

in missionary and fur trader references. The variety of spellings for clan in Ojibwe is the result not just of different orthographies, but also of the different forms of the noun. Although understanding the morphological composition of clan as the center of spiritual identity seems the most widely held view with the elders I interviewed, it is still possible that that clan (*doodem*) and village (*oodena*) share both a cultural and a linguistic root. Certain clans did dominate certain villages to the point where those villages were identified by their totemic assignations. Over time the difference in the concept of clan and village could have conflated in some areas. Nicolas Perrot and Ruth Landes refer to use of a clan symbol as a symbol for the entire village. It is still possible that those symbols were being used to represent the chiefs of the village, who spoke for everyone, rather than to ascribe them to everyone living there. See Blair, *Indian Tribes*, 1:37, 62, 347; Landes, *Ojibwa Sociology*, 31.

According to Edward Benton-Banai, the deer clan (waawaashkeshi) was, according to legend, completely exterminated for having violated the taboo about marriage. William W. Warren relates a similar story, although he claims it was the moose clan (mooz) that was wiped out. If there were married couples and families in a village, there had to be at least two clans in the village, and typically five or more.

10.   Archie Mosay interview (1992); Thomas Stillday Jr. interview (1995); Anna Gibbs interview (1995); Edward Benton-Banai interview (1989); Mary Roberts interview (1990); Nancy Jones interview (1994); William (Billy) Daniels interview (2006); Warren, *History of the Ojibway People*, 41–53; Keesing, *Kin Groups*, 60; Radcliffe-Brown, *Structure and Function*, 117; Schenck, *Voice of the Crane*, 29; Hickerson, *Southwestern Chippewa*, 88; Bishop, *Northern Ojibwa*, 343; Cleland, *Rites of Conquest*. The eagle is still the adopting clan today in Red Lake and most surrounding communities. In some first nations of northwestern Ontario, the marten clan (waabizheshi) is the adopting clan for children with a nonnative father. In some other communities of Ontario, the adopting clan is determined at a *jiisakaan* (shake tent), where the practitioner divines the adopting clan, which can vary for each individual. At Red Lake and most other places in Ojibwe country, the patrilineal structure of clan inheritance is never altered with the introduction of a non-Indian father. Warren cites five original clans (*History of the Ojibway People*, 44); Benton-Banai cites seven (*Mishomis Book*, 74). Some Ojibwe and Oji-Cree villages in northern Ontario saw successive waves of missionaries who spoke tribal languages and achieved high conversion rates, nearing 100 percent in some places. As a result, the importance of clan became devalued and was eventually forgotten. In Bearskin Lake, Ontario, for example, fluency rates remain near 100 percent even today, but the clan system is virtually nonexistent. The very meaning of the word *doodem* has changed at Bearskin Lake as well. Instead of "clan," or literally, "spiritual heart or center," *doodem* means simply "friend" (Thomas Beardy interview, 1992). My conversation with Beardy about *doodem* began as I observed his Ojibwe-language class at Lakehead University in Thunder Bay, Ontario, in June 1992. He had written on the blackboard, "Awenen gidoodem?" He asked what that meant, so I replied, "Who is your clan?" He responded, "'Who is your clan?' No.

What is 'clan'? That means 'Who is your friend?'" Not only had the word changed, but the concept of clan had been erased from the collective memory of his community. Beardy showed no shame or offense during our conversation. For him, the concept of clan and the meaning of the word *doodem* were simply different in his part of Ojibwe country. This helps explain why John Long, who stayed at Nipigon, Ontario, from 1777 to 1779, believed that *doodem* meant "friend" or "animal friend," rather than "clan" or "spiritual heart or center." See Quaife, *John Long's Voyages,* 110–12. Long's writings were initially published in 1791. The dynamic of religious and cultural change came early for some of the eastern Ojibwe communities, and it did not necessarily follow language loss.

11.   Thomas Stillday Jr. interviews (1995, 1998); Anna Gibbs interviews (1995, 2000); Eugene Stillday interview (2006); Lawrence Henry interviews (1990, 1994); Mary Roberts interview (1991); Melvin Eagle interview (2000); Archie Mosay interview (1992); Edward Benton-Banai interview (1989); Warren, *History of the Ojibway People,* 41–53, 87–88; Benton-Banai, *Mishomis Book,* 74–78.

12.   Copway, *Traditional History,* 140; Doty, "Northern Wisconsin in 1820," 197. Extract from Schoolcraft, *Narrative Journal,* now widely available in many reprinted forms. For reference and citation, I used the reprint, which has numbered pages, rather than the formal report to John C. Calhoun in 1821. For this quote, which is from Charles Christopher Trowbridge and is included with Schoolcraft's journal in the Calhoun report, see Williams, *Schoolcraft's Narrative Journal,* 486.

13.   Thomas Stillday Jr. interviews (1995, 1998); Anna Gibbs interviews (1995, 2000); Eugene Stillday interview (2006); Lawrence Henry interviews (1990, 1994); Mary Roberts interview (1991); Melvin Eagle interview (2000); Archie Mosay interview (1992); Edward Benton-Banai interview (1989); Warren, *History of the Ojibwe People,* 41–53, 87–88; Benton-Banai, *Mishomis Book,* 74–78.

14.   Referring to sturgeon, *name* is pronounced nah-may.

15.   Copway, *Traditional History,* 144; Mason, *Schoolcraft's Expedition,* xvi, 59; Warren, *History of the Ojibway People,* 36; Baraga, *Chippewa Indians,* 9; Thwaites, *Jesuit Relations,* 15:157; Kohl, *Kitchi-Gami,* 270; Danziger, *Chippewas of Lake Superior,* 23; Howard, *Plains-Ojibwa,* 7:74; Buck, *Indian Outbreaks,* 19. Leadership— *ogimaawiwin*—literally means to be "esteemed" or "held to high principle," from the morpheme *ogi,* meaning "high," found in other Ojibwe words such as *ogichidaa* (warrior), *ogidakamig* (on top of the earth), and *ogidaaki* (hilltop).

16.   See Black-Rogers, "Dan Raincloud." The cliff behind the White Sand Dunes is called the Precipice (Negawajiw).

17.   Thomas Stillday Jr. interview (1996).

18.   McKenney, *Sketches,* 315–16.

19.   Bray, *Nicollet Journals,* 155; Warren, *History of the Ojibway People;* Susan Jackson interview (1996); Hilger, *Chippewa Child Life,* 39–55. Names had spiritual power and gave direction and meaning to one's life. They were acquired by either fasting or dreaming. The name giver and the name receiver both used the word *niiyawe'enh* (my namesake) to refer to each other. *Niiyaw* (my body) carries the

critical meaning in the word. When someone gave a name, the name giver took part of his or her spiritual essence and put it into the body of the name recipient. They became spiritually related for life. The name giver then functioned much like a godparent in Christian tradition.

20.   Thomas Stillday Jr. interview (1996); Anna Gibbs interview (1996); Mary Roberts interviews (1989, 1991). Male leaders were called *ogimaa*, female leaders, *ogimaakwe*.

21.   Child, *Holding Our World Together*; Child, *My Grandfather's Knocking Sticks*.

22.   Kohl, *Kitchi-Gami*, 111; Baraga, *Chippewa Indians*, 45; Parker, *Carver Journals*, 106-7; Thomas Stillday Jr. interview (1996).

23.   Pond, *The Dakota*, 124, 140-41; Mittelholtz, *Historical Review*, 136; Bray, *Nicollet Journals*, 165. Forever Queen (Gaagige-ogimaansikwe) of the Pembina Band had a formal political position and even signed the Pembina Band Treaty in 1878. Men who functioned as women were called *ikwekaazo*, meaning "one who endeavors to be like a woman." Women who functioned as men were called *ininiikaazo*, meaning "one who endeavors to be like a man." *Ikwekaazo* and *ininiikaazo* had significant influence in politics. Earl Otchingwanigan (Nyholm) interview (1992); Archie Mosay interview (1993); Williams, *The Spirit and the Flesh*, 67-68, 110, 167-68; Henry and Thompson, *New Light*, 1:163-65; Kellogg, *Early Narratives*, 221-81; Kinietz, *Chippewa Village*, 155; Grant, "Saulteux Indians," 2:357; McKenney, *Sketches*, 315-16; Catlin, *Letters and Notes*, 2:214-15; Pond, *The Dakota*, 124; Thwaites, *Jesuit Relations*, 59:129, 185-211, 310; Folwell, *History of Minnesota*, 1:18-20; James, *Tanner Narrative*, 105-6; Kugel, *To Be the Main Leaders*, 71-73, 92n.

24.   Kappler, *Laws and Treaties*, 2:482-86, 567-71, 648-52, 685-90, 839-42, 853-55, 862-65, 974-76; Tanner, *Atlas*, 156; Blegen, *Minnesota*, 171-73; Folwell, *History of Minnesota*, 1:320-21.

25.   Smith, *Leadership among the Southwestern Ojibwa*, 7:11.

26.   Copway, *Traditional History*, 144.

27.   Paul LeJeune in Thwaites, *Jesuit Relations*, 6:243. See also Thwaites, *Jesuit Relations*, 38:265; Warren, *History of the Ojibway People*, 127-28, 319; Copway, *Traditional History*; James, *Tanner Narrative*, 313-16; Stout, "Ethnohistorical Report" 97. Treaty Council Minutes of 1837, National Archives, Washington, DC, microfilm 234, p. 12; Mason, *Schoolcraft's Expedition*, 207; Diedrich, *The Chiefs Hole-in-the-Day*, 6, 10; Schoolcraft Papers, Reel 4, 1827, Library of Congress; Birk, *John Sayer Journal*, 46; Thomas L. McKenney, *Sketches*, 315-16.

28.   Jameson, *Winter Studies*, 136; Kohl, *Kitchi-Gami*, 66.

29.   Thwaites, *Jesuit Relations*, 6:243, 20:155, 66:221; Blair, *Indian Tribes*, 1:145, 264.

30.   Pond, *The Dakota*, 60; Robinson, *History of the Dakota*, 111; Schulenberg, *Indians of North Dakota*, 43; Folwell, *History of Minnesota*, 1:86.

31.   Bray, *Nicollet Journals*, 199-211; Warren, *History of the Ojibway People*, 264; Densmore, *Chippewa Customs*, 87-89; Pond, *The Dakota*, 70, 93-96; Parker, *Carver Journals*, 108-10; Baraga, *Chippewa Indians*, 24; Gilman, Gilman, and Stultz, *Red*

River Trails, 46; White, *The Middle Ground,* 76-77, 151; Howard, *Plains-Ojibwa,* 82; Wheeler-Voeglin, "Anthropological Report," 67; Mason, *Schoolcraft's Expedition,* 55; Evangelical Society of Missions of Lausanne, "Report of June 11, 1835: The Mission of Canada," 118-19, Grace Lee Nute Papers, Minnesota Historical Society; William W. Warren to Alexander Ramsey, August 28, 1850, R 5, Alexander Ramsey Papers, Minnesota Historical Society.

32.   Baraga, *Chippewa Indians,* 24; Densmore, *Chippewa Customs,* 132; Johnston, *Ojibway Ceremonies,* 59-60; Pond, *The Dakota,* 61, 69-70; Mason, *Schoolcraft's Expedition,* xvi, 55; Kohl, *Kitchi-Gami,* 67, 272; Warren, *History of the Ojibway People,* 264; Danziger, *Chippewas of Lake Superior,* 23-24, 37, 73; Bray, *Nicollet Journals,* 154, 168, 277; Diedrich, *The Chiefs Hole-in-the-Day,* 2; Lund, *Chief Flat Mouth,* 19; Howard, *Plains-Ojibwa,* 81; Kellogg, *French Regime,* 125; Thwaites, *Jesuit Relations,* 47:223; James, *Tanner Narrative,* 113.

33.   Catlin, *Letters and Notes,* 1:238-40; Warren, *History of the Ojibway People,* 139, 264, 313; Densmore, *Chippewa Customs,* 135; Featherstonhaugh, *Canoe Voyage,* 1:362-63; Johnston, *Ojibway Ceremonies,* 75-76; Danziger, *Chippewas of Lake Superior,* 24-25; Lewis, *Valley of the Mississippi,* 173-75; Pond, *The Dakota,* 130-31, 133; Sibley, "Memoir of Jean Nicollet," 223, 224; Howard, *Plains-Ojibwa,* 104; Eastman, *Dahcotah,* xx; Thwaites, *Jesuit Relations,* 47:223; Boutwell, "Schoolcraft's Exploring Tour," 1:130-31; Milner, "Warfare in Eastern North America," 105-51; Strezewski, "Patterns of Interpersonal Violence," 249-80; Catlin, *Letters and Notes,* 1:245-46; Mason, *Schoolcraft's Expedition,* xvi, 253; Williams, *Schoolcraft's Narrative Journal,* 202-3; Kellogg, *Early Narratives,* 155; Bray, *Nicollet Journals,* 275; Thomas Stillday Jr. interview (1994); Anna Gibbs interview (1994); Kohl, *Kitchi-Gami,* 67, 170.

34.   Henry, *Travels and Adventures,* 203-4. This quote appears on page 195 of the repaginated reprint. Bray, *Nicollet Journals,* 180; Wahlberg, *The North Land,* 29.

35.   Warren, *History of the Ojibway People,* 106-7, 171-72, 219-20, 267-69; Kohl, *Kitchi-Gami,* 271-72; Robinson, *History of the Dakota,* 65; Zapffe, *Indian Days,* 116-17; Keesing, *Menomini Indians,* 102; James, *Tanner Narrative,* 72; Hickerson, "Chippewa of Lake Superior," 48; Schulenberg, *Indians of North Dakota,* 47.

36.   Ewers, "Ethnological Report," 40; Robinson, *History of the Dakota,* 28; Hurt, "Dakota Sioux Indians," 101; David Thompson quoting a Red Lake chief in 1798 cited in Howard, *Plains-Ojibwa,* 7:16.

37.   *To Walk the Red Road,* 86; *We Choose to Remember,* 50.

38.   James, *Tanner Narrative,* 142; Howard, *Plains-Ojibwa,* 18.

39.   George Anthony Belcourt as cited in Indian Claims Commission, "Findings on the Chippewa," 116; Kane, Holmquist, and Gilman, *Northern Expeditions,* 182; Mason, *Schoolcraft's Expedition,* 244; Howard, *Plains-Ojibwa,* 14, 17-19; Ewers, "Ethnological Report," 35; Mittelholtz, *Historical Review,* 16; Schulenberg, *Indians of North Dakota,* 13. The word *pembina* is corrupted from the Ojibwe word *aniibiiminan,* meaning highbush cranberries, of which there was a great abundance near the village. The Ojibwe name for the place was Gaa-aniibiiminikaag, or "the place where there are a lot of highbush cranberries."

40. Ewers, "Ethnological Report," 34; Howard, *Plains-Ojibwa*, 17; Mason, *Schoolcraft's Expedition*, 357.

41. Ewers, "Ethnological Report," 43; Indian Claims Commission, "Findings on the Chippewa," 107, 462; Howard, *Plains-Ojibwa*, 18; James, *Tanner Narrative*, 141, 197.

42. Hickerson, *Chippewa and Their Neighbors*, 71, 95; Diedrich, *Famous Chiefs*, 29; Ewers, "Ethnological Report," 61–62; Mittelholtz, *Historical Review*, 19, 133, 136; Indian Claims Commission, "Findings on the Chippewa," 117, 446–64; Sharrock and Sharrock, "History of the Cree," 297; Danziger, *Chippewas of Lake Superior*, 8, 220n; Howard, *Plains-Ojibwa*, 21; Goiffon, "Autobiography: 1824–25," translated by Charlotte Huot, unpublished manuscript, 67, Grace Lee Nute Papers, Minnesota Historical Society.

43. Nute, *Documents*, 303, 308, 310, 328, 371; Keating, *Narrative*, 2:149; Kane, Holmquist, and Gilman, *Northern Expeditions*; Mittelholtz, *Historical Review*, 10, 17; Mason, *Schoolcraft's Expedition*, 18, 326; Gilman, Gilman, and Stultz, *Red River Trails*, 9.

44. Howard, *Plains-Ojibwa*, 21–22; Catlin, *Letters and Notes*, 1:53, 57–58, 262–63; Ewers, "Ethnological Report," 53, 56–57; Sharrock and Sharrock, "History of the Cree," 269; Mittelholtz, *Historical Review*, 133; Indian Claims Commission, "Findings on the Chippewa," 113.

45. Indian Claims Commission, "Findings on the Chippewa," 113.

46. Mittelholtz, *Historical Review*, 130; *Treaty with the Pillager Band of Chippewa Indians, 1847* (August 21, 1847); Kappler, *Laws and Treaties*, 2:567–69; for further analysis of the treaty, see Tanner, *Atlas*, 156; Blegen, *Minnesota*, 171–73; Folwell, *History of Minnesota*, 1:320–21; Gilman, Gilman, and Stultz, *Red River Trails*, 40.

47. Norton, *Catholic Missionary Activities*.

48. Nute, *Documents*, 175; Gilman, Gilman, and Stultz, *Red River Trails*, 34; Folwell, *History of Minnesota*, 1:213; Kellogg, *British Regime*, 296. In 1811, the Earl of Selkirk (a Scottish philanthropist and utopian idealist) purchased a controlling interest in the Hudson's Bay Company. The company purchased settlement rights to a 116,000 square-mile stretch of land encompassing most of Manitoba, part of North Dakota, and a sliver of Minnesota, including Pembina. No Indian agreed to this land cession and neither did the U.S. government. The international border between the United States and Canada had not yet been surveyed.

49. Folwell, *History of Minnesota*, 1:214.

50. Alfred Brunson to Missionary Society of the Methodist Episcopal Church, "The North Red River Settlement," September 15, 1837, 1, Grace Lee Nute Papers, Minnesota Historical Society; Brunson, "Upper Mississippi Missions"; John Fritzen, "History of Fond du Lac and Jay Cooke State Park," unpublished manuscript, 1964, 3, Minnesota Historical Society; Goiffon, "Autobiography," 41–42; Williams, *Schoolcraft's Narrative Journal*, 139; Grace Lee Nute, "Missionaries among the Indians of the Northwest," *Hamline Radio Hour* 28 (November 27, 1928), Minnesota Historical Society; Tanner, "History of Fort Ripley," 10:191; Meyer, *History of the Santee Sioux*, 69; Dickason, *Canada's First Nations*, 265.

51.	Vandersluis, *History of Beltrami County*, 2.

52.	Mittelholtz, *Historical Review*, 19.

53.	Vandersluis, *History of Beltrami County*, 2; Mittelholtz, *Historical Review*, 16.

54.	Warren, *History of the Ojibway People*, 289. In addition to being a significant informant for Warren, Feathers in Different Directions met Schoolcraft in 1832.

55.	Vandersluis, *History of Beltrami County*, 2; Mittelholtz, *Historical Review*, 22.

56.	Vandersluis, *History of Beltrami County*, 6; Mittelholtz, *Historical Review*, 17.

57.	Commissioner of Indian Affairs, *Reports*, 1850: 58. See also Roger Jourdain, "Early History of Red Lake Reservation," 2, 3, undated historical sketch, submitted to Red Lake Tribal Council, January 31, 1985, Red Lake Archives; Vandersluis, *History of Beltrami County*, 6; Mittelholtz, *Historical Review*, 17, 18. The Commissioner of Indian Affairs report further elaborated on fields of winter wheat cultivated by the Red Lake Indians and a substantial agricultural effort under way. S. T. Bardwell to American Missionary Association, May 31, 1851, included with Commissioner of Indian Affairs, *Reports*, 1851: 88.

58.	Mittelholtz, *Historical Review*, 21; Commissioner of Indian Affairs, *Reports*, 1869: 38; Jourdain, "Early History of Red Lake Reservation," 5; Brill, *Red Lake Nation*, 21.

59.	Mittelholtz, *Historical Review*, 17, 19, 21, 135; Wub-e-ke-niew, *We Have the Right*, 41.

60.	Warren, *History of the Ojibway People*, 356-57; Mittelholtz, *Historical Review*, 11; *To Walk the Red Road*, 8-9; Wub-e-ke-niew, *We Have the Right*, xvii-xix. Warren suggests 1810 as the date for this battle, but Dan Needham Sr., Red Lake hereditary chief and grandson of Sun Shining Through, confirms the participation of his grandfather as a leader in that battle. Sun Shining Through died in 1902, advanced in years. His birth date is not known, but was around 1810. The late 1820s would be the earliest he could have led such a battle.

61.	*To Walk the Red Road*, 8-9; "Chippewa Indians in Minnesota," 51st Congress, 1st Session, House Exec. Doc., Serial 2747, Exec. Doc. 247.

62.	Fruth, *Century of Missionary Work*, 20; *To Walk the Red Road*, 8-9; "Chippewa Indians in Minnesota," 51st Congress, 1st Session.

NOTES TO CHAPTER 2: THE STRATEGIST

1.	Opening quote, "Articles of a Treaty Made and Concluded at the Old Crossing of the Red Lake River," 39, 36th Congress, 1st Session, Senate Exec. Doc. Hereafter, "Articles of a Treaty."

2.	http://sites.mnhs.org/historic-sites/alexander-ramsey-house/history.

3.	Major Edwin Clark, letter to the editor, *Minneapolis Journal*, December 4, 1916; Smith, *Leadership among the Southwestern Ojibwa*, 7:21; Diedrich, *The Chiefs Hole-in-the-Day*, 32.

4.	The original Red Lake chief Little Rock, for whom the village is named, was chief in the early 1800s. It is probable that Sitting Rock was actually his son, and used his father's name to validate his own hereditary right to chieftainship.

5.   George Bonga to Henry Whipple, August 12, 1866, box 4, Whipple Papers, Minnesota Historical Society; Henry Bartling to R. B. Van Valkenburgh, Acting Commissioner of Indian Affairs, October 12, 1865, National Archives Microfilm Publication, RG 75, microfilm 234, roll 154, p. 131; James Harlan to Dennis N. Cooley, October 26, 1865, National Archives Microfilm Publication, RG 75, microfilm 234, roll 154, p. 223.

6.   At Peguis, a ninety-year-old chief encouraged an attack on the Dakota refugee villages on the Red River, but there were no serious military campaigns. See Dickason, *Canada's First Nations*, 266; Schultz, *Over the Earth I Come*, 268, 270; Fannie Johns interview with Charles Grolla (April 7, 2004); Meyer, *White Earth Tragedy*, 240; Howard, *Plains-Ojibwa*, 7:22.

7.   Archie Mosay interviews (1992, 1994); Melvin Eagle interview (1995); Vennum, *Ojibwa Dance Drum*. The Ojibwe and Dakota had a long history of cultural exchange. The Ojibwe gave the Dakota the medicine dance, which the Dakota called the wakan dance. It proliferated and dominated Dakota religious experience in Minnesota for at least a hundred years. See Treuer, *Ojibwe in Minnesota*, 20, 89n15; Pond, *The Dakota*, 86–99, 110–11, 159–61.

8.   Adam Lussier interview (1993); Adam Lussier, "The Legend of the Drum," unpublished story, 1990, Red Lake Archives.

9.   Commissioner of Indian Affairs, Annual Report, 1863, 449; Folwell, *History of Minnesota*; Meyer, *White Earth Tragedy*; Wilson, *Remember This*; Wilson, *Footsteps of Our Ancestors*; Meyer, *History of the Santee Sioux*; Schultz, *Over the Earth I Come*, 28; Gibson, *The American Indian*; Radin, *The Winnebago Tribe*.

10.   Whipple, *Lights and Shadows*, 29; Tanner, *Fifty Years*, 299–301, 511–15.

11.   Mittelholtz, *Historical Review*, 130, 133.

12.   Kappler, *Laws and Treaties*, 1:851–54, 2:482–93; Folwell, *History of Minnesota*, 4:190; Tanner, *Atlas*, 156; Royce, *Indian Land Cessions*, 802, 804, 828, 840, 844; Winchell, *Aborigines of Minnesota*, 2:619–31; Office of Indian Affairs, *Reports*, 1863: 328–31, 341–46, 1867: 397, 1868: 301, 1870: 305, 1871: 588, 1872: 209, 210, 1874: 195, 1875: 53, 298, 1876: 84, 1878: 78, 81, 1880: 103–5, 1884: 103, 1885: 114–16, 1886: 168–70; Nichols, *Lincoln and the Indians*, 72–74.

13.   *Treaty with the Pillager Band of Chippewa Indians, 1847* (August 21, 1847); Kappler, *Laws and Treaties*, 2:567–71, 648–51, 685–90, 853–55, 861–62; Tanner, *Atlas*, 156; Blegen, *Minnesota*, 171–73; Folwell, *History of Minnesota*, 1:320–21, 4:190–91, 305–7; *Treaty with the Chippewa Indians, 1854* (September 30, 1854); *Treaty with the Chippewa Indians, 1855* (February 22, 1855); David Herriman to Willis Gorman, May 29, 1854, enclosed with Willis Gorman to Commissioner of Indian Affairs, June 5, 1854, M1101, National Archives Microfilm Publications, microfilm 234, roll 150; *Galena Daily Advertiser*, March 20, 1855; *Weekly Minnesotan*, October 21, 1854; *Minnesota Democrat*, October 18, 1854; *St. Anthony Falls Minnesota Republican*, October 19, 1854; *Washington Evening Star*, February 17, 1855; *Minnesota Weekly Times*, January 17, 1855; Kvasnicka, "From Wilderness to Washington," 56–57; Dunn, *The St. Croix*, 21–22; *Treaty with the Chippewa of the Mississippi and Lake Superior*, August 2, 1847 (9 Stat. 904, Ratified April 3, 1848,

Proclaimed April 7, 1848), in Kappler, *Laws and Treaties,* 2:567-69; Henry Dodge to William Medill, October 8, 1846, included in Commissioner of Indian Affairs, *Reports,* 1846. See also Jourdain, "Early History of Red Lake Reservation"; Schultz, *Over the Earth I Come,* 279; Ewers, "Ethnological Report," 160; *Treaty with the Chippewa—Red Lake and Pembina Bands, 1863* (October 2, 1863).

14.   Josephy, *500 Nations,* 374-79.

15.   Thwaites, *Jesuit Relations,* 6:243, 20:155, 66:221; Flat Mouth to Commissioner, National Archives, Commissioner of Indian Affairs, Letters Received, microfilm roll 234, p. 387; Blair, *Indian Tribes,* 1:264; Kugel, *To Be the Main Leaders;* Joseph A. Wheelock editorial, *St. Paul Daily Press* (October 15, 1863); Mittelholtz, *Historical Review,* 22; Major C. P. Adams to Lieutenant D. Scott, December 4, 1865, Moses N. Adams Papers, Minnesota Historical Society.

16.   Official records, including the original treaty, correspondence of Alexander Ramsey, treaty commissioner, and William P. Dole, commissioner of Indian Affairs, and the Journal of Proceedings for the treaty are all archived as "Articles of a Treaty Made and Concluded at the Old Crossing of the Red Lake River," 36th Congress, 1st Session, Senate Exec. Doc. See also *Treaty with the Chippewa—Red Lake and Pembina Bands, 1863* (October 2, 1863); Kappler, *Laws and Treaties,* 2:853-55, 861-62. See also Blegen, *Minnesota,* 172; Robinson, *Early Economic Conditions,* 3:63, 85, 115; 49th Congress, 2nd Session, Senate Exec. Doc. 115 (Serial 2449): 53.

17.   "Articles of a Treaty," 8.

18.   "Articles of a Treaty," 9.

19.   "Articles of a Treaty," 11, 12.

20.   Hole-in-the-Day to President Abraham Lincoln, June 7, 1863, 38th Congress, 1st Session, House Documents, 1863-64, Serial 1182, 3:448-51.

21.   "Articles of a Treaty," 13, 14.

22.   "Articles of a Treaty," 22.

23.   "Articles of a Treaty," 29.

24.   Henry B. Whipple Diary, January 13, 1862, Whipple Papers, Minnesota Historical Society.

25.   Nichols, "Translation of Key Phrases," 514-24. Nichols's arguments are well substantiated in other places, including Van Antwerp, "Negotiations for the Chippewa Treaty"; Satz, *Chippewa Treaty Rights,* 131-53; Auger and Beardy, *Glossary of Legal Terms.*

26.   "Articles of a Treaty," 18-30.

27.   "Articles of a Treaty," 32, 35.

28.   "Articles of a Treaty," 21.

29.   "Articles of a Treaty," 39.

30.   Wub-e-ke-niew [Francis Blake], *We Have the Right,* xix.

31.   "Articles of a Treaty," 5, 45.

32.   Henry B. Whipple as cited in Hawkinson, "The Old Crossing Chippewa Treaty," 298-99.

33.   Whipple, *Lights and Shadows,* 74, 143; *Grand Forks Herald,* September 25, 1988; "Red Lake History: The Beginning," *Red Lake Nation News* (http://www.rlnn.org/MajorSponsors/HistoryProjectBeginning.html).

34.   Beaulieu genealogy in this and the following paragraph taken from Ransom Judd Powell Papers, Genealogy Microfilm 455, Family 93, Minnesota Historical Society; U.S. Census listing for Paul H. Beaulieu (1940); U.S. Indian Census Roll for Paul H. Beaulieu (1885–1940); John Clement Beaulieu and Bernadeen Kirt, "Beaulieu Family Genealogy," undated manuscript, Anton Treuer Papers, Red Lake Archives.

35.   Whipple, *Lights and Shadows,* 143–45; Henry B. Whipple to Joel Bassett, November 14, 1866, Joel Bassett Papers, Minnesota Historical Society.

36.   David Thorstad, "The Sad Legacy of Moose Dung and Red Robe," *Monthly Review* (September 11, 2012), http://mrzine.monthlyreview.org/2012/thorstad 091112.html.

37.   Borgerding, "Father Thomas' History," 1.

NOTES TO CHAPTER 3: THE NATION BUILDER

1.   Opening quote: Hawkinson, "The Old Crossing Chippewa Treaty." Bad Day and Frank English depositions (August 21, 1930), Court of Claims Doc. H-76, p. 13–15, 135, Peter Graves Papers, Red Lake Archives; Borgerding, "Red Lake St. Mary's Mission."

2.   "Chippewa Indians in Minnesota," House Exec. Doc., 51st Congress, 1st Session, Serial 2747, Exec. Doc. 247:133–34; "1890s Reports Describe Chippewa Treaty Talks," *Minneapolis Star Tribune,* March 31, 1986, 1.

3.   "Chippewa Indians in Minnesota," Exec. Doc. 247; Depositions (August 21, 1930), Court of Claims Doc. H-76, p. 13–135, Peter Graves Papers, Red Lake Archives; Borgerding, "Red Lake St. Mary's Mission."

4.   The 1930 depositions should be filed in the National Archives, but are conspicuously missing. The reason why these documents are not to be found in U.S. government archives is the subject of much conjecture because their absence has made it difficult for Red Lake to document its understanding of this history while so many nonnative people have financially and personally profited from the taking of the lake, but what really happened to the government's copies remains a mystery. Peter Graves kept the copies provided to Red Lake's attorneys, which are now stored in Red Lake.

5.   "Chippewa Indians in Minnesota," Exec. Doc. 247:24; Captain Hassler to Commissioner of Indian Affairs, October 12, 1869, as cited in Mittelholtz, *Historical Review,* 23.

6.   *Treaty with the Chippewa—Red Lake and Pembina Bands, 1863* (October 2, 1863); *Treaty with the Chippewa of the Mississippi and the Pillager and Lake Winnibigoshish Bands, 1863* (March 11, 1863); Kappler, *Laws and Treaties,* 2:839–42, 974–76; Folwell, *History of Minnesota,* 4:193–96; Warren, *History of the Ojibway People,* 267–69; Report of Ashley C. Morrill, August 18, 1862, as cited in Winchell, *Aborigines of Minnesota,* 2:656; *Treaty with the Chippewa of the Mississippi, 1867* (March 19, 1867); John Johnson to Edwin A. Hatch, September 13, 1867, Henry Whipple Papers, Minnesota Historical Society; *Pioneer,* August 27, 1867; *St. Cloud Times,* July 11, 1868.

7.   Kappler, *Laws and Treaties,* 2:862–65, 974–76.

8.   John Johnson to Henry Whipple, July 7, 1864, box 3, Henry Whipple Papers, Minnesota Historical Society; Ashley C. Morrill, Indian Agent, to Clark W. Thompson, Superintendent of Indian Affairs, May 7, 1863, Commissioner of Indian Affairs, Correspondence File, National Archives; Bagone-giizhig Affidavit in Joel Bassett Papers, Minnesota Historical Society; George C. Whiting to George W. Manypenny, February 20, 1856, National Archives Microfilm Publications, RG 75, microfilm 234, roll 151:0158-59; James Lloyd Breck to William Chauncey Langdon, September 30, 1857, box 46, vol. 42, Protestant Episcopal Church Papers, Minnesota Historical Society; Hole-in-the-Day to President Abraham Lincoln, June 7, 1863, House Doc., 38th Congress, 1st Session, Serial 1182, 3:448-51; *Minneapolis State Atlas,* May 4, 1864; *Washington Evening Star,* April 26, 1864; Alexander Ramsey to William P. Dole, October, 1863, House Doc., 38th Congress, 1st Session, Serial 1182, 553-54; John Johnson to Henry B. Whipple, April 28, 1864, Henry Whipple Papers, Minnesota Historical Society; Commissioner of Indian Affairs, *Reports,* 1863: 449; Article 12, *Treaty with the Chippewa, Mississippi, Pillager, and Lake Winnibigoshish Bands, 1864* (May 7, 1864); Kappler, *Laws and Treaties,* 2:862-65; Folwell, *History of Minnesota,* 4:194.

9.   Mittelholtz, *Historical Review,* 23.

10.   McClurken, *Fish in the Lakes,* 357.

11.   Henry Whipple to Commissioner of Indian Affairs, March 14, 1866, National Archives Microfilm Publications, microfilm 234, roll 599:1408-17.

12.   Borgerding, "Father Thomas' History," 1.

13.   Article 4, *Treaty with the Chippewa of the Mississippi, 1867* (March 19, 1867); Kappler, *Laws and Treaties,* 2:975.

14.   Treuer, *Ojibwe in Minnesota,* 35; St. Germain, *Indian Treaty-Making Policy.* Ojibwe land cession by executive order includes "Chippewa Indians in Minnesota," Exec. Doc. 247:2-3, 14-15, 25, 95-110; Folwell, *History of Minnesota,* 4:233.

15.   Chief of Engineers, *Reports,* Serial 1447 (1870), 282-89; "Damages to Chippewa Indians," House Exec. Doc., 48th Congress, 1st Session, Serial 2200 (1884), 76:1-21; "Findings of the Northwest Indian Commission," Senate Exec. Doc., 49th Congress, 2nd Session, Serial 2449, 115:1-82; "Chippewa Indians in Minnesota," Exec. Doc. 247:1-12 (includes a full report from Henry Rice on flooding from dams, survey problems, and abortive legislation on arrearages and compensation); Folwell, *History of Minnesota,* 4:210, 234.

16.   23 Stat. 385; "Chippewa Indians in Minnesota," Exec. Doc. 247:35.

17.   Lucius Q. C. Lamar to Grover Cleveland, February 17, 1887, enclosed with "Findings of the Northwest Indian Commission," Serial 2449 (1887), 115:2; Whipple, *Lights and Shadows,* 314. Whipple's other letters advocating greater effort at White Earth removal can be found in Senate Exec. Doc., 49th Congress, 1st Session, Serial 2333 (1886), vol. 44; Senate Exec. Doc., 49th Congress, 2nd Session, Serial 2449, 115:53; 24 Stat. 44. See also Folwell, *History of Minnesota,* 4:201. Many historians laud Whipple as a brave hero who defended the Indian from politicians when he actually stood up to anyone who thwarted assimilation and relocation.

See the Minnesota Public Radio documentary on Whipple that aired several times in November 1994 and Folwell, *History of Minnesota*.

18. "Chippewa Indians in Minnesota," Exec. Doc. 247:72. In Minnesota, chipmunks were commonly called ground squirrels until after World War I, which explains the translation of *agongos* as ground squirrel rather than chipmunk when the Northwest Indian Commission and later Nelson himself came to Red Lake. The Ojibwe used the word *agongos* to refer to Norwegians because of the chipmunk-like sounds in their language.

19. 24 Stat. 388–91.

20. "Findings of the Northwest Indian Commission," Serial 2449, 115:1–82; 44 Stat. 24; Senate Exec. Doc., 49th Congress, 1st Session, Number 44, Serial 2333; Folwell, *History of Minnesota*, 4:205–11; 17 Stat. 189, 539; 18(3) Stat. 173–74; Office of Indian Affairs, *Reports,* 1869: 49, 1873: 182, 1874: 195, 1875: 53, 298, 1876: 84, 1877: 129, 1878: 78, 82, 1880: 103–5, 1882: 98, 1884: 103, 1885: 114–16, 1886: 168–70; Commissioner of Indian Affairs to Secretary of the Interior, January 16, 1886, in Senate Exec. Doc., 49th Congress, 1st Session, Number 44, Serial 2333, 5; Meyer, *White Earth Tragedy,* 57–61.

21. This and the following two paragraphs: "Proceedings of the Northwest Indian Commission," Senate Exec. Doc., 49th Congress, 2nd Session, Serial 2449, 90, 91.

22. "Proceedings of the Northwest Indian Commission," Serial 2449, 90–92.

23. Commissioner of Indian Affairs, *Reports,* 1871: 593, 1874: 30, 1877: 127; Mittelholtz, *Historical Review,* 27.

24. Commissioner of Indian Affairs, *Reports,* 1885: lxi; Mittelholtz, *Historical Review,* 27.

25. Mittelholtz, *Historical Review,* 28; 50 Cong. Rec., 273, 396–400, 829 (includes testimony for the Nelson Act about exploitative lumber harvest in Minnesota); Folwell, *History of Minnesota,* 4:224.

26. "Proceedings of the Northwest Indian Commission," Serial 2449, 93; John D. C. Atkins to Grover Cleveland, enclosed with "Findings of the Northwest Indian Commission," Serial 2449, 115:3.

27. Senate Exec. Doc., 49th Congress, 2nd Session, Serial 2449, also known as the *Northwest Indian Commission Report,* 115:12, 14, 22–25, 82–95.

28. "Proceedings of the Northwest Indian Commission," Serial 2449, 84.

29. "Agreement with the Red Lake Band of Chippewa" (August 23, 1886), in "Proceedings of the Northwest Indian Commission," Serial 2449, 115, 8; "Proceedings of the Northwest Indian Commission," Serial 2449, 93.

30. "Agreement with the Red Lake Band of Chippewa" (August 23, 1886), 6.

31. "Proceedings of the Northwest Indian Commission," Serial 2449, 94.

32. "Agreement with the Red Lake Band of Chippewa" (August 23, 1886), Article I.

33. "Findings of the Northwest Indian Commission," Serial 2449, 115:9.

34. Mittelholtz, *Historical Review,* 27.

35. 25 Stat. 642; 50th Congress, 1st Session, House Journal, Serial 2529,

Number 204; Agreement signed July 8, 1889; House of Representatives, Exec. Doc. 247, 51st Congress, 1st Session, 27, 32; Exec. Order, November 21, 1892.

36.   48th Congress, 1st Session, House Reports, Serial 2253, Number 183; 49th Congress, 1st Session, Serial 2435, Number 176; Senate Exec. Doc., 49th Congress, 2nd Session, Serial 2449, 1:2-22, 115.

37.   50th Congress, 1st Session, House Journal, Serial 2529, Number 999; "Red Lake Chippewa Indians of Minnesota," 50th Congress, 1st Session, House Journal, Serial 2600, Number 789.

38.   "Chippewa Indians in Minnesota," Exec. Doc. 247:2; Hilger, *Chippewa Families*, 5.

39.   50 Cong. Rec., 273, 336, 396-400, 829; 25 Stat. 642-46.

40.   Primary records about the Nelson Act of 1889, its incorporation of the Northwest Indian Commission findings, implementation of the allotment provisions of the Dawes Act, redress for damages caused by the dams, and the unique situation at Red Lake are in the government documents for findings of the Northwest Indian Commission, debate over the act, and the legislation itself. See "Findings of the Northwest Indian Commission," Serial 2449, 115:1-82; House Journal, 50th Congress, 1st Session, Serial 2529, 204, 789, 999; 50 Cong. Rec., (1886-89), 1971, 9129-31, 9353, 9616; Chief of Engineers, *Reports,* Serial 1447 (1870), 282-89; "Damages to Chippewa Indians," House Exec. Doc., 48th Congress, 1st session, Serial 2200, 76:1-21. See also Folwell, *History of Minnesota,* 4:219-35. The Nelson Act is 25 Stat. 642. Full findings of the Chippewa Commission are available at "Chippewa Indians in Minnesota," Exec. Doc. 247. See also Mittelholtz, *Historical Review,* 4.

41.   "Chippewa Indians in Minnesota," Exec. Doc. 247:72.

42.   "Message of the President of the United States" in "Chippewa Indians in Minnesota," Exec. Doc. 247:1.

43.   "Chippewa Indians in Minnesota," Exec. Doc. 247:75-76.

44.   "Chippewa Indians in Minnesota," Exec. Doc. 247:77-78.

45.   Statement of Father Thomas Borgerding, St. Mary's Mission, Red Lake, winter 1948, 1, Red Lake Archives.

46.   Nichols, "Translation of Key Phrases," 514-24. Nichols's arguments are well substantiated in other places, including Van Antwerp, "Negotiations for the Chippewa Treaty," 131-53, and Auger and Beardy, *Glossary of Legal Terms.*

47.   "Chippewa Indians in Minnesota," Exec. Doc. 247:13-14, 70.

48.   "Chippewa Indians in Minnesota," Exec. Doc. 247:15.

49.   "Chippewa Indians in Minnesota," Exec. Doc. 247:85.

50.   "Chippewa Indians in Minnesota," Exec. Doc. 247:73, 79.

51.   Father Thomas Borgerding statement, 1; Father Thomas Borgerding deposition (August 23, 1930), Court of Claims Doc. H-76, p. 16-17, Peter Graves Papers, Red Lake Archives.

52.   "Chippewa Indians in Minnesota," Exec. Doc. 247:81.

53.   "Chippewa Indians in Minnesota," Exec. Doc. 247:67. When Rice opened council at Leech Lake, he was even more offensive, telling the chiefs, "Talk about

your land, about not parting with your land, you don't know what you are saying; you do not own a foot of land. This land was taken from you and from the British, and the Great Father has never given it back to you, but as a kind father, has permitted you to live here as his children." Fifth Council at Leech Lake, August 13, 1889; "Proceedings of the Northwest Indian Commission," Serial 2449, 46.

54. "Chippewa Indians in Minnesota," Exec. Doc. 247:68, 69, 78.

55. "Chippewa Indians in Minnesota," Exec. Doc. 247:71.

56. "Chippewa Indians in Minnesota," Exec. Doc. 247:69.

57. "Chippewa Indians in Minnesota," Exec. Doc. 247:69.

58. "Chippewa Indians in Minnesota," Exec. Doc. 247:68–71.

59. "Message of the President of the United States," in "Chippewa Indians in Minnesota," Exec. Doc. 247:2.

60. "Chippewa Indians in Minnesota," Exec. Doc. 247:71, 72.

61. For information on this and the next two paragraphs, see "Chippewa Indians in Minnesota," Exec. Doc. 247:83, and Father Thomas Borgerding deposition, 18–20.

62. "Chippewa Indians in Minnesota," Exec. Doc. 247:83, 85.

63. "Chippewa Indians in Minnesota," Exec. Doc. 247:83, 85. See also Fruth, *Century of Missionary Work,* 37.

64. Henry M. Rice to T. J. Morgan, Commissioner of Indian Affairs, in "Chippewa Indians in Minnesota," Exec. Doc. 247:3; Mittelholtz, *Historical Review,* 135.

65. "Chippewa Indians in Minnesota," Exec. Doc. 247:2; Hilger, *Chippewa Families,* 5.

66. Mittelholtz, *Historical Review,* 31, 130; Fruth, *Century of Missionary Work,* 5.

67. Genealogy Microfilm 455, Family 93, Ransom Judd Powell Papers, Minnesota Historical Society; U.S. Census Listing for Paul H. Beaulieu (1940); U.S. Indian Census Roll for Paul H. Beaulieu (1885–1940). Robert Treuer, "Jourdain of Red Lake: Profile of an Indian Leader," unpublished manuscript, 2003; John Clement Beaulieu and Bernadeen Kirt, "Beaulieu Family Genealogy," undated manuscript—both Anton Treuer Papers, Red Lake Archives.

68. Thomas J. Morgan to John W. Noble with map attachments, July 1890, Secretary of the Interior Correspondence Files, 1890, National Archives, Washington, DC, enclosed with Jim Walker, "Red Survey Report," 2003, Red Lake Archives.

69. Don Allery, "Roger Jourdain," unpublished manuscript, Anton Treuer Papers, Red Lake Archives; Robert Treuer, "A Passion to Protect," *Minneapolis Star Tribune,* March 31, 2002, A21.

70. *To Walk the Red Road,* 5–6.

71. Father Thomas Borgerding deposition, 12–96. See also Borgerding, "Red Lake St. Mary's Mission."

72. Bad Day deposition; Joseph C. Roy deposition (August 21, 1930), Court of Claims Doc. H-76, 45, Peter Graves Papers, Red Lake Archives.

73. M. R. Baldwin to Secretary of the Interior, February 26, 1896, National

NOTES TO PAGES 108-12

Archives, Kansas City, RG 75 as cited in Child, *My Grandfather's Knocking Sticks,* 8.

74. John F. Norrish to George A. Burbank, January 1891; W. C. Smiley to U.S. Surveyor General, August 14, 1903—both Jim Walker Survey Papers, Red Lake Archives; Commissioner of Indian Affairs, *Reports,* 1921: 104.

75. Field Operations to John F. Norrish, Surveyor General, October 1891, Jim Walker Survey Papers, Red Lake Archives.

76. General Land Office to Surveyor General, January 1901, Jim Walker Survey Papers, Red Lake Archives (emphasis in original). Major Red Lake surveys include the 1872 Merrill Survey, 1873 Adley Survey, 1879 Hamilton Survey, 1885 Butler Survey, 1885 Darling Survey, 1892 Wilcox and Ralph Survey, 1928 General Land Office Map. "Red Lake Boundary and Survey Historical Discussion," Jim Walker Survey Papers, Red Lake Archives.

77. Office of Indians Affairs, *Reports,* 1890: 112, 1892: 277, 1894: 152; "Correspondence Relating to Timber on the Chippewa Indian Reservations," 55th Congress, 3rd Session, Senate Doc. No. 70, Serial 3731, 25-47, 84-88; *Crookston Times,* December 12, 1898, 8.

78. Folwell, *History of Minnesota,* 4:298.

79. Secretary of the Interior, *Reports,* 1891: xliii, 1895: xi, 1896: xx, 1898: xxxiii. A flurry of editorial letters and reports in local newspapers is thoroughly discussed in Folwell, *History of Minnesota,* 4:236n45, including Crookston *Daily Times,* April 27, 1893, 3; *Mississippi Valley Lumberman* (Minneapolis), April 28, 1893, 6, and May 19, 1893, 4; *Pioneer Press,* May 18, 1893, 2; *Crookston Times,* May 19, 1893, 1; *Anoka County Union,* September 27, 1893, 1; *Minneapolis Journal,* October 6, 1893, 9.

80. Vandersluis, *History of Beltrami County,* 6; Hagg, "Logging Line," 127.

81. Thomas J. Morgan, Brainerd, Minnesota, August 5, 1889, National Archives, Kansas City, RG 75. See also "Chippewa Indians in Minnesota," 53rd Congress, 2nd Session, House Reports, Serial 3269, Number 459; 54th Congress, 1st Session, House Reports, Serial 3457, Number 119; Secretary of the Interior, *Reports,* 1895: xi-xii; Mittelholtz, *Historical Review,* 33.

82. Commissioner of Indian Affairs, *Reports,* 1896: 51.

83. Hagg, "Logging Line," 127; Mittelholtz, *Historical Review,* 33.

84. John G. Morrison Jr., "My Forbears and the World They Lived In," in Bourgeois, Morrison, and Wight, *Mainly Logging,* 74. Information on this and the following paragraph is well documented in Secretary of the Interior, *Reports,* 1896: xxi, 1899: xvii, 1900: lvi, 1901: lxxiii, 1902: 29; Land Office, *Reports,* 1896: 101-3, 1898: 68, 104-6, 1904: 340; House of Representatives, "Report in the Matter of the Investigation of the White Earth Reservation," 62nd Congress, 3rd Session, Report Number 1336, Serial 6336, submitted January 16, 1913, 5, also known as the Graham Report. See also *Mississippi Valley Lumberman,* July 25, 1896, 14; *Crookston Times,* July 15, 1896, 4, 17. The Graham Report did much to expose the collusion and fraud in sales of Red Lake lands in the 1890s, even though it was never acted upon or used to seek justice.

85.   Indian Appropriation Act, 30 Stat. 924; Commissioner of Indian Affairs, *Reports,* 69th Annual Report (June 30, 1900), 71; Mittelholtz, *Historical Review,* 34.

86.   Minnesota State Demographic Center, Census Data by County; Minnesota Digital Library, "Minnesota's Logging History."

87.   Mittelholtz, *Historical Review,* 45.

88.   Chippewas of Minnesota: U.S. Congress Committee on Indian Affairs, 1920, 247, 345; 63 Cong. Rec., Serials 1095, 3773; 39 Stat. 123-37; Mittelholtz, *Historical Review,* 45.

89.   House Doc. 645, 62nd Congress, 2nd Session; 35 Stat. 268.

90.   64 Cong. Rec. (1916) 137; Mittelholtz, *Historical Review,* 54.

91.   64 Cong. Rec., 1752, 2310, 4759, 7846, 7865, 8275, and appendix 1100-1102.

92.   Mittelholtz, *Historical Review,* 34, 43.

93.   Commissioner of Indian Affairs, *Reports,* 1901: 69; Mittelholtz, *Historical Review,* 35. Timber harvests were included in every report to the commissioner in this time period. See the improving return to the people of Red Lake starting in 1904 in Commissioner of Indian Affairs, *Reports,* 1904: 218.

94.   Mittelholtz, *Historical Review,* 37; Commissioner of Indian Affairs, *Reports,* 1905: 79.

95.   Commissioner of Indian Affairs, *Reports,* 1906: 245; Mittelholtz, *Historical Review,* 28, 44; Folwell, *History of Minnesota,* 4:298.

96.   Minnesota Department of Natural Resources, "Peak Logging Years," http://www.dnr.state.mn.us/forestry/anniversary/peaklogging.html.

97.   Whipple, *Lights and Shadows,* 148.

98.   Thomas J. Morgan to John W. Noble, November 17, 1892, Commissioner of Indian Affairs Correspondence File; "Chippewa Indians in Minnesota," Exec. Doc. 247:27, 32; Exec. Order, November 21, 1892; Mittelholtz, *Historical Review,* 4; Folwell, *History of Minnesota,* 4:298.

99.   31 Stat. 134; Commissioner of Indian Affairs, *Reports,* 69th Annual Report (June 30, 1900), 89, 522; Department of the Interior, *Reports,* 1899: 212.

100. Vandersluis, *History of Beltrami County,* 8.

101. Steve Mosbeck, "The History of Moose Dung's Section and How the Section Influenced the Settlement of Thief River Falls," unpublished manuscript, March 27, 1975, Red Lake Archives.

102. *Jones v. Meehan* (175 U.S. 1); *Thief River Falls Times,* April 21, 23, 28, 30, 1975.

103. 31 Stat. 1077; *Thief River Falls News,* December 5, 1901, 1, December 26, 1901, 1; "Chippewas of Minnesota." This report includes a huge array of testimony from January 21 to March 22, 1920.

104. *Minnesota v. Hitchcock* (U.S. Supreme Court, docket 185); commission authorized by 32 Stat. 400.

105. "Chippewa Indians in Minnesota," Exec. Doc. 247:2-3, 14-15, 25, 95-110, 822-27; "Report in the Matter of the Investigation of the White Earth Reservation," 62nd Congress, 3rd Session, House Reports, Serial 6336, submitted

January 16, 1913, 1336:524–649; 56 Cong. Rec., 56, 2566; 58 Cong. Rec., 685, 3660, 4413, 5546, 5825; 33 Stat. 539; Folwell, *History of Minnesota,* 4:231–33, 265–68; Meyer, *White Earth Tragedy,* 51–52, 64–65; Joseph Auginaush interview (1994); White Earth Land Recovery Project, Research Division, Winona LaDuke interview (November 28, 1994).

106. "Proceedings with the Chippewa Belonging to the Red Lake Reservation," embedded in 57 Cong. Rec., 5 Serial 2183, 204, 227.

107. "Proceedings with the Chippewa," 225–26.

108. "Proceedings with the Chippewa," 226.

109. "Proceedings with the Chippewa," 221.

110. Mittelholtz, *Historical Review,* 4, 131, 133.

111. Information on this and the following paragraph are taken from "Signature Roll for Chippewa Belonging to the Red Lake Reservation," embedded in 57 Cong. Rec., Serial 2183, 229. Fred Dennis, a young, aspiring white lawyer, is recorded in the council log as stenographer. Years later he developed a friendly relationship with Peter Graves, and eventually worked on Red Lake's fishing rights and land case with the Court of Claims.

112. *Thief River Falls News,* May 8, 1903; 57 Cong. Rec., Doc. R532; 32 Stat. 1009; William W. Folwell to Hubert Work, July 29, 1927, Commissioner of Indian Affairs Correspondence Files; E. B. Merritt to William W. Folwell, August 16, 1927, Commissioner of Indian Affairs Correspondence Files.

113. 35 Stat. 46–50; 57 Cong. Rec., Serial 2183; H.R. 15804; "Red Lake Indian Reservation," special report, 58th Congress, 2nd Session, Senate Report 36, Serial 4570; 58 Cong. Rec., 358; "Indians of Red Lake Reservation," House Reports, 58th Congress, 2nd Session, Report 735, Serial 4578; *Thief River Falls News,* December 24, 1903, 1.

114. "Looks Like an Early Opening," *Thief River Falls News-Press,* April 7, 1904, 1; Wub-e-ke-niew, *We Have the Right,* 146; Thorstad, "The Sad Legacy of Moose Dung and Red Robe."

115. William H. Bishop to Commissioner of Indian Affairs, February 2, 1908, Red Lake Archives; "Bicentennial Observance Is Held in Thief River Falls Saturday," *Thief River Falls Times,* July 12, 1976, 4.

116. "Bicentennial Observance."

117. 31 Stat. 134; Commissioner of Indian Affairs, *Reports,* 69th Annual Report (June 30, 1900), 89, 522; Department of the Interior, *Reports,* 1899: 212; King, "Logging Railroads," 104–5; Hagg, "Logging Line," 124.

118. Vandersluis, *History of Beltrami County,* 8.

119. Mittelholtz, *Historical Review,* 1, 4, 38–39.

120. Vandersluis, *History of Beltrami County,* 12; "Chippewas of Minnesota," 112, 160, 353.

121. General Land Office, Homestead Circular, 1895; "NOW GIT! That Is What Uncle Sam Says to Red Lake Sooners," *Crookston Times,* May 9, 1896, 1; Mittelholtz, *Historical Review,* 32.

122. "Statement of Halvor Steenerson," 57 Congr. Rec., 5 Serial 2183, 242.

123. 57 Cong. Rec., 5 Serial 2183, 242.

124. The most complete list of correspondence on ditching and land issues in Red Lake's ceded lands is compiled in the legal briefs and supporting documents for 25 U.S.C. §70, *Red Lake Band of Chippewa Indians v. United States* and U.S. Court of Claims Docket 388-82L (Docket 189-C in settlement). More than one hundred letters and several studies are compiled there relating to this issue. See also Vandersluis, *History of Beltrami County,* 13.

125. Vandersluis, *History of Beltrami County,* 13; General Council Resolution 7, November 25, 1933, Red Lake Archives; Mittelholtz, *Historical Review,* 31. Sixteen named steamboats operated at Red Lake, and many smaller craft as well. *To Walk the Red Road,* 52.

126. Hagg, "Logging Line," 129; *Bemidji Pioneer,* August 3, 6, 13, 20, 1906.

127. House of Representatives, "Report in the Matter of the Investigation of the White Earth Reservation" ("Graham Report"), 5.

128. Mittelholtz, *Historical Review,* 3; Brill, *Red Lake Nation,* 20; Daniel M. Browning to W. F. Campbell, February 8, 1895; Daniel M. Browning to Hoke Smith, March 12, 1895—both Red Lake Archives.

129. Father Thomas Borgerding deposition, 31–32; M. L. Burns deposition, August 22, 1930, Court of Claims Doc. H-76, 102, Peter Graves Papers, Red Lake Archives. McPherson to M. R. Baldwin, March 25, 1896; Daniel M. Browning to Hoke Smith, March 12, 1895; Charles H. Burke to Hubert Work, January 19, 1925—all Red Lake Archives; Wahlberg, *The North Land,* 1–59. White settlers started squatting on tribal land before the Nelson Act was even signed. In 1888, Esther D. Goldner was the first white person born in Roseau County, in a house built by her family on tribal land before the land was ceded, sold, or homesteaded. Daniel M. Browning to Hoke Smith, March 12, 1895, Red Lake Archives.

130. Mittelholtz offers "The Old Chief's Village" as a translation of Ondatamaaning, which is likely how it was differentiated to him in English, although "The Source" is a more literal translation. Mittelholtz, *Historical Review,* 1.

NOTES TO CHAPTER 4: THE UNITER

1.   Opening quote, Don Allery, "Roger Jourdain," unpublished manuscript, 4, Anton Treuer Papers, Red Lake Archives. Nodin Wind's obituary appeared in the *Bemidji Pioneer,* February 2, 1981. There are conflicting details on the precise date of his birth as it appears in the 1930 federal census, the Minnesota Death Index, and the Indian Census Roll, Red Lake (1885-1940), but the family's stated birth date of April 15, 1874, appears the most reliable and is substantiated by the death index. Wind was first married at age eighteen in 1892, but the fate of his first wife is not known. By 1930, he was married to Circling Thunderbird Woman (Gezhibinesiikwe), who was ten years younger than him and the mother of his children as they appear in subsequent census data and his obituary. See Department of Commerce, Census Bureau, Population Schedule, 15th U.S. Census, 1930; Office of Indian Affairs, Indian Census Roll, Red Lake, 1885-1940; Minnesota Death Index, 1908-2002. At time of his death, Nodin Wind had twelve grandchildren, including

Leonard Hawk, who became a prominent spiritual leader at Ponemah in his own right; forty-nine great-grandchildren; and forty-four great-great-grandchildren. See also *Bemidji Pioneer,* May 6, 1977, 2; Brill, *Red Lake Nation,* 41, 100.

2.   The last known funeral conducted by Nodin Wind outside of Red Lake was in Mille Lacs, for Peter Sam (June 22, 1904–April 18, 1961). See U.S. Indian Census Roll for Peter Sam, 1885-1940; U.S. Census for Peter Sam, 1930; Minnesota Death Index; William Blackwell Sr. interview (August 2, 1996).

3.   Wind's role in the parade is reported in the *Bemidji Pioneer,* July 3, 1976, 11. Maude Wind married a Spears and Dorothy married a Martin: *Bemidji Pioneer,* February 2, 1981.

4.   Anna C. Gibbs interview (February 4, 2015).

5.   The saying about seeing the world, popularized in various forms by Henrik Scharling (1876), H. M. Tomlinson (1931), Anaïs Nin (1961), and recently by Stephen Covey, has unattributable authorship. Fruth, *Century of Missionary Work,* 14.

6.   Information on Ramsey's position and politics on Indian education in this and the following paragraph is available in Mittelholtz, *Historical Review,* 20.

7.   Mittelholtz, *Historical Review,* 21.

8.   Mittelholtz, *Historical Review,* 70-75.

9.   The ordinance translates as follows: "The descendants of the French who are accustomed to this country, together with all the Indians who will be brought to the knowledge of the faith and will profess it, shall be deemed and renowned natural Frenchmen, and as such may come to live in France when they want, and acquire, donate, and succeed and accept donations and legacies, just as true French subjects, without being required to take letters of declaration of naturalization." Acte pour l'établissement de la Compagnie des Cent Associés pour le commerce du Canada, contenant les articles accordés à la dite Compagnie par M. le Cardinal de Richelieu, le 29 avril 1627.

10.   See, for example, the compelling story of Lutiant LaVoye (French–Ojibwe from Red Lake) in Child, *My Grandfather's Knocking Sticks,* 150-59.

11.   Mittelholtz, *Historical Review,* 70-72.

12.   Norton, *Catholic Missionary Activities.*

13.   Baraga, *Diary.*

14.   Norton, *Catholic Missionary Activities,* 129.

15.   Mittelholtz, *Historical Review,* 21-22.

16.   Norton, *Catholic Missionary Activities,* 135.

17.   Fruth, *Century of Missionary Work,* 23, 53, 67; Mittelholtz, *Historical Review,* 27-28.

18.   Allery, "Roger Jourdain," 16.

19.   Fruth, *Century of Missionary Work,* 102.

20.   Mittelholtz, *Historical Review,* 33, 72-75.

21.   Mittelholtz, *Historical Review,* 26.

22.   Whipple, *Lights and Shadows,* 145.

23.   Whipple, *Lights and Shadows,* 146.

24.   Mittelholtz, *Historical Review*, 44, 75.

25.   Bigglestone, "Oberlin College," 27. Frederick Ayer grew up in Massachusetts and New York and served in mission work at Mackinac Island beginning in 1822 and then at La Pointe by 1830. In spite of Theodore Blegen's assertion that Edmund F. Ely was the primary advocate for the mission to Red Lake, historical records make it clear that Ayer was in fact the impetus for the mission and brought in Ely as a partner. See *Oberlin Evangelist*, September 27, 1843; Boutwell, Ely, Ayer, and Hall to David Greene, March 6, 1843, American Board of Commissioners for Foreign Missions Papers, Houghton Library, Harvard University. The mission at Pokegama was opened in 1836. After the Ojibwe left, Ely was among the missionaries who maintained the mission in spite of its abandonment by the Indians. See William T. Boutwell to Samuel Pond, June 29, 1842, Samuel Pond Papers, Minnesota Historical Society; Neill, "Battle of Lake Pokegama"; Pond, "Indian Warfare in Minnesota," 133–34; Larpenteur, "Recollections"; S. Freightner Sharp, "Tenting on Pokegama Lake," unpublished, undated manuscript, Minnesota Historical Society; Grace Lee Nute, "Missionaries among the Sioux and Chippewa," *Hamline Radio Hour* 26 (November 20, 1928), Minnesota Historical Society. See also Meyer, *White Earth Tragedy*, 61–62, 69; Danziger, *Chippewas of Lake Superior*, 74; Blegen, *Minnesota*, 146; Folwell, *History of Minnesota*, 1:179–81.

26.   Mittelholtz, *Historical Review*, 130; Wright, "Reminiscences," 46–48; William T. Boutwell to Samuel W. Pond, June 29, 1842, Manuscripts Relating to Northwest Missions, Grace Lee Nute Papers, Minnesota Historical Society; Schell, *In the Ojibway Country*, 5–6; Frank Hugh Foster, "The Oberlin Ojibway Mission," 1892, 2–3, Papers of the Ohio Church History Society, Oberlin; "Frederick Ayer"; *Oberlin Evangelist*, May 10, 1843; Elizabeth Ayer to Robert Stuart, February 23, 1843, Michigan Superintendency, Office of Indian Affairs, Letters Received, National Archives RG 75, microfilm 54; Hickerson, "William T. Boutwell."

27.   Bigglestone, "Oberlin College," 30; Vandersluis, *History of Beltrami County*, 2; Mittelholtz, *Historical Review*, 17.

28.   John P. Bardwell (American Missionary Association) to Luke Lea (Commissioner of Indian Affairs), September 1, 1851, in Commissioner of Indian Affairs, *Reports*, 1851: 179, 440; Roger Jourdain, "Early History of Red Lake Reservation," 3, undated historical sketch, submitted to Red Lake Tribal Council, January 31, 1985, Red Lake Archives; Mittelholtz, *Historical Review*, 20.

29.   John P. Bardwell, American Missionary Association, report, included with Commissioner of Indian Affairs, *Reports*, 1852: 341; Jourdain, "Early History," 4.

30.   Wright, "Reminiscences," 2–9; *Oberlin Evangelist*, March 13 and 27, 1844; Bigglestone, "Oberlin College," 30–31; Mittelholtz, *Historical Review*, 1, 20.

31.   Mittelholtz, *Historical Review*, 25.

32.   Mittelholtz, *Historical Review*, 76.

33.   Mittelholtz, *Historical Review*, 2.

34.   Eugene Stillday interview (May 7, 2015); E. B. Hickstrom to Roger Jourdain, September 4, 1979, Red Lake Archives; Wah-Bun Chapel, Gubernatorial Citation of Honor, July 19, 1978, Red Lake Archives.

35.   Borgerding, "Priest Expelled," 1. Fruth gives a parallel version of this event in *Century of Missionary Work*, 16. White, *We Are at Home*, 146–56; Priscilla Buffalohead, "Peace Queens, Women Warriors, and Resistance Fighters: Women in Native Communities of the Eastern Woodlands and Great Plains," undated, unpublished manuscript, Anton Treuer Papers, Red Lake Archives.

36.   Allery, "Roger Jourdain," 3.

37.   Allery, "Roger Jourdain," 4.

38.   Allery, "Roger Jourdain," 4; Charles H. Burke Powwow Prohibition, February 24, 1923, Red Lake Archives; Code of Indian Offenses, March 30, 1883, Office of Indian Affairs, http://en.wikisource.org/wiki/Code_of_Indian_Offenses.

39.   Allery, "Roger Jourdain," 4.

40.   Senate Committee on Indian Affairs, Special Commission on the Chippewa Indian Tribes of Minnesota, 68th Congress, 1st Session, Senate Resolution 24 (December 10, 1923), Minnesota Field Hearings, Official Transcripts (August 26–29, 1924), 596.

41.   In 1935, the government widened the road from Red Lake to Redby and forced several families to exhume the remains of buried relatives and move them. Hilger, *Chippewa Child Life*, 82.

42.   Hilger, *Chippewa Families*, 82.

43.   Dan Raincloud, Ponemah spiritual leader, annually traveled to Nett Lake to pick rice in addition to harvesting local Red Lake river beds. See Vennum, *Wild Rice and the Ojibway People*, 187.

44.   Debilitating waves of smallpox were documented in the Red Lake region in 1824, 1835, 1837, 1838, and 1839. See Evangelical Society of Missions of Lausanne, "Report of June 11, 1835"; Burpee, *Journals and Letters*, 257n; Sharrock and Sharrock, "History of the Cree," 286–88; Blegen, *Minnesota*, 117; Tanner, *Atlas*, 170.

45.   Mittelholtz, *Historical Review*, 22, 24, 26, 28, 35.

46.   Commissioner of Indian Affairs, *Reports*, 1905; Mittelholtz, *Historical Review*, 35.

47.   E. B. Merritt to William H. Bishop, March 19, 1912, Red Lake Archives.

48.   Mittelholtz, *Historical Review*, 1, 45.

49.   Child, *My Grandfather's Knocking Sticks*, 126.

50.   Dr. Thomas Rodwell, as cited in Child, *My Grandfather's Knocking Sticks*, 139–40.

51.   Reverend Lyman Abbott, "Education for the Indian," Lake Mohonk Conference Keynote Address, 1988, as cited in Wub-e-ke-niew [Francis Blake], *We Have the Right*, 109.

52.   Child, *My Grandfather's Knocking Sticks*, 53.

53.   Captain Hassler to Commissioner of Indian Affairs, October 12, 1869, and Lieutenant George Atcheson, both as cited in Mittelholtz, *Historical Review*, 23.

54.   Commissioner of Indian Affairs, *Reports*, 1896: 51, 1900: 18, 24; also Mittelholtz, *Historical Review*, 24–25, 30.

55.   Commissioner of Indian Affairs, *Reports*, 1900: 35; Mittelholtz, *Historical Review*, 32.

56.   Wub-e-ke-niew [Francis Blake], *We Have the Right,* 117-20.

57.   Commissioner of Indian Affairs, *Reports,* 1900: 40; *To Walk the Red Road,* 49.

58.   Eugene Stillday interview (May 2, 2015). Joe Dick and other older Ponemah speakers frequently called Ponemah Aazhooding, although Obaashiing is more common among younger speakers there today.

59.   Commissioner of Indian Affairs, *Reports,* 1900: 259.

60.   Commissioner of Indian Affairs, *Reports,* 1900: 687; Captain William A. Mercer to William A. Jones, Commissioner of Indian Affairs, July 20, 1900, Correspondence Files.

61.   Mittelholtz, *Historical Review,* 35, 37, 41.

62.   Mittelholtz, *Historical Review,* 37.

63.   Child, *My Grandfather's Knocking Sticks,* 150-59.

64.   Commissioner of Indian Affairs, *Reports,* 1900: 427.

65.   Commissioner of Indian Affairs, *Reports,* 1900: 260, 662.

66.   Hilger, *Chippewa Families,* xi, 78.

67.   Mittelholtz, *Historical Review,* 48.

68.   Senate Committee on Indian Affairs, Special Commission on the Chippewa Indian Tribes of Minnesota, 61.

69.   Mittelholtz, *Historical Review,* 44-47, 50-51. Dickinson Construction of Bemidji got the contract for the construction job.

70.   Erika Bailey-Johnson interview (April 1, 2015); Mittelholtz, *Historical Review,* 52.

71.   Mittelholtz, *Historical Review,* 52.

72.   Brookings Institution, "The Problem of Indian Administration: Report of a Survey made at the request of Honorable Hubert Work, Secretary of the Interior, and submitted to him, February 21, 1928" (Baltimore: The Johns Hopkins Press, 1928).

73.   Mittelholtz, *Historical Review,* 46-47.

74.   Mittelholtz, *Historical Review,* 53-55. The availability of impact aid monies began in 1950, with passage of Public Law 81-815.

75.   Charles H. Burke Powwow Prohibition; Code of Indian Offenses; Allery, "Roger Jourdain," 3; Mittelholtz, *Historical Review,* 27.

76.   Serving in Red Lake were George Highlanding, Stands Forever (Gabegaabaw), Lewis Jourdain, Striped Day (Beshi-giizhig), Joseph Bellanger, Henry Taylor, Joseph Mason, Little Frenchman (Wemitigoozhiins), John Martin, William Jourdain, David Lajeunesse, Clifford Sitting, Peter Graves, Joseph V. Roy, Norman Kelly, Charles A. Beaulieu, Michael Lussier, Bazile Maxwell, Francis Gurneau, Bazile Lawrence, Little Chief (Ogimaans), Patrick Lussier, Baptiste Thunder, Leo DesJarlait, William Blue, William Fineday, Warren Greenleaf, Augustus Lajeunesse, Peter Sitting, Edward Prentice, Frank Prentice, Charles Prentice, John Squirrel, Alex Jourdain, Geoffery Chase, Albert Jones, John A. Smith, Louis Yellow, Louis Barrett, Llewelyn Parkhurst, Herman Smith, Herman English, Charles White, Marvin Yellow, Simon Beaulieu, Thomas Barrett, John English, Louis Cas-

well, Louis Jourdain, Louis B. Harwood, Charles Harkins, Lizziam Archambeau, Earl Robinson, Theodore Murphy, Royce Graves, Matthew Sayers, Melvin Strong, Frank Stately, Albert Stately Jr., and Thomas Cain. Serving in Ponemah were Joseph Brown, Charles Jackson, John Stillday, George Blakely, James Downwind, Charles Dick, Michael Blakely, Spencer Whitefeather, John Signa, Peter Martin, Daniel Perkins, George Oldman, Charles Bug Sr., John George, Harold Johnson Sr., Alfred Wind, and Thomas Cain. See Mittelholtz, *Historical Review*, 40.

77.   Mittelholtz, *Historical Review*, 133-34.

78.   Nodin Wind's recognition as chief is well recorded in the communication around creating the constitution for the General Council of the Red Lake Band of Chippewa Indians, reprinted in Mittelholtz, *Historical Review*, 85-86. See also references in the Indian Appropriation Bill (January 10, 1919), 72; and General Council Resolutions 4 (November 29, 1920), 6 (March 14, 1921), 1 (August 23, 1924), 1 (January 16, 1937)—all Red Lake Archives. We do not know the details of every meeting he had with various chiefs at Ponemah to obtain permission to represent the community in 1909, but he did have their sanction, as evidenced in his words at subsequent meetings in Washington and Red Lake and the absence of any objection to them by Every Wind and King Bird at the time and any of the other many representatives from Ponemah active in Red Lake's political process afterward.

79.   The 1930 census shows Nodin Wind's occupation as a commercial fisherman at Red Lake. See Department of Commerce, Census Bureau, Population Schedule, 15th U.S. Census, 1930. Bobby Whitefeather and Darrell Seki, both of Ponemah, have been elected as tribal chairmen at Red Lake in recent years.

NOTES TO CHAPTER 5: THE REFORMER

1.   Opening quote: David B. O'Rear, "In Memoriam: A Tribute to the Memory of My Friend, Peter Graves," Red Lake Archives, reprinted in *Bemidji Pioneer*, March 14, 1991. Details of Collins Oakgrove's encounter with Peter Graves are taken from Collins W. Oakgrove interview (April 23, 1996). For more bibliographical information on Oakgrove, see Treuer, *Living Our Language*, 165-77; "Collins Wayne Oakgrove," *Red Lake Nation News* 10.206 (June 19, 2014). Collins Wayne Oakgrove was born March 16, 1944, and died June 15, 2014. His parents were Francis W. Oakgrove and Julia Dolly Johnson. Oakgrove was a veteran of the U.S. Navy, doing one tour in Vietnam in 1967, and worked for many years as instructor of Ojibwe at the University of Minnesota and the Leech Lake Bug-O-Nay-Geshick School. Details about the Ponemah store, Thomas and Mary Spears, kerosene lamp use, electrical service, and Peter Graves were corroborated by Anna C. Gibbs interview (February 4, 2015). Anna C. Gibbs (Waasabiikwe, or Moonlight Shining on the Water Woman) was born on December 17, 1944, and was a contemporary and classmate of Collins Oakgrove. The REA contract to establish electrical service to Ponemah in 1952 is referenced in Mittelholtz, *Historical Review*, 3, 54.

2.   Peter Graves interview with Arch Grahn (October 5, 1950), Minnesota Historical Society. Information in this paragraph and through this chapter is taken from several primary sources: Peter Graves to Mark L. Burns, January 9, 1939,

Peter Graves Papers, Red Lake Archives. This letter is on the letterhead of the General Council of the Red Lake Band of Chippewa Indians, which also lists the Hereditary Chiefs as Okemahwahjewabe (Ogimaawajiweb, or Chief Going over the Hill), Nayaytowub (Na'etoowab, or Sits in Deliberation), William Sayers, Mayskogwon (Miskogwan, or Red Feather), Payshegeshig (Bezhigiizhig, or Solitary Sky), John F. Smith, and Alfred Wind. It also lists Xavier Downwind as chairman and Peter Graves as secretary-treasurer. The four-page letter is an autobiography and stands as one of the most reliable primary source documents of Graves's career because it is in his own words and full of details, names, and dates for critical events. Peter Graves also gave a long and substantive autobiographical interview that details his early life and personal views; see Graves interview. Peter Graves drafted a position paper and issued it as a formal statement of the General Council. It was presented to the Minnesota Indian Conference in Bemidji on April 11, 1950, and also at the Indian Affairs conference in Bemidji on June 1, 1956. It provides great insight into Graves's position on several critical issues and his relationship with the Bureau of Indian Affairs. See "Statement of the General Council," June 1, 1956, Red Lake Archives. In addition, there are numerous newspaper articles and a well-researched biography of Peter Graves in Mittelholtz, *Historical Review*, 110-11. See also Jack Newman, "Temporary Post Lasts Six Years: Indian Judge Is Still on the Job," *Bemidji Daily Pioneer*, July 6, 1942; Jay Edgerton, "Death Comes for Peter Graves," *Minneapolis Star Tribune*, March 16, 1957; *Bemidji Daily Pioneer*, February 7, 1958, 1; Vandersluis, *History of Beltrami County*; David B. O'Rear, "In Memoriam" and "Death of Peter Graves," Red Lake Archives; Minnesota Chippewa Tribal Council, Resolution 36: Tribute to Peter Graves; *To Walk the Red Road*, 11-13; Vincent Staples-Graves interview (May 9, 2015); Peter Strong interview with Robert Treuer and Gary Fuller (June 20, 2003). Strong is a grandson of Peter Graves and also a half brother to Roger Jourdain. Graves claims May 20, 1872, as his birth date in his interview with Arch Grahn, but provides June 1872 in his letter to Mark Burns.

    3.   White Crane's daughter Madeline, who married Michel Cadotte, had two daughters who married Warrens. Charlotte and Marie Cadotte married Truman and Lyman Warren. The Cadottes were strict Catholics, but the Warrens, true to their Puritan roots, were Protestants. Most of the Warren clan followed Protestant traditions as they spread out to Red Lake. Child, *Holding Our World Together*, 33, 37, 62; Densmore, *Chippewa Customs*, 3.

    4.   Omen was more Scottish than English and held fast to Scottish Catholicism rather than Anglican, Methodist, or Presbyterian religious beliefs.

    5.   Peter Strong reported that Omen went back to Canada to retrieve personal belongings and was caught, tried, and hanged, presumably for his role in the Riel Rebellion. Strong interview.

    6.   Mittelholtz, *Historical Review*, 111.

    7.   Mittelholtz, *Historical Review*, 111.

    8.   Matsen, "Battle of Sugar Point," 269-75; King, *Seeds of War*, 83; Gardner, *Minnesota Treasures*, 16-19; Greiner, *Minnesota Book of Days*, 203; Associated

Press, "Emma Bear, Last Survivor of Battle of Sugar Point, Dead at 103," *Brainerd Daily Dispatch,* July 17, 2001.

9.   Graves interview; *To Walk the Red Road,* 13.

10. Peter Graves to Mark L. Burns, January 9, 1939.

11. Graves interview; Peter Graves to Mark L. Burns, January 9, 1939.

12. Mittelholtz, *Historical Review,* 111.

13. *Bemidji Daily Pioneer,* July 12, 1912.

14. Don Allery, "Roger Jourdain," unpublished manuscript, 1, 2, Anton Treuer Papers, Red Lake Archives. The general council referred to here was the general council for all Minnesota Ojibwe; Red Lake's general council had not yet been formed.

15. Allery, "Roger Jourdain," 2. The petition of the chiefs was reported on in the *Minneapolis Journal,* December 24, 1913.

16. Allery, "Roger Jourdain," 2.

17. Peter Graves to Mark L. Burns, January 9, 1939. The entire constitution for the General Council of the Red Lake Band of Chippewa Indians is reprinted in Mittelholtz, *Historical Review,* 85–86. Graves submitted to the U.S. Congress all charter documents and the first dozen tribal resolutions, which were appended to the Indian Appropriation Bill (January 10, 1919), 72.

18. For a good overview of the OIA dynamics discussed in this paragraph and the next, see Hoxie, *A Final Promise.*

19. Senate Committee on Indian Affairs, Special Commission on the Chippewa Indian Tribes of Minnesota, 68th Congress, 1st Session, Senate Resolution 24 (December 10, 1923), Minnesota Field Hearings, Official Transcripts (August 26–29, 1924), 568, 569, 577.

20. Mittelholtz, *Historical Review,* 131.

21. Anna C. Gibbs interview (February 4, 2015).

22. *Woodlands: The Story of the Mille Lacs Ojibwe.*

23. General Council Resolutions 4 (November 29, 1920), 6 (March 14, 1921), 1 (August 23, 1924), 1 (January 16, 1937)—all Red Lake Archives.

24. Brill, *Red Lake Nation,* 36.

25. Peter Graves to Mark L. Burns, January 9, 1939.

26. Roger Jourdain, "Mis-qua-ga-me-we-saga-eh-ganing," undated historical sketch, Red Lake Archives.

27. Senate Committee on Indian Affairs, Special Commission on the Chippewa Indian Tribes of Minnesota, 579. See also Mittelholtz, *Historical Review,* 3.

28. "Statement of the General Council," June 1, 1956, Red Lake Archives.

29. Edgerton, "Death Comes for Peter Graves"; Minnesota Pollution Control Agency, "Statewide Baseline Study," 1996, http://www.pca.state.mn.us/index.php /water/water-types-and-programs/groundwater/groundwater-monitoring-and -assessment/statewide-baseline-study.html.

30. Peter Graves to Mark L. Burns, January 9, 1939.

31. "Chippewa Indians of Minnesota," Committee on Indian Affairs, House of Representatives, Testimony Transcripts on House Resolution 26, March 1, 1924.

NOTES TO PAGES 202–11

32.   Senate Committee on Indian Affairs, Special Commission on the Chippewa Indian Tribes of Minnesota, 1–584.

33.   Senate Committee on Indian Affairs, Special Commission on the Chippewa Indian Tribes of Minnesota, 139, 582.

34.   Office of Indian Affairs Internal Memo, 1924, Red Lake Archives. See also Jourdain, "Mis-qua-ga-me-we-saga-eh-ganing."

35.   Senate Committee on Indian Affairs, Special Commission on the Chippewa Indian Tribes of Minnesota, 583.

36.   For information on the Red Lake claims case in this and following paragraphs, see *The Chippewa Indians of Minnesota v. U.S.* (U.S. Court of Claims, H76), filed with the Court of Claims February 26, 1927; Jourdain, "Mis-qua-ga-me-we-saga-eh-ganing"; 44 Stat. 555; 45 Stat. 423; 45 Stat. 601. There are more than one hundred letters pertaining to Red Lake's Court of Claims case in Fred Dennis Correspondence File, Red Lake Archives. Legislative enablement of the claims process is documented in 75th Congress, 3rd Session, Chapter 777, No. 755 (June 28, 1938); 49 Stat. 1826; 35 Stat. 268.

37.   60 Stat. 149.

38.   G. E. E. Lindquist to Harold Ickes, July 7, 1933, Red Lake Archives.

39.   Brill, *Red Lake Nation,* 35–36.

40.   Child, *My Grandfather's Knocking Sticks,* 56.

41.   Mittelholtz, *Historical Review,* 47, 50.

42.   43 Stat. 412; 39 Stat. 138; 44 Stat. 475.

43.   *Bemidji Sentinel,* February 27, 1925, 1.

44.   Mittelholtz, *Historical Review,* 49.

45.   For information in this and the next few paragraphs on the cyclical impact of fire on soil fertility, see Diamond, *Collapse.* On the trophic cascade effect, see John Terborgh and James Estes, *Trophic Cascades.* On the process at Red Lake, see Mittelholtz, *Historical Review,* 49; Vandersluis, *History of Beltrami County,* 14.

46.   Mittelholtz, *Historical Review,* 50.

47.   Red Lake Superintendent to Francis E. Leupp, April 18, 1908; Carlos Avery to C. F. Darrall, April 10, 1908; C. F. Larrabee to Carlos Avery, April 5, 1908; C. F. Larrabee to Red Lake Agency Superintendent, April 13 and 30, 1908; Carlos Avery to Francis E. Leupp, March 25, 1908; Francis E. Leupp to Halvor Steenerson, April 4, 1908—all Red Lake Archives. See also Commissioner of Indian Affairs, *Reports,* 1863–1934.

48.   *To Walk the Red Road,* 55.

49.   Mittelholtz, *Historical Review,* 51–52.

50.   "Statement of Halvor Steenerson," *Congressional Record,* 57th Congress, 2nd Session, Serial 2183, 242; 25 U.S.C. §70, *Red Lake Band of Chippewa Indians v. United States* and U.S. Court of Claims Docket 388–82L (Docket 189-C in settlement); Vandersluis, *History of Beltrami County,* 13.

51.   Graves interview; Vandersluis, *History of Beltrami County,* 14.

52.   25 U.S.C. §70, *Red Lake Band of Chippewa Indians v. United States*; 25 U.S.C. §§1401, "Funds Appropriated in Satisfaction of Indian Claims Commission"; Tom

Robertson, "Red Lake Band to Reforest 50,000 Acres," *Minnesota Public Radio,* August 25, 2011; Michael Meuers, "Red Lake to Restore Great Pine Forests," *The Circle,* September 10, 2011.

53.   Child, *My Grandfather's Knocking Sticks,* 95–96.

54.   Information on the development of Red Lake's commercial fishery in this and subsequent paragraphs is taken from Van Oosten and Deason, "History of Red Lake's Fishery"; Vandersluis, *History of Beltrami County,* 15; Mittelholtz, *Historical Review,* 46–48; Child, *My Grandfather's Knocking Sticks,* 38–42, 85–124; Hagg, "Logging Line," 132.

55.   Van Oosten and Deason, "History of Red Lake's Fishery"; Child, *My Grandfather's Knocking Sticks,* 87, 98.

56.   S. A. Selvog, February 21, 1925, Bureau of Indian Affairs Correspondence Files, National Archives, Kansas City. The full text of commercial regulations imposed at Red Lake by the state is available in Van Oosten and Deason, "History of Red Lake's Fishery." Senate Committee on Indian Affairs, Special Commission on the Chippewa Indian Tribes of Minnesota, 565–631.

57.   James F. Gould, Minnesota State Game and Fish Commissioner, to A. C. Kvennes, September 14, 1926, Bureau of Indian Affairs Correspondence Files, National Archives, Kansas City.

58.   Senate Committee on Indian Affairs, Special Commission on the Chippewa Indian Tribes of Minnesota, 607; Snyder Act, 43 Stat. 233.

59.   Van Oosten and Deason, "History of Red Lake's Fishery."

60.   Charles H. Burke, Commissioner of Indian Affairs, to James F. Gould, January 19, 1926, Bureau of Indian Affairs Correspondence Files, National Archives, Kansas City.

61.   Peter Graves to Edward L. Rogers, January 13, 1927, Bureau of Indian Affairs Correspondence Files, National Archives, Kansas City; Mittelholtz, *Historical Review,* 49; Child, *My Grandfather's Knocking Sticks,* 103–4.

62.   Child, *My Grandfather's Knocking Sticks,* 101.

63.   Child, *My Grandfather's Knocking Sticks,* 103–4, 107; Peter Graves to Edward L. Rogers, January 13, 1927.

64.   General Council Resolution 1 (February 19, 1927), Red Lake Archives; Child, *My Grandfather's Knocking Sticks,* 109.

65.   The law passed on March 22, 1929: Chapter 84, Section 5592, Subsections 1–8. See Van Oosten and Deason, "History of Red Lake's Fishery."

66.   Graves interview.

67.   The General Council of the Red Lake Band of Chippewa Indians approved of the arrangement on March 1, 1929, almost a month before the contract was executed, which enabled them to move quickly after the contract with the state was in place. See "The Proceedings of the General Council of the Red Lake Band of Chippewa Indians," March 1, 1929, Red Lake Archives.

68.   Van Oosten and Deason, "History of Red Lake's Fishery"; Fred Dennis, "Semi-Final Story Pertaining to the Acquiring of the Land around the North and Eastern Shores of Upper Red Lake," undated manuscript, Red Lake Archives.

69.　Child, *My Grandfather's Knocking Sticks,* 117.

70.　Frederic L. Kirgis to Harold L. Ickes, June 30, 1936, Secretary of the Interior Correspondence File; Fred Dennis to Governor Harold Stassen, January 24, 1939, Bureau of Indian Affairs Correspondence Files, National Archives, Kansas City.

71.　Peter Graves to Harry E. Speakes, May 11, 1939, Bureau of Indian Affairs Correspondence Files, National Archives, Kansas City.

72.　Raymond H. Bitney to Peter Graves, General Council of the Red Lake Band of Chippewa Indians, February 2, 1939, Bureau of Indian Affairs Correspondence Files, National Archives, Kansas City.

73.　Minnesota State Senate Bill 697, 51st Session (1939). Raymond Bitney to Fred Dennis, April 19, 1939; Theodore Quale to Raymond H. Bitney, April 14, 1939; E. L. Tungseth to Fred Dennis, April 15, 1939—all National Archives, Kansas City, RG 75, box 517485. Fred Dennis to Tom C. White, January 19, 1945; R. T. Buckler Memo, November 19, 1934; William Heritage to Raymond H. Bitney, February 21, 1936; Raymond H. Bitney to John Collier, March 30, 1936—all Red Lake Archives; Dennis, "Semi-Final Story."

74.　Fred Dennis to Richard T. Buckler, November 19, 1934; Fred Dennis to Richard T. Buckler, May 23, 1941; Fred Dennis to Ed Rogers, May 23, 1941—all Red Lake Archives.

75.　Dennis, "Semi-Final Story."

76.　Reclamation and condemnation proceedings and strategies are well documented in tribal correspondence. See especially Fred Dennis to Raymond H. Bitney, April 25, 1935; Fred Dennis to John Collier, April 25, 1935; Fred Dennis to Robert C. Bell, April 25, 1935; Raymond H. Bitney to John Collier, May 27, 1935; Fred Dennis to E. V. Willard, June 14, 1935; Fred Dennis to Peter Graves, June 14, 1935; Erling Swenson to Fred Dennis, June 20, 1935; E. V. Willard to Fred Dennis, June 18, 1935; Fred Dennis to Erling Swenson, June 22, 1935—all Red Lake Archives; Fred Dennis, "Report to Red Lake Fisheries Association," July 1, 1935–June 30, 1936, Red Lake Archives.

77.　Van Oosten and Deason, "History of Red Lake's Fishery."

78.　Mittelholtz, *Historical Review,* 54; Child, *My Grandfather's Knocking Sticks,* 41.

79.　*Return of the Red Lake Walleye,* documentary film (University of Arizona: Native Nations Institute, 2012); Red Lake Department of Natural Resources, "Red Lake Fisheries Program," http://www.redlakednr.org/Fisheries.html; Larry Oakes, "'87 Walleye Case," *Minneapolis Star Tribune,* May 23, 1999, 1.

80.　Peter Graves to Mark L. Burns, January 9, 1939; Graves interview.

81.　Graves interview; "Statement of the General Council," June 1, 1956.

82.　W. Barton Greenwood to Marlys Kingbird, August 29, 1954, Red Lake Archives.

83.　Wheeler-Howard Act, 48 Stat. 984 (June 18, 1934), codified as 25 U.S.C. §461. Raymond H. Bitney to David G. Mandelbaum, July 6, 1939; Raymond Bitney to Fred Dennis, July 7, 1939; Raymond H. Bitney to Mark L. Burns, July 7, 1939;

Raymond H. Bitney to Peter Graves, July 8, 1939; Raymond H. Bitney to Mark L. Burns, July 14, 1939—all Red Lake Archives.

84.   Fred Dennis to R. T. Buckler, November 19, 1934, December 18, 1935, May 21, 1936; Fred Dennis to Peter Graves, November 14 and December 18, 1935, January 29, 1937; Raymond H. Bitney to Peter Graves, January 10, 1935, February 2 and 16, 1939; Raymond H. Bitney to Commissioner of Indian Affairs, January 21, 1935, February 24 and December 23, 1936, January 29 and July 30, 1937, January 13, 1938, March 16, May 19, and June 13, 1939; Raymond H. Bitney to Fred Dennis, January 24, March 19, and May 2, 1936, February 1, 1937, February 16 and 23, 1939; Raymond H. Bitney to John Gunderson Rockwell, September 29, 1938; Raymond H. Bitney to A. L. Hook, October 3, 1938; J. H. Brott to Peter Graves, January 3, 1939; Raymond H. Bitney to Benjamin E. Youngdahl, March 11, 1939; Agency Superintendent to Fred Dennis, June 2, 1943; Fred Dennis to Tom White, January 19, 1945; Peru Faver to D. E. Murphy, June 11, 1947; E. K. Burlew Memorandum, October 22, 1940—all in Submarginal Land File, Red Lake Archives.

85.   10 Fed. Reg. 2448 (1945); House of Representatives Bill 4540, 75th Congress, 1st Session (February 9, 1937); 56 Stat. 1039 (December 4, 1942).

86.   Brad Swenson, "Red Lake Gains 32,000 Acres," *Bemidji Pioneer,* January 8, 1989, 1, 14; Jourdain, "Mis-qua-ga-me-we-saga-eh-ganing."

87.   Mittelholtz, *Historical Review,* 52–53.

88.   Vandersluis, *History of Beltrami County,* 24.

89.   *Ex Parte Crow Dog,* 109 U.S. Supreme Court 556; Major Crimes Act, 23 Stat. 385.

90.   Public Law 280, as it is commonly known, is properly cited at PL 83–280 (18 USC §1162 and 28 USC §1360). Bois Forte was later exempted from Public Law 280 by act of Congress on May 23, 1973 (25 USC §1323). For analysis, see Sarah N. Cline, "Sovereignty under Arrest? Public Law 280 and Its Discontents," master's thesis, Oregon State University, May 20, 2013. 39 Minn. 853, 867 in *Sigana v. Bailey,* 282 Minn. 367.

91.   *Sigana v. Bailey,* 282 Minn. 367, went all the way to the Minnesota Supreme Court. *Roman Sigana, Respondent v. Allen Bailey and Isaac Johnson, Appellants.* There is a great review of the case law on Public Law 280 in Christopher Lundberg, "Public Law 280 and Its Relevance for State Courts: Jurisdictional Limits on the State and the Importance of Ensuring Tribal Court Adjudication When Appropriate," unpublished manuscript, December 2006, Red Lake Archives, also available at http://www.lsej.org/documents/118871Public%20Law%20280%20Final%20Paper.pdf. See also *State v. Holthusen,* 261 Minn. 536, 113 N. W.2d 180; *In re Settlement of Beaulieu,* 264 Minn. 406, 119 N.W.2d 25; and *State v. Lussier,* 269 Minn. 176, 130 N.W.2d 484.

92.   Newman, "Temporary Post Lasts Six Years."

93.   Mittelholtz, *Historical Review,* 111; Edgerton, "Death Comes for Peter Graves."

94.   Graves interview.

95.   Commissioner of Indian Affairs, *Reports,* 69th Annual Report (1900), 687.

96.   Peter Graves to Mark L. Burns, January 9, 1939.

97. Graves interview; Peter Graves to Mark L. Burns, January 9, 1939.

98. Mittelholtz, *Historical Review,* 44.

99. General Council Resolutions 1 (June 27, 1927), 1 (September 18, 1944), 9 (September 4, 1945), 4 (September 14, 1947), 3 (July 30, 1950), 2 (September 24, 1950)—all Red Lake Archives.

100. "Statement of the General Council," June 1, 1956, Red Lake Archives; Senate Committee on Indian Affairs, Special Commission on the Chippewa Indian Tribes of Minnesota, 589; Peter Graves to Mark L. Burns, January 9, 1939.

101. Edgerton, "Death Comes for Peter Graves."

102. Frell M. Owl to Don C. Foster, April 18, 1952; Frell M. Owl to Brigadier-General J. E. Nelson, April 17, 1952; General Council Resolution 5 (April 6, 1952); Tribal Council Resolution 115-59 (October 13, 1959)—all Red Lake Archives; Anna Gibbs interview (April 14, 2015).

103. O. D. Morken to Peter Graves, July 20, 1956; W. McLaughlin to Peter Graves, October 5, 1956; BIA Mineral Prospecting Permit, May 29, 1956—all Red Lake Archives.

104. McClurken, *Fish in the Lakes,* 383.

105. Kathryn "Jody" Beaulieu interview with Robert Treuer (June 20, 2003).

106. Mittelholtz, *Historical Review,* 55.

107. Strong interview.

108. Mittelholtz, *Historical Review,* 110; Edgerton, "Death Comes for Peter Graves"; Raymond H. Bitney to Mrs. Marion Gridley, February 21, 1939, Red Lake Archives.

109. Harlan Beaulieu interview (April 5, 2013).

NOTES TO CHAPTER 6: THE REVOLUTIONARY

1. Opening quote from Brill, *Red Lake Nation,* 154; Susan Stanich, "Red Lake's Chief: Roger Jourdain's Friends, Foes Agree He Puts Reservation First," *Duluth News-Tribune,* undated press clipping, Red Lake Archives. Information on Roger Jourdain throughout this chapter is taken from several key sources. Jourdain was widely covered by the press. There are two great biographies of him: Chavers, "The Last Great Warrior," 79-97; Robert Treuer, "Jourdain of Red Lake: Profile of an Indian Leader," unpublished manuscript, 2003, Anton Treuer Papers, Red Lake Archives. I also relied on Floyd Jourdain interview (April 23, 2012); Kathryn "Jody" Beaulieu interview with Robert Treuer (June 20, 2003); Chuck Haga, "Roger Jourdain, 1912-2002," *Minneapolis Star Tribune,* March 23, 2002, 1; Pat Doyle, "Residency Rule Foiled Would-Be Tribal Leader," *Minneapolis Star Tribune,* August 7, 1990, 1; Rodney Jourdain to Robert Treuer, June 15, 1970, Anton Treuer Papers, Red Lake Archives; Brad Swenson, "Roger Jourdain, 1912-2002," *Bemidji Pioneer,* March 23, 2002, 1, 9; Molly Miron, "Friends Remember Jourdain: First Chairman of Red Lake Band of Chippewa Admired," *Bemidji Pioneer,* March 24, 2002, 1, 7; Linda Greer, "Bemidji Recognizes Roger Jourdain Day," *Bemidji Pioneer,* April 4, 2002, 3; Roger Jourdain interview with Wilf Cyr and Red Lake High School Students (1993), video, Red Lake Archives.

2. Floyd Jourdain interview (June 8, 2015).

3.   Ruth Fevig, Gladys Graves, and Alice Tatum. Ruth was previously married to Calvin Beaulieu.

4.   Roger Jourdain interview with Wilf Cyr.

5.   Don Allery, "Roger Jourdain," unpublished manuscript, 14, Anton Treuer Papers, Red Lake Archives.

6.   Allery, "Roger Jourdain," 15-16.

7.   *To Walk the Red Road,* 17.

8.   *Lakota Times,* 1991, as cited in Chavers, "The Last Great Warrior," 80; John Greeting Spears Sr. (1908-68) was four years older than Roger Jourdain. Jourdain gives a nearly identical interview in Roger Jourdain interview with Wilf Cyr.

9.   Allery, "Roger Jourdain," 21.

10.   Nathan Head received the nickname "Scan" because he frequently used the word *scandalous.* Kathryn "Jody" Beaulieu interview with Robert Treuer; Allery, "Roger Jourdain," 23.

11.   Allery, "Roger Jourdain," 23.

12.   Allery, "Roger Jourdain," 7, 14.

13.   Roger Jourdain interview with Wilf Cyr. Paul H. Beaulieu was born July 30, 1889, and died on April 8, 1955. Ransom Judd Powell Papers, Genealogy Microfilm 455, Family 93, Minnesota Historical Society.

14.   Allery, "Roger Jourdain," 7, 14.

15.   Allery, "Roger Jourdain," 8.

16.   Allery, "Roger Jourdain," 8.

17.   Roger Jourdain interview with Wilf Cyr.

18.   Stanich, "Red Lake's Chief."

19.   Peter Graves interview with Arch Grahn (October 5, 1950), Minnesota Historical Society.

20.   "Red Lake Nation: A Status Report," Red Lake Band of Chippewa Indians, May 23, 1990, 3; Roger Jourdain interview with Wilf Cyr.

21.   U.S. Census listing for Paul H. Beaulieu (1940); U.S. Indian Census Roll for Paul H. Beaulieu (1885-1940); Allery, "Roger Jourdain," 12.

22.   "New Council Held Out as Reservation Possibility: Rival Groups Could Both Lose, Indians Told," and "Red Lake Governing Rights Argued before Committee," *Bemidji Daily Pioneer,* February 7, 1958, 1.

23.   Shirley M. Cain, "Red Cloak: Tom Cain, Warrior and Teacher," *The Circle,* May 1990; Mark Boswell, "Tom Cain, Portrait of an Ojibwe Man," *Ojibwe News,* March 21, 1990, 6.

24.   Information on this and the next chapter is documented in "Report and Recommendations," Departmental Hearing Committee on Red Lake Tribal Governance Dispute to Secretary of the Interior, March 5, 1958. R. W. Quinn, Bureau of Indian Affairs Field Trip Report, June 23, 1958; R. D. Holtz, "Red Lake Band of Chippewa Tribal Government Meeting," March 19, 1958—both Red Lake Archives.

25.   "Hereditary Chiefs Council Spokesman Arrested, Freed as Power Inquiry Proceeds," *Bemidji Daily Pioneer,* February 8, 1958, 1.

26.   "Report and Recommendations," Departmental Hearing Committee;

Quinn, Field Trip Report, June 23, 1958; Holtz, "Red Lake Band of Chippewa"; D. S. Myer and Red Lake Tribal Business Association, Meeting Minutes, July 8, 1952, Red Lake Archives.

27. "Rival Red Lake Factions Await Result of Hearings," *Bemidji Daily Pioneer*, February 10, 1958, 1.

28. "Department of Interior Holds Fate of Councils," *Bemidji Daily Pioneer*, February 10, 1958, 1.

29. *Minneapolis Journal,* June 15, 1953; "Rival Red Lake Factions Await Result of Hearings," 1.

30. "Rival Red Lake Factions Await Result of Hearings," 1.

31. "Rival Red Lake Factions Await Result of Hearings," 1; "Guide Course for Indians Is Proposed at College," *Bemidji Daily Pioneer*, February 7, 1958.

32. "Red Lake Band Must Form New Government," *Bemidji Daily Pioneer*, March 20, 1958, 1-2; Findings and Recommendations of Special Departmental Committee on Controversy over the Governing Body of the Red Lake Band of Chippewa Indians, Secretary of the Interior, *Reports,* March 5, 1958.

33. "Red Lake Band Must Form New Government," 2.

34. Findings and Recommendations of Special Departmental Committee; "Red Lake Band Must Form New Government," 2.

35. "Red Lake Group Organized for Closed Reservation," *Bemidji Daily Pioneer,* March 25, 1958, 1; "Red Lake Fisheries Holds Election," *Bemidji Daily Pioneer,* April 1, 1958, 1.

36. "Red Lake Election to Be Held on May 22," *Bemidji Daily Pioneer,* April 19, 1958, 1-2; "Let's Help Them," *Bemidji Daily Pioneer,* May 2, 1958, 8; "Closed Red Lake Reservation Group to Meet Sunday," *Bemidji Daily Pioneer,* May 8, 1958, 1; *Bemidji Daily Pioneer,* March 20, 1958, 2; "Candidates for Red Lake Poll May 22," *Bemidji Daily Pioneer,* May 16, 1958, 2; "Jourdain and Jahnke Win at Red Lake," *Bemidji Daily Pioneer,* May 21, 1958, 1; "Meetings on New Indian Bylaws Set," *Bemidji Daily Pioneer,* June 18, 1958, 2.

37. "Indian Affairs Committee to Meet in Bemidji," *Bemidji Daily Pioneer,* January 24, 1958; "Indian Meet Slated Here Wednesday," *Bemidji Daily Pioneer,* February 3, 1958; "Chippewas Will Discuss Property Titles Wednesday," *Bemidji Daily Pioneer,* May 28, 1958, 2; "Decision on Appeal from Settlement Voted to Law Firm at Red Lake Meeting," *Bemidji Daily Pioneer,* June 12, 1958, 1-2.

38. "Jourdain Is Voted Head of Red Lake Indian Band," *Bemidji Daily Pioneer,* January 8, 1959, 1; Wub-e-ke-niew [Francis Blake], *We Have the Right,* 143; "Indians Vote for Amended Constitution," *Bemidji Daily Pioneer,* October 18, 1958, 1; "Tribal Council of Red Lake to Be Elected January 6," *Bemidji Daily Pioneer,* November 28, 1958, 1, 3; "New Tribal Council Installed," *Bemidji Daily Pioneer,* January 22, 1959, 1.

39. Information for this section is taken from Beito, *Coya Come Home;* Dan Gunderson, "Coya's Story," May 3, 2004, Minnesota Public Radio; Treuer, "Jourdain of Red Lake," 4; Allery, "Roger Jourdain," 10-14.

40. There were several thousand enrolled members at Red Lake and even more at White Earth in Knutson's district. Most enrolled members were not

registered voters, but many of the adults were. Jourdain did not dictate their voting, but he did exert significant influence among tribal voters.

41.   Termination persisted as a policy until the middle of the 1960s. Fifty tribes were reinstated after termination in the 1970s. The Chinook and many others never were. See Fixico, *Termination and Relocation*.

42.   Beito, *Coya Come Home*; Dan Gunderson, "Coya's Story," May 3, 2004, Minnesota Public Radio.

43.   Chavers, "The Last Great Warrior," 79; "Hospital at Red Lake Is Reopened," *Bemidji Sentinel*, January 23, 1959, 1.

44.   Mittelholtz, *Historical Review*, 99.

45.   Chavers, "The Last Great Warrior," 83; Roger Jourdain speech to students at St. Cloud State University in 1990, as cited in Chavers, "The Last Great Warrior," 82.

46.   *Red Lake Band of Chippewa Indians v. Earl J. Barlow*, 846 F.2d 474.

47.   Red Lake Tribal Council, Press Release, May 1, 1967, Red Lake Archives.

48.   The Red Lake Tribal Employment Rights Ordinance is posted on the tribe's website and codified in Tribal Council Resolutions 231-88 (September 22, 1988), 170-12 (August 14, 2012), 44-13 (March 12, 2013)—all Red Lake Archives. The national legislative effort and Roger Jourdain's role in advocating for it is documented in Title 18, Part 1, Chapter 53, USC § 1151; Smith, *Labor and Employment Law*; Chavers, "The Last Great Warrior," 83.

49.   *To Walk the Red Road*, 18.

50.   Information on the boycott throughout this section is taken from Sam Newlund, "Indians to Boycott Bemidji Merchants after Broadcast," *Minneapolis Tribune*, October 28, 1966, 1, 9; "Tribal Council Votes to Boycott Bemidji," *Bemidji Daily Pioneer*, October 28, 1966, 1; Roger Jourdain, Letter to the Editor, *Bemidji Daily Pioneer*, October 29, 1966; "Indians Protest Broad Cast, Vow Longer Boycott," *Minneapolis Tribune*, October 30, 1966, 1, 18A; "Indians Continue Bemidji Boycott," *Bemidji Daily Pioneer*, October 31, 1966, 1-2; Jim Daman, Letter to the Editor, *Bemidji Daily Pioneer*, November 1, 1966; "Boycott Continues," *Bemidji Daily Pioneer*, November 4, 1966, 1; "Harmful Boycott," *Bemidji Daily Pioneer*, November 2, 1966, 2; "Boycott against Bemidji Lifted," *Bemidji Daily Pioneer*, November 5, 1966, 1; Chuck Haga, "A Long Year at Red Lake: From Condemnation to Compassion during a Crisis," *Minneapolis Star Tribune*, March 14, 2006; Roger Jourdain, Formal Complaint to Federal Communications Commission, October 25, 1966; FCC to Roger Jourdain, October 28, 1966; James R. Hambacher to Roger Jourdain, October 28, 1966; Roger Jourdain to James Hambacher, October 26, 1966; Roger Jourdain to Eugene McCarthy, October 26, 1966—all Red Lake Archives. Thomas Stillday Jr. interview (2006).

51.   Robert Kohl, KBUN Commentary Program, October 25, 1966. The entire text was reproduced and shared in many venues, including a full reprint in the *Red Lake News*. Copies are archived with the Federal Communications Commission in Washington, DC, and the Red Lake Archives. For Miller quote, see Red Lake Tribal Council Meeting Minutes, October 29, 1966, Red Lake Archives.

52. "Indians Protest Broad Cast."

53. Roger Jourdain, Letter to the Editor, *Bemidji Daily Pioneer*, October 29, 1966.

54. "Kohl Quits, Boycott Ends," *Red Lake News* 1.13 (November 4, 1966): 1. Margaret Seelye represented Red Lake's new Community Action Program (CAP) at the meetings, and her mother, Luella Seelye, deputy assistant director of Community Action Program, was there for Leech Lake.

55. "Harmful Boycott," *Bemidji Daily Pioneer*, November 2, 1966, 2.

56. Roger Jourdain, Letter to the Editor, *Bemidji Daily Pioneer*, October 29, 1966; Jim Daman, Letter to the Editor, *Bemidji Daily Pioneer*, November 1, 1966; David E. Umhauer, Letter to the Editor, *Bemidji Daily Pioneer*, November 2, 1966.

57. "LeVander Says Bemidji Station Supports Rolvaag," *Minneapolis Tribune*, October 30, 1966. Archived at Red Lake are copies of more than fifty letters of support for the boycott from business and political leaders sent to Roger Jourdain.

58. "Statement by Bob Kohl to Red Lake Tribal Council," November 3, 1966, Red Lake Archives.

59. Bob Schranck, "Indian Critic Quits Bemidji Radio Post," *Minneapolis Star*, November 4, 1966.

60. Joint Resolution by the Beltrami County Board of Supervisors, the Council of the City of Bemidji, and the Tribal Council of the Red Lake Band of Chippewa Indians, November 4, 1966.

61. Tribal Council Resolution 167-66 (November 4, 1966), Red Lake Archives; Thomas Stillday Jr. interview (2006); Haga, "A Long Year at Red Lake."

62. Brad Swenson, "Remarks at Two Public Meetings Called Racist," *Bemidji Pioneer*, March 20, 1992.

63. Tribal Council Resolutions 76-60 (September 14, 1960), 136-66 (September 14, 1966), 25-67 (February 9, 1967); General Council Resolution 3 (February 21, 1943)—all Red Lake Archives.

64. Tribal Council Resolutions 163-66 (November 3, 1966), 98-66 (July 13, 1966)—both Red Lake Archives. One Redby parcel was purchased from the Episcopal mission by the tribe during the Graves administration prior to Jourdain's effort. See General Council Resolution 6 (December 19, 1948), Red Lake Archives.

65. Robert Treuer's profile of Roger Jourdain ("Jourdain of Red Lake") during the housing boom is a great combination of personal observations and historical research. Treuer served as community organizer for the Bemidji Office of the Bureau of Indian Affairs (1963-66), as director of Red Lake's Community Action Program (1966-68), and as director of personnel for the Office of Economic Opportunity in Washington, DC (1968-78). For details on housing policy, see "Red Lake Nation: A Status Report," 2.

66. Treuer, "Jourdain of Red Lake," 12.

67. Treuer, "Jourdain of Red Lake," 13; Robert Treuer, "A Passion to Protect," *Minneapolis Star Tribune*, March 31, 2002, A21.

68. Treuer, "Jourdain of Red Lake," 15; "Red Lake Nation: A Status Report," 2.

69. Treuer, "A Passion to Protect."

70. "People Are Coming to Walk Taller," *Minneapolis Tribune,* November 14, 1967. Roger Jourdain to Hubert H. Humphrey, March 15, 1966; Roger Jourdain to Walter Mondale, March 15, 1966; Red Lake Tribal Council Resolution 187-66 (October 26, 1966); Red Lake Tribal Council, Press Release, November 1, 1967; Roger Jourdain to Myron Hutchinson (University of South Dakota), November 10, 1966—all Red Lake Archives.

71. Information on this and the next three paragraphs is taken from Chuck Haga, "A Champion of His People," *Minneapolis Star Tribune,* March 23, 2002, A1, A18; Treuer, "A Passion to Protect"; Wahlberg, *The North Land,* 24.

72. Commissioner of Indian Affairs, *Reports,* 1905; Mittelholtz, *Historical Review,* 35.

73. Mittelholtz, *Historical Review,* 1, 45.

74. Margaret Seelye Treuer interview (April 11, 2015). She is the author's mother.

75. Margaret Seelye Treuer interview (April 11, 2015).

76. "Jourdain-Perpich Extended Care Facility among Highest Rated in Minnesota," *Red Lake Nation News,* August 10, 2006.

77. Chuck Haga, "A Champion of His People"; Treuer, "A Passion to Protect"; Wahlberg, *The North Land,* 24.

78. Kathryn "Jody" Beaulieu interview with Robert Treuer; Tim Giago, "Are We Becoming Nations of Sheep," *Lakota Journal,* January 9-16, 2004.

79. Kathryn "Jody" Beaulieu interview with Robert Treuer.

80. Kermit Pattison, "Tribal Leader Left Big Legacy," *St. Paul Pioneer Press,* March 23, 2002, 1; Kathryn "Jody" Beaulieu interview with Robert Treuer; Roger Jourdain interview with Wilf Cyr.

81. *Red Lake Band v. State,* 248 NW 2d 722, MSC (1976).

82. Red Lake Tribal Council Passport, Passport No. 1265, Robert Treuer, Issued September 1, 1987, Anton Treuer Papers, Red Lake Archives; *U.S. v. Jackie White,* 508 U.S. Court of Appeals, 8th Circuit 453; *To Walk the Red Road,* 20. The White case was a jurisdictional one in which White shot at and missed a live bald eagle and was charged under federal statute, but argued that the federal government lacked jurisdiction at Red Lake, except for crimes under the Major Crimes Act.

83. Roger A. Jourdain to Ted Thorson, May 3, 1985, Red Lake Archives.

84. Roger Jourdain interview with Wilf Cyr.

85. Pattison, "Tribal Leader Left Big Legacy," 1, 12A; Tribal Council Resolution 110-67 (July 4, 1967), Red Lake Archives.

86. Pattison, "Tribal Leader Left Big Legacy," 1, 12A.

87. Brill, *Red Lake Nation,* 154.

88. Public Law 93-638; 28 U.S.C. § 450-8.

89. Full text of Nixon's policy statement is available at http://www.epa.gov/tribal/pdf/president-nixon70.pdf. It was transmitted to Congress as "Special Message to the Congress on Indian Affairs," July 8, 1970. See Gerhard Peters and

John T. Woolley, *The American Presidency Project*, http://www.presidency.ucsb.edu /ws/?pid=2573.

90. Treuer, "A Passion to Protect"; Robert Treuer interview (April 2, 2014). Robert Treuer is the author's father.

91. Brill, *Red Lake Nation*, 147-48; Tribal Council Resolution 203-90 (September 17, 1990), Red Lake Archives; Bureau of Indian Affairs official website, http://www.indianaffairs.gov/; "Hallett Killed in Auto Accident," *Bemidji Pioneer*, February 5, 1992; 543 U.S. 631 (Supreme Court, 2005).

92. Public Law 92-318, Title IV (1972); "The Indian Education Act of 1972," *Journal of American Indian Education* 14.2 (January 1975). Public Law 93-380 added teacher training and fellowship opportunities to the IEA in 1974. In 1988, Public Law 100-297 made BIA schools eligible for formula funding and gifted and talented programs. Public Laws 103-382 in 1994 and 107-110 in 2001 reauthorized the program.

93. Daniel K. Inouye to family of Roger Jourdain, March 27, 2002, Red Lake Archives.

94. Public Law 95-341 (August 11, 1978); 92 Stat. 469; 42 U.S.C. § 1996.

95. "Roger Alfred Jourdain, Biographical Sketch," unpublished biography, 1966, Anton Treuer Papers, Red Lake Archives. There is a note on the manuscript that reads: "Read to Roger at 3:15 P.M. on December 15, 1966, authorized this a true quote."

96. All of the statistics on adoption and foster care of native children, including the Minnesota-specific figures, are taken from expert testimony on the bill Public Law 95-608 (Indian Child Welfare Act), 9-10, 336-37. Information on impacts of the act and caseload numbers is taken from Graves and Ebbott, *Indians in Minnesota*, 227, 238; Child, *Holding Our World Together*, 151.

97. ICWA advocacy and legislative effort in this and the following paragraph are taken from Public Law 95-608; 92 Stat. 3069 (November 8, 1978); 25 Stat. Codified §1901-63; Esther Wattenberg, "Sovereignty: The Heart of the Matter, Critical Considerations on the Interface between ICWA and ASFA" (unpublished conference proceedings, University of Minnesota, May 17, 2000).

98. John Redhorse in Esther Wattenberg, "Sovereignty."

99. *Seminole Tribe of Florida v. Butterworth*, 658 F. 2d 310 (5th Circuit Court of Appeals, 1981); *California v. Cabazon Band of Mission Indians*, 480 U.S. 202 (1987); Indian Gaming Regulatory Act, Public Law 100-497; 25 U.S.C. § 2701.

100. Brad Swenson, "Gambling Law Challenged," *Bemidji Pioneer*, January 29, 1989, 1; Susan Landon, "N.M. Tribe Leads Challenge against Gambling Law," *Albuquerque Journal*, January 28, 1989, 1; "Perpich Signs Pacts Regulating Gambling on State Reservations," *Duluth News-Tribune*, October 26, 1989, 3A; Bill Johnson, "Jourdain Urges Other Tribes to Join Lawsuit against Gaming Law," Associated Press via *Bemidji Pioneer*, October 6, 1989, 1, 3; Don Jacobson, "Indian Lawsuit Says Gaming Act Unconstitutional," *Duluth News-Tribune*, January 28, 1989, 1; Brad Swenson, "Reagan Asked to Veto Indian Gambling Bill," *Bemidji Pioneer*, October 2, 1988, 1, 3.

101. The act was originally passed as Public Law 93-638; 28 U.S.C. § 450-8. Reauthorization is Public Law 100-297 (1988).

102. Michael Meuers, Red Lake Political Education Committee, "Reservation Turnout Data Report, 2000–2012," Red Lake Archives.

103. Information throughout this section is taken from *Red Lake Band of Chippewa Indians v. United States,* 800 F.2d 1187 (September 6, 1986); Jim Parsons, "Nepotism Charge Is Part of Red Lake Dissension," *Minneapolis Tribune,* June 10, 1979, 1, 8A; George White, "Fires, Shootings Destroy Much of Red Lake," *Minneapolis Tribune,* May 21, 1979, 1, 4A; George White, "New Reservation Agent Says Federal Funds Were Misused," *Minneapolis Tribune,* May 22, 1979, 1, 8A; Jim Parsons, "Red Lake Leader May Be Ousted like Predecessor He Helped Oust," *Minneapolis Tribune,* May 22, 1979, 1, 9A; Jim Parsons, "Red Lake Revolt Leader Waives His Rights," *Minneapolis Tribune,* May 23, 1979, 1, 4B; Jim Parsons, "Red Lake Buries Victims of Violence; Hiding Chairman Freezes Tribal Funds," *Minneapolis Tribune,* May 24, 1979, 2B, 10B; Finlay Lewis, "Red Lake Violence Rekindles Controversy over BIA Role," *Minneapolis Tribune,* May 27, 1979, 1, 4A; Joe Kimball, "Jourdain Says He Is Still Red Lake Chairman," *Minneapolis Tribune,* May 27, 1979, 1, 4A; George White, "Indians Burn Reservation Jail," *Minneapolis Tribune,* May 20, 1979, 1, 8A; Brill, *Red Lake Nation,* 154–55; Eugene Stillday interview (July 11, 2006).

104. *Roger A. Jourdain and Margaret E. Jourdain v. Commissioner of Internal Revenue,* 617 U.S. Court of Appeals, 8th Circuit 507; *Commissioner of Taxation v. Brun,* 174 NW 2d, MSC 120 (1970).

105. The background for this paragraph is taken from note 98, above, and "Alvin R. Oliver," *Bemidji Pioneer,* August 3, 1981, 3. The political action around Hanson's job censure is taken from Tribal Council Resolutions 1-78 (February 28, 1978), 2-78 (February 28, 1978), 5-79 (May 21, 1979), 4-80 (January 16, 1980)—all Red Lake Archives; Don Allery, "The Red Lake Band of Chippewa Indians: May 19, 1979," Red Lake Archives.

106. Eugene Stillday interview (July 11, 2006).

107. *Minneapolis Tribune,* July 24, 1979.

108. Brill, *Red Lake Nation,* 155.

109. Treuer, "Jourdain of Red Lake," 6.

110. Tribal Council Resolution 181-71 (December 16, 1971), Red Lake Archives.

111. "A Man Called," *Lakota Times* 10.50 (1991); Coleman, Frogner, and Eich, *Ojibwa Myths and Legends,* 103; Tribal Council Resolutions 115-59 (October 13, 1959), 59-78 (May 4, 1978)—both Red Lake Archives; Treuer, "Jourdain of Red Lake," 6.

112. Tribal Council Resolutions 148-60 (July 12, 1960), 135-73 (September 19, 1973), 90-76 (September 24, 1976), 141-77 (September 15, 1977)—all Red Lake Archives.

113. Public Law 97-425; Red Lake Band of Chippewa Indians, "Policy Statement on Nuclear Waste Disposal Sites," 1982, Red Lake Archives.

114. Stanich, "Red Lake's Chief"; Wub-e-ke-niew [Francis Blake], *We Have the*

Right, 187–88; Pat Doyle, "BIA Urges Red Lake to Open Reservation for Jobs," *Minneapolis Star Tribune,* 1, 8B.

115. Treuer, "Jourdain of Red Lake," 7; Treuer, "A Passion to Protect."

116. Treuer, "A Passion to Protect," 8.

117. Brad Swenson, "Jourdain Re-elected by 21 Votes," *Bemidji Pioneer,* May 23, 1986, 1; "Jourdain Is Winner in Tribal Election," *Minneapolis Star Tribune,* May 23, 1986, 1B.

118. "Judge to Decide Red Lake Reservation Election Issue," *Grand Forks Herald,* July 18, 1990, 1.

119. Amended Red Lake Band of Chippewa Constitution, Article 5b (May 24, 1978); Tribal Council Resolution 78-78 (May 24, 1978), Red Lake Archives. Other amendments to the tribe's 1958 constitution were passed in 1974, lowering the voting age from twenty-one to eighteen and, in 1982, prohibiting felons from running for office. Amended Red Lake Band of Chippewa Constitution, Article 5a (May 22, 1974); Tribal Council Resolution 62-74 (May 22, 1974); Amended Red Lake Band of Chippewa Constitution, Article 5b (May 26, 1982); Tribal Council Resolution 107-82 (May 26, 1982)—all Red Lake Archives.

120. Brill, *Red Lake Nation,* 155; "Remembering Roger Jourdain," *Bemidji Pioneer,* April 1, 2003, 3; Walter Mondale to Robert Treuer, August 31, 1970, and Robert Treuer to Walter Mondale, July 19, 1970—both Anton Treuer Papers, Red Lake Archives.

121. Linda Greer, "Royal Funeral Planned Today: Politicians, Dignitaries Expected to Pay Respects to Jourdain," *Bemidji Pioneer,* March 27, 2002, 1; Brad Swenson, "Whitefeather Discusses Legacy of Roger Jourdain," *Bemidji Pioneer,* March 27, 2002, 10; Brad Swenson, "Jourdain Recalled as People's Leader," *The American,* March 31, 2002, 1-2; Brenda Child, "Roger Jourdain Passes On," *The Circle,* May 2002; Pattison, "Tribal Leader Left Big Legacy," 1, 12A; "Roger Jourdain," *Bemidji Pioneer,* March 24, 2002; Robert Treuer, "Jourdain Saved Red Lake Nation and Changed U.S. Indian Policy," undated, unpublished manuscript, Anton Treuer Papers, Red Lake Archives.

122. "Minnesota Journalist Who Was Tribal Watchdog Dies after Cancer Fight," *Park Rapids Enterprise,* March 5, 2010. Jourdain's conflict with Lawrence ran deep. Lawrence was relentless in his political and personal criticism of Jourdain. Jourdain eventually fought back and even ran background checks on Lawrence's employment history at Fort Mojave, obtaining statements from political officials and supervisors about alleged misconduct when Lawrence was an employee at Mojave. Jourdain pulled criminal background checks on Gary E. Blair, including a first-degree criminal sexual conduct complaint filed February 12, 1982 (Beltrami County, Ninth Judicial District). Blair sometimes assisted Lawrence in political investigation and reporting on Jourdain. See Elmer Seville to Roger A. Jourdain, March 28, 1986, Anton Treuer Papers, Red Lake Archives.

NOTES TO CHAPTER 7: THE DREAMER

1.   Opening quote, Anna C. Gibbs interview (May 13, 2015). Gibbs's account of the bombing throughout this section is taken from Anna C. Gibbs interview (May 13, 2015). For corroborating documentation of the bombings and tribal politics around them, see Frell M. Owl to Don C. Foster, April 18, 1952; Frell M. Owl to Brigadier General J. E. Nelson, April 17, 1952; General Council Resolution 5 (April 6, 1952); Tribal Council Resolution 115-59 (October 13, 1959)—all Red Lake Archives. The bombings annually killed thousands of fish on Upper Red Lake; they floated up in the ordnance-testing zone every spring when the ice melted.

2.   This section is based on Anna Gibbs interviews (1992-2015), and a biography of her by the author reworked and published here with permission, originally published in *Oshkaabewis Native Journal* 7.2 (Spring 2010).

3.   Nenabozho, or Wenabozho in other dialects of Ojibwe, is a figure from traditional legends—half human, half spirit, and a positive spiritual force. He is also famous for his tricks on animals, birds, and Ojibwe people.

4.   Biographical information on Thomas Stillday Jr. is taken from Thomas Stillday Jr. interviews (1992-2006), and a biography of him by the author reworked and published here with permission, originally published in *Oshkaabewis Native Journal* 7.1 (Fall 2009).

5.   This story is a firsthand account experienced by the author and his brother, David Treuer.

6.   Molly Miron, "Red Lake Spiritual Leader Stillday Dies," *Bemidji Pioneer,* October 15, 2008, 1; Ben Cohen, "Thomas Stillday, Jr., Spiritual Leader of Red Lake Ojibwe," *Minneapolis Star Tribune,* October 15, 2008, 1.

7.   Mike Mosedale, "Same Country, Different Nation: The Real Red Lake," *City Pages,* May 4, 2005; John Enger, "A Day They Can't Forget: Legacy of Red Lake Shootings Complex, Difficult to Grasp," Minnesota Public Radio, reprinted in *Bemidji Pioneer,* March 22, 2015, 1, 6-7.

8.   "Language Policy for the Red Lake Band of Chippewa Indians," General Council of the Red Lake Band of Chippewa Indians, 5-6, emphasis in the original; Proposed Resolution 14 (January 7, 2014)—both Red Lake Archives.

9.   The Sela G. Wright Papers are housed at Oberlin College and a copy of the Josselin De Jong Papers is available at the Minnesota Historical Society.

10.   Curriculum included, for example, Tom Cain's *Chippewa Language Series,* published by the Bemidji State College Press in the 1970s.

11.   *Why the Bear Has a Short Tail.*

12.   Title translations are *The Little Animals, Helping, Making Friends,* and *How It Is Said.*

13.   Waadookodaading means "where we help one another."

14.   Molly Miron, "Red Lake Nation College: College President Appreciates His Humble Beginnings," *Bemidji Pioneer,* December 22, 2012, 1.

15.   Michael Barrett, "Seki Sworn in as 6th Chairman of the Red Lake Nation," *Red Lake Nation News,* July 7, 2014.

16.   *Red Lake Band of Chippewa Indians v. United States,* 25 U.S.C. §70; 25 U.S.C. §§1401; Tom Robertson, "Red Lake Band to Reforest 50,000 Acres," Minne-

sota Public Radio, August 25, 2011; Michael Meuers, "Red Lake to Restore Great Pine Forests," *The Circle*, September 10, 2011.

17.   William M. Blair, "Changes in U.S. Agency Stir Anger among Indians," *New York Times*, August 16, 1971.

18.   Rob Capriccioso, "Indian Affairs Experts Jockeying to be President Hillary's Native Guru," *Indian Country Today*, August 14, 2013.

19.   Brill, *Red Lake Nation*, 147-48; Tribal Council Resolution 203-90 (September 17, 1990), Red Lake Archives; Bureau of Indian Affairs official website, http://www.indianaffairs.gov/; "Hallett Killed in Auto Accident," *Bemidji Pioneer*, February 5, 1992.

20.   John Hageman, "Opening New Restaurant in Bemidji a Perfect Fit for Marv Hanson," *Bemidji Pioneer*, April 27, 2013; Zach Kayser, "Marv Hanson Dies at Age 60," *Bemidji Pioneer*, December 30, 2013, 1.

21.   Anna C. Gibbs interview (May 13, 2015).

22.   Aloysius Thunder interview (2006); Wub-e-ke-niew [Francis Blake], *We Have the Right*, 187; Pat Doyle, "BIA Urges Red Lake to Open Reservation for Jobs," *Minneapolis Star Tribune*, June 19, 1986, 1, 8B.

23.   M. L. Burns deposition (August 22, 1930), Court of Claims Doc. H-76, 102, Peter Graves Papers, Red Lake Archives; Wahlberg, *The North Land*, 1-59; "KaKay-Geesick," *Warroad Pioneer*, January 27, 1999, 1; Ryan Bakken, "High-Stakes Game," *Grand Forks Herald*, November 20, 2000, 1, 7A; Tom Robertson, "Warroad Ojibwe Want Federal Recognition," Minnesota Public Radio, October 24, 2005. Tribal Council Resolution 54-73 (April 26, 1973); McPherson to M. R. Baldwin, March 25, 1896; Daniel M. Browning to Hoke Smith, March 12, 1895; Daniel M. Browning to W. F. Campbell, February 8, 1895; Charles H. Burke to Hubert Work, January 19, 1925; Raymond Bitney to George F. Sullivan, January 2, 1936; J. H. Brott to Commissioner of Indian Affairs, March 19, 1941; Raymond Bitney to Victor E. Anderson, August 26, 1938; Raymond Bitney to Max Jones, March 16, 1939—all Red Lake Archives.

24.   Tribal Council Resolution 54-73 (April 26, 1973), Red Lake Archives; Floyd Jourdain interview (June 8, 2015).

25.   "Indians Seek Home on Reserve in Canada," *Bemidji Pioneer*, December 12, 1990; Tribal Council Resolution 89-08 (May 28, 2008), Red Lake Archives; Tom Robertson, "Ojibwe Family Fights Land Sale for Tribal Casino," Minnesota Public Radio, November 4, 2010.

26.   Wilhelm Murg, "Tito Ybarra's Medicine Is His Comedy," *Indian Country Today*, September 27, 2012; Wilhelm Murg, "On the Cutting Edge of Native Comedy with the 1491s," *Indian Country Today*, September 2, 2012.

27.   Wub-e-ke-niew [Francis Blake], *We Have the Right*, xlv, xlvii, 1.

28.   John Gilbert, "Warroad's Boucha Wins Election to U.S. Hockey Hall of Fame," *Minneapolis Star Tribune*, August 12, 1995, 10C.

29.   Floyd Jourdain interview (June 8, 2015).

30.   Andy Nelson, "Saving the Lost Arts of the Chippewa Indians," *Northern Collector*, April 1985, 24-29.

31.   DesJarlait and Williams, *Patrick DesJarlait*.

32. DesJarlait and Williams, *Patrick DesJarlait*, back cover quote.

33. Floyd Jourdain interview (June 9, 2015).

34. "KaKayGeesick's Seeking Recognition," *Warroad Pioneer*, October 4, 2000, 1; Anne Louise Meyerding, "Traditional Art as Fresh as the Artist's Vision," *Bemidji Pioneer*, March 7, 1986, 4; English and Dallman, *Sam English;* Jamie Keith, "Sam English's Big Dream," *The Circle*, July 30, 2012.

35. Child, *My Grandfather's Knocking Sticks.*

36. Minnesota Pollution Control Agency, "Statewide Baseline Study," 1996,   http://www.pca.state.mn.us/index.php/water/water-types-and-programs /groundwater/groundwater-monitoring-and-assessment/statewide-baseline -study.html.

NOTES TO APPENDIX 1: WHEN THE DAKOTA RULED RED LAKE

1. Opening quote, Diedrich, *Ojibway Oratory*, 15. Bear Heart (Le Cœur d'Ours in French) was chief at La Pointe. Turney and Brown, "Catastrophic Early Holocene Sea Level Rise"; Sansome, *Minnesota Underfoot*, 174-79.

2. Mittelholtz, *Historical Review*, 7. The Mandan likely visited Red Lake but did not live there. There were Mandan villages at the mouth of the Minnesota River observed by Perrot in 1689 and Le Sueur in 1701.

3. When the Ojibwe attacked the Dakota at Mille Lacs in 1745, they encountered many of them still living in the A'aninin earthen lodges there. The Ojibwe drove them out by storming the village, dropping gunpowder wrapped in cloth through the smoke holes of the earthen lodges, and clubbing the survivors when they emerged from the explosions. Warren, *History of the Ojibway People*, 157-62, 178-82, 261.

4. The Tuscarora joined the Iroquois Confederacy in 1717. For details on the Iroquois Wars and their impact on Ojibwe-Dakota relations prior to 1679, see Thwaites, *Jesuit Relations*, 5:290, 55:97; Hickerson, "Mdewakanton Band," 41; Kellogg, *French Regime*, 95, 99, 153-54; Warren, *History of the Ojibway People*, 193; Archie Mosay interview, 1994; Earl Otchingwanigan interview, 1993; Mason, *Schoolcraft's Expedition*, 115; Parker, *Carver Journals*, 189; Adams, *Radisson Explorations*, 94; Danziger, *Chippewas of Lake Superior*, 28; Folwell, *History of Minnesota*, 1:80; Gilman, *Grand Portage Story*, 31-32; Sharrock and Sharrock, "History of the Cree," 205-6.

5. Kellogg, *French Regime*, 163; Thwaites, *Jesuit Relations,* 50:279, 54:167, 205, 217, 55:133, 56:115, 117, 57:203, 58:257-63; Hickerson, "Mdewakanton Band," 41-42, 49; Dunn, *The St. Croix*, 10; Danziger, *Chippewas of Lake Superior*, 30; Gilman, *Grand Portage Story*, 31; Folwell, *History of Minnesota*, 1:43; Edmunds, *The Potawatomis*, 8.

6. Tanner, *Atlas*, 65-66; Upham, "Groseilliers and Radisson," 504.

7. Blair, *Indian Tribes*, 1:160-63, 277. See also Densmore, *Chippewa Customs*, 133; Gilman, *Grand Portage Story*, 27, 33; Danziger, *Chippewas of Lake Superior*, 36; Hickerson, "Chippewa of Lake Superior," 58; Upham, "Groseilliers and Radisson," 501; Hill, "Geography of Perrot," 2:207. Most people do not think of buffalo and

caribou inhabiting the lands south of Lake Superior. They were there, however, and in great numbers. The buffalo were primarily along the St. Croix Valley region and the caribou mainly in northern Minnesota. There was a state license to hunt woodland caribou in Minnesota as late as 1906.

8.   Burpee, *Journals and Letters*, 117, 134-35; White, *The Middle Ground*, 77; Hickerson, "Chippewa in Central Minnesota," 41, 57, 59; Sharrock and Sharrock, "History of the Cree," 66; Edmunds, *The Potawatomis*, 13; Hickerson, "Mdewakanton Band," 59-60; Folwell, *History of Minnesota*, 1:39; Blair, *Indian Tribes*, 2:112; Danziger, *Chippewas of Lake Superior*, 29; Blegen, *Minnesota*, 53.

9.   Adams, *Radisson Explorations*, 91; Bishop, "Northern Chippewa," 317.

10.   Meyer, *History of the Santee Sioux*, 10; Folwell, *History of Minnesota*, 1:39, 42-43; Thwaites, *Jesuit Relations*, 68:329; Baerreis, Wheeler-Voeglin, and Wycoco-Moore, "Anthropological Report," 24; Kellogg, *French Regime*, 282, 323, 331-33; Kellogg, *Early Narratives*, 81; Hickerson, "Mdewakanton Band," 76-78, 82-84; Zapffe, *Indian Days*, 40; White, *The Middle Ground*, 82, 168; Blegen, *Minnesota*, 54; "The Fox and Ojibwa War," 1:283; Edmunds, *The Potawatomis*, 26.

11.   The evolution of French trade and exploration policy is easily accessed in the records of early explorers and the documents of New France, including information on the expeditions of Brule and Grenoble (Isle Royale, 1620), Fathers Isaac Jogues and Charles Raymbault (Sault Ste. Marie, 1641), Radisson and Groseilliers (1659), Nicolas Perrot (Lake Superior, 1665 and 1699), Louis Joliet (Lake Superior, 1673), Tonti and La Salle (1678-83 and 1684-87), Du Lhut (Lake Superior, 1678-80), Hennepin (1680), De Noyon (Lake of the Woods, 1687-89), De la Noue (Rainy Lake, 1717); Thwaites, *Jesuit Relations*, 9:313, 55:320; Kellogg, *Early Narratives*, 17-27; Folwell, *History of Minnesota*, 1:28-29, 73.

12.   Burpee, *Journals and Letters*, 136-37, 179; Kavanagh, *La Vérendrye*, 92, 95-97; Norton, *Catholic Missionary Activities*, 15-16. Fort St. Charles is marked on most maps, but the precise location was uncertain from 1800 to 1908, when a major excavation of the site successfully located most of the buildings.

13.   Lund, *Lake of the Woods II*, 42; Blegen, *Minnesota*, 58; Burpee, *Journals and Letters*, 25; Dickason, *Canada's First Nations*, 148; Gilman, *Grand Portage Story*, 142.

14.   For details on the construction of the fort, see Kellogg, *French Regime*, 337.

15.   Crouse, *La Vérendrye*, 88-90; Lund, *Lake of the Woods II*, 35-36.

16.   Burpee, *Journals and Letters*, 175-76, 211; Kavanagh, *La Vérendrye*, 105.

17.   Burpee, *Journals and Letters*, 211.

18.   Burpee, *Journals and Letters*, 238; Hickerson, "Chippewa of Lake Superior," 42.

19.   Burpee, *Journals and Letters*, 211-12, 238, 264-65; Laut, *Pathfinders*, 213-14. See also Crouse, *La Vérendrye*, 107-9; Kavanagh, *La Vérendrye*, 127; Mittelholtz, *Historical Review*, 9; Hickerson, "Chippewa of Lake Superior," 42; Zapffe, *Indian Days*, 45. After the 1736 Dakota attack at Lake of the Woods, large numbers of Dakota returned to the Lake Pepin area boasting of the deed and even sporting a medallion taken from a Frenchman they had killed. This is probably the most

solid evidence there is that the Dakota were the largest contingent. The report of La Vérendrye from June 2, 1736, states that the French encountered an Ojibwe at Lake Vermilion, Minnesota, who claimed to have been present at the incident. Several Ojibwe from Chequamegon were also reported to have been present. René Bourassa's report of the incident says that the war party was composed of Prairie Sioux, Lake Sioux, and Chequamegon Ojibwe.

20. Burpee, *Journals and Letters*, 213-66; Danziger, *Chippewas of Lake Superior*, 36; Gilman, *Grand Portage Story*, 37; Norton, *Catholic Missionary Activities*, 17.

21. Burpee, *Journals and Letters*, 219.

22. Zapffe, *Indian Days*, 45.

23. Burpee, *Journals and Letters*, 228-29, 231.

24. Zapffe, *Indian Days*, 36; Gilman, *Grand Portage Story*, 37.

25. Burpee, *Journals and Letters*, 212-13, 221, 224, 259-60, 266; Blegen, *Minnesota*, 56; Lund, *Lake of the Woods II*, 39.

26. Burpee, *Journals and Letters*, 258; Hickerson, *Chippewa and Their Neighbors*, 71; Gilman, *Grand Portage Story*, 38; Vennum, *Wild Rice and the Ojibway People*, 9.

27. Hickerson, "Chippewa in Central Minnesota," 62; Danziger, *Chippewas of Lake Superior*, 36.

28. Densmore, *Chippewa Customs*, 133; Warren, *History of the Ojibway People*, 158, 159-60.

29. Tanner, *Atlas*, 42; Dunn, *The St. Croix*, 11; Woolworth, "Ethnohistorical Report," 30; Hurt, "Dakota Sioux Indians," 101; Robinson, *History of the Dakota*, 28; Meyer, *History of the Santee Sioux*, 13; Danziger, *Chippewas of Lake Superior*, 37; Warren, *History of the Ojibway People*, 157. As the fur trade put pressure on animal populations on the eastern fringes of the Dakota territory, the Dakota began to move westward. Big game animals such as buffalo were in great abundance on the prairies. According to Mdewakantonwan Dakota oral history, this was the primary causal factor for Dakota westward migrations in the late seventeenth and early eighteenth century. Adaptation to plains hunting practices was greatly augmented by the introduction of the horse to the Dakota around 1700. The primary motive for relocation was the pull of better resources, not the push of enemy warfare. In fact, some scholars believe that the Dakota had begun to shift westward as early as 1650.

30. Hickerson, "Chippewa of Lake Superior," 45; Danziger, *Chippewas of Lake Superior*, 27, 36; Gilman, *Grand Portage Story*, 38; Hickerson, "Mdewakanton Band," 92.

31. Lund, *Lake of the Woods II*, 73; Burpee, *Journals and Letters*, 256-57; Zapffe, *Indian Days*, 128; Ewers, "Ethnological Report," 20.

32. Burpee, *Journals and Letters*, 234, 238; Hickerson, "Chippewa of Lake Superior," 163; Bishop, "Northern Chippewa," 319; Tanner, *Atlas*, 43; Gilman, *Grand Portage Story*, 38, 43.

33. Burpee, *Journals and Letters*, 274; Hickerson, "Mdewakanton Band," 91; Mittelholtz, *Historical Review*, 9.

34. Kegg, "Nookomis Gaa-inaajimotawid," 29-35, 41-43, 49-51, 65, 69; Warren, *History of the Ojibway People*, 106-7, 127-29, 158-62, 170-78, 219-20, 248; Thwaites, *Jesuit Relations*, 51:53, 69:39; Hickerson, "Chippewa of Lake Superior," 45-47; McKenney, *Sketches*, 291; Tanner, *Atlas*, 43; Kellogg, *French Regime*, 356-57; Danziger, *Chippewas of Lake Superior*, 33, 37; Zapffe, *Indian Days*, 128; Mittelholtz, *Historical Review*, 9-10; Diedrich, *The Chiefs Hole-in-the-Day*, 1; Meyer, *History of the Santee Sioux*, 13-14; Folwell, *History of Minnesota*, 1:80; Hurt, "Dakota Sioux Indians," 104; Dunn, *The St. Croix*, 11; Densmore, *Chippewa Customs*, 133; Howard, *Plains-Ojibwa*, 7:99.

NOTE TO APPENDIX 2: RED LAKE RESERVATION POST OFFICES

1. U.S. Postal Service, Postmasters by City, Redlake Post Office, Redby Post Office, and Ponemah Post Office (Beltrami County, Minnesota); U.S. Postal Service, Department of Records, Appointment of Postmasters, microfilm 16, roll 63, number 841, Minnesota Historical Society; "First Postoffice [*sic*] Established at Red Lake in 1875," *Northland Times*, March 26, 1954, 1; Mittelholtz, *Historical Review*, 1, 24-55. The formal name of the post office at Red Lake has the words conflated as "Redlake." The last name Gurno is a common one at Red Lake, and usually is spelled Gurneau, although the postal service records and those at the Minnesota Historical Society spell it as Gurno. Seline Arnold held the postmaster position at Redby in 1944 on a temporary basis while her husband, Datus M. Arnold, was in active military service during World War II. He resumed his former position and she stepped down when he returned.

NOTE TO APPENDIX 4: RED LAKE HEREDITARY CHIEFS

1. Kathryn "Jody" Beaulieu, "Hereditary Chiefs," August 3, 1994, Red Lake Archives; Harlan Beaulieu interview (August 1, 2015); Floyd Jourdain interview (August 2, 2105); James Loud interview (August 15, 2015).

Research Notes
and Bibliography

Researching Red Lake History

I have spent a great deal of time at Red Lake over the past thirty years, much of it in Ponemah, helping Thomas Stillday Jr. and Anna Gibbs at ceremonies. My passion for Red Lake history and language is lifelong. But I did not decide to write a book on Red Lake by myself. Floyd "Buck" Jourdain (who was tribal chairman at the time), Donald "Dude" May, Harlan Beaulieu, and Sam Strong approached me and asked me to take on the project on behalf of the tribe. I then had a sustained working relationship with the tribal council through the duration of Jourdain's administration and the beginning of Darrell Seki's tenure as chairman. The entire tribal council and many staff members at Red Lake commented on and participated in editorial decisions about the book, although any mistakes or omissions are my own.

The tribal council at Red Lake wanted *Warrior Nation* to identify and document the evolution of Red Lake's political culture. They want their tribal citizens to have a new and powerful tool for understanding their political patrimony, history, and culture. They also wanted to document not just stories of loss and trauma, but the collective achievements of their people. I organized *Warrior Nation* in seven main chapters, each a biography of an important Red Lake leader at a different point in time. Red Lake had hundreds of important leaders, and the decisions to focus on seven were designed to accomplish the objectives stated by the council rather than to diminish any other historical figures. Each biographical feature should be seen not as the most important person of his or her time, but as a window into the evolving political culture of the Red Lake nation.

Women and men shared equally in making Red Lake what it is, but most of Red Lake's early politicians were men. That posed special challenges in trying to balance the contributions of both men and women without straying from the goal established by the council to write a political history rather than a social, cultural, or labor history. *Warrior Nation* tries to navigate this by drawing upon the political contributions of women wherever possible, and most powerfully in the chapter on Anna Gibbs, which includes not just her narrative, but those of many other women who shaped Red Lake's polity.

Red Lake has an amazing history. Researching it is a challenge. Red Lake opened its tribal archives for this project and it made a huge difference. In the Red Lake Archives are some documents that can only be found there: Jim Walker's survey analysis from the 1889 Nelson Act, the Peter Graves Papers, 1930 Indian Claims Commission depositions of 1889 Nelson Act witnesses, three major oral-history projects, all resolutions from the General Council of the Red Lake Band of Chippewa Indians (1918–57), all resolutions from the Red Lake Tribal Council (1958–present), correspondence files with Red Lake's attorneys (1920–present), dozens of video recordings of tribal leaders, and hundreds of original photographs. These documents made it possible for me to do two things. First, I used as many quotes and stories as I could from Red Lakers like Dan Needham Sr., Nodin Wind, Vernon Whitefeather, Anna Gibbs, and Thomas J. Stillday Jr. to tell this history. The goal was to have the book reflect authentic Red Lake perspective as much as the records allow. The second thing that these records did for the book was to show and give reliable evidence that explains how Upper Red Lake was illegally excluded from the reservation. All of the depositions for Court of Claims should be in at least a few major archives but were not always where they should be. The documents in Red Lake helped validate and support the history as it is written here in a way not otherwise possible.

There are also records that I placed in the archives at Red Lake that I uncovered in the course of this work. The most significant of these are some of the oral histories I gathered from Red Lake elders. I interviewed dozens of tribal elders for this project and have spent more than twenty-five years collecting oral histories, including many from Red Lake elders that have informed this work. Some were published in the *Oshkaabewis Native Journal* or other places, but some were unique to this project. Also of great importance for this work were numerous oral histories with tribal members gathered by others. Red Lake High School students published two collections of oral histories that were also very helpful for this book: *To Walk the Red Road* and *We Choose to Remember*. Three major oral-history projects in the Red Lake Archives also contained very useful historical material.

My father, Robert Treuer, began research on Red Lake history many years ago, and in his papers, which are now archived at Red Lake, were the only copies I was able to locate of an incomplete rough draft autobiography by Roger Jourdain, given in dictation to Don Allery. Robert Treuer also kept his personal correspondence files, some of which I placed in the Red Lake Archives. His letters from Walter Mondale are the only evidence I found documenting Mondale's consideration of nominating Roger Jourdain for a Nobel Peace Prize. His own biographical essays were useful in supplementing research and perspectives on Jourdain since he spent so much time working with and for the chairman as an employee of the BIA, the tribe, and the Office of Economic Opportunity.

Most of the primary research for this book came from classic archival work at the Minnesota Historical Society, the National Archives (Washington, Chicago, and Kansas City branches), Oberlin College, and the State Historical Society of Wisconsin. The *Bemidji Pioneer* and other periodicals have a great deal of information on the Peter Graves and Roger Jourdain eras as well.

Secondary sources on Red Lake history are pretty scant. The most useful is Erwin F. Mittelholtz's *Historical Review of the Red Lake Reservation: Centennial Souvenir Commemorating a Century of Progress, 1858–1958*. Charles Brill's *Red Lake Nation: Portraits of Ojibway Life* has some original interview material and many gorgeous pictures. Francis Blake's *We Have the Right to Exist* had some important personal recollections on Red Lake history. Brenda Child's *Holding Our World Together: Ojibwe Women and the Survival of Community* and *My Grandfather's Knocking Sticks: Ojibwe Family Life and Labor on the Reservation* are impactful works on Ojibwe women, labor, and family life that include a great archival history of the Red Lake Fisheries. William W. Warren's *History of the Ojibway People* is the most thorough collection of Ojibwe oral history recorded and published in the nineteenth century, and there is plenty on Red Lake in his work.

Warrior Nation is an attempt to tell Red Lake's story and illumi-
nate the contributions of pivotal leaders, with an eye on how the Red
Lake Nation has and continues to evolve. The research and documentary process I employed merges the archives and the Indians. As
much as possible, I try to tell this story with native sources and perspectives, and then try to exhaust the archives for a well-rounded,
authentic, and reliable history. Historians usually let the archives do
all the talking, and this often makes Indian voices scarce in history
books. Doing both has been a challenge but is also a great contribution of *Warrior Nation*. It doesn't just tell Red Lake's stories. It shows
historians a better way to research tribal history.

Bibliography

ARCHIVAL COLLECTIONS CITED

National Archives
  Congressional Record
  Files of the Department of the Interior
    Commissioner of Indian Affairs Correspondence Files
    Commissioner of Indian Affairs Reports
    Indian Agent Report Files
    Office/Bureau of Indian Affairs Classified Files
    Office/Bureau of Indian Affairs Correspondence Files
    Office/Bureau of Indian Affairs Segregated Files
  House Correspondence Files
  House Executive Documents
  Presidential Correspondence Files
  Senate Correspondence Files
  Senate Executive Documents
  Works Progress Administration Papers
Library of Congress
  Henry Rowe Schoolcraft Papers
Minnesota Historical Society
  Alexander Ramsey Papers
  American Board of Commissioners for Foreign Missions Papers
  American Fur Company Papers
  Collections of the Minnesota Historical Society (published series)
  Edwin Clark Papers
  Grace Lee Nute Papers
    Manuscripts Relating to Northwest Missions
  Henry Benjamin Whipple Papers
  Henry H. Sibley Papers

Joel Basset Papers
Julia Warren Spears Papers
Mary Spears Papers
Moses N. Adams Papers
Protestant Episcopal Church Papers
Ransom Judd Powell Papers
North Dakota Historical Society
  North Dakota Historical Collections (published series)
Oberlin College
  Rev. Sela G. Wright Papers
State Historical Society of Wisconsin
  Charles Francis Xavier Goldsmith Papers
  Collections of the State Historical Society of Wisconsin (published series)

INTERVIEWEES CITED

Ammann, Dora. St. Croix Band of Ojibwe, Wisconsin. Tribal Elder. Interviews conducted in Ojibwe and in English, 1991–2015.

Auginaush, Joseph (Joe Maude). White Earth Band of Ojibwe, Minnesota. Tribal Elder. Interviews conducted in Ojibwe, 1992–97.

Bailey-Johnson, Erika. Red Lake Band of Chippewa, Minnesota. Descendant. Interviews conducted in English, 2015.

Beardy, Thomas. Bearskin Lake Oji-Cree, Ontario. Tribal Elder. Interviews conducted in Ojibwe and English, 1992.

Beaulieu, Harlan. Red Lake Band of Chippewa. Tribal Citizen. Interviews conducted in English, April 5, 2013, August 1, 2015.

Beaulieu, Kathryn. Red Lake Band of Chippewa. Former tribal secretary. Interview conducted in English with Robert Treuer, June 20, 2003.

Benton-Banai, Edward. Lac Courte Oreilles Band of Ojibwe, Wisconsin. Tribal Elder. Interviews conducted in Ojibwe, 1986–2007.

Blackwell, William Sr. Grand Portage Band of Chippewa, Minnesota. Tribal Elder. Interview conducted in English, August 2, 1996.

Clark, James. Mille Lacs Band of Ojibwe, Minnesota. Tribal Elder. Interviews conducted in Ojibwe, 1992–2007.

Daniels, William (Billy). Forest County Potawatomi, Wisconsin. Tribal Elder, Drum Chief. Interview conducted in Potawatomi, 2006.

Eagle, Melvin. Mille Lacs Band of Ojibwe, Minnesota. Tribal Elder, Drum Chief, Hereditary Chief. Interviews conducted in Ojibwe, 1992–2013.

Gibbs, Anna. Red Lake Band of Chippewa, Minnesota. Tribal Elder. Interviews conducted in Ojibwe, 1991–2015.

Graves, Peter. Red Lake Band of Chippewa, Minnesota. Former secretary-treasurer, General Council. Interview conducted in English with Arch Grahn, October 5, 1950.

Grolla, Charles. Bois Forte Band of Ojibwe, Minnesota. Interviews conducted in English, 2004–15.

Henry, Lawrence. Roseau River First Nation, Manitoba. Tribal Elder. Interviews conducted in Ojibwe, 1986–96.

Jackson, Susan. Leech Lake Band of Ojibwe, Minnesota. Tribal Elder. Interviews conducted in Ojibwe, 1991–2001.

Johns, Fannie. Red Lake. Interviews conducted in English with Charles Grolla, 1985–2004.

Jones, Nancy. Nigigoonsiminikaaning First Nation, Ontario. Tribal Elder. Interviews conducted in Ojibwe, 1991–2007.

Jourdain, Floyd. Red Lake Band of Chippewa, Minnesota. Tribal Chair. Interviews conducted in English, 1992–2015.

Jourdain, Roger. Red Lake Band of Chippewa, Minnesota. Former Tribal Chairman. Interview conducted in Ojibwe with Wilf Cyr, 1993.

Kingbird, Ona. Red Lake Band of Chippewa, Minnesota. Tribal Elder. Interviews conducted in Ojibwe, 1993.

LaDuke, Winona. White Earth Band of Ojibwe, Minnesota. Executive Director, White Earth Land Recovery Project. Interviews conducted in English, 1994.

Loud, James. Red Lake Band of Chippewa, Minnesota. Hereditary Chief. Interview conducted in English, August 15, 2015.

Lussier, Adam. Red Lake. Interviews conducted in English, 1991–93.

May, William. Red Lake Band of Chippewa, Minnesota. Tribal Elder. Interviews conducted in English, 2005–15.

Mosay, Archie. St. Croix Band of Ojibwe, Wisconsin. Tribal Elder, Drum Chief, Lodge Chief. Interviews conducted in Ojibwe, 1991–96.

Oakgrove, Collins. Red Lake Band of Chippewa, Minnesota. Tribal Elder. Interviews conducted in Ojibwe, 1992–2008.

Otchingwanigan (Nyholm), Earl. Keweenaw Bay Band of Ojibwe, Michigan. Tribal Elder, Professor of Ojibwe Emeritus, Bemidji State University. Interviews conducted in Ojibwe and English, 1991–2000.

Porter, Margaret. Red Lake Band of Chippewa, Minnesota. Tribal Elder. Interviews conducted in Ojibwe, 1988–2015.

Roberts, Mary. Roseau River First Nation, Manitoba. Tribal Elder. Interviews conducted in Ojibwe and English, 1986–96.

Schommer, Carolyn. Dakota, Granite Falls, Minnesota. Tribal Elder. Interviews conducted in English, 1992–94.

Seaboy, Daniel. Dakota, Sisseton, South Dakota. Tribal Elder. Interviews conducted in English, 2006–07.

Staples-Graves, Vincent. Red Lake. Tribal Citizen. Interviews conducted in English, 2015.

Stillday, Eugene. Red Lake Band of Chippewa, Minnesota. Tribal Elder. Interviews conducted in Ojibwe, 1995–2008.

Stillday, Thomas Jr. Red Lake Band of Chippewa, Minnesota. Tribal Elder. Interviews conducted in Ojibwe, 1992–2008.

Strong, Peter. Red Lake. Tribal Elder. Interview conducted in English with Robert Treuer and Gary Fuller, 2003.

Thunder, Aloysius. Red Lake. Tribal Judge. Interview conducted in Ojibwe and English, 2006.

Treuer, Margaret Seelye. White Earth Band of Chippewa. Tribal Citizen. Interview conducted in English, April 11, 2015.

White, Walter (Porky). Leech Lake Band of Ojibwe, Minnesota. Tribal Elder. Interviews conducted in Ojibwe, 1986–2001.

Whitefeather, Vernon. Red Lake Band of Chippewa, Minnesota. Tribal Elder. Interviews conducted in Ojibwe with David Treuer, 1995.

Wilson, Angela. Dakota, Granite Falls, Minnesota. Interviews conducted in English, 1991–97.

WORKS CITED

Adams, Arthur T. *The Explorations of Pierre Esprit Radisson from the Original Manuscript in the Bodleian Library and the British Museum.* Minneapolis: Ross and Haines, 1967.

America's Lost Landscape: The Tallgrass Prairie. Video documentary. Cedar Falls, IA: New Light Media, 2004.

Auger, Donald J., and Thomas Beardy. *Glossary of Legal Terms Translated into Northwestern Ojibwe.* Thunder Bay, ON: Nishnawbe-Aski Legal Services Corporation, 1993.

Baerreis, David A., Erminie Wheeler-Voeglin, and Remedios Wycoco-Moore. "Anthropological Report on the Chippewa, Ottawa, and Potawatomi Indians in Northeastern Illinois and the Identity of the Mascoutens." In *Indians of Northeastern Illinois.* New York: Garland Publishing, 1974.

Baraga, Frederic. *Chippewa Indians in 1847.* New York: Studia Slovenica, 1976.

———. *The Diary of Bishop Frederic Baraga: First Bishop of Marquette, Michigan.* Edited by Regis M. Walling and Rev. N. Daniel Rupp. Detroit, MI: Wayne State University Press, 1990.

Beito, Gretchen Urnes. *Coya Come Home: A Congresswoman's Journey.* Los Angeles: Pomegranate Press, 1990.

Belcourt, George A. "A Sketch of the Red River Mission." *Collections of the Minnesota Historical Society* 1 (1902): 121–40.

Benton-Banai, Edward. "Indinawemaaganag," *Oshkaabewis Native Journal* 8.1 (spring 2011): 88–102.

———. *The Mishomis Book: The Voice of the Ojibway.* Hayward, WI: Indian Country Communications, 1988.

Bigglestone, William E. "Oberlin College and the Beginning of the Red Lake Mission." *Minnesota History* 45 (spring 1976): 21–31.

Birk, Douglas A. *John Sayer's Snake River Journal, 1804–1805.* Minneapolis: Institute for Minnesota Archaeology, 1989.

Bishop, Charles Aldrich. "The Northern Chippewa: An Ethnohistorical Study." Dissertation, State University of New York, 1969.

———. *The Northern Ojibwa and the Fur Trade: An Historical and Ecological Study.* Toronto: Holt, Rinehart and Winston, 1974.

Black-Rogers, Mary. "Dan Raincloud: Keeping Our Indian Way." In Clifton, *Being and Becoming Indians, 226-48.*

Blair, Emma Helen. *The Indian Tribes of the Upper Mississippi Valley and Region of the Great Lakes as Described by Nicolas Perrot, French Commandant of the Northwest; Bacqueville de La Potherie, French Royal Commissioner to Canada; Morrell Marston, American Army Officer; and Thomas Forsyth, United States Agent at Fort Armstrong.* 2 vols. Cleveland: Arthur H. Clark, 1912.

Bleed, Peter. "The Archaeology of Petaga Point: The Preceramic Component." MA thesis, University of Minnesota—Twin Cities, 1967.

Blegen, Theodore C. *Minnesota: A History of the State.* Minneapolis: University of Minnesota Press, [1963] 1975.

Bloomfield, Leonard. *Eastern Ojibwa: Grammatical Sketch, Text, and Word List.* Ann Arbor: University of Michigan Press, 1958.

Borgerding, Thomas. "Father Thomas' History of Early Red Lake Indians." *Northland Times,* January 15, 1954.

———. "Priest Expelled from Duty on Reservation in Early Logging Boundary Dispute." *Northland Times,* April 9, 1954.

———. "Red Lake St. Mary's Mission: Treaty of 1889." Unpublished manuscript, winter 1918.

Boutwell, William T. "Schoolcraft's Exploring Tour of 1832." *Collections of the Minnesota Historical* Society 1 (1902): 121-40.

Bray, Martha Coleman. *The Journals of Joseph N. Nicollet: A Scientist on the Mississippi Headwaters with Notes on Indian Life, 1836-37.* Translated by André Fertey. St. Paul: Minnesota Historical Society Press, 1970.

Brill, Charles. *Red Lake Nation: Portraits of Ojibway Life.* Minneapolis: University of Minnesota Press, 1992.

Brower, Jacob V. *Memoirs of Explorations in the Valley of the Mississippi.* Vols. 3-4. St. Paul: H. L. Collins Company, 1901.

Brunson, Alfred. "Upper Mississippi Missions." *Christian Advocate and Journal* 12.4 (September 15, 1837): 7.

Buck, Daniel. *Indian Outbreaks.* Minneapolis: Ross and Haines, 1965.

Buffalohead, Roger, and Priscilla Buffalohead. *Against the Tide of American History: The Story of the Mille Lacs Anishanabe.* Cass Lake, MN: Minnesota Chippewa Tribe, 1985.

Burpee, Lawrence J., ed. *Journals and Letters of Pierre Gaultier de Varennes de La Vérendrye and His Sons with Correspondence between the Governors of Canada and the French Court, Touching the Search for the Western Sea.* Toronto: Champlain Society, 1968.

Campbell, Lyle. *American Indian Languages: The Historical Linguistics of Native America.* New York: Oxford University Press, 1997.

Catlin, George. *Letters and Notes on the Manners, Customs, and Conditions of North American Indians.* 2 vols. New York: Dover Publications, 1973.

Chavers, Dean. "The Last Great Warrior." In *Modern American Indian Leaders: Their Lives and Their Work.* 2 vols. Lewiston, NY: Edwin Mellen, 2007.

Child, Brenda. *Holding Our World Together: Ojibwe Women and the Survival of Community*. New York: Penguin, 2012.

———. *My Grandfather's Knocking Sticks: Ojibwe Family Life and Labor on the Reservation*. St. Paul: Minnesota Historical Society Press, 2014.

Chute, Janet. *The Legacy of Shingwaukonse: A Century of Native Leadership*. Toronto: University of Toronto Press, 1998.

Cleland, Charles E. *Rites of Conquest: The History and Culture of Michigan's Native Americans*. Ann Arbor: University of Michigan Press, 1992.

Clifton, James A. *Being and Becoming Indians: Biographical Studies of North American Frontiers*. Urbana: University of Illinois Press, 1991.

Coleman, Bernard, Ellen Frogner, and Estelle Eich. *Ojibwa Myths and Legends*. Minneapolis: Ross and Haines, 1962.

Combet, Denis. *In Search of the Western Seas: Selected Journals of La Vérendrye*. Winnipeg: Great Plains Publications, 2001.

Cooper, Leland R. "Archaeological Survey and Excavation at Mille Lacs Kathio State Park." Department of Anthropology, University of Minnesota–Twin Cities, 1965.

Copway, George. *Life, Letters and Speeches*. 1847. Reprint, Lincoln: University of Nebraska Press, 1997.

———. *The Traditional History and Characteristic Sketches of the Ojibway Nation*. London: Charles Gilpin, 1850.

Crouse, Nellis M. *La Vérendrye: Fur Trader and Explorer*. Ithaca, NY: Cornell University Press, 1956.

Cutler, Charles L. *O Brave New Words: Native American Loanwords in Current English*. Norman: University of Oklahoma Press, 1992.

Danziger, Edmund Jefferson Jr. *The Chippewas of Lake Superior*. Norman: University of Oklahoma Press, 1979.

Densmore, Frances. *Chippewa Customs*. St. Paul: Minnesota Historical Society Press, 1979.

———. *Chippewa Music*. 2 vols. Minneapolis: Ross and Haines, 1973.

DesJarlait, Patrick, and Neva Williams. *Patrick DesJarlait: Conversations with a Native American Artist*. Minneapolis: Runestone Press, 1994.

Diamond, Jared. *Collapse: How Societies Choose to Fail or Succeed*. New York: Penguin, 2005.

Dickason, Olive Patricia. *Canada's First Nations: A History of Founding Peoples from Earliest Times*. Norman: University of Oklahoma Press, 1992.

Diedrich, Mark. *The Chiefs Hole-in-the-Day of the Mississippi Chippewa*. Rochester, MN: Coyote Books, 1986.

———. *Famous Chiefs of the Eastern Sioux*. Rochester, MN: Coyote Books, 1987.

———. *Ojibway Oratory: Great Moments in the Recorded Speech of the Chippewa, 1695–1889*. Rochester, MN: Coyote Books, 1989.

Doty, James D. "Northern Wisconsin in 1820." *Collections of the State Historical Society of Wisconsin* 7 (1876): 195–206.

Dunn, James Taylor. *The St. Croix: Midwest Border River*. St. Paul: Minnesota Historical Society Press, 1979.

Eastman, Mary. *Dahcotah; or, Life and Legends of the Sioux around Fort Snelling.* Minneapolis: Ross and Haines, 1962.

Edmunds, Russell David. *The Potawatomis: Keepers of the Fire.* Norman: University of Oklahoma Press, 1978.

English, Samuel F., and Ann Dallman. *Sam English: The Life, Work, and Times of an Artist.* Albuquerque, NM: Sam English Arts, 2008.

Ewers, John C. "Ethnological Report on the Chippewa Cree Tribe of the Rocky Boy Reservation and the Little Shell Band of Indians." In Indian Claims Commission, *Chippewa Indians* 6.

Featherstonhaugh, George W. *A Canoe Voyage up the Minnay Sotor with an Account of the Lead and Copper Deposits in Wisconsin; of the Gold Region in the Cherokee Country; and Sketches of Popular Manners.* 2 vols. St. Paul: Minnesota Historical Society Press, 1970.

Fixico, Donald L. *Termination and Relocation: Federal Indian Policy, 1945-1960.* Albuquerque: University of New Mexico Press, 1986.

Folwell, William W. *A History of Minnesota.* 4 vols. St. Paul: Minnesota Historical Society Press, 1956.

Fortunate Eagle, Adam. *Alcatraz! Alcatraz! The Indian Occupation of 1969-1971.* Denver, CO: Heydey Books, 1992.

———. *Heart of the Rock.* Norman: University of Oklahoma Press, 2002.

———. *Pipestone: My Life in an Indian Boarding School.* Norman: University of Oklahoma Press, 2010.

"The Fox and Ojibwa War." *Collections of the Minnesota Historical Society* 1 (1902): 283-85.

"Frederick Ayer: Teacher and Missionary to the Ojibway Indians, 1829-1850." *Collections of the Minnesota Historical Society* 6 (1894): 429-37.

Fruth, Albin. *A Century of Missionary Work among the Red Lake Chippewa Indians.* Red Lake, MN: St. Mary's Mission, 1958.

Gardner, Denis P. *Minnesota Treasures: Stories behind the State's Historic Places.* St. Paul: Minnesota Historical Society Press, 2004.

Gibbon, Guy, and Christy A. H. Caine. "The Middle to Late Woodland Transition in Eastern Minnesota." *Midcontinental Journal of Archaeology* 5.1 (1980): 57-72.

Gibbs, Anna C. Special Issue. *Oshkaabewis Native Journal* 7.2 (spring 2010).

Gibson, Arrell M. *The American Indian: Prehistory to the Present.* Lexington, MA: D. C. Heath, 1980.

Gilman, Carolyn. *The Grand Portage Story.* St. Paul: Minnesota Historical Society Press, 1992.

Gilman, Rhoda R., Carolyn Gilman, and Deborah M. Stultz. *The Red River Trails: Oxcart Route between St. Paul and the Selkirk Settlement, 1820-1870.* St. Paul: Minnesota Historical Society Press, 1979.

Gold, Debra L. "St. Cloud State University Archaeological Investigations at the Petaga Point Site" (21-ML-0011). Mille Lacs County, Minnesota. Final Report, Department of Sociology and Anthropology, St. Cloud State University, 2004.

Grant, Peter. "The Saulteux Indians about 1804." In Masson, *Les Bourgeois.*

Graves, Kathy Davis, and Elizabeth Ebbott. *Indians in Minnesota*. Minneapolis: University of Minnesota Press, 2006.

Greiner, Tony. *The Minnesota Book of Days: An Almanac of State History*. St. Paul: Minnesota Historical Society Press, 2001.

Hagg, Harold T. "Logging Line: A History of the Minneapolis, Red Lake and Manitoba." *Minnesota History* 43 (winter 1972): 123-35.

Hawkinson, Ella. "The Old Crossing Chippewa Treaty and Its Sequel." *Minnesota Historical Society Collections* 15 (September 1934): 282-300.

Hennepin, Louis. *Description of Louisiana: Newly Discovered to the Southwest of New France by Order of the King*. Translated by Marion E. Cross. Minneapolis: University of Minnesota Press, 1938.

Henry, Alexander. *Travels and Adventures in Canada and the Indian Territories between the Years 1760 and 1776*. 1809. Ann Arbor, MI: University Microfilms, 1966.

Henry, Alexander, and David Thompson. *New Light on the Early History of the Greater Northwest*. Edited by Elliott Coues. New York: Harper, 1897.

Hickerson, Harold. *The Chippewa and Their Neighbors: A Study in Ethnohistory*. Prospect Heights, IL: Waveland Press, 1988.

———. "Ethnohistory of Chippewa in Central Minnesota." In Indian Claims Commission, *Chippewa Indians* 4.

———. "Ethnohistory of Chippewa of Lake Superior." In Indian Claims Commission, *Chippewa Indians* 3.

———. "Mdewakanton Band of Sioux Indians." In Indian Claims Commission, *Sioux Indians* 1: 1-301.

———. *The Southwestern Chippewa: An Ethnohistorical Study*. Memoir 92. Menasha, WI: American Anthropological Association, 1962.

———. "William T. Boutwell of the American Board and the Pillager Chippewa: The History of a Failure." *Ethnohistory* 12 (winter 1965): 1-29.

Hilger, M. Inez. *Chippewa Child Life and Its Cultural Background*. St. Paul: Minnesota Historical Society Press, 1992.

———. *Chippewa Families: A Social Study of White Earth Reservation, 1938*. St. Paul: Minnesota Historical Society Press, 1938.

Hill, Alfred J. "The Geography of Perrot; So Far as It Relates to Minnesota and the Regions Immediately Adjacent." *Collections of the Minnesota Historical Society* 2 (1867): 200-214.

Hiller, Wesley R. "Reminiscences of Two Mille Lacs Trips." *Minnesota Archaeologist* 2 (1936): 8-10.

Howard, James H. *The Plains-Ojibwa or Bungi*. Reprints in Anthropology 7. Vermillion: University of South Dakota Press, 1977.

Hoxie, Frederick E. *A Final Promise: The Campaign to Assimilate the Indians, 1880-1920*. Lincoln: University of Nebraska Press, 2001.

Hurt, Wesley R. "Dakota Sioux Indians." In Indian Claims Commission, *Sioux Indians* 2.

Indian Claims Commission. "Commission Findings on the Chippewa Indians." *Chippewa Indians*. 7 vols. New York: Garland Publishing, 1974.

————. "Commission Findings on the Sioux Indians." *Sioux Indians*. 4 vols. New York: Garland Publishing, 1974.

James, Edwin, ed. *A Narrative of the Captivity and Adventures of John Tanner during Thirty Years Residence among the Indians in the Interior of North America*. London: Carvill, 1830. Reprint, Minneapolis: Ross and Haines, 1956.

Jameson, Anna. *Winter Studies and Summer Rambles in Canada*. 3 vols. New York: Wiley and Putnam, 1839.

Jameson, J. Franklin. *Early Narratives of the Northwest, 1634–1699* New York: Scribner's, 1917.

Johnson, Elden. "Cultural Resource Survey of the Mille Lacs Area." St. Paul: Minnesota Historical Society, 1983.

Johnston, Basil. *Ojibway Ceremonies*. Lincoln: University of Nebraska Press, 1990.

Josephy, Alvin Jr. *500 Nations: An Illustrated History of North American Indians*. New York: Alfred A. Knopf, 1994.

Juneau, Denise. "Indian Education for All: Montana Indians, Their History and Location." Montana Office of Public Instruction, April 2009.

Kane, Lucile M., June D. Holmquist, and Carolyn Gilman. *The Northern Expeditions of Stephen H. Long: The Journals of 1817 and 1823 and Related Documents*. St. Paul: Minnesota Historical Society Press, 1978.

Kappler, Charles J. *Laws and Treaties*. 2 vols. Washington, DC: U.S. Government Printing Office, 1904.

"Kathio State Park Archaeology." Mille Lacs Kathio State Park Interpretive Pamphlet Series. Onamia, MN, 1989.

Kavanaugh, Martin. *La Vérendrye: His Life and Times*. Brandon, MB: Fletcher & Son, 1967.

Keating, William H. *Narrative of an Expedition to the Source of the St. Peters River*. 2 vols. London: George B. Whittaker, 1825.

Kegg, Maude. "Nookomis Gaa-inaajimotawid." Edited by John D. Nichols. *Oshkaabewis Native Journal* 1.2 (1990).

Keesing, Felix M. *The Menomini Indians of Wisconsin: A Study of Three Centuries of Cultural Contact and Change*. Madison: University of Wisconsin Press, 1987.

Keesing, Roger M. *Kin Groups and Social Structure*. New York: Holt, Rinehart, and Winston, 1975.

Kellogg, Louise Phelps. *The British Regime in Wisconsin and the Old Northwest*. Madison: State Historical Society of Wisconsin Press, 1935.

————. *Early Narratives of the Northwest, 1634–1699*. New York: Charles Scribner's Sons, 1917.

————. *The French Regime in Wisconsin and the Northwest*. Madison: State Historical Society of Wisconsin Press, 1925.

King, Franklin A. "Logging Railroads of Northern Minnesota." (Railway and Locomotive Historical Society) *Bulletin* 93 (October 1955): 94–115.

King, Steven C. *Seeds of War*. Bloomington, IN: Author House, 2007.

Kinietz, Vernon W. *Chippewa Village*. Bloomfield, MI: Cranbrook Press, 1947.

Kohl, Johann Georg. *Kitchi-Gami: Life among the Lake Superior Ojibway.* 1860. Reprint, St. Paul: Minnesota Historical Society Press, 1985.

Kugel, Rebecca. *To Be the Main Leaders of Our People: A History of Minnesota Ojibwe Politics, 1825-1898.* East Lansing: Michigan State University Press, 1998.

Kvasnicka, Robert M. "From Wilderness to Washington—and Back Again: The Story of the Chippewa Delegation of 1855." *Kansas Quarterly* 3.4 (fall 1971): 56-63.

Landes, Ruth. *Ojibwa Sociology.* New York: Columbia University Press, 1937.

Larpenteur, Auguste L. "Recollections of the City and People of St. Paul, 1843-1898." *Collections of the Minnesota Historical Society* 9 (1901): 363-94.

Laut, Agnes. *Pathfinders of the West,* New York: Freeport, 1904.

Leustig, Jack. *500 Nations.* Video documentary. Los Angeles: Warner Home Video, 1995.

Lewis, Henry. *The Valley of the Mississippi Illustrated.* Translated by Hermina Poatgieter. St. Paul: Minnesota Historical Society Press, 1967.

Lund, Duane R. *Lake of the Woods II: Featuring Translations of Pierre La Vérendrye's Diaries and Father Alneau's Letters.* Staples, MN: Nordell Graphic Communications, 1984.

———. *Minnesota's Chief Flat Mouth of Leech Lake.* Staples, MN: Nordell Graphic Communications, 1983.

Mann, Charles C. *1491: New Revelations of the Americas before Columbus.* New York: Vintage Books, 2006.

Mason, Philip P. *Schoolcraft's Expedition to Lake Itasca: The Discovery of the Source of the Mississippi.* East Lansing: Michigan State University Press, 1993.

Masson, L. R. *Les Bourgeois de la Compagnie du Nord-Ouest: Récits de Voyages, Lettres et Rapports Inédits Relatifs au Nord-Ouest Canadien.* 2 vols. New York: Antiquarian Press, 1960.

Mather, David J. "Archaeological Overview of the Mille Lacs Locality Report." Minnesota Department of Transportation, 2000.

Matsen, William E. "Battle of Sugar Point: A Re-examination." *Minnesota History* 50 (fall 1987): 269-75.

McClurken, James M., ed. *Fish in the Lakes, Wild Rice and Game in Abundance: Testimony on Behalf of the Mille Lacs Ojibwe Hunting and Fishing Rights.* East Lansing: Michigan State University Press, 2000.

McKenney, Thomas L. *Sketches of a Tour to the Lakes, of the Character and Customs of the Chippeway Indians and of Incidents Connected with the Treaty of Fond du Lac.* 1827. Reprint, Minneapolis: Ross and Haines, 1959.

Meyer, Melissa L. *The White Earth Tragedy: Ethnicity and Dispossession at a Minnesota Anishinaabe Reservation, 1889-1920.* Lincoln: University of Nebraska Press, 1994.

Meyer, Roy W. *History of the Santee Sioux: United States Indian Policy on Trial.* Lincoln: University of Nebraska Press, 1993.

Milner, George R. "Warfare in Prehistoric and Early Historic Eastern North America." *Journal of Archaeological Research* 7.2 (1999): 105-51.

Mittelholtz, Erwin F. *Historical Review of the Red Lake Indian Reservation: Centennial Souvenir Commemorating a Century of Progress, 1858-1958*. Bemidji, MN: General Council of the Red Lake Band of Chippewa Indians and the Beltrami County Historical Society, 1957.

Moose, Leonard L., et al. *Aaniin Ekidong: Ojibwe Vocabulary Project*. St. Paul: Minnesota Humanities Center, 2009.

Neill, Edward D. "Battle of Lake Pokegama." *Collections of the Minnesota Historical Society* 1 (1902): 141-45.

Nichols, David. *Lincoln and the Indians*. Columbia: University of Missouri Press, 1978.

Nichols, John D. "The Translation of Key Phrases in the Treaties of 1837 and 1855." In McClurken, *Fish in the Lakes*, 514-24.

Nichols, John D., and Earl Nyholm (Otchingwanigan). *A Concise Dictionary of Minnesota Ojibwe*. Minneapolis: University of Minnesota Press, 1995.

Norton, Mary Aquinas. *Catholic Missionary Activities in the Northwest, 1818-1864*. Washington, DC: Catholic University of America, 1930.

Ojakangas, Richard W., and Charles L. Mastch. *Minnesota's Geology*. Minneapolis: University of Minnesota Press, 1982.

Parker, John, ed. *The Journals of Jonathan Carver and Related Documents*. St. Paul: Minnesota Historical Society Press, 1976.

Parkman, Francis. *La Salle and the Discovery of the Great West*. New York: New American Library, 1963.

Pinker, Steven. *The Language Instinct: How the Mind Creates Language*. New York: HarperPerennial, 1994.

Pond, Samuel W. *The Dakota or Sioux in Minnesota: As They Were in 1834*. St. Paul: Minnesota Historical Society Press, 1986.

———. "Indian Warfare in Minnesota." *Collections of the Minnesota Historical Society* 3 (1880): 129-38.

Quaife, Milo Milton. *John Long's Voyages and Travels in the Years 1768-1788*. 1791. Reprint, Chicago: Lakeside, 1922.

Radcliffe-Brown, A. R. *Structure and Function in Primitive Society*. New York: Free Press, 1952.

Radin, Paul. *The Winnebago Tribe*. Lincoln: University of Nebraska Press, 1970.

Rhodes, Richard. *Eastern Ojibwa-Chippewa-Ottawa Dictionary*. Berlin: Mouton de Gruyter, 1985.

Robinson, Doane. *A History of the Dakota or Sioux Indians: From Their Earliest Traditions and First Contact with White Men to the Final Settlement of the Last of Them upon Reservations and the Consequent Abandonment of the Old Tribal Life*. Minneapolis: Ross and Haines, 1967.

Robinson, Edward V. *Early Economic Conditions and the Development of Agriculture in Minnesota*. Minneapolis: University of Minnesota Studies in the Social Sciences, 1915.

Royce, Charles C. *Indian Land Cessions in the United States*. New York: Arno, 1900.

St. Germain, Jill. *Indian Treaty-Making Policy in the United States and Canada, 1867-1877.* Lincoln: University of Nebraska Press, 2001.

Sansome, Constance. *Minnesota Underfoot: A Field Guide to the State's Outstanding Geologic Features.* Stillwater, MN: Voyageur Press, 1983.

Satz, Ronald N. *Chippewa Treaty Rights: The Reserved Rights of Wisconsin's Chippewa Indians in Historical Perspective.* Wisconsin Academy of Sciences, Arts and Letters, 1991.

Schell, James Peery. *In the Ojibway Country: A Story of the Early Missions on the Minnesota Frontier.* Walhalla, ND: Charles H. Lee, 1911.

Schenck, Theresa M. *The Voice of the Crane Echoes Afar: The Sociopolitical Organization of the Lake Superior Ojibwa, 1640-1855.* New York: Garland Publishing, 1997.

———. *William W. Warren: The Life, Letters, and Times of an Ojibwe Leader.* Lincoln: University of Nebraska Press, 2007.

Schulenberg, Raymond F. *Indians of North Dakota.* Bismarck: State Historical Society of North Dakota Press, 1956.

Schultz, Duane. *Over the Earth I Come: The Great Sioux Uprising of 1862.* New York: St. Martin's Press, 1992.

Sharrock, Floyd W., and Susan R. Sharrock. "History of the Cree Indian Territorial Expansion from the Hudson Bay Area to the Interior Saskatchewan and Missouri Plains." In Indian Claims Commission, *Chippewa Indians* 6.

Sibley, Henry H. "Memoir of Jean Nicollet." *Collections of the Minnesota Historical Society* 1 (1902): 146-56.

Smith, James G. E. *Leadership among the Southwestern Ojibwa.* Publications in Ethnology 7. Ottawa: National Museums of Canada, 1973.

Smith, Kaighn Jr. *Labor and Employment Law in Indian Country.* Portland, ME: Drummond, Woodsum, and MacMahon, 2011.

Stillday, Thomas J. Special Issue. *Oshkaabewis Native Journal* 7.1 (fall 2009).

Stout, David B. "Ethnohistorical Report on the Saginaw Chippewa." In Indian Claims Commission, *Chippewa Indians* 5.

Streiff, Jan. "Mille Lacs Kathio: A Minnesota State Park Development Project Reconnaissance Survey." Department of Anthropology, University of Minnesota—Twin Cities, 1981.

Strezewski, Michael. "Patterns of Interpersonal Violence at the Fisher Site." *Midcontinental Journal of Archaeology* 31.22 (2006): 249-80.

Tanner, George C. *Fifty Years of Church Work in the Diocese of Minnesota, 1857-1907.* St. Paul: W. C. Pope, 1909.

———. "History of Fort Ripley, 1849 to 1859, Based on the Diary of Rev. Solon W. Manney, D.D., Chaplain of This Post from 1851 to 1859." *Collections of the Minnesota Historical Society* 10 (1905): 179-202.

Tanner, Helen Hornbeck, ed. *Atlas of Great Lakes Indian History.* Norman: University of Oklahoma Press, 1987.

Terborgh, John, and James A. Estes. *Trophic Cascades: Predators, Prey, and the Changing Dynamics of Nature.* Washington, DC: Island Press, 2010.

Thwaites, Reuben Gold, ed. *The Jesuit Relations and Allied Documents.* 73 vols. New York: Pageant Book Company, 1959.

To Walk the Red Road: Memories of the Red Lake Ojibwe People. Red Lake Board of Education: Project Preserve, 1989.

Treuer, Anton S. *Living Our Language: Ojibwe Tales and Oral Histories.* St. Paul: Minnesota Historical Society Press, 2001.

———. *Ojibwe in Minnesota.* St. Paul: Minnesota Historical Society Press, 2010.

Turney, C. S. M., and H. Brown. "Catastrophic Early Holocene Sea Level Rise, Human Migration and the Neolithic Transition in Europe." *Quaternary Science Reviews* 26 (2007): 2036–41.

Upham, Warren. "Groseilliers and Radisson, the First White Men in Minnesota, 1655–56, and 1659–60, and Their Discovery of the Upper Mississippi River." Part 2. *Collections of the Minnesota Historical Society* 10 (1905): 449–594.

———. *Minnesota Geographic Names: Their Origin and Historic Significance.* 1969. Reprint, St. Paul: Minnesota Historical Society Press, 2001.

Valentine, J. Randolph. *Nishnaabemwin Reference Grammar.* Toronto: University of Toronto Press, 2001.

Van Antwerp, Ver Planck. "Negotiations for the Chippewa Treaty of July 29, 1837." In Satz, *Chippewa Treaty Rights,* 131–53.

Van Kirk, Sylvia. *Many Tender Ties: Women in Fur-Trade Society.* Norman: University of Oklahoma Press, 1980.

Van Oosten, John, and Hilary J. Deason. "History of Red Lake's Fishery, 1917–1938." Special Scientific Report: Fisheries 229, August 1957, U.S. Department of the Interior.

Vandersluis, Charles. *A Brief History of Beltrami County.* Bemidji, MN: Beltrami County Historical Society, 1997.

Vandersluis, Charles, Euclid J. Bourgeois, John G. Morrison, and Charles L. Wight. *Mainly Logging.* Minneota, MN: Minnesota Clinic, 1974.

Vennum, Thomas Jr. *The Ojibwa Dance Drum: Its History and Construction.* St. Paul: Minnesota Historical Society Press, 2010.

———. *Wild Rice and the Ojibway People.* St. Paul: Minnesota Historical Society Press, 1988.

Vogel, Virgil J. *Indian Names in Michigan.* Ann Arbor: University of Michigan Press, 1986.

Wahlberg, Hazek. *The North Land: A History of Roseau County.* Warroad, MN: Roseau County Historical Society, 1975.

Walling, Regis M., and N. Daniel Rupp. *The Diary of Bishop Frederic Baraga.* Detroit, MI: Wayne State University Press, 1990.

Warren, William W. *History of the Ojibway People.* 1885. St. Paul: Minnesota Historical Society Press, 1984.

Waziyatawin. *What Does Justice Look Like: The Struggle for Liberation in Dakota Homeland.* St. Paul: Living Justice Press, 2008.

We Choose to Remember: More Memories of the Red Lake Ojibwe People. Red Lake Board of Education: Project Preserve, 1991.

Wheeler-Voegelin, Erminie. "An Anthropological Report on Indian Use and Occupancy of Northern Michigan." In Indian Claims Commission, *Chippewa Indians* 5.

Whipple, Henry B. "Civilization and Christianization of the Ojibways in Minnesota." *Collections of the Minnesota Historical Society* 9 (1901):129-42.

———. *Lights and Shadows of a Long Episcopate*. New York: Macmillan, 1899.

White, Bruce. *We Are at Home: Pictures of the Ojibwe People*. St. Paul: Minnesota
Historical Society Press, 2007.

White, Richard. *The Middle Ground: Indians, Empires and Republics in the Great
Lakes Region, 1650-1815*. New York: Cambridge University Press, 1991.

Whitefeather, Vernon. "Gaa-danapinaniding." *Oshkaabewis Native Journal* 8.1
(spring 2011): 16-19.

———. "Waabi-bines." *Oshkaabewis Native Journal* 8.1 (spring 2011): 20-23.

Wilford, Lloyd A. "The Prehistoric Indians of Minnesota: The Mille Lacs Aspect."
Minnesota History 25.4 (1944): 329-41.

———. "A Revised Classification of the Prehistoric Cultures of Minnesota." *American Antiquity* 21.2 (1955): 130-42.

Williams, Mentor L., ed. *Schoolcraft's Narrative Journal of Travels: Through the
Northwestern Regions of the United States Extending from Detroit through the
Great Chain of American Lakes to the Sources of the Mississippi River in the Year
1820*. East Lansing: Michigan State University Press, 1992.

Williams, Walter L. *The Spirit and the Flesh: Sexual Diversity in American Indian
Culture*. Boston: Beacon Press, 1992.

Wilson, Angela. *In the Footsteps of Our Ancestors: The Dakota Commemorative
Marches of the 21st Century*. St. Paul: Living Justice Press, 2006.

———. *Remember This: Dakota Decolonization and the Eli Taylor Narratives*. Lincoln:
University of Nebraska Press, 2005.

Winchell, Newton H. *The Aborigines of Minnesota: A Report Based on the Collections
of Jacob V. Brower, and on the Field Surveys and Notes of Alfred J. Hill and Theodore
Lewis*. St. Paul: Minnesota Historical Society Press, 1911.

Woodlands: The Story of the Mille Lacs Ojibwe. Oral history video documentary.
Onamia, MN: Mille Lacs Band of Ojibwe, 1994.

Woolworth, Alan R. "Ethnohistorical Report on the Yankton Sioux." In Indian
Claims Commission, *Sioux Indians* 3.

Wright, Sela G. "Some Reminiscences of the Early Oberlin Missionaries in Northwestern Minnesota." Unpublished manuscript, Oberlin College Library.

Wub-e-ke-niew [Francis Blake]. *We Have the Right to Exist: A Translation of Aboriginal Indigenous Thought*. New York: Black Thistle Press, 1995.

Zapffe, Carl Andrew. *Indian Days in Minnesota's Lake Region: A History of the
Great Sioux-Ojibwe Revolution, from Invasion to the Intertribal Boundary of 1825*.
Brainerd, MN: Historic Heartland Association, 1991.

Index

Picture Credits

pages 8, 57
   Matt Kania, Map Hero

pages 29, 47, 63, 133, 147, 149, 155, 212
   Minnesota Historical Society

pages 42 (gn-00574), 80 (gn-00567a), 93 (gn-00577a)
   National Anthropological Archives, Smithsonian Institution

pages 68 (BCHS-520), 117 (BCHS-404), 178-79 (BCHS 403)
   Beltrami County Historical Society

pages 136, 240, 251, 329
   Charles Brill, published in *Red Lake Nation: Portraits of Ojibway Life* (University of Minnesota Press, 1992)

pages 170, 190-91, 214, 283, 342
   Red Lake Tribal Archives

pages 172-73 (NARA-285702), 207 (NARA-285749), 223 (NARA-285729), 258 (NARA-285701)
   National Archives, Kansas City, Department of the Interior, Bureau of Indian Affairs, Red Lake Agency (1964)

page 182
   Jerome Liebling Photography

page 278
   AP Photo/The Pioneer of Bemidji, Monte Draper

page 304
   Anton Treuer

About the Author

Anton Treuer is professor of Ojibwe at Bemidji State University and author of fourteen books. He has a BA from Princeton University and an MA and PhD from the University of Minnesota. He is editor of the *Oshkaabewis Native Journal*, the only academic journal of the Ojibwe language. Dr. Treuer has presented all over the United States and Canada and in several foreign countries on "Everything You Wanted to Know about Indians But Were Afraid to Ask," cultural competence and equity, strategies for addressing the "achievement" gap, and tribal sovereignty, history, language, and culture. His books published by the Minnesota Historical Society Press are *Everything You Wanted to Know about Indians But Were Afraid to Ask*, *Ojibwe in Minnesota* ("Minnesota's Best Read for 2010" by the Center for the Book in the Library of Congress), *The Assassination of Hole in the Day* (Award of Merit winner from the American Association for State and Local History), and *Living Our Language: Ojibwe Tales and Oral Histories*. Connect with him at faculty.bemidjistate.edu/atreuer/.